QUESTIONS & ANSWERS:
Contracts

Multiple Choice and Short Answer
Questions and Answers

REVISED FIRST EDITION

By

Keith A. Rowley
Professor of Law
William S. Boyd School of Law
University of Nevada, Las Vegas

ISBN#: 082057080X

Editorial Offices
744 Broad Street, Newark, NJ 07102 (973) 820-2000
201 Mission St., San Francisco, CA 94105-1831 (415) 908-3200
701 East Water Street, Charlottesville, VA 22902-7587 (434) 972-7600
www.lexis.com

(Pub.3175)

To Katherine and James, who both give so generously and ask so little in return.

ABOUT THE AUTHOR

Keith A. Rowley is Professor of Law at the William S. Boyd School of Law, University of Nevada Las Vegas, having previously taught at Emory University School of Law and Mississippi College School of Law. A former lecturer in economics and public policy at Baylor University, Professor Rowley graduated from the University of Texas School of Law, where he served as Executive Editor of the *Texas Law Review* and interned with then-Justice Lloyd Doggett of the Texas Supreme Court. Following law school, Professor Rowley clerked for Judge Thomas M. Reavley of the U.S. Fifth Circuit Court of Appeals and then practiced commercial litigation in Houston for five years before accepting his first law teaching position.

Professor Rowley is the author of Volume 10 of the Revised Edition of *Corbin on Contracts* — forthcoming from LexisNexis — covering breach of contract and anticipatory repudiation. He has published more than 25 other books and articles on a variety of legal, economic, and public policy topics. His current teaching and research focuses on contract law, commercial law, and securities regulation.

In addition to contributing this book to the *Questions & Answers* series, Professor Rowley also serves as an editorial consultant for the series, working with Professor Tim Zinnecker (South Texas College of Law) and LexisNexis Acquisitions Editor Leslie Levin to identify subjects for the series, recruit authors, and review manuscripts prior to their publication.

PREFACE

The law changes constantly. Most of the changes come in the form of small steps, rather than giant leaps. But some changes alter the legal landscape. In the area of contract law, the past 150 years have seen

- "objective" theories of contract supplant more "subjective" approaches,

- legal "realism" supplant "formalism" (though this battle is ongoing, with formalism — or as it is now often called "conceptualism" — regaining some of the ground lost during the Legal Realist revolution) as the divining rod courts use to ascertain "objective" reality,

- relational, economic, sociological, behavioral, and critical theories vying to rewrite some or all of legal realism's past, present, and future,

- increasing codification of a body of law that was once an almost entirely common law,

- increasing internationalization, creating new challenges and opportunities for reconciling fundamental differences between civil and common law systems, between domestic and international law, and between public and private law.

In May 2003, the American Law Institute ("ALI") approved comprehensive revisions to Articles 2 and 2A of the Uniform Commercial Code ("UCC"), governing contracts for, respectively, the sale and lease of goods. In 2002, the National Conference of Commissioners on Uniform State Laws ("NCCUSL") approved the same revisions. Forty-nine states and the District of Columbia have in place their own versions of Articles 2 and 2A that vary to differing degrees from the uniform versions that the ALI recently voted to replace. Consequently, it is reasonable to assume that state legislatures will begin considering adopting parts or all of Revised Articles 2 and 2A as early as 2004, depending on how quickly the official comments that accompany all UCC Articles are finalized. In 2001, the ALI and NCCUSL rewrote UCC Article 1, which contains general provisions applicable, *inter alia*, to contracts governed by Articles 2 and 2A. As of January 1, 2006, 14 states have adopted Revised Article 1, and as many as twenty more states' legislatures are expected to consider Revised Article 1 during their 2006 legislative sessions.

In 1999, NCCUSL promulgated the Uniform Electronic Transactions Act ("UETA"), designed to facilitate forming, memorializing, and enforcing contracts by electronic means. As of January 1, 2006, 46 states and the District of Columbia have adopted UETA. Congress also enacted, and President Clinton signed into law, the Electronic Signatures in Global and National Commerce Act, 15 U.S.C. §§ 7001-7006 (commonly referred to as "E-SIGN"), which serves the same basic functions as UETA (and, in a somewhat unusual twist, yields to UETA if the state whose law governs a particular transaction or dispute has adopted UETA). Thus, between UETA and E-SIGN, electronic contract formation, memorialization, and enforcement are a statutory reality in every U.S. jurisdiction.

In 1999, NCCUSL also promulgated the Uniform Computer Information Transactions Act ("UCITA"), which NCCUSL intended to standardize the law governing software licenses and other contracts involving rights in computer information. UCITA has met with decidedly less success than UETA. As of January 1, 2006, more states (four: Iowa, North Carolina, Vermont, and West Virginia) have enacted so-called "UCITA Shield" or "UCITA Bomb Shelter" legislation, designed to insulate their citizens from the possible effects of UCITA, than have enacted UCITA (two: Maryland and Virginia).

In 1988, the United Nations Convention on Contracts for the International Sale of Goods ("CISG") first took effect. As of January 1, 2006, the United States and 65 other countries have acceded, accepted, approved, ratified, or succeeded to the CISG. Two other countries have signed the Convention, but have not yet acceded, accepted, approved, or ratified it. Because it is a treaty of the United States, the CISG supersedes contrary state law (by operation of the Supremacy Clause — Article VI, clause 2 — of the U.S. Constitution). In the wake of the CISG, the International Institute for the Unification of Private Law ("UNIDROIT") promulgated the Principles of International Commercial Contracts in 1994. In 2004, UNIDROIT promulgated a second edition of its Principles of International Commercial Contracts. While they do not carry the force of law, the UNIDROIT Principles are often referred to as a "Restatement" of the law governing international commercial contracts.

These changes in the theory underlying contract law and the sources of contract law — combined with other forces that are beyond the scope of this discussion — have caused changes in the way American law schools teach contract law. What was once a fairly uniform course of study devoted almost exclusively to examining the incremental evolution of common law has transformed into one or more heterogeneous course(s) involving a significant amount of statutory analysis, considering at least some of the issues involved in transnational contracts, and injecting jurisprudential, ethical, economic, political, historical, sociological, anthropological, and psychological perspectives into the discussion of some or all of the common law and statutory doctrines studied.

This tremendous diversity of source material and perspectives makes Contracts a delightful course to teach, but poses quite a challenge to someone trying to write a book such as this. I must make some editorial decisions and some simplifying assumptions.

Who Should Use This Book?

I have written this book primarily for students taking the basic course in Contracts, though it should also be useful to students taking a course in one or more of Sales, Leases, Electronic Transactions, and International Sales and to readers looking for materials to review in preparing for the Contracts portion of the Multistate Bar Exam.

What Does it Cover?

Contract theory, contract drafting, and transactional counseling are topics worthy of considerable discussion in the basic Contracts course. However, I do not think the format of this book is particularly well suited to addressing them. As a consequence, this book focuses on contract doctrine, and generally leaves matters of theory and practice to other fora.

The Not-So-Common Law of Contracts

Because the common law is inherently state-specific, we need a proxy. Therefore, unless the question indicates otherwise, you should assume that the common law of the jurisdiction whose law governs any question accords with the **Restatement (Second) of Contracts ("R2")**.

Alphabet Soup: The Statutory Law of Contracts

While some professors — particularly those now given only three or four hours to teach Contracts — eschew the UCC and other statutory sources of law and devote their entire course to the common law (and, perhaps, some theory and drafting issues), I assume that the basic course in Contracts includes some discussion of UCC Articles 1 and 2 (and, perhaps, Article 2A), UETA (and, perhaps, E-SIGN), and the CISG.

This book does not devote significant attention to UETA or the CISG, but both figure into several questions and answers. Absent a statement to the contrary, you should assume that any domestic jurisdiction involved in a question has adopted UETA and, in a question involving more than one country, that all countries involved have ratified the CISG.

The UCC is another kettle of fish. Just as some professors choose to minimize statutory coverage, others teach a significant part of the course using UCC Article 2. Most Contracts casebooks devote considerable space to Article 2. Some interlace statutory and common law. Others reserve the UCC materials for separate chapters. In any event, Article 2 deserves substantial coverage in this book. The problem is: *Which Article 2?* Because I see both the merits and demerits of assuming either quick, widespread adoption of Revised Article 2 (along the lines of UETA) or, essentially, ignoring Revised Article 2 until it actually becomes the law in enough jurisdictions to consider it part of the body of contract law (something UCITA, for example, has not yet accomplished outside of Maryland and Virginia), I have tried to ask questions so that the best answer is the same regardless of which version of Article 2 applies.[1] Absent a statement to the contrary, you should apply the pre-2003 version of Articles 2 and 2A and the pre-2001 version of Article 1.

What is the Book's Format?

Like the other books in the *Questions & Answers* series, this book presents a number of multiple choice and short answer questions, arranged by major topics, followed by answers to those questions, again arranged by major topics. The Table of Contents guides you through the major topics (*e.g.*, "Offer and Acceptance," "Remedies") and the Index identifies which questions and answers discuss more discrete topics (*e.g.*, "Mailbox Rule," "Reliance Damages"). In addition, the book also includes a comprehensive "Practice Final Exam" that should take you between 1-1/2 and 2 hours to complete.

While most of the questions in this book will have an answer that is, once analyzed carefully, superior to other answers (at least taking the foregoing simplifying assumptions as given), sometimes — particularly when dealing with some of the topics I address with short answer questions — the best we can do is narrow the field. At times, to borrow a phrase from one of my favorite Crosby, Stills & Nash tunes, "Just beneath the surface of the mud, there's more mud."[2] Or, to use a more contemporary reference, "There is no spoon."[3]

Acknowledgments

---

[1] I have also tried to note, the first time we encounter a UCC provision — and again, when the answer might differ applying Revised Article 1, 2, or 2A — the extent to which the text of that provision has been revised or relocated. Please realize that I am doing so without the benefit of any official comments or transition guide and that I am focusing on those changes to Articles 1, 2, and 2A that I believe may be relevant to a first-year Contracts class.

[2] Crosby, Stills & Nash, *Anything at All*, on CSN (Atlantic Records 1977).

[3] The Matrix (Warner Brothers 1999). If you find that revelation unsettling, then allow me another quote from the same movie: "I didn't say it would be easy, . . . I just said it would be the truth." *Id.*

Many of the questions and answers in this book have been "field-tested" on my Contracts and Sales students over the last several years. I want to thank them for being (mostly) willing subjects and for their help in identifying concepts that are relatively easier and relatively more difficult for law students to master. I also want to thank Ira David, Colt Dodrill, Sally Galati, and Tiffani McDonald for their help proofreading this book (and other books in this series, too), as well as Scott Burnham, Heather Dean, Bruce Markell, and Tim Zinnecker for their comments and suggestions.

The Final Pitch

I enjoy teaching Contracts. I enjoy writing about Contracts. I see this book as an opportunity to do both. I hope my enjoyment will be infectious. But, more importantly, I hope that you will find the scope and substance of this book useful. I welcome your comments, questions, and suggestions.

Keith A. Rowley
Las Vegas, Nevada
keith.rowley@unlv.edu
March 2006

TABLE OF CONTENTS

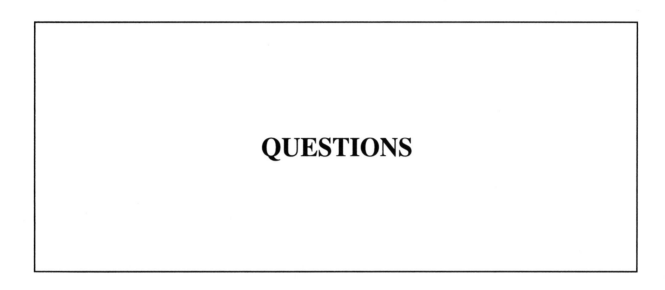

QUESTIONS

On May 1, 2003, All Things Greene ("ATG"), a professional landscaper doing business in Iowa, telephoned Jumping Junipers ("JJ"), a commercial tree farm in Colorado, and ordered 100 juniper saplings, at a price of $9 per sapling, with JJ to deliver the saplings to ATG no later than June 15th. Later that day, JJ faxed an acknowledgment to ATG, agreeing to deliver 100 juniper saplings to ATG no later than June 15th, with ATG paying $9 per sapling.

1. Absent a contrary agreement between the parties, what substantive body of law governs the contract between ATG and JJ?

   (A) UCC Article 2, because both ATG and JJ were merchants when they entered into the contract.

   (B) Article 2, because the juniper saplings were goods when ATG and JJ entered into the contract.

   (C) Article 2, because the juniper saplings were goods when ATG and JJ entered into the contract and the contract price is $500 or more (or $5,000 or more, if applying Revised Article 2).

   (D) Common law, because the juniper saplings were affixed to real property when ATG and JJ entered into the contract.

2. Assuming that all relevant jurisdictions have enacted it, is the contract between ATG and JJ also subject to the Uniform Electronic Transactions Act?

   (A) No, because Article 2 preempts UETA.

   (B) No, because the Electronic Signatures in Global and National Commerce Act (E-SIGN) preempts UETA.

   (C) Yes, because ATG and JJ consented to transact electronically by using the telephone and the fax machine, respectively, to form their contract.

   (D) Yes, if ATG and JJ consented to transact electronically by using the telephone and the fax machine, respectively, to form their contract.

Shortly after ATG confirmed receipt of JJ's fax and its terms, ATG contracted with several landscaping clients who had expressed their desire to include juniper saplings in their landscaping. One client, Cindy Redleaf, had recently bought a home and wanted to completely re-landscape the backyard. She paid ATG $2,500 to prepare a comprehensive landscape plan for her backyard; and, after approving the plan, she paid ATG to remove most of the existing landscaping (such as it was), re-contour the soil, build several flower beds, install an irrigation system, install curbing and stepping stones, plant new grass, flowers, shrubs, and trees (including

3

several of the juniper saplings ATG was purchasing from JJ), and pour the foundation for and construct a gazebo in her backyard. The cost of the backyard makeover, above and beyond the fee for preparing the plan, was $10,000, $2,500 of which was for materials and $7,500 of which was for labor.

3. If a dispute subsequently arose between Cindy and ATG over ATG's workmanship in building Cindy's gazebo (for which ATG charged Cindy $350 for materials and $650 for labor), what body of law would most likely govern their dispute?

    (A) Article 2, because the materials for the gazebo were goods when Cindy and ATG entered into the contract.

    (B) Article 2, because ATG's re-landscaping of Cindy's yard included installing new grass, numerous flowers, shrubs, and trees, the irrigation system, and the gazebo, all of which were goods when Cindy and ATG entered into the contract.

    (C) Common law, because, despite the large number of goods installed by ATG, the predominant purpose of Cindy's contract with ATG was to pay for ATG's expertise in designing and installing new backyard landscaping.

    (D) Common law, because, once installed, the gazebo and other goods became improvements to real property.

Using the same facts as Question 3, suppose that the Iowa courts apply the "gravamen of the action" test for determining whether a dispute arising out of a contract for both goods and services is governed by Article 2 or by common law.

4. If a dispute subsequently arose between Cindy and ATG over ATG's workmanship in installing Cindy's gazebo (for which ATG charged Cindy $350 for materials and $650 for labor), what body of law should govern?

    (A) Article 2 would govern the entire contract, because the materials for the gazebo were goods when Cindy and ATG entered into the contract.

    (B) Article 2 would govern the dispute over ATG's workmanship in building Cindy's gazebo, because the materials for the gazebo were goods when Cindy and ATG entered into the contract.

    (C) Common law would govern the entire contract, because Cindy's complaint is over the installation of the gazebo, not the materials used to build it.

    (D) Common law would govern the dispute over ATG's workmanship in building Cindy's gazebo, because Cindy's complaint is over the installation of the gazebo, not the materials used to build it.

Suppose, instead, that the problem with the gazebo was that the wood ATG used to build it deteriorated and discolored much more rapidly than Cindy reasonably expected.

5. If Iowa courts apply the "gravamen of the action" test, what body of law would most likely govern?

    (A) Article 2 would govern the entire contract, because the wood was goods when Cindy and ATG entered into the contract.

    (B) Article 2 would govern the dispute over the quality of the wood ATG used to build Cindy's gazebo, because the wood was goods when Cindy and ATG entered into the contract.

    (C) Common law would govern the entire contract, because ATG would not have needed to use the wood but for Cindy's desire that ATG install a gazebo.

    (D) Common law would govern the dispute over the quality of the wood, because ATG would not have needed to use the wood but for Cindy's desire that ATG install a gazebo.

Another of ATG's clients, Reitz, Burton & Andersen, L.L.P. ("RBA"), a prominent Iowa City law firm, wanted to provide its best clients and its staff with the best Christmas trees money can buy. One of the partners, who had recently vacationed in and around Vancouver, British Columbia (Canada), convinced his colleagues that Canadian Spruce could not be beat. The partners authorized him to contract with ATG to purchase 100 6-to 7-foot tall Canadian Spruce trees for $75 each, to be delivered to various addresses during the first week of December 2003. ATG, in turn, contracted with McKenzie Brothers Trees and More ("McKenzie"), in Whiskey Springs, British Columbia, to purchase 125 6-to 7-foot tall Canadian Spruce trees for US$50 to US$55 (depending on height), to be delivered to ATG no later than November 30th, with ATG to pay all shipping expenses.

6. Absent a contrary agreement between the parties, what body of law governs ATG's contract with McKenzie for the trees?

    (A) The U.N. Convention on Contracts for the International Sale of Goods ("CISG"), because the trees were goods sold by a foreign seller to a U.S. buyer and the U.S. has ratified the CISG.

    (B) The CISG, because the trees were goods sold by a Canadian seller to a U.S. buyer and both Canada and the U.S. have ratified or otherwise adopted the CISG.

    (C) The CISG, because the trees were goods sold by a Canadian seller to a U.S. buyer, both Canada and the U.S. have ratified or otherwise adopted the CISG, and ATG did not purchase the trees for its own personal, family, or household use.

    (D) Article 2, because ATG did not know or have reason to know that McKenzie's principal place of business is in Canada.

At the same time it ordered the trees, ATG also ordered from McKenzie — at RBA's request — 50 custom-made, blown-glass Christmas ornaments with the year and RBA's firm logo to be hand-painted onto each ornament. RBA wanted the ornaments as mementos for each of the firm's attorneys and employees. McKenzie agreed to make and sell the ornaments to ATG for US$40 each.

7. Absent a contrary agreement between the parties, what body of law governs ATG's contract with McKenzie for the ornaments?

    (A) The CISG, because the ornaments were goods sold by a Canadian seller to a U.S. buyer, both Canada and the U.S. have ratified or otherwise adopted the CISG, and ATG did not purchase the ornaments for its own personal, family, or household use.

    (B) Article 2, because, while the ornaments were goods sold by a Canadian seller to a U.S. buyer, and both Canada and the U.S. have ratified or otherwise adopted the CISG, ATG was merely acting as a proxy for RBA, which was purchasing the ornaments for its own personal, family, or household use.

    (C) Article 2, because each ornament had to be made by hand; and, therefore, the service performed by the craftsperson was the predominant purpose of the contract to buy the ornaments.

    (D) Common law, because each ornament had to be made by hand; and, therefore, the service performed by the craftsperson was the predominant purpose of the contract to buy the ornaments.

ATG's business had been flourishing, despite the minor setback involving Cindy Redleaf, and ATG's owner, Tom Greene, wanted to expand. Tom contracted with Rita Estrich to locate the record owner of the lot immediately east of ATG's existing location and to arrange ATG's purchase of the property. Tom agreed to pay Rita four percent (4%) of the purchase price if she could successfully arrange ATG's purchase of the property.

8. Absent a contrary agreement between the parties, what body of law governs ATG's contract with Rita the realtor?

    (A) Article 2, because ATG is a merchant dealing in goods.

    (B) Article 2, because both ATG and Rita are merchants.

    (C) Common law, because ATG's contract with Rita was for the purchase of real property.

    (D) Common law, because ATG's contract with Rita was for Rita's personal services.

After searching the county real property records, Rita found that the Sixth National Bank of Iowa ("Sixth National") was the record owner of the lot in question, which it obtained through foreclosure.

9. Assuming that ATG and Sixth National reached an agreement on the terms of ATG's purchase of the lot in question, what body of law would most likely govern ATG's contract with Sixth National?

ANSWER:

When ATG and Sixth National reached their agreement for ATG's purchase of the subject lot from Sixth National, there were a couple of storage buildings and some other personal property on the lot, which Sixth National told ATG it was free to keep or dispose of as it wished.

10. Does their presence on the lot change your answer to Question 9?

ANSWER:

ATG has decided to demolish and remove the storage buildings and other personal property situated on the lot and to install several prefabricated buildings that ATG contracted to purchase from Buildings-R-Us ("BRU"). When installed, the buildings will become fixtures attached to real property.

11. Absent a contrary agreement between the parties, what body of law will govern ATG's contract with BRU for the purchase, delivery, and installation of the buildings?

   (A) UCC Article 1, because the buildings are personal property, but they are not "movables," and therefore are not goods.

   (B) Article 2, because the buildings were goods when ATG and BRU contracted for ATG's purchase and BRU's delivery and installation.

   (C) Common law, because the buildings, as installed, will become improvements to real property.

   (D) Common law, because the predominant purpose of the contract is for BRU's services in fabricating, delivering, and installing the buildings.

After consummating its purchase of the lot from Sixth National and agreeing to purchase several new prefabricated buildings from BRU, ATG set about to clear the lot. Rather than hiring someone to demolish and remove the old storage buildings and other personal property situated on the lot, ATG decided to do the work itself. Needing equipment to do the job, ATG agreed to lease a bulldozer from Rent-All Equipment Leasing. The term of the lease was two weeks, and the agreed weekly rental payment was $1,000 (including insurance). The lease allowed ATG to renew the lease indefinitely, at the same weekly rate, but required ATG to give Rent-All seven days notice prior to returning the bulldozer.

12. Absent a contrary agreement between the parties, what body of law will govern ATG's contract with Rent-All?

   (A) UCC Article 2A, because the bulldozer is a good and both ATG and Rent-All are merchants.

(B)   Article 2A, because the bulldozer is a good and the agreement between ATG and Rent-All is a lease agreement.

(C)   Article 2A, because the bulldozer is a good and the agreement between ATG and Rent-All is a lease agreement for $1,000 or more.

(D)   Article 2, because the bulldozer is a good and ATG's agreement with Rent-All effectively permits ATG to purchase the bulldozer from Rent-All on credit.

On March 1, 2003, Gwyneth and Russell agreed that Gwyneth would pay Russell $100 each for two tickets to the March 15th New York premiere of *The Orange Pumpernickel*. They further agreed that Russell would deliver the tickets to Gwyneth no later than March 14th. The New York premiere of Cameron Ridley's new movie, *The Orange Pumpernickel*, was scheduled for March 15th at the Radikal City Musik Hall. That same night, the 41st Street Playhouse scheduled the premiere of a stage production of *The Orange Pumpernickel*, directed by David Marmoset.

On March 2nd, Russell purchased two tickets from the 41st Street Playhouse for $75 each. On March 14th, when Russell delivered the tickets to Gwyneth, she refused to pay, claiming that Russell had agreed to sell her tickets to the movie, not the play. Russell did not have any tickets to the movie, and none were commercially available at that late date. Russell tried unsuccessfully to find another buyer for the play tickets and to obtain a refund from the Playhouse. Unable to use the tickets himself, Russell left them with Gwyneth in case she changed her mind.

13.   Suppose that, when they formed their agreement, Gwyneth knew about the movie premiere, but not about the play, and Russell knew about the play premiere, but not the movie. Did Gwyneth and Russell have an enforceable contract?

ANSWER:

Jenny Beasley wants to sue her former employer, Owl's Nest, for breaching its promise to award a new Mitsubishi to the winner of a March 2003 sales contest. Jenny claims that her manager, Jason Boone, told her and the other waitresses at the Paradise Road Owl's Nest that whoever sold the most margaritas at each participating Owl's Nest location during March 2003 would have her name entered in a drawing, and that the winner of the drawing would receive a new Mitsubishi. As the contest progressed, Jason told the waitresses that he did not know whether the winner would receive a Mitsubishi car, truck, or SUV, but that the winner would have to pay any registration fees on the vehicle. On or about April 8th, Jason informed Jenny that she had sold more margaritas during March than any other waitress at the Paradise Road Owl's Nest, and that he had submitted her name for the drawing. Two weeks later, Jason informed Jenny that she had won the drawing. He proceeded to blindfold her and lead her to the parking lot outside the restaurant. Waiting for her there was not a Mitsubishi car, truck, or SUV, however, but a plastic model of a Mitsubishi Zero, a World War II Japanese fighter airplane. Jason was laughing. Jenny was not.

Owl's Nest pays its waitresses $5.00 per hour for each hour they work, and allows them to keep 75% of their tips. The restaurant keeps the other 25%. Waitresses are scheduled to work between 35 and 40 hours per week. They can work extra shifts when another waitress wants or needs time off, but are not allowed to work more than 50 hours per week. In the three months prior to March 2003, Jenny worked an average of 40 hours per week, and earned an average of $1,600 per month in tips ($1,200 of which she kept). During March 2003, Jenny worked an average of 50 hours per week, and earned $2,000 in tips ($1,500 of which she kept).

Owl's Nest waitresses are at-will employees, who work without written employment contracts. The company's policy manual requires any employee to give two weeks notice prior to terminating her employment, and requires Owl's Nest to give any employee two weeks notice prior to terminating her employment, unless Owl's Nest is terminating the employee for cause. Every employee receives a copy of the policy manual when she is hired. Jenny received a copy of the policy manual when she began working at Owl's Nest in January 2002.

Assume for purposes of the following questions that Jason acted with apparent, if not actual, authority; therefore, his words and actions are attributable to Owl's Nest.

14. Did Jason make an offer that, if accepted, could have obligated Owl's Nest to award the contest winner a new Mitsubishi car, truck, or SUV if she won the sales contest?

  (A) No, it should have been obvious that Jason was only joking.

  (B) No, all that Jason offered was to enter the winning waitress from his restaurant in a drawing for a chance at a new Mitsubishi.

  (C) No, because the disparity in value between a new Mitsubishi car, truck, or SUV and the marginal increase in profits the restaurant might realize if the waitresses tried to outsell one another during the contest month was too great for a reasonable person in Jenny's position to believe Jason's offer was genuine.

  (D) Yes. Because Jason was not obviously joking, the fact that his offer was conditional did not prevent it from inviting acceptance to form a conditional contract, and employers often run promotional contests that award one or a small number of employees prizes that are significantly more valuable than whatever the employee(s) had to do to win the prize.

15. Regardless of your answer to Question 14, assuming that Jason did make an offer that invited Jenny (and the other waitresses) to accept, and thereby form a contract (conditional or otherwise), did Jenny accept Jason's offer?

  (A) No, because she failed to timely notify Jason that she intended to accept his offer and participate in the sales contest.

  (B) No, because she never promised Jason that she would exert any additional effort or continue to work at Owl's Nest beyond her two-week-notice period (even though, in fact, she did both).

  (C) Yes, because she continued to work at Owl's Nest during the entire contest period, despite the fact that she could have quit at any time on two weeks notice.

(D)   Yes, because she worked more hours, sold more margaritas, and earned more tip income for Owl's Nest than she typically did in the average month prior to the contest period.

Kerwin Smith is a self-styled "tax rebel," who has made a career out of, and substantial income from, his tax protest activities. His basic contention is that the federal income tax is a voluntary tax, which no one is required to pay. Smith has published various books espousing his views, and has promoted the books by appearing on numerous radio and television programs.

On February 6, 2003, Smith appeared on *Mary Prince Live!*, a television program broadcast nationally by the DMM television network, which invites viewers to call during the show with questions for, and comments directed to, its guests. Host Mary Prince interviewed Smith from approximately 11:00 p.m. to 12:00 a.m. EST. The words "Live Phone-In" and the telephone number "(202) 555-5555" flashed on the screen periodically during Smith's appearance. In addition, Prince repeated the phone number and encouraged viewers to call and speak directly with Smith on the air. During the course of the program, Smith offered the following challenge: "I will pay $100,000 to the first person who calls during this show and cites any section of the Internal Revenue Code that requires an individual to file a federal tax return."

The following morning, Ingrid Neumann saw a two-minute taped segment of Smith's *Mary Prince Live!* interview, including the part where Smith said he would pay $100,000 to the first caller who could prove him wrong, on the *DMM Wakeup News*. Neumann felt certain that Smith's statements regarding the Internal Revenue Code were incorrect. She researched the issue and located several provisions that, to her satisfaction, demonstrated the mandatory nature of the federal income tax. The next day, February 8th, Neumann wrote to the *DMM Wakeup News*, citing numerous Internal Revenue Code provisions as authority for her position that individuals are required to pay federal income tax. DMM responded to Neumann's letter on March 3rd, informing her that it had forwarded her letter to Smith. On April 15th (ironically enough), Smith wrote to Neumann, stating:

> I did make an offer during the February 6th *Mary Prince Live!* program to pay $100,000 to the first person who could call during the show and produce a section of the Internal Revenue Code that requires an individual to file a tax return. I do not believe that the sections you cite in your letter obligate an individual to file an income tax return. But, even if they do, you did not call me during the show, as my offer required. As a result, I do not owe you any money.

16.   Did Neumann's February 8th letter form a contract obligating Smith to pay Neumann $100,000?

(A)   No, Smith's offer was not made so as to justify *Mary Prince Live!* viewers to understand that they were invited to form a contract by accepting Smith's offer.

(B)   No, because Neumann failed to accept Smith's offer on its terms.

(C)   No. As Smith's reply to Neumann's letter made clear, he reserved to himself the right to decide whether a caller's response satisfied the terms of his offer.

(D)　No, it should have been obvious that Smith was only joking.

Sandra Ypres is a realtor living and working in San Dimas, California. Bosworth Hallifax, a personal injury attorney based in nearby Riverside, knows Sandra casually through mutual acquaintances. At 9:00 a.m. on Monday, June 30, 2003, Sandra faxed Bosworth a letter stating that she had 100 acres of undeveloped land, at the intersection of Wyld Stallyns Drive and No Way, which she would sell him for $1,000 per acre. Sandra's letter also stated: "Unless I receive your written acceptance by 5:00 p.m. on Thursday, July 3, 2003, my offer will expire. I will not offer this same acreage to any other prospective buyer until 5:00 p.m. on Thursday, July 3, 2003, or until you reject this offer, whichever occurs first." Across the bottom of Sandra's letter was printed

"Sandra Ypres, Realtor
2400 Baja Grande Dr., Suite 150, San Dimas, CA 90735
Tel: (562) 555-1234
Fax: (562) 555-9876
E-Mail: sandra2400@yippie.com."

At 1:00 p.m. on July 3rd, just before he rushed out of the house to catch a flight to Akron, Bosworth sent an e-mail to "sandra2400@yippie.com" stating: "I agree to buy your 100 acres for $1,000 per acre. Have a great Fourth of July!" Bosworth's e-mail reached Sandra's e-mailbox less than a minute later, but she did not check her e-mail until after 5:00 p.m. on July 3rd.

17.　Was Sandra's fax an offer to sell Bosworth 100 acres of undeveloped land for $1,000 per acre?

ANSWER:

18.　Regardless of your answer to Question 17, if Sandra offered to sell Bosworth 100 acres of undeveloped land for $1,000 per acre, was she obligated to offer the land exclusively to Bosworth until 5:00 p.m. on Thursday, July 3rd, or until he rejected the offer, whichever happened first?

(A)　Yes, because she promised to do so.

(B)　Yes, because her written offer was a "firm offer."

(C)　Yes, because her offer created a binding, exclusive option in Bosworth's favor.

(D)　No, because her offer was not a firm offer and did not create a binding, exclusive option in Bosworth's favor; therefore, she was not contractually bound by her promise to offer the land exclusively to Bosworth until the deadline stated in the offer.

19.　Returning to the facts of Question 17, assuming Sandra offered to sell Bosworth 100 acres of undeveloped land for $1,000 per acre, did Bosworth accept her offer by the terms of his July 3rd e-mail?

ANSWER:

20.   Assuming Sandra offered to sell Bosworth 100 acres of undeveloped land for $1,000
      per acre, if Bosworth died before 5:00 p.m. on July 3rd, and before responding to
      Sandra's offer, could his son, Rochester, have accepted Sandra's offer, provided he
      did so according to its terms?

ANSWER:

21.   Returning to the facts of Question 17, assuming Sandra offered to sell Bosworth 100
      acres of undeveloped land for $1,000 per acre, did Bosworth accept Sandra's offer
      by a permissible means?

      (A)   No. Having received Sandra's offer by fax, the "mirror image rule" required
            Bosworth to accept by fax.

      (B)   No. Bosworth's e-mail was not a "written acceptance," as Sandra's offer required.

      (C)   Yes, because common law permits an offeree to accept an offer by any reasonable
            means, and e-mail was reasonable under these circumstances.

      (D)   Yes, because Sandra insisted on a written acceptance and Bosworth's e-mail was
            a written acceptance.

22.   Assuming Sandra offered to sell Bosworth 100 acres of undeveloped land for $1,000
      per acre, and that Bosworth accepted Sandra's offer by a permissible means, was
      Bosworth's acceptance timely?

      (A)   Yes, because Bosworth sent his acceptance to Sandra prior to 5:00 p.m. on July
            3rd.

      (B)   Yes, because Sandra received Bosworth's acceptance prior to 5:00 p.m. on July
            3rd.

      (C)   Yes, because Bosworth sent his acceptance to Sandra prior to any act by Sandra
            that would have revoked the offer and prior to 5:00 p.m. on July 3rd.

      (D)   Yes, because Sandra received Bosworth's acceptance prior to revoking the offer
            and prior to 5:00 p.m. on July 3rd.

Suppose that, despite having heard nothing from Bosworth, Sandra met her friend Trina at 9:00
a.m. on July 3rd for a round of golf at Wyld Stallyns Golf Course. At 2:00 p.m., over post-round
drinks, without Bosworth's knowledge, Sandra sold the land to Trina for $1,100 per acre. When
Sandra returned to her office around 3:00 p.m. that same day, she sent an e-mail to Bosworth's

office e-address informing him that she was revoking her offer because she had already sold the land to Trina.

23.   Assuming Sandra offered to sell Bosworth 100 acres of undeveloped land for $1,000 per acre, and that Bosworth timely accepted Sandra's offer by a permissible means, was Sandra's revocation effective?

   (A)   No, because Bosworth sent his acceptance to Sandra before 5:00 p.m. on July 3rd.

   (B)   No, because Bosworth sent his acceptance to Sandra before he received her revocation.

   (C)   No, because Sandra received Bosworth's acceptance before she sent Bosworth her revocation.

   (D)   No, because Sandra received Bosworth's acceptance before Bosworth received her revocation.

Suppose, instead, that Sandra cancelled her July 3rd tee time with Trina and started working the phones, anxious to sell the property before she left town for the July 4th holiday weekend. Before noon, she exchanged faxes with Fausto, who agreed to purchase the land for $1,050 per acre. At 12:00 p.m., by which time Bosworth had already left the office in order to pack for his trip to Akron and his staff had gone home early for the holiday weekend, Sandra sent a fax to Bosworth's office revoking her offer. No one returned to Bosworth's office (and, therefore, no one saw the fax) until 8 a.m. on Monday, July 7th.

24.   Was Sandra's revocation effective?

ANSWER:

Returning to the facts of Question 17, suppose now that, despite having sent his e-mail to Sandra's correct address at 1:00 p.m. on July 3rd, due to the fault of Bosworth's Internet service provider, Bosworth's e-mail did not reach Sandra's Internet service provider until after 5:00 p.m. on July 3rd.

25.   Assuming Sandra offered to sell Bosworth 100 acres of undeveloped land for $1,000 per acre, and that Bosworth accepted Sandra's offer by a permissible means, was Bosworth's acceptance timely?

   (A)   Yes, because Bosworth sent his acceptance to Sandra prior to 5:00 p.m. on July 3rd.

   (B)   Yes, because Sandra received Bosworth's acceptance prior to 5:00 p.m. on July 3rd.

   (C)   Yes, because Sandra received Bosworth's acceptance prior to 5:00 p.m. on July 3rd, and prior to any act by Sandra that would have revoked the offer.

(D) No, because Sandra did not receive Bosworth's acceptance prior to 5:00 p.m. on July 3rd.

26. Suppose, instead, that, despite having sent his e-mail to Sandra's correct e-address at 1:00 p.m. on July 3rd, Bosworth's e-mail did not "arrive" in Sandra's inbox until after 5:00 p.m. on July 3rd due to the fault of *Sandra's* Internet service provider. Was Bosworth's acceptance timely?

    (A) No, because Sandra did not receive Bosworth's acceptance until after 5:00 p.m. on July 3rd.

    (B) No, because Bosworth assumed the risk of untimely delivery when he elected to attempt to accept Sandra's offer via e-mail.

    (C) Yes, because Sandra received Bosworth's acceptance before the 5:00 p.m., July 3rd deadline.

    (D) Yes, because Sandra received Bosworth's acceptance before she revoked her offer.

Returning to the facts of Question 17, suppose that, in response to Sandra's June 30th fax, Bosworth mailed her a letter on Tuesday, July 1st stating: "Thank you for your offer. Unfortunately, I am financially overextended and unable to accept it at this time." When he went home to pack and eat lunch prior to leaving for Akron on July 3rd, Bosworth found a letter in his mail slot from the San Francisco law firm of Bhagwat, Dodge, Knapp, Martinez & Prince, P.C., informing Bosworth that he had just inherited $250,000 from a distant relative. At 1:00 p.m. on July 3rd, just before he rushed out of the house to catch his flight to Akron, Bosworth sent Sandra an e-mail, addressed to "sandra2400@yippie.com," stating: "Please disregard my earlier letter. I hereby agree to buy your 100 acres for $1,000 per acre. Have a great Fourth of July!" Bosworth's e-mail reached Sandra's inbox a few minutes later. The postal carrier delivered Bosworth's July 1st letter at 4:00 p.m. on July 3rd.

27. Did Bosworth timely accept Sandra's offer by means of his July 3rd e-mail?

    (A) No, because he had already sent Sandra a written rejection, terminating his power to accept.

    (B) Yes, because Sandra received his acceptance before she received his rejection.

    (C) Yes, because Sandra received his acceptance before she received his rejection, before the deadline stated in her offer, and before Sandra revoked the offer.

    (D) Yes, because, regardless of when she received his rejection, Sandra received his acceptance before the deadline stated in her offer, and before Sandra revoked the offer.

Starting again with the facts of Question 17, suppose that, in response to Sandra's June 30th fax, Bosworth mailed her a letter on Tuesday, July 1st stating: "I will purchase your 100 acres for $800.00 per acre." While eating lunch just before leaving for the airport on July 3rd, Bosworth read in *The San Dimas Wasp* about a zoning change approved by the city council that would make the land Sandra was trying to sell him substantially more valuable. At 1:00 p.m. on July 3rd, just before he rushed out of the house to catch his flight to Akron, Bosworth sent Sandra an e-mail, addressed to "sandra2400@yippie.com," stating: "Please disregard my earlier letter. I agree to buy your 100 acres for $1,000 per acre. Have a great Fourth of July!" Bosworth's e-mail reached Sandra's inbox a few minutes later. The postal carrier delivered Bosworth's July 1st letter at 4:00 p.m. on July 3rd.

28. Did Bosworth timely accept Sandra's offer by means of his July 3rd e-mail?

    (A) No, because he had already sent Sandra a written counteroffer, terminating his power to accept.

    (B) Yes, because Sandra received his acceptance before she received his counteroffer.

    (C) Yes, because Sandra received his acceptance before she received his counteroffer, before the deadline stated in her offer, and before Sandra revoked the offer.

    (D) Yes, because, regardless of when she received his counteroffer, Sandra received his acceptance before the deadline stated in her offer, and before Sandra revoked the offer.

Suppose instead that, at 9:00 a.m. on Monday, June 30th, Sandra faxed Bosworth and 29 other people (whose names appeared on the fax cover sheet accompanying the letter) a letter stating that she had 500 acres of undeveloped land that she would sell for $1,000 per acre, and that her offer was good "until 5:00 p.m. on Thursday, July 3, 2003, or until I have received written commitments to purchase all of the available acreage, whichever comes first." The letter was addressed "Dear Client," and across the bottom of Sandra's letter was printed

"Sandra Ypres, Realtor
2400 Baja Grande Dr., Suite 150, San Dimas, CA 90735
Tel: (562) 555-1234
Fax: (562) 555-9876
E-Mail: sandra2400@yippie.com."

29. If Bosworth sent Sandra a fax at 12:00 p.m. on June 30th, stating "I agree to buy 100 acres of the undeveloped land you are presently offering to sell for $1,000 per acre," would Bosworth have an enforceable contract with Sandra obligating her to sell him 100 acres of undeveloped land for $1,000 per acre?

ANSWER:

Suppose that, instead of stating that she had 500 acres of undeveloped land for sale, Sandra's letter stated that she had five vintage 1966 and 1967 Corvette Sting Ray convertibles for sale for $50,000 each, first come, first served. Suppose, further, that Bosworth owns a vintage automobile dealership in Canada, and that he received Sandra's fax at his Canadian place of business.

30. Was Sandra's June 30th fax an offer to sell one or more of the Corvettes to Bosworth?

  (A) No, because common law would deem it to be merely an invitation to offer.

  (B) No, because Article 2 would deem it to be merely an invitation to offer.

  (C) No, because the CISG would deem it to be merely an invitation to offer.

  (D) Yes, because the CISG would deem it to be an offer.

Mercury Rising ("Mercury") is an Illinois manufacturer of indoor and outdoor thermometers. Tubular Glass ("Tubular") is a Michigan manufacturer of precision glass tubing. On March 14, 2003, following telephone negotiations between the two, Will Bruce, Mercury's purchasing agent, faxed a purchase order to Tubular for 5,000 one-foot lengths of glass tubing, at a price of $5.00 per foot, to be delivered to Mercury's plant no later than May 1st. Later that same day, Tubular faxed a written acknowledgment, agreeing to manufacture and deliver 5,000 one-foot lengths of glass tubing, at a price of $5.00 per foot, to Mercury's plant no later than May 1st. The terms of Tubular's acknowledgment also (1) disclaimed all implied warranties, and (2) required Mercury to pay the full contract price, including the cost of shipping the tubing from Tubular's plant to Mercury's plant, when Mercury received the tubing. The parties did not correspond further. Mercury received the goods on May 1st and paid the carrier in full, including transportation costs.

31. Did Mercury and Tubular form a contract by their exchange of correspondence, their actions, or both?

  (A) No, because Tubular's acknowledgment contained terms that were not included in Mercury's offer, making Tubular's acknowledgment a counteroffer that Mercury never accepted in writing.

  (B) Yes, because Tubular's acknowledgment contained terms that were not included in Mercury's offer, making Tubular's acknowledgment a counteroffer, which Mercury accepted when it paid the carrier for the goods and for the cost of shipping the goods from Tubular to Mercury.

  (C) No, because Tubular expressly conditioned its acceptance of Mercury's offer on Mercury's agreement to the additional terms contained in Tubular's acknowledgment.

  (D) Yes, because Tubular did not expressly condition its acceptance of Mercury's offer on Mercury's agreement to the additional terms contained in Tubular's acknowledgment.

Suppose, instead, that Mercury's purchase order specifically stated: "We hereby reserve all warranties set forth in Article 2 of the Uniform Commercial Code."

32. Did Mercury and Tubular form a contract by their exchange of correspondence?

(A)   No, because Tubular's acknowledgment contained additional terms not included in Mercury's offer, making Tubular's acknowledgment a counteroffer that Mercury never accepted in writing.

(B)   No, because the disclaimer of warranties in Tubular's acknowledgment conflicted with the reservation of warranties in Mercury's purchase order, making Tubular's acknowledgment a counteroffer that Mercury never accepted in writing.

(C)   No, because Tubular expressly conditioned its acceptance of Mercury's offer on Mercury's agreement to the additional and conflicting terms contained in Tubular's acknowledgment.

(D)   Yes, because Tubular did not expressly condition its acceptance of Mercury's offer on Mercury's agreement to the additional and conflicting terms contained in Tubular's acknowledgment.

Returning to the facts of Question 31, suppose that Tubular's acknowledgment clearly stated that it would accept Mercury's purchase order only on the condition that Mercury agree to the terms set forth in Tubular's acknowledgment.

33.   Did Mercury and Tubular form a contract by their exchange of correspondence, their actions, or both?

(A)   No, because Tubular expressly conditioned its acceptance of Mercury's offer on Mercury's agreement to the additional terms contained in Tubular's acknowledgment.

(B)   No, because Tubular expressly conditioned its acceptance of Mercury's offer on Mercury's agreement to the additional terms contained in Tubular's acknowledgment and Mercury did not accept Tubular's additional terms.

(C)   Yes, because Tubular shipped the goods to Mercury and Mercury paid the carrier for the goods and for the cost of shipping the goods from Tubular to Mercury.

(D)   Yes, because Mercury accepted the additional terms contained in Tubular's acknowledgment when it paid the carrier for the goods and for the cost of shipping the goods from Tubular to Mercury.

Suppose that, rather than faxing a purchase order for 5,000 one-foot lengths of glass tubing to Tubular, Bruce faxed it to Philippe Glass ("PG"), a manufacturer of precision glass tubing located in Windsor, Ontario (Canada).

34.   If PG's acknowledgment contained the same terms set forth in Tubular's acknowledgment in Question 31, would Mercury and PG have formed a contract by their correspondence, their actions, or both?

(A)   No, because PG's acknowledgment contained terms that were not included in Mercury's offer, making PG's acknowledgment a counteroffer that Mercury never accepted in writing.

(B)   No, because PG's acknowledgment contained additional terms that materially altered the terms of Mercury's offer, making PG's acknowledgment a counteroffer that Mercury never accepted in writing.

(C)   Yes, because PG's acknowledgment was a seasonable acceptance of Mercury's offer, despite the fact that PG's acknowledgment contained additional terms that materially altered the terms of Mercury's offer, because Mercury did not, without undue delay, object to PG's additional terms.

(D)   Yes, because PG's acknowledgment contained additional terms that materially altered the terms of Mercury's offer, making PG's acknowledgment a counteroffer, which Mercury accepted when it paid the carrier for the goods and for the cost of shipping the goods from PG to Mercury.

On August 1, 2003, Bobbie Barista engaged Pablo Paynter to strip, prep, repaint or stain (as appropriate), and seal Bobbie's new summer house, garage, deck, boat dock, and boathouse on Martha's Vineyard. Pablo came highly recommended by Bobbie's new summer neighbors, Hans and Helga Heimlich. Bobbie asked Pablo to begin work as soon as his schedule permitted following her departure for her primary home in Tallahassee, Florida, on or before August 31st, and promised to pay him $20,000 for the entire job.

Upon returning to Tallahassee, Bobbie found that her house had suffered some hail damage, which was not covered by her homeowner's insurance. Shortly thereafter, she learned that her employer, the law firm of Crossley, Garvin & Shepherd, Chtd., was disbanding effective September 30th. (Bobbie, despite her apparent financial well-being, was not a partner in the firm. Of course, that may be just as well, as a partner might not get to take three months off every summer. She inherited a substantial sum on the death of her parents, some of which she used to make the down payment on the Martha's Vineyard house.) Uncertain how much it would cost her to repair the hail damage to her primary residence and what the consequences of the firm's break-up would be on her income, Bobbie decided to hold off spending $20,000 (roughly two months' income in her present position) on a summer house she would not see again for several months until she had a better idea of what her monthly income would be after September 30th.

Unbeknownst to Bobbie, Pablo's schedule cleared very quickly, and he and his crew began work on Bobbie's house on September 1st. By the time Bobbie called Pablo on or about September 10th to tell him not to start the job until further notice, he and his crew were already more than 25% through with the project.

35.   Given that Pablo had substantially begun to perform, could Bobbie still revoke her offer?

(A)   Yes, because Bobbie offered Pablo a unilateral contract, which Bobbie could revoke at any time before Pablo completed the performance Bobbie requested.

(B)   Yes, because Bobbie offered Pablo a bilateral contract, which Bobbie could revoke at any time before Pablo promised to complete the requested work for the offered price.

(C) Yes, because Pablo failed to notify Bobbie that he had begun the work she offered to pay him to do.

(D) No, because Pablo had substantially begun to perform the work Bobbie offered to pay him to do.

Suppose that, shortly after Bobbie called Pablo, and before he had completed the entire contract, Pablo received a lucrative job offer that required him to move to Seattle, Washington.

36. If Pablo abandoned Bobbie's job, would Bobbie be obligated to pay Pablo the contract price?

ANSWER:

On May 1, 2003, Tom Greene, owner of All Things Greene ("ATG"), a professional landscaping business located in Iowa, wrote to Uncle Buck's Tree Farm ("Uncle Buck"), in Golden, Colorado, offering to purchase 500 juniper saplings from Uncle Buck at a price of $10 per sapling, provided that Uncle Buck deliver the saplings to ATG no later than June 15th and that Uncle Buck bear the cost of transporting the trees to ATG. On June 14th, Uncle Buck's truck pulled up to ATG's lot in order to deliver the saplings. Uncle Buck's driver presented ATG with an invoice for $5,000 for 500 juniper saplings. ATG refused delivery.

37. Did ATG and Uncle Buck form a contract as a result of ATG's written offer and Uncle Buck's delivery of the trees to ATG?

(A) No, because Uncle Buck never notified ATG that it had accepted and would fill ATG's order.

(B) No, because the contract between ATG and Uncle Buck was a unilateral one, entitling ATG to revoke its offer at any time before it accepted Uncle Buck's delivery.

(C) Yes, because Uncle Buck accepted ATG's offer by promptly shipping the goods ATG ordered.

(D) Yes, because ATG made a firm offer to Uncle Buck, precluding ATG from revoking its offer until the deadline had passed or Uncle Buck rejected the offer, whichever occurred first.

On July 14, 2003, Monica, a fruit merchant, mailed Chandler, a fruit stand operator, a written offer to sell him 100 crates of mangoes (approximately 30 per crate) for $6.00 per crate. By the terms of Monica's offer, Chandler had the exclusive right to accept or decline the offer until July 25th at 5:00 p.m. Chandler received Monica's written offer on July 16th at 2 p.m.

On July 17th, Monica wrote to Chandler revoking the offer. Monica promptly placed the letter in the mail, properly addressed, and with adequate postage. Later that same day, Monica sold all 100 crates of mangoes to Phoebe, a mango-loving vegetarian (or should it be "fruititarian"?), at a price of $7.50 per crate.

On July 19th, having no knowledge of Monica's transaction with Phoebe, Chandler faxed a letter to Monica stating that he would purchase 100 crates of mangoes from Monica for $6.00 per crate, provided that Monica deliver the mangoes no later than September 1st. Chandler added that he would be willing to take delivery at the same time of any additional mangoes in Monica's stock at the same price.

Monica received Chandler's July 19th fax at noon that day. Monica immediately sent a return fax to Chandler informing him that she had revoked her offer and sold the mangoes to Phoebe. Chandler received Monica's July 17th letter a few hours after receiving Monica's fax.

38. Assuming that Chandler otherwise effectively and timely accepted Monica's offer to sell Chandler 100 crates of mangoes for $6.00 per crate, what is the legal effect of Chandler's statement in his July 19th fax that he was willing to buy additional mangoes at the same price?

ANSWER:

39. Suppose that Chandler received Monica's July 17th letter before he sent Monica his July 19th fax. Did Chandler and Monica form a valid contract?

   (A) No, because Monica sent her revocation to Chandler before Chandler sent his acceptance to Monica.

   (B) No, because Chandler received Monica's revocation before Chandler sent his acceptance to Monica.

   (C) Yes, because Chandler sent his acceptance to Monica before July 25th.

   (D) Yes, because Monica made a firm offer that she could not revoke prior to July 25th.

40. Returning to the facts of Question 38, suppose, instead, that Chandler is a merchant but Monica is not. Did Chandler and Monica form a valid contract?

   (A) No, because Monica sent her revocation to Chandler before Chandler sent his acceptance to Monica.

   (B) Yes, because Chandler sent his acceptance to Monica before Chandler received Monica's revocation.

   (C) Yes, because Chandler sent his acceptance to Monica before July 25th.

   (D) Yes, because Monica made a firm offer that she could not revoke prior to July 25th.

Verbal received a package from the Home Video Outlet in the mail yesterday. Enclosed was a DVD and a letter. The letter read: "The enclosed DVD includes the first two episodes of *Who is Keyser Soze?* If you decide to keep this DVD, we will bill you $4.95 for these episodes. If you wish to receive additional installments in the future, do nothing, we will send you future episodes every 3-4 weeks at a price of $9.95 per one-hour DVD. If you wish to cancel your pre-approved subscription, return this letter, with the word 'CANCEL' written on it, in the enclosed self-addressed, postage-paid envelope."

41.   As a matter of contract law, what should Verbal do to avoid liability for the Home Video Outlet's offer to let him keep the first *Who is Keyser Soze?* DVD for only $4.95 and send him additional DVDs periodically for $9.95?

   (A)   Verbal need not do anything, because he did not order the DVD in the first place.

   (B)   Verbal should write "CANCEL" on the offer letter and return it to the Home Video Outlet in the enclosed self-addressed, postage-paid envelope.

   (C)   Verbal should return the unwanted DVD to the Home Video Outlet with the word "RETURN" (or words to that effect) written on the package.

   (D)   Verbal should do both (B) and (C).

Verbal's son, Keaton, wanted to learn to play the piano. Edie is a professional piano instructor. Verbal brought Keaton to Edie's studio for an introductory session. Edie agreed to accept Keaton as a student, and told Verbal that she charged $50 per hour. Thereafter, Verbal brought Keaton to Edie's studio twice a week for one-hour lessons. At the end of the first month, Edie sent Verbal an invoice for $400, or $50 per hour for the eight sessions after the introductory session. Verbal stopped taking Keaton to Edie's studio for piano lessons. When she called to inquire when Keaton will be returning and when she could expect to receive payment for the lessons she had already given Keaton, Verbal responded, "I never said I would pay you $50 per hour to teach my kid how to play the piano."

42.   Prior to telling her that he would no longer pay for her to teach Keaton to play the piano, did Verbal accept Edie's offer to teach Keaton for $50 per hour?

ANSWER:

Methuselah was getting along in years and wanted to provide for his grandson Noah's future. Over dinner one evening, Methuselah asked Noah what he would like Methuselah to leave him after Methuselah died. Noah replied that he was very fond of Methuselah's chinchilla ranch. "Very well," said Methuselah, "I will change my will to leave you the chinchilla ranch." "Thanks, Grandpa," Noah replied. "I'll make you proud."

43. Did Methuselah and Noah form a contract obligating Methuselah to amend his will to leave the chinchilla ranch to Noah?

    (A)   No, because Methuselah suffered no detriment from his promise.

    (B)   No, because Noah's promise to make Methuselah proud did not induce Methuselah to promise to will the chinchilla ranch to Noah.

    (C)   No, because Methuselah did not seek Noah's promise or performance in exchange for Methuselah's promise to will the chinchilla ranch to Noah.

    (D)   Yes, because Methuselah was morally obligated to keep his promise to Noah.

Suppose that Noah was a precocious 16-year old who was, in Methuselah's opinion, a bit too fond of cold beer, high stakes, and fast cars. Methuselah promised to will the chinchilla ranch to Noah if Noah would refrain from drinking and gambling and avoid speeding tickets for the rest of Methuselah's life. Noah promised to refrain from drinking and gambling and to avoid speeding tickets for the rest of Methuselah's life.

44. Did Methuselah and Noah form a contract obligating Methuselah to amend his will to leave the chinchilla ranch to Noah?

    (A)   Yes, because Noah's promise to refrain from activities that were not illegal, and in which he might otherwise have engaged, was a legal detriment to Noah.

    (B)   Yes, because Noah's promise to refrain from drinking, gambling, and speeding for the rest of Methuselah's life was the consideration Methuselah sought in exchange for his promise to will the chinchilla ranch to Noah.

    (C)   No, because Methuselah did not benefit from Noah's promise to refrain from drinking, gambling, and speeding for the rest of Methuselah's life.

    (D)   No, because Noah's promise to refrain from drinking, gambling, and speeding for the rest of Methuselah's life was not the consideration Methuselah sought in exchange for his promise to will the chinchilla ranch to Noah.

Suppose that, in addition to promising to refrain from drinking and gambling and to avoid speeding tickets for the rest of Methuselah's life, Noah actually did as he promised for the rest of Methuselah's life.

45. Did Methuselah and Noah form a contract obligating Methuselah to amend his will to leave the chinchilla ranch to Noah?

    (A)   Yes, because Noah's refraining from activities that were not illegal, and in which he might otherwise have engaged, was a legal detriment to Noah.

    (B)   Yes, because Noah's promise to refrain from drinking, gambling, and speeding for the rest of Methuselah's life was the consideration Methuselah sought in exchange for his promise to will the chinchilla ranch to Noah.

    (C)   Yes, because Noah's refraining from drinking, gambling, and speeding for the rest of Methuselah's life was the consideration Methuselah sought in exchange for his promise to will the chinchilla ranch to Noah.

    (D)   No, because Methuselah did not benefit from Noah's refraining from drinking, gambling, and speeding for the rest of Methuselah's life.

Returning to the facts of Question 44, suppose that Methuselah promised to will the chinchilla ranch to Noah if Noah would promise to refrain from drinking, gambling, and speeding for the rest of Methuselah's life. Noah replied that he promised to refrain from drinking, gambling, and speeding for the rest of Methuselah's life.

46. Did Methuselah and Noah form a contract obligating Methuselah to amend his will to leave the chinchilla ranch to Noah?

    (A)   Yes, because Methuselah sought Noah's promise to refrain from drinking, gambling, and speeding in exchange for Methuselah's promise to will the chinchilla ranch to Noah.

    (B)   No, because Noah suffered no detriment from his promise to refrain from drinking, gambling, and speeding.

    (C)   No, because Methuselah realized no benefit from his promise to will the chinchilla ranch to Noah.

    (D)   No, because Noah, who was a minor when he made his promise, had the legal right to avoid the contract, making his promise to Methuselah illusory.

When Methuselah's regular chinchilla herder told Methuselah that he required back surgery and that the doctor estimated it would take at least six months for him to recover sufficiently to resume work, Methuselah sought to hire Shem to tend the herd for a period of up to six months, or until Methuselah's regular chinchilla herder became physically able to resume his duties, if he was not able to do so for more than six months. In exchange for Shem's services, Methuselah promised to either (1) pay Shem $1,000 per month or (2) provide Shem's family with suitable rent-free housing for as long as Shem tended Methuselah's chinchilla herd.

47.   Was Methuselah's promise to either pay Shem or house Shem's family valid consider-
      ation for Shem's services as a chinchilla herder?

ANSWER:

Suppose that, rather than promising to either pay Shem $1,000 per month or provide Shem's
family with suitable, rent-free housing for as long as Shem tends Methuselah's herd, Methuselah
promised to either (1) pay Shem $1,000 per month or (2) pay Shem $500 per month and provide
Shem's family with suitable rent-free housing for as long as Shem tended Methuselah's herd.

48.   Would that promise constitute valid consideration for Shem's services as a chinchilla
      herder?

ANSWER:

Some of the fences on Methuselah's chinchilla ranch needed to be repaired or replaced and
Methuselah had to go out of town on other business. Before he left town, Methuselah called
the local hardware store and ordered the lumber and other materials needed to repair or replace
the damaged fencing. The owner of the store, Jared, had been thinking for some time about
selling the store, retiring to another state, and taking up chinchilla ranching as a (hopefully
profitable) diversion. The retail price for the items Methuselah ordered totaled $4,500. However,
Jared proposed to trade the lumber and other materials to Methuselah for a breeding pair of
chinchillas. At the time, a breeding pair of chinchillas sold for between $400 and $650 on the
open market, depending on the coloring of the male and the female. Knowing this, Methuselah
gladly accepted Jared's proposal and agreed to trade Jared a prime breeding pair for the lumber
and other materials. Jared told Methuselah that he would deliver the lumber and other materials
the next morning. Methuselah told Jared he could pick out his chinchillas whenever it was
convenient.

49.   Was Methuselah's promise to trade Jared a prime breeding pair of chinchillas adequate
      consideration for Jared's promise to trade Methuselah the lumber and other materials?

      (A)   Yes, because Jared sought Methuselah's promise to trade him the chinchillas in
            exchange for Jared's promise to provide Methuselah the materials he needed.

      (B)   No, because the materials were worth substantially more on the open market than
            the chinchillas.

      (C)   No, because the materials were goods, transactions which are governed by UCC
            Article 2, while chinchillas were animals, transactions in which are outside the
            scope of Article 2.

      (D)   No, because Methuselah and Jared agreed orally, and the materials were worth
            more than $500, requiring some writing to bind Jared to his promise.

Suppose that Methuselah agreed to trade Jared the breeding pair for the lumber and other materials, on the condition that Jared agree not to operate a competing chinchilla ranch within 100 miles of Methuselah's ranch. Jared told Methuselah that he was planning to retire to another state more than 100 miles away anyway, so he readily agreed to Methuselah's condition.

50. Was Methuselah's promise to trade Jared a breeding pair of chinchillas, subject to the condition that Jared not operate a competing chinchilla ranch within 100 miles of Methuselah's ranch, adequate consideration for Jared's promise to trade Methuselah the lumber and other materials?

ANSWER:

Before leaving town, Methuselah telephoned the local handyman, Enos, to discuss the fence repairs. Enos had done numerous jobs for Methuselah over the years, and his regular hourly rate was $20.00. Methuselah told Enos that Jared would deliver the materials the next morning and that he needed Enos to start work immediately after Jared delivered the materials. Gaps had opened in the fence line, allowing a neighboring cattle rancher's steers to stray onto Methuselah's land, where they had already trampled a few of Methuselah's "free range" chinchillas, and allowing Methuselah's chinchillas to stray onto the neighbor's land or onto an adjacent highway. Because Enos was already in the midst of a job for someone else and would have to work overtime to manage both jobs, Enos told Methuselah he would have to pay $40.00 per hour if he wanted Enos to start immediately. Having saved a bundle of money on his deal with Jared, Methuselah agreed to pay Enos double his normal rate. When Methuselah returned from his trip, Enos presented him with a bill for $1,200.00 ($40.00 per hour x 30 hours) for his time and labor spent repairing and replacing Methuselah's damaged fences.

51. Could Methuselah refuse to pay Enos on the grounds that Enos gave inadequate consideration for Methuselah's promise to pay him $40.00 per hour?

ANSWER:

Arnold owed Benedict $500, which the parties did not dispute. Arnold offered to pay Benedict the $500 if Benedict would promise to repaint Arnold's car. Benedict typically charged $250 to repaint a car the size, style, and condition of Arnold's.

52. Was Arnold's offer of $500 valid consideration for Benedict's promise to repaint Arnold's car?

(A) Yes, because Benedict promised to repaint Arnold's car in exchange for Arnold's promise to pay Benedict the $500 Arnold already owed Benedict.

(B) Yes, because the price Arnold promised to pay was twice the value of Benedict's services, so Arnold was obviously repaying a part of his debt as well as purchasing Benedict's services.

(C) Yes, because Benedict had not previously been able to induce or compel Arnold to pay his debt, so Arnold's offer to pay the $500 provided Benedict with value he might not otherwise have received.

(D) No, because Arnold's promise to pay a debt he already owed to Benedict cannot be consideration for an additional promise or performance by Benedict.

Suppose, instead, that Arnold offered to pay Benedict $750 to repaint Arnold's car and Benedict accepted. Both parties understood at the time that $500 of the $750 was the money Arnold already owed Benedict.

53. Was Arnold's offer of $750 valid consideration for Benedict's promise to repaint Arnold's car?

(A) No, because Arnold's promise to pay a debt he already owed to Benedict cannot be consideration for an additional promise or performance by Benedict.

(B) Yes, because Benedict had not previously been able to induce or compel Arnold to pay his debt, so Arnold's offer to pay the $750 provides Benedict with value he might not otherwise have received.

(C) Yes, because the price Arnold promised to pay equaled the amount of his outstanding debt plus the fair market value of Benedict's services.

(D) Yes, because Benedict promised to repaint Arnold's car in exchange for Arnold's promise to pay Benedict more than the $500 Arnold already owed Benedict.

Sandra Ypres is a realtor living and working in San Dimas, California. Bosworth Hallifax, a personal injury attorney based in nearby Riverside, knows Sandra casually through mutual acquaintances. At 9:00 a.m. on Monday, June 30, 2003, Sandra faxed Bosworth a letter stating that she had 100 acres of undeveloped land, at the intersection of Wyld Stallyns Drive and No Way, which she would sell him for $1,000 per acre. Sandra's letter also stated: "Unless I receive your written acceptance by 5:00 p.m. on Thursday, July 3, 2003, my offer will expire. I will not offer this same acreage to any other prospective buyer until 5:00 p.m. on Thursday, July 3, 2003, or until you reject this offer, whichever occurs first." Across the bottom of Sandra's letter was printed

"Sandra Ypres, Realtor
2400 Baja Grande Dr., Suite 150, San Dimas, CA 90735
Tel: (562) 555-1234
Fax: (562) 555-9876
E-Mail: sandra2400@yippie.com."

At 1:00 p.m. on July 3rd, just before he rushed out of the house to catch a flight to Akron, Bosworth sent an e-mail to "sandra2400@yippie.com" stating: "I agree to buy your 100 acres for $1,000 per acre. Have a great Fourth of July!" Bosworth's e-mail reached Sandra's e-mailbox less than a minute later, but she did not check her e-mail until after 5:00 p.m. on July 3rd.

54.   Was there sufficient consideration to bind Sandra to her offer to sell Bosworth 100 acres of undeveloped land for $1,000 per acre?

   (A)   No, because Sandra wanted Bosworth to purchase the land, not to promise to purchase the land.

   (B)   Yes, because Bosworth's promise to purchase the land was the consideration Sandra sought in exchange for her promise to sell the land to Bosworth.

   (C)   No, because Sandra did not receive Bosworth's reply until after the deadline.

   (D)   No. Bosworth's e-mail was legally inadequate to form a binding contract because Sandra's offer required him to respond in writing.

Bamm Bamm, age 25, lived with his parents, Barney and Betty, in a nice neighborhood in Bedrock. Bamm Bamm had his own bedroom, but wanted a place to play his drums. He contacted Slate Construction Company ("Slate") to get an estimate on adding a music room to the house. His parents had no particular need for the additional room, but they wanted to support his musical interests and preferred that he not play the drums in his bedroom.

Fred, one of Slate's supervisors, came to the house and met with Bamm Bamm to discuss the addition. Fred had Bamm Bamm fill out a credit application and explained that Slate would only agree to perform the work on credit if Bamm Bamm's credit rating was satisfactory. Fred also gave Bamm Bamm a written "offer" detailing the specifics of the project, the expected cost and time of completion, and the payment schedule. The "offer" clearly indicated that it was conditional on Bamm Bamm having satisfactory credit. It also stated: "This agreement shall become binding only upon written acceptance by Slate Construction Company or upon commencing performance of the work." The total cost was to be $10,000.

After a few weeks passed without word from Slate, Bamm Bamm assumed that his credit rating had proved unacceptable. (He was rather destructive, at times, and had promised to make amends to several neighbors and area businesses, but he was not always able to do so in a timely manner.) Bamm Bamm wrote to Fred: "I have changed my mind and no longer want the construction work done which we discussed." Slate never received the letter. Bamm Bamm sold his drums and took up power lifting at the local gym — a hobby that did not require adding on to his parents' house.

A month or so later, while Barney and Betty were vacationing at Yellowrock Park and Bamm Bamm was out of town at a power lifting competition, a Slate crew quickly (but in a workmanlike manner) built the addition, leaving behind an invoice billing Bamm Bamm for the work. When Barney, Betty, and Bamm Bamm returned to Bedrock, they discovered the new music room and the bill from Slate, with the first payment due in one month.

No longer needing the room, and unable to pay for the work (having squandered his meager savings on steroids and baby oil), Bamm Bamm telephoned Fred. Fred referred the call to in-house counsel, Stonewall, who replied: "Sorry, we did not receive your letter. According to our agreement, we were to perform the work once your credit check was approved. It was. We did. You owe us $10,000.00." Stonewall subsequently sent Bamm Bamm several letters demanding payment, and then threatening suit for nonpayment, but Bamm Bamm could not pay.

Betty eventually met with Stonewall and asked her to stop harassing Bamm Bamm. When Stonewall insisted that *someone* pay Slate for the work it performed, Betty orally agreed to pay Slate the remaining balance due ($10,000 plus interest), in 12 monthly installments of $950 each, if Slate would stop all efforts to collect from Bamm Bamm. Stonewall agreed, on Slate's behalf, not to pursue Bamm Bamm any further. Betty made only three payments. Meanwhile, Bamm Bamm fled the jurisdiction and was last seen working in a circus side show in a distant land.

55. Were the improvements that Slate made to Barney and Betty's house consideration to support Betty's agreement to pay Slate $11,400?

   (A) Yes, because Slate performed the work in exchange for Bamm Bamm's promise to pay, which promise Betty assumed.

   (B) Yes, because Slate gave value in exchange for Betty's promise to pay Bamm Bamm's debt.

   (C) No, because Slate had already completed its work before Betty promised to pay Slate.

   (D) No, because Betty and Barney did not authorize the work that Slate performed on their house.

56. Whether or not the improvements that Slate made to Barney and Betty's house were consideration to support Betty's promise to pay Slate, was Betty's promise supported by other consideration?

ANSWER:

Jenny Beasley wants to sue her former employer, Owl's Nest, for breaching its promise to award a new Mitsubishi to the winner of a March 2003 sales contest. Jenny claims that her manager, Jason Boone, told her and the other waitresses at the Paradise Road Owl's Nest that whoever sold the most margaritas at each participating Owl's Nest location during March 2003 would have her name entered in a drawing, and that the winner of the drawing would receive a new Mitsubishi. As the contest progressed, Jason told the waitresses that he did not know whether the winner would receive a Mitsubishi car, truck, or SUV, but that the winner would have to pay any registration fees on the vehicle. On or about April 8th, Jason informed Jenny that she had sold more margaritas during March than any other waitress at the Paradise Road Owl's Nest, and that he had submitted her name for the drawing. Two weeks later, Jason informed Jenny that she had won the drawing. He proceeded to blindfold her and lead her to the parking lot outside the restaurant. Waiting for her there was not a Mitsubishi car, truck, or SUV, however, but a plastic model of a Mitsubishi Zero, a World War II Japanese fighter airplane. Jason was laughing. Jenny was not.

Owl's Nest pays its waitresses $5.00 per hour for each hour they work, and allows them to keep 75% of their tips. The restaurant keeps the other 25%. Waitresses are scheduled to work between 35 and 40 hours per week. They can work extra shifts when another waitress wants or needs time off, but are not allowed to work more than 50 hours per week. In the three months prior to March 2003, Jenny worked an average of 40 hours per week, and earned an average of $1,600 per month in tips ($1,200 of which she kept). During March 2003, Jenny worked an average of 50 hours per week, and earned $2,000 in tips ($1,500 of which she kept).

Owl's Nest waitresses are at-will employees, who work without written employment contracts. The company's policy manual requires any employee to give two weeks notice prior to terminating her employment, and requires Owl's Nest to give any employee two weeks notice prior to terminating her employment, unless Owl's Nest is terminating the employee for cause. Every employee receives a copy of the policy manual when she is hired. Jenny received a copy of the policy manual when she began working at Owl's Nest in January 2002.

57. If Jason's statements and Jenny's actions were sufficient to constitute an offer and acceptance, did Jenny give consideration to bind Owl's Nest to the contract thus formed?

   (A) Yes, because she continued working at Owl's Nest for the duration of the contest, despite the fact that she was an at-will employee who could have quit at any time after giving two weeks notice.

   (B) Yes, because she worked additional hours during the contest period, generating additional sales revenue for Owl's Nest and increasing the "tip tax" collected by the restaurant.

   (C) Yes, because she sold additional margaritas during the contest period, generating additional sales revenue for Owl's Nest and increasing the "tip tax" collected by the restaurant.

   (D) All of the above.

Suppose that, in order to work the extra hours during March, Jenny had to pay a babysitter $7.00 per hour to stay with Jenny's daughter, Evelyn.

58. Would the $70 or so per week that Jenny paid the babysitter be part of Jenny's consideration for Jason's offer, on behalf of Owl's Nest?

   (A) Yes, because Jason should have foreseen that Jenny would have to pay someone to watch her small child while Jenny was working extra hours at Owl's Nest.

   (B) Yes, because it was a natural consequence of Jason's implied request that Jenny work extra hours at Owl's Nest.

   (C) No, because Jenny paid the $70 to a third party, rather than to Owl's Nest.

   (D) No, because Jason did not seek Jenny's employment of a babysitter in exchange for Jason's promise to enter Jenny in the Mitsubishi drawing if she won the sales contest at the Paradise Road Owl's Nest.

Carol and Dawson were recently divorced. Carol has primary custody of their minor children, Emilio and Francesca. The divorce decree and property settlement agreement require Dawson to pay Carol $500 per month "for the support of each minor child resulting from their former marriage." Dawson is also required, during the first two years following their divorce, to continue making monthly payments on the minivan he and Carol bought a year before they separated and "such other sums as may be required to keep the minivan safely operational, including scheduled maintenance."

Guillermo, a major client of Dawson's, provided Dawson with private box tickets for the big game Saturday, and Dawson wanted to take Emilio and Francesca to the game. Unfortunately, Dawson did not have visitation rights the weekend of the game. Dawson asked Carol if she would agree to let Dawson take the children to the game. Carol said "O.K., but I want you to do something for me first. I want a new set of tires for the minivan. I don't like the feel of the tires that are on it now. If you will pay for the tires, I'll let you take the kids to the game." Dawson agreed. Carol drove the minivan to get the new tires installed on Tuesday, and dropped by Dawson's office later that day with a receipt for four new tires, valve stems, and balancing. Dawson wrote her a check for the total amount. When Dawson called Carol on Friday to make arrangements to pick up the children on Saturday morning, Carol told him she had changed her mind and would not let him take the children to the game.

Assume, for purposes of the following questions, that there are no contractual or legal impediments to Carol and Dawson agreeing to modify the visitation terms of their divorce decree and property settlement agreement in order to allow Dawson one extra day's visitation with Carol's prior consent.

59. Did Dawson give valuable consideration in exchange for Carol's promise to let him have additional visitation time with Emilio and Francesca?

ANSWER:

Suppose, instead, that Carol promised to let Dawson take the children to the game in exchange for his promise to pay for having a DVD entertainment center installed in the minivan.

60. Was Dawson's promise to pay for a new DVD system installed in the minivan consideration to bind Carol to her promise to let Dawson take Emilio and Francesca to the game?

(A) No, because Dawson was contractually responsible for the upkeep of the minivan.

(B) No, because contracts that affect custody rights are, as a general rule, unenforceable as contrary to public policy.

(C) Yes, because paying to install a DVD entertainment center, unlike paying to install new tires, is beyond the scope of Dawson's pre-existing duties under the divorce decree and property settlement agreement.

(D)   Yes, as long as it was what Carol bargained for and Dawson gave his promise in exchange for Carol's promise to let Dawson take Emilio and Francesca to the game.

On February 15, 2002, Wallace Williams and Bruce Roberts entered into a written contract whereby Wallace, a professional entertainer, agreed to perform at Bruce's resort hotel in the Berkshires for the week of July 1-7, 2002 and Bruce agreed to pay Wallace $25,000 for performing. In early May, Wallace had a hit single that, virtually overnight, made him a star who could command at least $75,000 for a one-week engagement. On June 1st, Wallace telephoned Bruce demanding $75,000 for his July 1st-7th performances. Bruce told Wallace that "a deal is a deal," and would not agree to pay Wallace more than the previously-agreed $25,000.

61. If Wallace's 18th birthday was June 1, 2002, would he have been entitled to refuse to perform the contract?

    (A) Yes, because any contract Wallace entered into while he was a minor was void.

    (B) Yes, because any contract Wallace entered into while he was a minor was voidable at Wallace's option.

    (C) Yes, because this was not a contract for medical attention or other goods or services necessary to maintain his well-being, and Wallace was a minor when he entered into it.

    (D) No, because Wallace implicitly reaffirmed the contract when he asked Bruce for more money rather than telling Bruce he did not intend to be bound.

Suppose that, while Bruce initially refused to renegotiate, when Wallace said he would not perform unless Bruce agreed to pay him more money, Bruce relented. After a lengthy face-to-face discussion the morning of June 8th, Bruce dictated a new contract to his secretary, in the exact words of the first contract and running for the same period, with Wallace's compensation changed from $25,000 to $50,000. As they signed the new contract they tore up the old one. Thereafter, Wallace kept the engagement, but Bruce refused to pay more than the $25,000 he had originally promised. Wallace sued.

62. On what basis could Bruce successfully defend Wallace's suit by arguing that, because he had already spent considerable time, money, and resources — particularly after Wallace's single became a hit — advertising Wallace's upcoming appearance, he should not be held to the June 8th contract?

    (A) Bruce should not be bound by the June 8th contract because he signed it under duress.

    (B) Bruce should not be bound by the June 8th contract because he signed it under undue influence.

(C)   Bruce should not be bound by the June 8th contract because to do so would be unconscionable.

(D)   None of the above.

Suppose that, when Wallace met with Bruce on June 8th, Wallace was accompanied by a couple of older men, who he introduced to Bruce as his "advisors." When Bruce rejected Wallace's initial demand for more money, the elder of the two men motioned for Bruce to come closer. When he did, the younger of the two men casually unbuttoned his suit jacket and slid one side back to reveal a pistol. Threatened by the gesture, Bruce's negotiating strategy changed, and he and Wallace soon came to an accommodation and signed the new contract.

63.   Under these facts, would Bruce have grounds (assuming he had the nerve) to refuse to pay Wallace more than the original $25,000?

(A)   Bruce should not be bound by the June 8th contract because he signed it under duress.

(B)   Bruce should not be bound by the June 8th contract because he signed it under undue influence.

(C)   Bruce should not be bound by the June 8th contract because to do so would be unconscionable.

(D)   None of the above.

Returning to the facts of Question 62, suppose that Bruce drank heavily the day he and Wallace negotiated and signed the agreement increasing Wallace's compensation to $50,000.

64.   Can Bruce defend Wallace's suit by arguing that he was too intoxicated to form the requisite intent to be bound by the new contract?

(A)   No, because Bruce voluntarily became intoxicated, and should not now be able to argue that he was not responsible for his actions while voluntarily intoxicated.

(B)   No, because Bruce's actions gainsay his being sufficiently intoxicated to relieve him of his contractual obligations.

(C)   No, because Bruce reaffirmed the June 8th contract by letting Wallace perform at his hotel the week of July 1st-7th.

(D)   Yes, because Bruce was so intoxicated that he could not form the requisite intent to contract, and Wallace knew or should have known that Bruce was intoxicated.

Suppose that, within days of his hit single's release, Wallace signed a multi-album contract with Vestal Records. Wallace spent the whole week following his eighteenth birthday in Vestal's studios, recording and mixing songs. At the end of the week, Wallace called Vestal's president, Chick Hanson. Wallace told Hanson that he appreciated all that Vestal had done for him, but he had received a better offer from another label. When Hanson sputtered, "But we have a contract," Wallace replied, "I was underage when I signed it. Sorry, Chick."

65. Could Wallace disaffirm his contract with Vestal because he signed it when he was a minor?

    (A) Yes, because any contract Wallace entered into while he was a minor was void.

    (B) Yes, because any contract Wallace entered into while he was a minor was voidable at Wallace's option.

    (C) Yes, because this was not a contract for medical attention or other goods or services necessary to maintain his well-being, and Wallace was a minor when he entered into it.

    (D) No, because Wallace implicitly reaffirmed the contract when he used Vestal's studio time and equipment following his 18th birthday.

Having completed a very successful summer tour, including the week at Bruce's hotel (where all seven shows were sold out and made Bruce a healthy profit, despite having to pay Wallace more money than they had originally agreed) and having eventually signed a more lucrative contract with Hippo Records, one of Vestal's competitors (who bought out Vestal's interest in Wallace once Vestal made it clear they would fight Wallace's claim that he was not bound by the contract he signed before he turned 18), Wallace decided it was time to spend some of his hardly earned (that's a pun, not a typo) riches. Wanting to stay on the East Coast, he began hunting for housing befitting a rising music star. After some searching, he found an apartment on the Upper East Side with a nice view of Central Park. Anticipating an increasing flow of income, Wallace was not worried about living beyond his present means. Having agreed with the seller, Sam Sharman, on a price of $2.5 million, Wallace paid $250,000 cash and signed a five-year real estate installment purchase contract for the balance. The contract required Wallace to make 60 principal payments of $37,500 per month, plus interest, upon full satisfaction of which Sharman would deliver title to the apartment, free of any liens or encumbrances (other than those in favor of the apartment building owner or cooperative).

After moving into the apartment, Wallace was awakened one morning by a knock at the door. When he answered the door, he was greeted by an attorney, who introduced himself as a representative of Otis Owen, the owner of the apartment that Wallace was presently occupying. Owen, who had been abroad for several months, was preparing to return to the city, and had sent the attorney to notify Sharman, who was subletting from Owen, that he had 14 days to vacate the premises. When Wallace told the attorney he must be mistaken because Wallace had purchased the apartment from Sharman, the attorney responded, "I'm sorry, sir, but you're the one who is mistaken. Mr. Sharman has never owned this apartment, and had no right to sell it to you. You have 14 days to vacate." When Wallace received a payment due notice from Sharman a day or two later, he returned it unpaid with a note stating that Wallace would not pay Sharman one cent more and that he would see Sharman in court. Sharman sued Wallace for breach of the installment purchase contract. Wallace countersued for fraud and conversion, seeking judicial rescission of the installment purchase contract, the return of his $250,000 down payment, and damages to compensate him for the cost of locating and moving into new digs.

66. Was Wallace obligated to pay Sharman the remainder of the installments as promised, despite the fact that Sharman did not have the right to sell Wallace the apartment?

   (A)   No, because Wallace lacked the requisite capacity to form a binding contract.

   (B)   No, because Sharman breached the duty of good faith and fair dealing when he sold an apartment to Wallace that he did not have the right to sell.

   (C)   No, because Sharman misrepresented that he had title, or could give title, to the apartment to Wallace upon Wallace's satisfaction of the installment purchase contract.

   (D)   Yes, because Wallace did not ask Sharman whether he had title to the apartment before agreeing to purchase it from him.

Suppose, instead, that Sharman did have good title or the right to convey good title on Owen's behalf, and that Wallace has been comfortably ensconced in the apartment since moving in several months ago. Suppose, further, that the contract included a provision for interest on the unpaid balance at 18% per year, and that the maximum interest rate permitted by applicable New York law is 16% per year.

67. Would Wallace have grounds to avoid the contract with Sharman under these circumstances?

   (A)   Yes, because the contract rate of interest is usurious, and therefore illegal.

   (B)   Yes, because the contract rate of interest is usurious, and therefore unconscionable.

   (C)   Yes, because Sharman breached the duty of good faith and fair dealing he owed Wallace when he gave Wallace a contract to sign that contained a usurious interest rate.

   (D)   Yes, because Sharman actually or impliedly misrepresented that the interest rate included in the contract was not usurious.

While strolling down the street with some buddies one afternoon, a beautiful young woman approached Wallace, handed him a piece of paper, and asked for his autograph. Wallace obliged. A few days later, Wallace received a phone call from an attorney with the law firm of Cohen, Perillo & Sanger, outside counsel for Hippo Records (the label Wallace signed with after leaving Vestal). The attorney explained that a young woman had delivered what appeared to be an agreement, signed by Wallace, assigning her one-half of his royalties for the next five years in exchange for her domestic services. Wallace denied signing any such agreement, and asked the attorney to describe the young woman. When the attorney did so, Wallace realized it must have been the beautiful young woman who had asked for his autograph a few days earlier. The next morning, the same beautiful young woman appeared at Wallace's door, introduced herself as Sonya, and asked, "Where shall I begin?" Wallace responded, "What do you mean?" Sonya replied, "We have an agreement. I clean your apartment once a week, and you pay me one-half of your royalties. You signed it, remember?"

68. Assuming that the signature on the document in question is Wallace's, may he avoid being bound, despite his signature, because the contract is unconscionable?

ANSWER:

On March 1, 2003, Gwyneth and Russell agreed that Gwyneth would pay Russell $100 each for two tickets to the March 15th New York premiere of *The Orange Pumpernickel*. They further agreed that Russell would deliver the tickets to Gwyneth no later than March 14th. The New York premiere of Cameron Ridley's new movie, *The Orange Pumpernickel*, was scheduled for March 15th at the Radikal City Musik Hall. That same night, the 41st Street Playhouse scheduled the premiere of a stage production of *The Orange Pumpernickel*, directed by David Marmoset.

On March 2nd, Russell purchased two tickets from the 41st Street Playhouse for $75 each. On March 14th, when Russell delivered the tickets to Gwyneth, she refused to pay, claiming that Russell had agreed to sell her tickets to the movie, not the play. Russell did not have any tickets to the movie, and none were commercially available at that late date. Russell tried unsuccessfully to find another buyer for the play tickets and to obtain a refund from the Playhouse. Unable to use them himself, he left the tickets with Gwyneth in case she changed her mind.

Gwyneth sued Russell for failing to provide her with the movie tickets. Russell countersued Gwyneth for failing to pay for the tickets he delivered to her.

69. Assuming that, when they made their contract, Gwyneth knew about the movie, but not about the play, and Russell knew about the play, but not the movie, would Russell have a viable defense to Gwyneth's suit?

    (A) Yes, based on mutual mistake.

    (B) Yes, based on unilateral mistake.

    (C) Yes, based on lack of mutual assent.

    (D) No, because Russell assumed the risk of any disagreement between him and Gwyneth regarding the object of the contract.

Jenny Beasley wants to sue her former employer, Owl's Nest, for breaching its promise to award a new Mitsubishi to the winner of a March 2003 sales contest. Jenny claims that her manager, Jason Boone, told her and the other waitresses at the Paradise Road Owl's Nest that whoever sold the most margaritas at each participating Owl's Nest location during March 2003 would have her name entered in a drawing, and that the winner of the drawing would receive a new Mitsubishi. As the contest progressed, Jason told the waitresses that he did not know whether the winner would receive a Mitsubishi car, truck, or SUV, but that the winner would have to pay any registration fees on the vehicle. On or about April 8th, Jason informed Jenny that she had sold more margaritas during March than any other waitress at the Paradise Road Owl's Nest, and that he had submitted her name for the drawing. Two weeks later, Jason informed Jenny that she had won the drawing. He proceeded to blindfold her and lead her to the parking lot outside the restaurant. Waiting for her there was not a Mitsubishi car, truck, or SUV, however, but a plastic model of a Mitsubishi Zero, a World War II Japanese fighter airplane. Jason was laughing. Jenny was not.

70. Assuming that Jason's words and actions are attributable to Owl's Nest, can Owl's Nest successfully defend Jenny's breach of contract suit by claiming mutual mistake?

ANSWER:

In early June 2002, Rochelle Payne, the Dean of Missy's College of Law, located in the state of Magnolia, telephoned Hilda Rodriguez, a resident of South Mesquite (located in another state several hundred miles away from Magnolia), and offered her a two-year appointment as a visiting professor of law at an annual salary of $50,000, plus certain expenses, provided that Hilda could move to Magnolia in time to begin the Fall 2002 semester. Rochelle mentioned a remote possibility that the visiting position might become permanent, but she cautioned Hilda against considering that possibility when deciding whether to accept the visiting offer. Hilda accepted, quit her lucrative private practice in South Mesquite, sold her home in South Mesquite, and moved herself, her hubby, and their adorable child Lars, to Magnolia, incurring several thousand dollars in un-reimbursed moving expenses.

During the spring semester of her first year, Rochelle informed Hilda that the spring semester would likely be her last. While Hilda's job performance was satisfactory, former Supreme Court Justice Brilliant Foote, a Magnolia native, had inquired about teaching part-time at Missy's while he worked on his memoirs, and Rochelle decided to use the funds set aside for Hilda's salary to pay Foote.

71. Assuming that Rochelle and Hilda formed a contract supported by consideration, did that contract satisfy the relevant statute of frauds?

   (A) Yes, because Hilda's appointment was on an annual basis.

   (B) Yes, because Hilda detrimentally relied on Rochelle's promise to employ her for two years.

   (C) Yes, because Hilda could have quit, died, or become incapacitated during her first year at Missy's.

   (D) No, because it was a contract for services to be performed over a two-year period.

Suppose that Missy's policy is to pay professors their salaries in equal installments on the last business day of each month, beginning with the last day of the month in which a professor begins teaching. In order to process Hilda's first paycheck, Rochelle signed a payroll form prepared by her administrative assistant, Chet, who typed the words "Visiting Professor" on the line on the payroll form titled "Job Title" and "24 months" on the line titled "Duration of Contract." Rochelle signed the payroll form without making any changes to it.

72. Assuming that Missy's and Hilda formed a contract supported by consideration, would that contract satisfy the relevant statute of frauds?

   (A) No, because there was no written contract signed by both parties.

(B)   No, because there was no writing signed by both parties evidencing the contract.

(C)   No, because Chet created and Rochelle signed the payroll record after Hilda had already accepted and begun to perform.

(D)   Yes, because the payroll form evidenced a two-year employment contract between Missy's and Hilda.

Returning to the facts of Question 71, suppose that, instead of offering to employ Hilda for two years, Rochelle offered to employ Hilda "until she dies, becomes disabled, or voluntarily retires."

73.   Assuming that Missy's and Hilda formed a contract supported by consideration, would that contract satisfy the relevant statute of frauds?

(A)   No, because it was a contract for services that the parties anticipated would be performed over a period in excess of one year.

(B)   No, because the contract gave Hilda the option to terminate the contract early by voluntarily retiring; therefore, it was illusory and unenforceable.

(C)   Yes, but only if Hilda died, became disabled, or voluntarily retired during her first year of employment.

(D)   Yes, because Hilda could fully perform the contract in one year or less.

Returning to the facts of Question 71, suppose that, instead of offering to employ Hilda for two years, Rochelle offered to employ Hilda "for two years or until she dies, becomes disabled, or voluntarily retires, whichever transpires first."

74.   Assuming that Missy's and Hilda formed a contract supported by consideration, would that contract satisfy the relevant statute of frauds?

(A)   No, because it was a contract for services to be performed over a two-year period.

(B)   No, because the contract gave Hilda the option to terminate the contract early by voluntarily retiring; therefore, it was illusory and unenforceable.

(C)   Yes, but only if Hilda died, became disabled, or voluntarily retired during her first year of employment.

(D)   Yes, because Hilda could fully perform the contract in one year or less.

Sandra Ypres is a realtor living and working in San Dimas, California. Bosworth Hallifax, a personal injury attorney based in nearby Riverside, knows Sandra casually through mutual acquaintances. At 9:00 a.m. on Monday, June 30, 2003, Sandra faxed Bosworth a letter stating that she had 100 acres of undeveloped land, at the intersection of Wyld Stallyns Drive and No Way, which she would sell him for $1,000 per acre. Sandra's letter also stated: "Unless I receive your written acceptance by 5:00 p.m. on Thursday, July 3, 2003, my offer will expire. I will not offer this same acreage to any other prospective buyer until 5:00 p.m. on Thursday, July 3, 2003, or until you reject this offer, whichever occurs first." Across the bottom of Sandra's letter was printed

"Sandra Ypres, Realtor
2400 Baja Grande Dr., Suite 150, San Dimas, CA 90735
Tel: (562) 555-1234
Fax: (562) 555-9876
E-Mail: sandra2400@yippie.com."

At 1:00 p.m. on July 3rd, just before he rushed out of the house to catch a flight to Akron, Bosworth sent an e-mail to "sandra2400@yippie.com" stating: "I agree to buy your 100 acres for $1,000 per acre. Have a great Fourth of July!" Bosworth's e-mail reached Sandra's inbox less than a minute later, but she did not check her e-mail until after 5:00 p.m. on July 3rd. Sandra deemed Bosworth's acceptance to be untimely, and she sold the land to someone else. Bosworth sued.

75. Assuming that Sandra and Bosworth formed a contract supported by consideration, would that contract satisfy the relevant statute of frauds?

   (A) Yes. Sandra's June 30th fax satisfied the statute of frauds because she addressed it to Bosworth, set forth in it the contract's essential terms, and signed it.

   (B) No, because Sandra did not sign any writing that sufficiently evidenced her agreement with Bosworth.

   (C) Yes, because the composite document rule would allow Bosworth to use his e-mailed acceptance, along with Sandra's faxed offer, to satisfy the statute of frauds.

   (D) Yes. Bosworth's "signature" on his e-mailed acceptance was attributable to Sandra because she invited Bosworth to accept by e-mail and thereby conclude their contract.

In 1980, Edward Lewis began working at Sunny Dale nursing home, owned and operated by Mesquite Elder Care, Inc. ("MEC"). In 1986, Lewis became the administrator of Sunny Dale, in which position he continued until June 1, 2001, when MEC terminated his employment.

On September 1, 1987, Lewis and MEC executed a written contract, which recited MEC's desire to retain Lewis as an employee and provided what the contract called "assured rewards and incentives" to keep him employed, including obligating MEC's owners to give Lewis 20% of the proceeds of any sale of the company. However, the contract also stated:

Nothing in this Contract shall obligate the Employer to retain the Employee in its employment, or the Employee to remain in the Employer's employment, in any capacity, for any period.

One of the two original owners, Cal Billoway, entered into a stock redemption agreement in October 1989 with MEC. Because this buy-out might have required Lewis to be paid 20% of the proceeds under the terms of the September 1, 1987 contract, Lewis and MEC's sole remaining owner, Miriam Washington, amended the September 1, 1987 contract on October 1, 1989 to exclude the proceeds from Billoway's redemption, but otherwise reaffirmed the September 1, 1987 agreement. Lewis asserts that in return for relinquishing a claim to any part of the sale proceeds, Washington orally promised to retain him until age 65. Lewis further alleges that, on December 15, 1992, he and Washington made a handwritten amendment to the September 1, 1987 contract to provide that MEC would employ Lewis until age 65.

When MEC terminated Lewis prior to his 65th birthday, Lewis sued. MEC moved for summary judgment, arguing that Lewis was an at-will employee. Lewis opposed the motion on the basis of the alleged October 1, 1989 oral amendment and the alleged December 15, 1992 handwritten amendment to the September 1, 1987 contract. By affidavit, Lewis explained that, when Billoway sold his interest in October 1989, Washington orally promised Lewis employment until age 65 as consideration for his relinquishing a claim for 20% of the proceeds of the sale of Billoway's interest. The December 15, 1992 amendment allegedly was the belated recognition of this 1989 oral promise. Lewis does not have his own copy of the amended contract. The copy MEC attached to its summary judgment motion does not contain the alleged December 15, 1992 amendment.

76. Assuming that MEC promised to retain Lewis until age 65, can Lewis enforce MEC's promise under the applicable statute of frauds?

ANSWER:

Bamm Bamm, age 25, lived with his parents, Barney and Betty, in a nice neighborhood in Bedrock. Bamm Bamm had his own bedroom, but wanted a place to play his drums. He contacted Slate Construction Company ("Slate") to get an estimate on adding a music room to the house. His parents had no particular need for the additional room, but they wanted to support his musical interests and preferred that he not play the drums in his bedroom.

Fred, one of Slate's supervisors, came to the house and met with Bamm Bamm to discuss the addition. Fred had Bamm Bamm fill out a credit application and explained that Slate would only agree to perform the work on credit if Bamm Bamm's credit rating was satisfactory. Fred also gave Bamm Bamm a written "offer" detailing the specifics of the project, the expected cost and time of completion, and the payment schedule. The "offer" clearly indicated that it was conditional on Bamm Bamm having satisfactory credit. It also stated: "This agreement shall become binding only upon written acceptance by Slate Construction Company or upon commencing performance of the work." The total cost was to be $10,000.

After a few weeks passed without word from Slate, Bamm Bamm assumed that his credit rating had proved unacceptable. (He was rather destructive, at times, and had promised to make amends to several neighbors and area businesses, but he was not always able to do so in a timely manner.) Bamm Bamm wrote to Fred: "I have changed my mind and no longer want the construction work done which we discussed." Slate never received the letter. Bamm Bamm sold his drums and took up power lifting at the local gym — a hobby that did not require adding on to his parents' house.

A month or so later, while Barney and Betty were vacationing at Yellowrock Park and Bamm Bamm was out of town at a power lifting competition, a Slate crew quickly (but in a workmanlike manner) built the addition, leaving behind an invoice billing Bamm Bamm for the work. When Barney, Betty, and Bamm Bamm returned to Bedrock, they discovered the new music room and the bill from Slate, with the first payment due in one month.

No longer needing the room, and unable to pay for the work (having squandered his meager savings on steroids and baby oil), Bamm Bamm telephoned Fred. Fred referred the call to in-house counsel, Stonewall, who replied: "Sorry, we did not receive your letter. According to our agreement, we were to perform the work once your credit check was approved. It was. We did. You owe us $10,000.00." Stonewall subsequently sent Bamm Bamm several letters demanding payment, and then threatening suit for nonpayment, but Bamm Bamm could not pay.

Betty eventually met with Stonewall and asked her to stop harassing Bamm Bamm. When Stonewall insisted that *someone* pay Slate for the work it performed, Betty orally agreed to pay Slate the remaining balance due ($10,000 plus interest), in 12 monthly installments of $950 each, if Slate would stop all efforts to collect from Bamm Bamm. Stonewall agreed, on Slate's behalf, not to pursue Bamm Bamm any further. Betty made only three payments. Meanwhile, Bamm Bamm fled the jurisdiction and was last seen working in a circus side show in a distant land.

77. Assuming that Betty and Slate formed a contract supported by consideration, and that Betty's first payment under that contract was due by the last business day of the month in which it was formed, and subsequent installments were, likewise, due by the end of each month, would that contract satisfy the relevant statute of frauds?

    (A) No, because a writing signed by the party against whom enforcement is sought must evidence a contract to transfer an interest in real property.

    (B) No, because a writing signed by the party against whom enforcement is sought must evidence a contract to answer for the debt of another.

    (C) Yes, because a contract to pay a debt over a period of one year or less need not be evidenced by a writing.

    (D) Yes, because the three checks that Betty sent Slate are writings signed by Betty that evidence a contract — particularly if she wrote on the "memo" line of each check "1st Installment," "2nd Installment," etc.

The Yucca Museum of Art, located in a suburb of Las Vegas, decided the time had come to build a new wing onto its existing building in order to house its growing collection of fine origami (works of art made with folded paper). The Museum announced a $25 million fundraising campaign. The Museum's fundraising brochure stated that $20 million would be used to pay for the new wing. The brochure explained that Museum policy permits persons pledging $50,000 or more to designate a particular use for their donations. If they fail to do so, the Museum may use the funds as it sees fit. The brochure also stated that the Museum would name the new wing after the first donor to pledge $5 million toward the cost of the new wing, or the largest single donor if no one pledged $5 million.

The Museum mailed its fundraising brochure on September 1, 2002. On November 5th, Mary O'Mary sent the Museum her pledge card, having written on it "$4,750,000, on the condition that the funds may be used only for the new wing."

Museum policy requires that all pledges be paid no later than 120 days after the Museum receives the pledge, with the exception that pledges in excess of $50,000 may be paid in up to five equal installments, the first of which must be made within 120 days after the Museum receives the pledge. On March 1, 2003, the Museum sent Mary a reminder that she had pledged to pay no less than $950,000 (one-fifth of $4,750,000) on or before April 6th. On March 15th, Mary wrote to the Museum's board of directors, notifying them that, due to circumstances beyond her control, she would be unable to make the $950,000 payment due by April 6th, and wanted to cancel her entire pledge of $4,750,000. Museum officials want to know their legal options.

78. Assuming that Mary and the Museum formed a contract supported by consideration, can the Museum enforce that contract notwithstanding the statute of frauds?

(A) Yes, because promises to make charitable contributions are not subject to any statute of frauds.

(B) Yes, because promises to pay money over a period of one year or less are not subject to any statute of frauds.

(C) Yes, because the pledge card Mary completed and returned, coupled with her March 15th letter to the Museum, are sufficient to satisfy the statute of frauds.

(D) No, because the pledge card Mary completed and returned, coupled with her March 15th letter to the Museum are not sufficient to satisfy the statute of frauds.

Jenny Beasley wants to sue her former employer, Owl's Nest, for breaching its promise to award a new Mitsubishi to the winner of a March 2003 sales contest. Jenny claims that her manager, Jason Boone, told her and the other waitresses at the Paradise Road Owl's Nest that whoever sold the most margaritas at each participating Owl's Nest location during March 2003 would have her name entered in a drawing, and that the winner of the drawing would receive a new Mitsubishi. As the contest progressed, Jason told the waitresses that he did not know whether the winner would receive a Mitsubishi car, truck, or SUV, but that the winner would have to pay any registration fees on the vehicle. On or about April 8th, Jason informed Jenny that she had sold more margaritas during March than any other waitress at the Paradise Road Owl's Nest, and that he had submitted her name for the drawing. Two weeks later, Jason informed Jenny that she had won the drawing. He proceeded to blindfold her and lead her to the parking lot outside the restaurant. Waiting for her there was not a Mitsubishi car, truck, or SUV, however, but a plastic model of a Mitsubishi Zero, a World War II Japanese fighter airplane. Jason was laughing. Jenny was not.

Owl's Nest waitresses are at-will employees, who work without written employment contracts. The company's policy manual requires any employee to give two weeks notice prior to terminating her employment, and requires Owl's Nest to give any employee two weeks notice prior to terminating her employment, unless Owl's Nest is terminating the employee for cause.

Every employee receives a copy of the policy manual when she is hired. Jenny received a copy of the policy manual when she began working at Owl's Nest in January 2002.

79. Assuming that Jason's statements gave rise to a contract between Jenny and Owl's Nest, will Jenny's efforts to enforce it run afoul of any applicable statute of frauds?

ANSWER:

Buffy and Spike orally agreed that, for $10,000, Buffy would sell Spike her list of addresses and telephone numbers of vampires and slayers living in California. Buffy mailed the list to Spike. Spike received the list but refused to pay, arguing that their oral agreement was unenforceable under the applicable statute of frauds; therefore, he owed Buffy nothing.

80. Can Buffy enforce her contract with Spike despite the statute of frauds?

(A) No, because the list was a good, subject to UCC Article 2, and Buffy sold it for more than $500 (or $5,000, if applying Revised Article 2).

(B) No, because the list was non-goods personal property, subject to UCC Article 1, and Buffy sold it for more than $5,000.

(C) Yes, because the list was non-goods personal property, subject to UCC Article 1; therefore Buffy may enforce the contract up to $5,000 despite the lack of a signed writing.

(D) Yes, because Buffy performed a service in compiling the list, that service predominated her transaction with Spike, and their contract falls outside the scope of the common law statute of frauds.

Mercury Rising ("Mercury") is an Illinois manufacturer of indoor and outdoor thermometers. Tubular Glass ("Tubular") is a Michigan manufacturer of precision glass tubing. On March 14, 2003, following telephone negotiations leading to an oral agreement between the parties for the purchase and sale, respectively, of 5,000 one-foot lengths of glass tubing for $5.00 per foot, Will Bruce, Mercury's purchasing agent, faxed a purchase order to Tubular for 5,000 one-foot lengths of glass tubing, at a price of $5.00 per foot, to be delivered to Mercury's plant no later than May 1st. During their negotiations, Tubular informed Mercury that Tubular would have to specially manufacture the tubing in order to meet Mercury's specifications, which would take four to six weeks. The parties did not correspond further until April 28th, when Tubular notified Mercury that it would not honor Mercury's purchase order. (Tubular shipped the goods prior to April 28th, but stopped the shipment and rerouted it to another buyer willing to pay a better price.) Mercury wants to sue Tubular for breach of contract.

81. Assuming that Mercury and Tubular formed a contract by their correspondence, their actions, or both, would that contract satisfy the applicable statute of frauds?

(A)   No, because Mercury's inclusion of the delivery term changed the terms of the parties' prior agreement, so as to make the agreement unenforceable without Tubular's express consent.

(B)   No, because there is no writing signed by Tubular sufficient to satisfy the relevant statute of frauds against Tubular.

(C)   Yes, because Mercury's purchase order is sufficient to satisfy the statute of frauds against Tubular.

(D)   Yes, because Tubular had to specially manufacture the goods and did so prior to any breach.

Suppose that, rather than faxing a purchase order for 5,000 one-foot lengths of glass tubing to Tubular, Bruce faxed it to Philippe Glass ("PG"), a manufacturer of precision glass tubing whose plant is in Windsor, Ontario (Canada).

82.   Assuming that Mercury and PG formed a contract by their correspondence, their actions, or both, did that contract satisfy any applicable statute of frauds?

ANSWER:

Dharma and Greg recently agreed to lease the equipment they needed to set up their own microbrewery from Drew. The fair market value of the equipment at the inception of the lease was $500. Dharma and Greg agreed to pay Drew 10 monthly payments of $99 each. After 120 days, Dharma and Greg have the right to terminate the lease with 30 days notice without penalty (other than having to pay rent for the 30-day notice period). At the end of 10 months, Dharma and Greg will have the option to purchase the equipment for $25, or to return it to Drew. The expected fair market value of the equipment at the end of the lease is $250.

83.   Do Dharma and Greg need a writing signed by Drew and evidencing their agreement in order to ensure their rights?

(A)   No, because this contract is a lease of goods and total lease payments, excluding the purchase option, are less than $1,000.

(B)   Yes, because this contract is a lease of goods and total lease payments, including the purchase option, are more than $1,000.

(C)   Yes, because this contract is a sale of goods for $500 or more.

(D)   No, because this contract can be fully performed within one year.

On May 1, 2003, Tom Greene, owner of All Things Greene ("ATG"), a professional landscaping business located in Iowa, telephoned Uncle Buck's Tree Farm, in Golden, Colorado ("Uncle Buck"), and ordered 500 juniper saplings, with Uncle Buck to deliver the saplings to ATG's place of business no later than June 15th. Buck Russell, Uncle Buck's sole proprietor, orally agreed to deliver 500 juniper saplings to ATG no later than June 15th, with ATG paying reasonable delivery costs. Neither party said anything about price. Shortly thereafter, ATG contracted with several clients who wanted juniper saplings included in their landscaping at prices ranging from $12 to $18 per tree. The prevailing market price for juniper saplings on May 1st was $10.00 per sapling.

Bad weather struck, leaving Uncle Buck unable to deliver 500 juniper saplings by June 15th. Russell, realizing his predicament, called ATG on June 2nd, explaining the situation and offering to deliver 250 juniper saplings to ATG no later than June 15th at a price of $15.00 per sapling and another 250 saplings no later than August 1st. The prevailing market price for juniper saplings on June 2nd was $18.00 per sapling. Unaware of any substitute source on such short notice, and needing the saplings, ATG orally agreed to Uncle Buck's new terms. Russell, on behalf of Uncle Buck's, promptly signed and faxed a letter to ATG "confirming your agreement to a price of $15.00 per sapling for those saplings to be delivered no later than June 15th and the then-prevailing market price for those additional saplings delivered no later than August 1st." ATG did not respond in writing to Uncle Buck's June 2nd fax.

Uncle Buck delivered the first 250 saplings to ATG on June 14th, along with an invoice in the amount of $3,800.00 ($15.00 x 250 saplings, plus $50.00 delivery expenses). ATG accepted the trees and wrote a check to Uncle Buck in the amount of $3,800.

On July 15th, Uncle Buck called ATG to inform the latter that Uncle Buck was ready to deliver the remaining 250 saplings. ATG indicated it was ready to take delivery. Again, neither party discussed the price of the second batch of saplings. On July 16th, Uncle Buck delivered the remaining 250 saplings to ATG, along with an invoice in the amount of $4,550.00 ($18.00 x 250 saplings, plus $50.00 delivery expenses). The prevailing market price for juniper saplings on July 16th was $20.00 per sapling. ATG accepted the trees, crossed out the $18.00 per unit language on the invoice and wrote in "$15.00 per unit, per June 2nd agreement," and wrote a check to Uncle Buck in the amount of $3,800.

Uncle Buck called ATG to request payment of the additional $750.00. ATG refused. Uncle Buck sued. In its Answer filed in response to Uncle Buck's suit, ATG stated: "ATG admits an agreement to buy 500 juniper saplings from Uncle Buck, but denies ever agreeing to pay more than $15.00 per sapling, for a total contract price of $7,500.00 or less, plus shipping."

84. Assuming that ATG and Uncle Buck formed a contract over the telephone on May 1st, did that contract satisfy any applicable statute of frauds?

    (A) No, because this was a contract for the sale of non-goods personal property and there was no signed writing that defined or stated the price for the saplings.

    (B) No, because this was a contract for the sale of goods and there was no signed writing that defined or stated the price for the saplings.

(C)   No, because this was a contract for the sale of goods and there was no signed writing that specified the quantity of the saplings they had agreed to purchase and sell.

(D)   Yes, because both parties were merchants, meaning that either party who failed to object within a reasonable time to the lack of a written agreement could not later successfully use the statute of frauds to avoid the contract.

85.   Assuming, instead, that ATG and Uncle Buck formed a contract during or after Russell's June 2nd telephone call, may ATG successfully interpose a statute of frauds defense to Uncle Buck's claim for $18.00 per sapling for the second batch of 250 saplings?

(A)   Yes, because Uncle Buck's June 2nd fax failed to adequately indicate that a contract for the sale of goods had been agreed to between ATG and Uncle Buck.

(B)   Yes, because ATG did not sign, or otherwise acknowledge in writing, Uncle Buck's June 2nd fax.

(C)   Yes, because Uncle Buck's June 2nd fax failed to specify the quantity of the saplings that Uncle Buck had agreed to sell ATG.

(D)   No, because each of the foregoing is either untrue or insufficient to conclude that Uncle Buck has not satisfied UCC § 2-201 with respect to its claim against ATG.

86.   Regardless of your answer to Question 85, if Uncle Buck failed to satisfy UCC § 2-201(1) on the basis of the various writings it and ATG signed, can Uncle Buck take advantage of one or more exceptions set forth in UCC § 2-201(3)?

ANSWER:

The Yucca Museum of Art, located in a suburb of Las Vegas, decided the time had come to build a new wing onto its existing building in order to house its growing collection of fine origami (works of art made with folded paper). The Museum announced a $25 million fundraising campaign. The Museum's fundraising brochure stated that $20 million would be used to pay for the new wing. The brochure explained that Museum policy permits persons pledging $50,000 or more to designate a particular use for their donations. If they fail to do so, the Museum may use the funds as it sees fit. The brochure also stated that the Museum would name the new wing after the first donor to pledge $5 million toward the cost of the new wing, or the largest single donor if no one pledged $5 million. At the bottom of the brochure appeared the following language:

> *This new wing cannot become a reality unless we receive sufficient pledges to pay for it. We will not begin construction on the new wing until we have at least $10 million in total pledges toward the cost of the new wing or at least one "keystone" pledge toward the cost of the new wing in excess of $5 million.*

Museum policy requires the Museum to apply all undesignated (non-"earmarked") pledges to its general purpose fund until the general purpose portion of any particular fundraising campaign (here, $5,000,000) is satisfied, at which time any remaining undesignated funds may be used for a particular purpose (here, the new wing).

The Museum mailed its fundraising brochure on September 1, 2002. On September 20th, noted philanthropists Roy and Bai Golly pledged $750,000 to the Museum. The Gollys did not designate a particular use for their gift. On October 1st, Dr. Edwina Splunk, chief of medicine at Yucca Medical College and successful investor, pledged $2 million, with the notation that her funds were only to be used for the new wing. On October 15th, Dave & Aimee Flockenstein pledged $4,250,000 to the Museum's fundraising drive. The Flockensteins did not specify the use to which their gift must be put. As of October 15th, the Museum had received a number of smaller (less than $50,000 each) pledges totaling $500,000.

On November 1st, Leopard Tree, a world-famous professional ping-pong player, pledged $4,500,000 on the condition that her funds were to be used only for the new wing. A few days later, on November 5th, Mary O'Mary sent the Museum her pledge card, having written on it "$4,750,000, on the condition that the funds may be used only for the new wing."

By December 31st, the Museum had received three more large ($50,000 or more each) pledges and hundreds of additional small pledges totaling $9,000,000. None of the large pledges specified the use to which the donor's money must be put. Having raised more than its goal for both the total campaign and for the new wing, the Museum stopped soliciting funds for the new wing. A few days later, the Flockensteins offered to increase their total pledge to $5,000,000 if the

Museum would name its new wing in their honor. Museum officials thanked the Flockensteins for their generosity, but explained that, under the terms of the campaign brochure, the "naming rights" belonged to Mary, who had made the largest pledge to the new wing. The Flockensteins then "renewed" their original, undesignated pledge of $4,250,000. Around the same time, Museum officials notified Mary that the new wing would be named in her honor (or in honor of someone else if Mary so chose).

On November 6th, Museum officials approved a set of plans that had been prepared by a prominent local architect and hired a general contractor to oversee construction on the new wing. Ground was broken on December 1st, and construction was well under way by March 1, 2003.

Museum policy requires that all pledges be paid no later than 120 days after the Museum receives the pledge, with the exception that pledges in excess of $50,000 may be paid in up to five equal installments, the first of which must be made within 120 days after the Museum receives the pledge. On March 1, 2003, the Museum sent Mary a reminder that she had pledged to pay no less than $950,000 (one-fifth of $4,750,000) on or before April 6th. On March 15th, Mary wrote to the Museum's board of directors, notifying them that, due to circumstances beyond her control, she would be unable to make the $950,000 payment due by April 6th, and wanted to cancel her entire pledge of $4,750,000. Museum officials, finding their project now under-funded by $4,000,000, want to know their legal options.

87. Applying the *Restatement (Second)*, does the Museum have a viable promissory estoppel claim against Mary?

(A) No, because a charitable pledge is not a promise on which a charity can foreseeably rely to its detriment.

(B) No, because the facts do not suggest that the Museum relied to its detriment on Mary's pledge.

(C) No, because not enforcing Mary's promise will not result in injustice.

(D) Yes, because not enforcing Mary's promise will result in injustice.

Suppose, instead, that Nevada follows the majority pre-*Restatement (Second)* rule regarding the enforceability of charitable subscriptions, rather than Section 90(2) of the *Restatement (Second)*.

88. Does the Museum have a viable promissory estoppel claim against Mary?

(A) No, because the Museum gave no consideration to bind Mary to her pledge.

(B) No, because the Museum could not foreseeably rely to its detriment on Mary's pledge.

(C) No, because the Museum did not foreseeably rely to its detriment on Mary's pledge.

(D) Yes, because the Museum could and did foreseeably rely to its detriment on Mary's pledge.

Applying the same law as in Question 88, suppose that it was the Gollys, rather than Mary O'Mary, who are unable to honor their pledge.

89. Does the Museum have a viable promissory estoppel claim against the Gollys?

   (A) No, because the Museum gave the Gollys no consideration to bind them to their pledge.

   (B) No, because the Museum could not foreseeably rely to its detriment on the Gollys' pledge.

   (C) No, because the Museum did not foreseeably rely to its detriment on the Gollys' pledge.

   (D) Yes, because the Museum could and did foreseeably rely to its detriment on the Gollys' pledge.

Glenn Paisley and Nick Savage own adjoining lots along the Willamette River in Oregon. One day, while sitting on his boat dock, Glenn noticed that one of Nick's boats had broken loose from its moorings and was floating away down the river toward a set of rapids that would eventually propel it beyond rescue. Glenn called out to his friends, Will and Jean-Luc, to grab some rope and a gaffing hook and hop into his spare canoe to help him retrieve the stray boat. An hour or so later, Nick, who had been to town to buy provisions, returned just as Glenn, Will, and Jean-Luc were re-securing Nick's boat and the two canoes. Glenn explained what had happened and Nick thanked the three of them profusely for rescuing his too-expensive-to-be-so-poorly-secured boat.

90. Assuming that Nick did not offer to reward the lads for their effort, would Glenn, Will, and Jean-Luc have a viable equitable claim against Nick?

   (A) Yes, because Glenn and his mates acted without Nick's permission out of necessity and had no reason to believe that Nick would not consent if asked.

   (B) Yes, because Glenn and his mates acted lawfully and without owing Nick any pre-existing duty as a result of their relationship to him or their own acts or omissions.

   (C) No, because Glenn and his mates did not act with the intent of being rewarded for their actions.

   (D) Yes, because Nick accepted the boat when Glenn returned it to him.

91. Suppose that, after Glenn explained what had happened, Nick said he would pay Glenn, Will, and Jean-Luc $50 each the next day. If, when they came to receive their rewards, Nick refused to pay, would Glenn, Will, and Jean-Luc have a viable equitable claim against Nick?

   (A) Yes, Glenn, Will, and Jean-Luc could recover from Nick based on promissory estoppel.

(B)   Yes, Glenn, Will, and Jean-Luc could recover from Nick based on promissory restitution.

(C)   Yes, Glenn, Will, and Jean-Luc could recover from Nick under Section 117 of the *Restatement of Restitution.*

(D)   Yes, Glenn, Will, and Jean-Luc could recover from Nick based on quasi-contract.

Suppose, instead, that Nick was present when the boat floated away from the dock, but was unable to do anything about it because he had recently had knee surgery and was on crutches. Seeing his cherished boat begin to float away, he called out to Glenn, who was nearby: "If you will fetch my boat and bring it back to me, I'll pay you $100." Glenn, seeing an opportunity to make a few extra bucks, grabbed his friends Jean-Luc and Will, and they set out to retrieve the boat and return it to Nick. When they returned with Nick's boat, he thanked them, handed them $10 each, and said, "Sorry, that's all I have on me." Jean-Luc and Will are satisfied because Glenn never told them how much to expect. Glenn, on the other hand, was upset, and tried unsuccessfully the next day to get the rest of the money Nick promised him.

92.   Does Glenn have a viable equitable claim against Nick?

(A)   Yes, based on promissory estoppel.

(B)   Yes, based on promissory restitution.

(C)   Yes, based on *Restatement of Restitution* § 117.

(D)   No, because Glenn can recover from Nick for breach of contract.

Lestrade, an unusually virtuous insurance defense attorney, found Watson lying gravely injured and unconscious by the side of the road, where Watson had apparently crawled from his overturned car. The car was leaking fuel and appeared to be at risk of catching fire. Lestrade carefully placed Watson in the back of Lestrade's Range Rover and drove Watson to the local hospital, where Lestrade had Watson admitted and promised to pay Watson's expenses if he was unable to do so himself. Word of Lestrade's good deed soon spread, and the local DEF network affiliate ran a story on the evening news that was picked up a few days later by the network news. Watson's cousin, Holmes, saw the story and tracked down Lestrade, who told Holmes where to find Watson. Unable to attend to Watson personally, Holmes told both Lestrade and hospital officials to spare no effort or expense to return Watson to good health. Holmes promised to pay the hospital, or reimburse Lestrade, whatever the arrangement between Lestrade and the hospital might be, for all expenses. Alas, Watson did not recover, and Holmes met an untimely end while mountain climbing. The hospital sent Lestrade a bill for Watson's room and care, which Lestrade paid as he had promised to do. Lestrade has come to you seeking legal advice. Assume that the "rules" for suing Holmes's estate are the same as they would be for suing Holmes were he still alive, and that Watson died without any estate or kin to sue.

93.   Does Lestrade have a viable claim against Holmes' estate for the expenses he incurred in seeing to Watson's care *before* Holmes promised to reimburse him?

(A)   Yes, based on promissory estoppel.

(B)   Yes, based on promissory restitution.

(C)   Yes, based on *Restatement of Restitution* § 116.

(D)   No.

94.   Does Lestrade have a viable claim against Holmes' estate for the expenses he incurred in seeing to Watson's care *after* Holmes promised to reimburse him?

(A)   Yes, based on promissory estoppel.

(B)   Yes, based on promissory restitution.

(C)   Yes, based on *Restatement of Restitution* § 116.

(D)   Yes, based on breach of contract.

95.   If the hospital elected to pursue Holmes' estate rather than collecting from Lestrade, would the hospital have a viable claim against Holmes' estate for the reasonable expenses of Watson's care *before* Holmes promised to reimburse the hospital?

ANSWER:

Suppose that Holmes never told Lestrade and the hospital that he would pay for Watson's care, but that Holmes was Watson's sole heir; and, under applicable state law, Holmes' estate would be liable to the same extent as Watson (if he had survived) or Watson's estate (if there was one).

96.   Would Lestrade have a viable claim against Holmes' estate for the expenses he incurred in seeing to Watson's care?

(A)   Yes, based on breach of contract.

(B)   Yes, based on promissory estoppel.

(C)   Yes, based on *Restatement of Restitution* § 116.

(D)   No.

97.   Would the hospital have a viable claim against Holmes' estate for the expenses incurred in seeing to Watson's care?

(A)   Yes, based on breach of contract.

(B)   Yes, based on promissory estoppel.

(C)   Yes, based on *Restatement of Restitution* § 116.

(D) No.

In 1980, Edward Lewis began working at Sunny Dale nursing home, owned and operated by Mesquite Elder Care, Inc. ("MEC"). In 1986, Lewis became the administrator of Sunny Dale, in which position he continued until June 1, 2001, when MEC terminated his employment.

On September 1, 1987, Lewis and MEC executed a written contract, which recited MEC's desire to retain Lewis as an employee and provided what the contract called "assured rewards and incentives" to keep him employed, including obligating MEC's owners to give Lewis 20% of the proceeds of any sale of the company. However, the contract also stated:

> Nothing in this Contract shall obligate the Employer to retain the Employee in its employment, or the Employee to remain in the Employer's employment, in any capacity, for any period.

One of the two original owners, Cal Billoway, entered into a stock redemption agreement in October 1989 with MEC. Because this buy-out might have required Lewis to be paid 20% of the proceeds under the terms of the September 1, 1987 contract, Lewis and MEC's sole remaining owner, Miriam Washington, amended the September 1, 1987 contract on October 1, 1989 to exclude the proceeds from Billoway's redemption, but otherwise reaffirmed the September 1, 1987 agreement. Lewis asserts that in return for relinquishing a claim to any part of the sale proceeds, Washington orally promised to retain him until age 65. Lewis further alleges that, on December 15, 1992, he and Washington made a handwritten amendment to the September 1, 1987 contract to provide that MEC would employ Lewis until age 65.

When MEC terminated Lewis prior to his 65th birthday, Lewis sued. MEC moved for summary judgment, arguing that Lewis was an at-will employee. Lewis opposed the motion on the basis of the alleged October 1, 1989 oral amendment and the alleged December 15, 1992 handwritten amendment to the September 1, 1987 contract. By affidavit, Lewis explained that, when Billoway sold his interest in October 1989, Washington orally promised Lewis employment until age 65 as consideration for his relinquishing a claim for 20% of the proceeds of the sale of Billoway's interest. The December 15, 1992 amendment allegedly was the belated recognition of this 1989 oral promise. Lewis does not have his own copy of the amended contract. The copy MEC attached to its summary judgment motion does not contain the alleged December 15, 1992 amendment.

> 98. Could Lewis use the doctrine of promissory estoppel to overcome his inability to produce a writing signed by MEC promising to employ him until age 65?

ANSWER:

Bamm Bamm, age 25, lived with his parents, Barney and Betty Rubble, in a nice neighborhood in Bedrock. Bamm Bamm had his own bedroom, but wanted a place to play his drums. He contacted Slate Construction Company ("Slate") to get an estimate on adding a music room to the house. His parents had no particular need for the additional room, but they wanted to support his musical interests and preferred that he not play the drums in his bedroom.

Fred, one of Slate's supervisors, came to the house and met with Bamm Bamm to discuss the addition. Fred had Bamm Bamm fill out a credit application and explained that Slate would only agree to perform the work on credit if Bamm Bamm's credit rating was satisfactory. Fred also gave Bamm Bamm a written "offer" detailing the specifics of the project, the expected cost and time of completion, and the payment schedule. The "offer" clearly indicated that it was conditional on Bamm Bamm having satisfactory credit. It also stated: "This agreement shall become binding only upon written acceptance by Slate Construction Company or upon commencing performance of the work." The total cost was to be $10,000.

After a few weeks passed without word from Slate, Bamm Bamm assumed that his credit rating had proved unacceptable. (He was rather destructive, at times, and had promised to make amends to several neighbors and area businesses, but he was not always able to do so in a timely manner.) Bamm Bamm wrote to Fred: "I have changed my mind and no longer want the construction work done which we discussed." Slate never received the letter. Bamm Bamm sold his drums and took up power lifting at the local gym — a hobby that did not require adding on to his parents' house.

A month or so later, while Barney and Betty were vacationing at Yellowrock Park and Bamm Bamm was out of town at a power lifting competition, a Slate crew quickly (but in a workmanlike manner) built the addition, leaving behind an invoice billing Bamm Bamm for the work. When Barney, Betty, and Bamm Bamm returned to Bedrock, they discovered the new music room and the bill from Slate, with the first payment due in one month.

No longer needing the room, and unable to pay for the work (having squandered his meager savings on steroids and baby oil), Bamm Bamm telephoned Fred. Fred referred the call to in-house counsel, Stonewall, who replied: "Sorry, we did not receive your letter. According to our agreement, we were to perform the work once your credit check was approved. It was. We did. You owe us $10,000.00." Stonewall subsequently sent Bamm Bamm several letters demanding payment, and then threatening suit for nonpayment, but Bamm Bamm could not pay. Unlike most contemporary American jurisdictions, Bedrock does not recognize statutory liens for repairs and improvements to realty.

Betty eventually met with Stonewall and asked her to stop harassing Bamm Bamm. When Stonewall insisted that *someone* pay Slate for the work it performed, Betty orally agreed to pay Slate the remaining balance due ($10,000 plus interest), in 12 monthly installments of $950 each, if Slate would stop all efforts to collect from Bamm Bamm. Stonewall agreed, on Slate's behalf, not to pursue Bamm Bamm any further. Betty made only three payments. Meanwhile, Bamm Bamm fled the jurisdiction and was last seen working in a circus side show in a distant land.

99. Assuming that Slate cannot prevail against Betty on a breach of contract action, does Slate have a viable promissory estoppel claim against Betty?

   (A) No, because Slate built the addition to the Rubbles' house in reliance on Bamm Bamm's promise to pay, not Betty's promise.

  (B) No, because Betty promised to pay Slate after Slate had already built the addition to the Rubbles' house.

  (C) Yes, because Betty's promise to pay Slate induced Slate to forbear from attempting to collect the debt from Bamm Bamm.

  (D) Yes, because Betty's promise to pay Slate induced Slate to forbear from attempting to collect the debt from Bamm Bamm and injustice will result if Slate is not allowed to hold Betty to her promise.

100. Does Slate have a viable promissory restitution claim against Betty?

  (A) No, because Slate built the addition to the Rubbles' house before Betty promised to pay Slate.

  (B) No, because Slate built the addition to the Rubbles' house gratuitously.

  (C) No, because Betty promised to pay Slate more than the value of the addition to her and Barney.

  (D) Yes, because not enforcing Betty's promise would unjustly enrich the Rubbles and deny Slate compensation for work it did not perform gratuitously.

101. Does Slate have a viable restitution or quasi-contract claim against Betty?

  (A) Yes, under the rule of *Webb v. McGowin*.

  (B) Yes, based on *Restatement of Restitution* § 117.

  (C) Yes, based on quasi-contract.

  (D) No, because Betty has not been unjustly enriched by Slate.

102. In construing and interpreting a written contract, a court's primary concern should be to ascertain and give effect to

(A) the objective intent of the parties at the time of contracting, as expressed or apparent in their written agreement, in light of the circumstances surrounding its formation.

(B) the subjective intent of the parties at the time of contracting, as expressed or apparent in their written agreement, in light of the circumstances surrounding its formation.

(C) the objective intent of the parties at the time of contracting, whether or not it was accurately captured in their written agreement, in light of the circumstances surrounding its formation.

(D) the subjective intent of the parties at the time of contracting, whether or not it was accurately captured in their written agreement, in light of the circumstances surrounding its formation.

103. As a general rule, extrinsic evidence, whether written or oral, is inadmissible to prove either the intent of the parties to the contract or the meaning of contractual terms when the parties have executed

(A) an integrated written agreement.

(B) an integrated written agreement, the terms of which are unambiguous.

(C) a fully integrated written agreement.

(D) a fully integrated written agreement, the terms of which are unambiguous.

104. Whether and to what extent a writing is integrated and whether it is unambiguous are

(A) questions of fact, to be determined by the trial judge.

(B) questions of law, to be determined by the trial judge.

(C) questions of fact, to be determined by the jury.

(D) questions of law, to be determined by the jury.

105. In a "four corners" jurisdiction, what evidence should the trial judge consider when deciding whether a written agreement is fully integrated and unambiguous?

(A) Only the written agreement.

(B) The written agreement, plus any other documents incorporated therein by reference.

(C)   The written agreement, plus any other documents incorporated therein by reference, as well as other documents that appear to relate to the agreement.

(D)   The written agreement, plus any other documents incorporated therein by reference, as well as other documents that relate to the agreement, and any evidence a party wishes to proffer regarding the circumstances surrounding the contract's formation.

106.   In a *Restatement* or "modified objectivist" jurisdiction, what evidence may the trial judge consider when deciding whether a written agreement is fully integrated and unambiguous?

(A)   Only the written agreement.

(B)   The written agreement, plus any other documents incorporated therein by reference.

(C)   The written agreement, plus any other documents incorporated therein by reference, as well as other documents that appear to relate to the agreement.

(D)   The written agreement, plus any other documents incorporated therein by reference, as well as other documents that appear to relate to the agreement, and any other evidence a party wishes to proffer regarding the circumstances surrounding the contract's formation.

107.   A writing is ambiguous if

(A)   one or more of its terms or provisions are susceptible to more than one reasonable meaning based on the facts actually or constructively known by the parties when they executed the writing.

(B)   one or more of its terms or provisions are susceptible to more than one reasonable meaning based on the facts actually or constructively known by the parties when the court considers the writing.

(C)   the parties disagreed about the meaning of a term or provision when they executed the writing.

(D)   the parties disagree about the meaning of a term or provision when a court interprets the writing.

Bruce Roberts desired to insure the new concert hall he was building as part of his resort in the Berkshires. Bruce contacted Lacy Simms, the local agent for Good Hands Insurance ("GHI"), to discuss terms and rates. Bruce and Lacy settled on a three-year policy with premium payments due in monthly installments. Lacy submitted the paperwork to the underwriting department in GHI's main office, along with Bruce's check for the first month's premium, Bruce's completed policy application, and a "binder" (a document temporarily evidencing insurance coverage until the policyholder receives the actual policy from the insurer). Bruce signed all three of the foregoing, and Lacy signed the application and the binder. The binder accurately indicated coverage from July 1, 2002 through June 30, 2005. A few weeks later, when Bruce received the multi-page policy, he simply filed it away.

In August 2003, a fire broke out in one of the food service areas in the concert hall, causing significant fire, smoke, and water damage to the structure. When Bruce called Lacy to report the incident, Lacy took the relevant information over the phone and filed a claim with GHI's claims department. A week or two later, Bruce received a polite letter from GHI's claims department refusing his claim on the ground that the policy had lapsed. The claims analyst who wrote the letter attached a copy of a page from Bruce's policy, which indicated coverage from July 1, 2002 through June 30, 2003. Bruce, knowing this to be inaccurate, sat down and read through his copy of the policy. On another page not forwarded by GHI's claims analyst, the policy indicated that the policy would be effective "for a term of three years, from July 1, 2002 to June 30, 2003, provided that the Insured is not delinquent on premiums payments." When Bruce faxed that page to GHI's claims analyst, she politely replied that GHI's position was that the stated dates, "July 1, 2002 to June 30, 2003," rather than the less specific "for a term of three years," controlled the duration of the policy.

Assume for the purposes of the following questions that an insurance policy is, in all relevant respects, a contract.

108. Which of the following best describes the written policy's statement of the duration of Bruce's coverage?

(A) The policy is patently ambiguous.

(B) The policy is latently ambiguous.

(C) The policy is unambiguous.

(D) The policy is unintegrated.

Suppose, instead, the insurance policy itself said that Bruce was covered "from July 1, 2002 through June 30, 2003," but the application and binder that Bruce and Lacy signed, and Lacy submitted to GHI's underwriting department, showed Bruce being covered "from July 1, 2002 through June 30, 2005."

109. Assuming Bruce could introduce the binder into evidence, which of the following best describes the written policy's statement of the duration of Bruce's coverage?

(A) The policy is patently ambiguous.

(B) The policy is latently ambiguous.

(C) The policy is unambiguous.

(D) The policy is unintegrated.

Suppose that there was also a dispute over what property and perils the policy covered. Bruce's insurance policy described the covered premises as:

Business premises and other improvement to real property as more fully described in "Attachment A" affixed hereto, as amended, at the time of the loss.

The section of the policy titled "Perils Insured Against" stated:

> This policy insures against physical loss to the property described in the version of "Attachment A" in effect at the time of the loss caused by a peril listed below, unless the loss is excluded under the terms of the version of "Attachment B — Business Premises: Excluded Perils" in effect at the time of the loss.

The policy also stated:

> Except as subsequently amended in a writing signed or otherwise endorsed by GHI, this policy constitutes the entire agreement of the parties hereto with respect to GHI's obligations in the event of any property loss suffered by the Insured.

110. Which of the following best characterizes the policy's description of the covered premises and the excluded perils?

   (A) The policy is fully integrated.

   (B) The policy is only partially integrated, but it is integrated with respect to the covered premises and excluded perils.

   (C) The policy is only partially integrated, and it is not integrated with respect to the covered premises and excluded perils.

   (D) The policy is wholly unintegrated.

111. In a *Restatement* or "modified objectivist" jurisdiction, what is the legal effect of the final quoted clause in the facts preceding Question 110?

   (A) It is conclusive proof that the written agreement sets forth the parties' full and final agreement with respect to the subject matter of the written agreement, and that all prior negotiations, prior or contemporaneous oral agreements, and prior written agreements were merged into or superseded by the written agreement.

   (B) It is conclusive proof, in the absence of something on the face of the writing to the contrary, that the written agreement sets forth the parties' full and final agreement with respect to the subject matter of the written agreement, and that all prior negotiations, prior or contemporaneous oral agreements, and prior written agreements were merged into or superseded by the written agreement.

   (C) It creates a strong, but rebuttable, presumption that the written agreement sets forth the parties' full and final agreement with respect to the subject matter of the written agreement, and that all prior negotiations, prior or contemporaneous oral agreements, and prior written agreements were merged into or superseded by the written agreement.

   (D) It is evidence that the written agreement sets forth the parties' full and final agreement with respect to the subject matter of the written agreement, and that all prior negotiations, prior or contemporaneous oral agreements, and prior written agreements were merged into or superseded by the written agreement.

Global Chemicals ("Global") contracted with Falcon Crest Engineers ("Falcon Crest") to design a new chemical refinery and act as Global's consultants during the refinery's construction. Global hired Black & Shoot ("B&S") to act as general contractor, overseeing construction of the plant, and assuming primary responsibility to ensure that the plant was built to Falcon Crest's precise specifications. Falcon Crest's design included several multi-chambered vessels used to distill chemical feedstock into various end-product chemicals. Falcon Crest specified that the exterior shell of each vessel be fabricated using "Osaka steel." Falcon Crest's design also indicated that each chamber of each vessel was to be separated by a specific size and model number of bi-flow (two-way) valve manufactured by AccuValve, Inc.

A series of disputes subsequently arose among Global, Falcon Crest, and B&S over various aspects of the refinery's construction. B&S's contract with Global required B&S to strictly comply with Falcon Crest's specifications and permitted B&S to deviate from those specifications only after obtaining a written "change order" signed by either Falcon Crest or Global. The final paragraph of B&S's contract with Global stated:

> 36. This contract, including all exhibits attached hereto as of the date both parties sign the contract, constitutes the entire agreement between the parties with respect to the subject refinery. Both parties understand and agree that this contract supersedes any prior negotiations, drafts, or oral or written agreements between them relating to this project, and that any subsequent changes to this contract must be made in writing and be signed by both B&S and Global (or its designated consultant, Falcon Crest).

112.   In response to Global's complaint that B&S used steel manufactured by AmeriSteel, not by Osaka Steel Corporation, which of the following evidence should the trial court consider in deciding whether B&S's contract with Global is fully integrated, partially integrated, or unintegrated?

   (A)   Evidence that "Osaka" is a generic term for a particular type or grade of steel, as well as the name of a particular brand of that type or grade of steel (like "Kleenex" or "Xerox").

   (B)   A copy of a change order signed by Falcon Crest, after B&S and Global signed their contract, authorizing B&S to fabricate the refinery vessel shells using "Osaka or similar grade and type steel."

   (C)   A copy of a memo written by Falcon Crest's site supervisor attached to the invitation to bid sent to, among others, B&S, explaining that Falcon Crest's specification of "Osaka steel" meant "Osaka or similar grade and type steel."

   (D)   All of the above.

113.   Which of the following evidence should the trial court consider in deciding whether B&S's contract with Global is unambiguous?

   (A)   Evidence that "Osaka" is a generic term for a particular type or grade of steel, as well as the name of a particular brand of that type or grade of steel (like "Kleenex" or "Xerox").

(B) A copy of a memo written by Falcon Crest's site supervisor attached to the invitation to bid sent to, among others, B&S, explaining that Falcon Crest's specification of "Osaka steel" meant "Osaka or similar grade and type steel."

(C) Evidence that, in their past dealings on other projects, Falcon Crest had routinely allowed B&S to substitute like type and grade materials for those specified by Falcon Crest or called for in the contract between B&S and the project owner.

(D) All of the above.

Suppose Global's complaint was not that B&S used Osaka-grade steel manufactured by someone other than Osaka Steel Corporation; rather, it was that the steel B&S used was not Osaka-grade steel. Reasonably convinced by Falcon Crest's analysis of the steel it used on the Global project, B&S sued AmeriSteel for selling it inferior steel. The written contract between B&S and AmeriSteel is silent about whether the steel B&S purchased from AmeriSteel was "Osaka steel." Moreover, the contract contained a merger clause disclaiming the legal effect of any prior representations, negotiations, or agreements. B&S insists that the AmeriSteel sales representative repeatedly assured B&S that it was buying "Osaka steel," despite the fact that the salesperson must have known that the steel AmeriSteel was selling B&S was *not* "Osaka steel."

114. Should the trial court in *B&S v. AmeriSteel* consider B&S's testimony regarding the representations AmeriSteel's salesperson made, despite the fact that those representations were not repeated in or incorporated by the written contract between B&S and AmeriSteel?

(A) No, because the written contract, which B&S signed, expressly disavows, *inter alia*, any prior statements made by AmeriSteel's salesperson regarding the type or grade of steel B&S was buying.

(B) No, because the evidence B&S seeks to introduce does not relate to a trade usage, a prior course of dealing between B&S and AmeriSteel, or B&S and AmeriSteel's course of performance of the contract at issue.

(C) Yes, because the salesperson's assurances that B&S was buying "Osaka steel" constitute a consistent additional term, evidence of which is admissible under UCC § 2-202(b).

(D) Yes, because evidence that AmeriSteel fraudulently induced B&S to enter into the contract at issue is always admissible, notwithstanding the parol evidence rule.

On March 1, 2003, Gwyneth and Russell agreed that Gwyneth would pay Russell $100 each for two tickets to the March 15th New York premiere of *The Orange Pumpernickel*. They further agreed that Russell would deliver the tickets to Gwyneth no later than March 14th. The New York premiere of Cameron Ridley's new movie, *The Orange Pumpernickel*, was scheduled for March 15th at the Radikal City Musik Hall. That same night, the 41st Street Playhouse scheduled the premiere of a stage production of *The Orange Pumpernickel*, directed by David Marmoset.

On March 2nd, Russell purchased two tickets from the 41st Street Playhouse for $75 each. On March 14th, when Russell delivered the tickets to Gwyneth, she refused to pay, claiming that Russell had agreed to sell her tickets to the movie, not the play. Russell did not have any tickets to the movie, and none were commercially available at that late date. Russell tried unsuccessfully to find another buyer for the play tickets and to obtain a refund from the Playhouse. Unable to use them himself, he left the tickets with Gwyneth in case she changed her mind. Gwyneth sued Russell for failing to provide her with tickets to the movie premiere.

Suppose that, when they made their contract, Gwyneth knew about the movie premiere, but not the play opening; Russell knew that Gwyneth wanted tickets to the movie premiere; and, despite that knowledge, Russell provided her with tickets to the play.

115. Should Russell be able to avoid liability by arguing that their agreement was ambiguous with respect to which *The Orange Pumpernickel* Gwyneth wanted tickets?

ANSWER:

Suppose, instead, that Russell bought two tickets to the movie premiere for $75 per ticket. When Russell attempted to deliver the tickets to Gwyneth on March 14th, as agreed, she was not home, so he slipped them through her mail slot with a note saying: "You can pay me tomorrow." Gwyneth hoped to star in the much-anticipated sequel to *Titanic* and planned to schmooze its director, Cameron, while at the movie premiere. Unbeknownst to Russell, Gwyneth heard later that day on *Entertainment This Night* that Cameron had suddenly become ill and would not be coming to New York for the premiere. Gwyneth decided not to attend the premiere and returned the tickets to Russell the next day. Russell demanded to be paid for the tickets. Gwyneth refused.

116. If, when they made their contract, Gwyneth knew only about and wanted to attend the movie premiere, can she avoid liability by arguing that their agreement was ambiguous with respect to which *The Orange Pumpernickel* she wanted tickets?

ANSWER:

117. In a contract governed by UCC Article 2, which of the following types of evidence should a court refuse to allow the trier of fact to consider if the court finds the contract at issue to be fully integrated?

   (A) Consistent additional terms.

   (B) Course of dealing.

   (C) Course of performance.

   (D) Usage of trade.

Justin Thyme, who collects Volkswagens as a hobby, made a "handshake deal" to purchase four 1966 Volkswagen Beetles for $5,000 each from Belinda Waring, who owns Belinda's Car Aisle, a vintage Volkswagen dealership. Belinda and Justin agreed that Justin could pick up the cars at any time within 30 days of the sale. They also agreed that Justin would pay for each car when he picked it up from Belinda's lot.

The day after Justin and Belinda made their deal, Belinda sent Justin a signed letter purporting to confirm their oral agreement. Belinda's letter, however, described an agreement for the sale of two 1966 Volkswagen Beetles for $7,500 each. After receiving the letter, Justin tried for two weeks to reach Belinda to clear up the matter, but she was out of town on vacation. When Justin finally reached Belinda, Belinda insisted that the terms of the letter were the only ones on which she would perform — even though Justin told her that Justin's friend Magda, who accompanied him to Belinda's dealership the day that Justin and Belinda made their oral agreement, overheard their agreement and would testify that Belinda had agreed to sell Justin four 1966 Beetles for $5,000 each, not two 1966 Beetles for $7,500 each.

118.   If Justin sues Belinda for breach of contract, should Justin's and Magda's testimony regarding the terms of the oral agreement be admissible despite the signed writing?

(A)   Yes, because there is no writing evidencing the contract between Belinda and Justin, taking the parol evidence rule completely out of play.

(B)   Yes, because there is no writing evidencing the contract between Belinda and Justin that both Belinda and Justin intended to be a final expression of their agreement.

(C)   Yes, because Justin's and Magda's testimony that Belinda agreed to sell Justin four Beetles for $5,000 each will create ambiguity both with respect to the number of Beetles the parties agreed to buy and sell and the price that Justin agreed to pay and Belinda agreed to accept.

(D)   No, because Belinda's letter is a written confirmation, within the meaning of UCC § 2-201(2), and Justin's failure to object to it means, as a matter of law, that he agreed to its contents.

119.   Regardless of your answer to the Question 118, if the trial court permits Justin and Magda to testify, how many Beetles should the trier of fact find that Justin was entitled to buy and at what price?

(A)   Four Beetles for $5,000 each.

(B)   Four Beetles for $7,500 each.

(C)   Two Beetles for $5,000 each.

(D)   Two Beetles for $7,500 each.

Suppose Belinda's vintage Volkswagen dealership is in El Paso, Texas, and Justin lives in Ciudad Juarez, Mexico. Suppose, further, that Justin was purchasing the Beetles for the purpose of reselling them.

120. Assuming the same disagreement arose between Justin and Belinda regarding the number of Beetles Belinda had agreed to sell Justin and the price at which Belinda agreed to sell them, how many Beetles should the trier of fact find that Justin was entitled to buy and at what price?

ANSWER:

Mercury Rising ("Mercury") is an Illinois manufacturer of indoor and outdoor thermometers. Tubular Glass ("Tubular") is a Michigan manufacturer of precision glass tubing. On March 14, 2003, following telephone negotiations between the two, Will Bruce, Mercury's purchasing agent, faxed a purchase order to Tubular for 5,000 one-foot lengths of glass tubing, at a price of $5.00 per foot, to be delivered to Mercury's plant no later than May 1st. Later that same day, Tubular faxed a written acknowledgment, agreeing to manufacture and deliver 5,000 one-foot lengths of glass tubing, at a price of $5.00 per foot, to Mercury's plant no later than May 1st. The terms of Tubular's acknowledgment also (1) disclaimed of all implied warranties, and (2) required Mercury to pay the full contract price, including the cost of shipping the tubing from Tubular's plant to Mercury's plant, when Mercury received the tubing. The parties did not correspond further. Mercury received the goods on May 1st and paid the carrier in full, including transportation costs. Later, Mercury determined that nearly 80% of the glass tubing was of inferior quality and unfit for the use for which Mercury bought it.

121. Assuming that Mercury and Tubular had a contract, and that Tubular's shipment of nonconforming tubing violated one or more UCC Article 2 implied warranties, did Mercury's contract with Tubular permit Mercury to sue Tubular for breach of warranty?

    (A) No, because Tubular's acknowledgment disclaimed all implied warranties.

    (B) No, because Tubular's acknowledgment was actually a counteroffer, the terms of which Mercury agreed to by accepting and paying for the tubing.

    (C) No, because Tubular's disclaimer of all warranties did not materially alter the terms of Mercury's offer and Mercury did not timely object to the disclaimer.

    (D) Yes, because Tubular's disclaimer of all warranties materially altered the terms of Mercury's offer; therefore, the disclaimer did not become a part of the parties' contract.

Suppose that Mercury's purchase order specifically stated: "All warranties set forth in Article 2 of the Uniform Commercial Code apply to this transaction."

122. Should Mercury prevail against Tubular on a claim of breach of warranty?

    (A) Yes, because Mercury expressly reserved its right to enforce any applicable implied warranty against Tubular.

    (B) No, because Tubular's acknowledgment, which followed Mercury's purchase order, expressly disclaimed all implied warranties.

(C)   No, because Mercury accepted and paid for the goods despite the fact that Tubular's acknowledgment, which followed Mercury's purchase order, expressly disclaimed all implied warranties.

(D)   Yes, because, given the conflicting terms in Mercury's purchase order and Tubular's acknowledgment, UCC § 2-207 will operate to preserve Mercury's right to enforce any applicable implied warranty against Tubular.

Returning to the facts of Question 121, suppose, instead, that Tubular's acknowledgment clearly stated that it would accept Mercury's purchase order only if Mercury agreed to all terms set forth in Tubular's acknowledgment.

123.   Should Mercury prevail against Tubular on a claim of breach of warranty?

(A)   Yes, because Mercury expressly reserved its right to enforce any applicable implied warranty against Tubular.

(B)   No, because Tubular's acknowledgment, which followed Mercury's purchase order, expressly disclaimed all implied warranties.

(C)   No, because Mercury accepted and paid for the goods despite the fact that Tubular's acknowledgment, which followed Mercury's purchase order, expressly disclaimed all implied warranties.

(D)   Yes, because, given the conflicting terms in Mercury's purchase order and Tubular's acknowledgment, UCC § 2-207 will operate to preserve Mercury's right to enforce any applicable implied warranty against Tubular.

Returning again to the facts of Question 121, suppose that, rather than purchasing the glass tubing in question from Tubular Glass, Mercury purchased it from Philippe Glass ("PG"), a manufacturer of precision glass tubing whose plant is in Windsor, Ontario.

124.   Assuming that the other facts in Question 121 remain unchanged, that Mercury and PG formed an enforceable contract for the glass tubing, and that their contract is governed by the CISG, what are the terms of that contract?

ANSWER:

On March 1, 2003, Whit and Suzy Sample placed a "For Sale" sign in the front yard of the house in Paradise that they bought two years earlier from its builder, Thomas Homes. The very same day, the Burgers, who were on a house hunting trip from Tennessee where they were then living, saw the "For Sale" sign and offered the Samples $150,000 for the house, which the Samples accepted. No realtor represented either party. The Burgers and the Samples sat down in the living room and prepared a contract by copying paragraphs from a standard-form real estate contract that Suzy borrowed from the local library, making certain changes and additions agreed to by both the Samples and the Burgers.

The contract that the Burgers and the Samples signed contains the following language:

1. Hamilton ("Ham") and Patty Burger (collectively "Buyers") agree to purchase from Whitman ("Whit") and Suzy Sample (collectively "Sellers"), and Sellers agree to sell to Buyers, all right and title to Sellers' house and real property located at 425 Mesquite Lane, Paradise City, Paradise, for the purchase price of $150,000, to be paid by Buyers to Sellers on May 31, 2003 (the "closing date"), at which time Sellers will convey to Buyers an unencumbered deed and clear title to said house and real property.

. . . .

8. Sellers agree to transfer the following personal property to Buyers along with the house: (1) all window treatments; (2) all appliances, including the oven, stove, refrigerator/freezer, and dishwasher; (3) the furniture in the upstairs game room; and (4) all lawn and patio furniture.

. . . .

16. Sellers make no warranty, other than those required by law, about the condition of the house. Buyers agree to assume responsibility for any defects not discovered by Buyers prior to the closing date. Sellers agree to make the house available for one or more inspection(s), arranged and paid for by Buyers, prior to the closing date.

. . . .

20. This contract constitutes the entire agreement between the Buyers and the Sellers with respect to the purchase and sale of the aforementioned house and related real and personal property, and the parties hereby agree that any prior drafts of, or discussions relating to, this contract will have no legal effect.

Notwithstanding paragraph 20, the Burgers claim the Samples agreed to make the Burgers' obligation to complete the purchase conditional on Ham's mother selling her house in Tennessee. (His mother was then to move into Ham and Patty's old home in Tennessee and assume the mortgage payments on it.) When asked, the Samples say they never agreed to such a condition. When the Burgers moved into the house on May 1st, Patty noticed that the Samples had taken the eight exterior solar window screens that Whit had told Patty he had custom-made for the house, as well as the washer and dryer that Suzy told Patty were only a few months old.

125. Based solely on the portions of the contract reproduced above, to what extent does this written contract appear on its face to be integrated?

(A) The written contract appears to be unintegrated.

(B) The written contract appears to be partially integrated.

(C) The written contract appears to be fully integrated.

(D) It is impossible to tell based solely on the document itself.

126.   Assuming, for present purposes, that the Samples did agree to make the Burgers'
        obligation to purchase the Samples' house contingent on Mrs. Burger selling her house
        in Tennessee, should the trial judge permit the Burgers to testify about that condition?

   (A) No, because this is a contract for the sale of an interest in real property. As such,
        a writing must evidence it, and there is no writing evidencing the alleged condition.

   (B) No, because the written contract that the parties signed is fully integrated, and
        the Burgers' attempt to introduce evidence of an additional term — the condition
        precedent — is barred by the parol evidence rule.

   (C) Yes, because the fact that the parties had discussed the condition precedent but
        failed to include it in their written agreement indicates that they did not intend
        the written agreement to be fully integrated, notwithstanding the language of
        paragraph 20.

   (D) Yes, because competent evidence relating to a condition precedent is freely
        admissible, notwithstanding the parol evidence rule, even if the parties have
        executed what appears to be a fully integrated, unambiguous written agreement.

127.   Assuming that the Samples and the Burgers formed an enforceable contract, did that
        contract obligate the Samples to convey the custom-made solar screens to the Burgers
        with the house?

ANSWER:

Suppose that, at all relevant times up to and including when the parties executed their written
agreement, the Samples had no awnings, blinds, curtains, drapes, shades, UV film, valences,
or other interior or exterior window treatments except the custom-made exterior solar screens.

128.   If the trial court were to use the fact that the custom-made exterior solar screens were
        the only window treatments the Burgers were aware of when they contracted with the
        Samples to resolve the ambiguity regarding the solar screens against the Samples,
        which of the following principles of construction and interpretation would the trial
        court *least* likely rely upon in so doing?

   (A) Accounting for the circumstances surrounding the contract's formation.

   (B) Favoring express terms over implied terms or subsequent conduct.

   (C) Giving each contractual provision meaning and purpose.

   (D) *Noscitur a sociis.*

Returning to the facts of Question 125. Assume that the Samples drafted the entire written
agreement, and the Burgers simply read and signed the agreement the Samples provided.

129. If the trial court were to use the fact that the Samples drafted the entire agreement to resolve the ambiguity regarding the solar screens, which of the following principles of construction and interpretation would the trial court *most* likely rely upon in so doing?

    (A) Accounting for the circumstances surrounding the contract's formation.

    (B) *Contra proferentem.*

    (C) Giving each contractual provision meaning and purpose.

    (D) *Noscitur a sociis.*

Returning to the facts of Question 125, assume that the Samples and the Burgers formed an enforceable contract.

130. Did that contract obligate the Samples to convey the washer and dryer to the Burgers with the house?

    (A) Yes, because a washer and dryer clearly fit within the plain meaning of the phrase "all appliances, including the oven, stove, refrigerator/freezer, and dishwasher."

    (B) Yes, because the principle of *ejusdem generis* provides that, where a list of items follows, or is followed by, a generic term that would, without the list, encompass the listed items, then the effect of the generic term is to include unlisted items of the same genre as the listed items.

    (C) No, because the Burgers failed to ensure that the washer and dryer were specifically included in one of the conveyance clauses in paragraph 8, and the principle of *expressio unius est exclusio alterius* provides that, when certain items of a genre are listed and others are not, only those listed items are part of the contract.

    (D) No, because the parties' actions in the course of performing the contract clearly indicate that they did not consider the washer and dryer to be included in the items to be conveyed under paragraph 8.

Leon James is developing a subdivision near Houston. On February 14, 2003, he entered into a written contract to sell a lot in the subdivision to Paola Thomas for $50,000. During negotiations, Leon assured Paola that the property was zoned outside of the 50-year flood plain. The written contract, which contained a conspicuous merger clause, made no mention of this. When, after signing the contract and paying Leon for the lot, Paola applied for a building permit, she was notified that the lot was within the 50-year flood plain (meaning both that it was substantially more prone to flooding and that it would be much more expensive to insure the house that Paola intended to build on the lot).

131. If Paola sued Leon for breach of contract, would evidence of Leon's oral representation be admissible at trial, notwithstanding the parol evidence rule?

ANSWER:

In 1980, Edward Lewis began working at Sunny Dale nursing home, owned and operated by Mesquite Elder Care, Inc. ("MEC"). In 1986, Lewis became the administrator of Sunny Dale, in which position he continued until June 1, 2001, when MEC terminated his employment.

On September 1, 1987, Lewis and MEC executed a written contract, which recited MEC's desire to retain Lewis as an employee and provided what the contract called "assured rewards and incentives" to keep him employed, including obligating MEC's owners to give Lewis 20% of the proceeds of any sale of the company. However, the contract also stated:

> Nothing in this Contract shall obligate the Employer to retain the Employee in its employment, or the Employee to remain in the Employer's employment, in any capacity, for any period.

One of the two original owners, Cal Billoway, entered into a stock redemption agreement in October 1989 with MEC. Because this buy-out might have required Lewis to be paid 20% of the proceeds under the terms of the September 1, 1987 contract, Lewis and MEC's sole remaining owner, Miriam Washington, amended the September 1, 1987 contract on October 1, 1989 to exclude the proceeds from Billoway's redemption, but otherwise reaffirmed the September 1, 1987 agreement. Lewis asserts that in return for relinquishing a claim to any part of the sale proceeds, Washington orally promised to retain him until age 65. Lewis further alleges that, on December 15, 1992, he and Washington made a handwritten amendment to the September 1, 1987 contract to provide that MEC would employ Lewis until age 65.

When MEC terminated Lewis prior to his 65th birthday, Lewis sued. MEC moved for summary judgment, arguing that Lewis was an at-will employee. Lewis opposed the motion on the basis of the alleged October 1, 1989 oral amendment and the alleged December 15, 1992 handwritten amendment to the September 1, 1987 contract. By affidavit, Lewis explained that, when Billoway sold his interest in October 1989, Washington orally promised Lewis employment until age 65 as consideration for his relinquishing a claim for 20% of the proceeds of the sale of Billoway's interest. The December 15, 1992 amendment allegedly was the belated recognition of this 1989 oral promise. Lewis does not have his own copy of the amended contract. The copy of the original contract MEC attached to its summary judgment motion does not contain the alleged December 15, 1992 amendment.

132. Could a reasonable finder of fact conclude that MEC's agreement with Lewis required MEC to employ Lewis until age 65?

(A) No, because the September 1, 1987 contract signed by both Lewis and MEC clearly stated that he is an at-will employee.

(B) No, because Lewis has not produced a copy of the alleged December 15, 1992 amendment to the September 1, 1987 contract; therefore, even if MEC had agreed to employ Lewis until age 65, he cannot bind them to that promise, because doing so would violate the statute of frauds.

(C) Yes, because Lewis may be able, following discovery, to produce a copy of the September 1, 1987 contract that includes the December 15, 1992 amendment.

(D) Yes, because, regardless of whether Lewis can produce a copy of the September 1, 1987 contract that includes the December 15, 1992 amendment, the parol evidence rule does not bar testimonial evidence about an amendment entered into by the parties after they executed a purportedly fully integrated, unambiguous written agreement.

Suppose that, during discovery, Lewis's attorneys locate in MEC's files a copy of the September 1, 1987 contract that includes the handwritten December 15, 1992 amendment. The amendment is written in the margin of the typed and signed contract. Written in blue pen, it reads: "For valuable consideration, MEC hereby agrees to employ Mr. Lewis for as long as he desires, up to age 65." Immediately beneath this sentence are the initials "M.W." and "E.L."

133. Assuming that Washington, as the sole remaining owner of MEC after Billoway redeemed his stock, had the authority to bind MEC, should the trial judge find, as a matter of law, that the December 15, 1992 amendment bound MEC to employ Lewis until his 65th birthday?

(A) No, because the handwritten amendment conflicts with the at-will provision in the original contract. Therefore, the amendment creates an ambiguity regarding MEC's ability to terminate Lewis prior to his 65th birthday, and the trial judge should permit the jury to resolve the ambiguity in light of all relevant evidence and testimony.

(B) No, because the handwritten amendment was unsupported by separate consideration and is, therefore, unenforceable.

(C) Yes, because the trial court should construe the contract, as amended, to give every provision therein meaning and purpose, and the only way to give the handwritten amendment meaning and purpose is to find that it binds MEC to employ Lewis for as long as he desires, up to age 65.

(D) Yes, because when a typewritten or printed provision in a contract conflicts with a handwritten provision, the trial court should enforce the handwritten provision, rather than the typewritten or printed one.

Following Wallace Williams's meteoric rise up the charts in the spring of 2002, he signed a multi-album contract with Vestal Records. Wallace, who was only 17 years old at the time, did not bother shopping around for a better deal because Vestal had a good reputation among recording artists and it gave him a chance when other labels had not. Wallace's contract with Vestal included promises (1) by Vestal to promote Wallace and his music "at such times and by such means as Vestal, in the exercise of its professional judgment, deems appropriate," and (2) by Wallace to record and perform solely for Vestal. The contract provided that Vestal would pay Wallace $500,000 for signing the contract and $250,000 per album, plus a percentage of net revenues from all CD, album, and tape sales, and a percentage of net revenues from all non-charity performances. The contract granted Vestal a percentage of gross revenues from all of the foregoing, as well as final authority over whether a particular single or album would be released.

The bloom was soon off the rose. While Wallace had a successful nationwide tour during the summer of 2002, he felt that Vestal was booking him into too many small venues and too many small towns, when larger venues in bigger cities sat idle. When Wallace raised his concerns with Chick Hanson, Vestal's president, Hanson assured him that Vestal was "looking after his best interests" because Vestal considered him "an important long-term investment." "Be patient," Hanson told Wallace, "you'll be playing stadium shows in Cleveland and Atlanta soon enough." Not prone to patience (like most teens), Wallace began to pay attention to the entreaties he was receiving from other recording labels. When Wallace told Hanson that he wanted to move to Hippo Records as soon as both labels' attorneys could sort out the details, Hanson instructed Vestal's staff to stop advertising Wallace's records, to stop scheduling promotional events, and to ask radio stations to take Wallace's music out of their regular rotation. During the two months it took the two labels to agree to the terms of Hippo's buy-out of Wallace's contract with Vestal, revenues from the sale of Wallace's CDs and royalties paid by radio stations and other outlets for the right to play Wallace's music dropped precipitously.

134. Assuming that Wallace's contract with Vestal was valid and enforceable against both parties, did Vestal's behavior during the final two months of its relationship with Wallace violate any actual or implied term of that contract?

   (A) No, because Wallace's contract with Vestal explicitly gave Vestal complete discretion to promote or not promote Wallace's music.

   (B) No, because Vestal's behavior was only in response to Wallace's clear repudiation of his contract with Vestal.

   (C) Yes, because Vestal's behavior violated its duty to use "reasonable efforts" on Wallace's behalf.

(D)   Yes, because Vestal's behavior violated the duty of good faith and fair dealing it owed Wallace.

Global Chemicals ("Global") operates a number of chemical refineries along the Texas and Louisiana Gulf Coasts. Wanting to expand its operations into southern Mississippi, in January 2003 Global entered into a long-term contract to supply benthahexelene, a chemical preservative used in hot dogs, sausages, and other packaged meat products, to Byron Meats, a major packaged-meat producer based in Mississippi. The contract provided that Byron would purchase as much benthahexelene as Global's planned Waveland, Mississippi plant could produce, up to 100,000 gallons per month, at $5.00 per gallon for the first 50,000 gallons per month, with the per-gallon price decreasing to $4.00 per gallon for the next 20,000 gallons, $3.50 per gallon for the next 15,000 gallons, and $3.00 per gallon for the next 15,000 gallons. If Global was able to produce more than 100,000 gallons of benthahexelene in a given month, the contract gave Byron a right of first refusal to purchase as much of the additional output as it wanted for $3.00 per gallon. Global and its design engineers, Falcon Crest, estimated it would take six to eight months to build the new plant and make it operational, so Byron's contract with Global provided that Byron's obligation to purchase, and Global's obligation to sell, benthahexelene would commence on October 1, 2003. When Global and Byron signed their contract, the market price of benthahexelene was $4.75 per gallon, and over the preceding year it had varied between $4.50 per gallon and $5.25 per gallon.

As construction of the new plant was ongoing, the market price of benthahexelene was rising, due to a trade embargo imposed by the United States on the tiny nation of Luxembourg (surprisingly, the world's leading producer of benthahexelene) after Luxembourg declared war on Great Britain. By the time construction of the Waveland plant was two-thirds complete, the market price of benthahexelene had risen to $10.00 per gallon. Global realized that it could make more profit by shifting its resources to maximizing the output and expanding the capacity of its other benthahexelene plants, rather than completing construction of the Waveland plant and being locked into an output contract with Byron that grew less and less lucrative every day.

135.   If Global decided to delay construction of the Waveland plant or to let it sit idle, until the market price of benthahexelene fell to a level that made the Byron contract economically sound for Global, would that decision have violated any actual or implied term of its contract with Byron?

(A)   No, because Global did not promise to produce any benthahexelene at its Waveland plant; it only promised to sell whatever benthahexelene it did produce at its Waveland plant to Byron.

(B)   No, because Global owed Byron no duty to produce benthahexelene at its Waveland plant; it only owed Byron a duty to sell whatever benthahexelene it did produce at its Waveland plant to Byron.

(C)   No, because Global's decision was economically sound for Global and consistent with Global's duty of good faith and fair dealing.

(D)   Yes, because, by agreeing to sell Byron the benthahexelene output of its Waveland plant, Global assumed a duty to use its best efforts to produce commercially reasonable quantities of benthahexelene at its Waveland plant.

Around the same time it entered into its contract to supply benthahexelene to Byron, Global entered into a contract to purchase all of the hypobutatetridiene it needed for the Waveland plant from Bubba Gump Chemicals in nearby Bay St. Louis, Mississippi. Hypobutatetridiene is a chemical feedstock that evaporates rapidly during transport. As a consequence, Global and other producers of benthahexelene and other refined chemicals that require hypobutatetridiene as a feedstock either must order substantially more hypobutatetridiene than they actually need, to account for evaporation, or must find a supplier of hypobutatetridiene located near them. The cost of purchasing hypobutatetridiene from Bubba Gump and shipping it to any of Global's existing benthahexelene plants (the nearest of which to Bay St. Louis is in Cameron, Louisiana) is too high to be economically feasible, even with benthahexelene selling for $10.00 per gallon.

136.   If Global decided to delay construction of the Waveland plant or to let it sit idle, until the market price of benthahexelene fell to a level that made the Byron contract economically sound for Global, would that decision have violated any actual or implied term of its contract with Bubba Gump?

(A)   No, because Global did not promise to purchase any hypobutatetridiene from Bubba Gump; it only promised to purchase whatever hypobutatetridiene it required for its Waveland plant from Bubba Gump.

(B)   No, because Global owed Bubba Gump no duty to purchase hypobutatetridiene for its Waveland plant; it only owed Bubba Gump a duty to purchase whatever hypobutatetridiene it required for its Waveland plant from Bubba Gump.

(C)   No, because Global's decision was economically sound for Global and consistent with Global's duty of good faith and fair dealing.

(D)   Yes, because, by agreeing to purchase the hypobutatetridiene requirements of its Waveland plant from Bubba Gump, Global assumed a duty to use its best efforts to ensure that it would require commercially reasonable quantities of hypobutatetridiene for its Waveland plant.

Not surprisingly, Luxembourg's "war" with Great Britain did not last long and, by September 2003, Luxembourgian benthahexelene was once again flooding the world market, driving the spot market price back into the $5.00-$6.00 per gallon range and prompting Global to resume construction on the Waveland plant. One of the final phases of the construction involved painting the exterior of the refinery structure and installing siding panels on and painting several buildings to match. Global contracted with Pete's Paints and Panels ("PPP"), from Pascagoula, Mississippi, to supply paint matching Falcon Crest's specifications for the job and to apply the paint and siding panels "in a manner satisfactory to Global (or its designated agent, Falcon Crest)."

137.   If a dispute subsequently arose about PPP's performance of the painting and paneling portion of its contract with Global, what standard should a court use to decide whether PPP performed satisfactorily?

    (A)   Whether Global was honestly dissatisfied with PPP's performance.

    (B)   Whether a reasonable person in Global's position would have been dissatisfied with PPP's performance.

    (C)   Whether PPP's performance met industry standards.

    (D)   Whether PPP performed in good faith.

Sally Rich, age 22, told her parents that she would have their dining room wallpapered while they were on vacation. Sally hired Wally Hanger to put wallpaper on the walls in Sally's parents' house. When Sally hired Wally, the walls were unpapered, but tastefully painted.

Their written contract provided, in relevant part:

> Hanger agrees to paper the walls of Mr. & Mrs. Rich's dining room to Sally Rich's satisfaction, using any paper Sally Rich selects from Hanger's sample book, for a total price of $1,000.

> In the event that the quality of Hanger's work does not meet Sally Rich's satisfaction, Hanger agrees, at its election, (i) to repair any defective paper and/or defectively installed paper at Hanger's own expense; (ii) to remove the defective paper and/or defectively installed paper and refinish and paint the walls, as they were prior to Hanger's work, at Hanger's own expense; or (iii) to refund the contract price, less the cost of all nondefective paper and other materials. Alternatively, Sally Rich may demand that Hanger pay her liquidated damages in the amount of $500, the payment of which by Hanger will discharge Hanger of any further liability.

Sally selected wallpaper with a rustic scene with dancing nymphs and satyrs. Wally promptly papered the dining room with paper like the sample. The paper and materials expended cost Wally $900. There were no visible defects in any of the installed wallpaper.

When the room was done, Sally showed it to her father, who was shocked at the nude nymphs and satyrs. Sally then wrote to Wally, stating:

> I am not satisfied with the wallpaper because it shocks my father and because some of the paper panels are out of alignment. I will not pay your bill unless and until you repaper the dining room to my satisfaction and at your expense.

In fact, some panels were out of alignment, but the problem could only be seen with a magnifying glass. It would cost Wally (1) $500 to remove the "nymph and satyrs" wallpaper, (2) $1,000 to install new wallpaper (which can be installed over the existing paper), (3) $300 to refinish and repaint the walls the way they were once the wallpaper was removed, and (4) $250 to repair those panels that are out of alignment. Uncertain whether Wally would comply with her demand, Sally solicited bids from other wallpaper companies to repaper the dining room and, in the alternative, to remove the paper and repaint the room as it was. The lowest bids she received from a reputable company were from WallCo, which bid (1) $1,250 to remove the "nymph and satyrs" wallpaper and install replacement wallpaper and (2) $900 to remove the "nymph and satyrs" wallpaper, then refinish and repaint the walls.

138. If Wally sued Sally for the payment she owes under their contract and Sally defended or countersued on the ground that Wally failed to perform their contract to her satisfaction, who should prevail?

(A) Sally, because she is honestly dissatisfied with the quality of Wally's work.

(B) Sally, because a reasonable person in her position would be dissatisfied with the quality of Wally's work.

(C) Wally, because Sally is not honestly dissatisfied with the quality of Wally's work.

(D) Wally, because a reasonable person in Sally's position would be satisfied with the quality of Wally's work.

139. Which of the following implied warranties is not found in UCC Article 2?

(A) The implied warranty of fitness for a particular purpose.

(B) The implied warranty of good title.

(C) The implied warranty of habitability.

(D) The implied warranty of merchantability.

Returning to the facts of Question 137, suppose, instead, that the dispute was not about PPP's painting and paneling proficiency, but over the quality of the paint and paneling PPP procured or produced for the project. Assume that UCC Article 2 would govern any dispute between Global and PPP regarding the quality of the paint and paneling materials PPP used, and that PPP made no express warranties to Global or Falcon Crest regarding the quality of the paint and paneling materials.

140. Would PPP's use of poor quality paint and paneling materials on the Waveland plant have violated any UCC Article 2 implied warranty?

(A) Yes, PPP would have violated the implied warranty of merchantability.

(B) Yes, PPP would have violated the implied warranty of fitness for a particular purpose.

(C) Yes, PPP would have violated the implied warranty of workmanlike performance.

(D) No, PPP would not have violated any implied warranty.

Pennybakers is a small, but successful, interior design business located in Athens, Georgia. Wanting to expand into graphic design and advertising, Pennybakers' principal, Petunia Pennybaker, contracted with an upstart computer engineering firm, Scott & Co. ("S&C"), to design customized graphics software. S&C's chief engineer, Adam Scott — who Petunia met on a flight from Atlanta to San Jose, California (where S&C is headquartered) — promptly designed and tested the software. Claiming that he was dissatisfied with the software's performance on Pennybakers' existing computers, Adam suggested that Pennybakers buy a new computer specially designed for graphics software, the Scott GR8 ("GR8"), to run the new software. S&C manufactures the GR8. Delighted with Adam's demonstration of the custom software using the GR8, Petunia willingly agreed to buy the GR8 to run the software. The parties amended their contract to include Pennybakers' purchase and S&C's delivery of the GR8.

Less than two weeks after taking delivery of the software and the GR8, Petunia began to notice a recurrent glitch that caused a small, bespectacled dog to appear randomly in the graphical layouts she designed using the GR8. Acting on a hunch, Petunia discovered the same glitch while running other software that had been installed on the GR8. When she called S&C to complain, her call was directed to S&C's customer service specialist, Bob, who was unable to solve Petunia's problem. The problem persisted, causing Pennybakers to lose a lucrative advertising contract for the Greater Atlanta Garfield Fan Club. Finally fed up with it all, and wanting to prevent any further loss of business, Pennybakers purchased a MicroSpaz 3000GT computer for $3,000 and new graphics software for $2,000. Pennybakers also filed suit against S&C, alleging breach of any and all applicable express or implied warranties.

The parties' pleadings and discovery reveal, in addition to the foregoing, that: (1) Pennybakers paid S&C $25,000 to design the custom software; (2) Pennybakers paid S&C $2,500 for the GR8 computer; (3) Pennybakers paid S&C the entire $27,500 prior to taking delivery of the software and the GR8; (4) the parties agree that any glitch is a "hardware" problem with the GR8, not a "software" problem; (5) Pennybakers' expert witness has opined that the software designed by S&C would have performed as well or better on any number of other commercially-available computers as it did on the GR8 before the glitch appeared; (6) Petunia's assistant, Cleo, loaded the software onto another computer and ran it for several weeks without ever encountering the glitch; (7) the warranty card that accompanied the GR8 computer did not disclaim any implied warranties and expressly warranted that the computer would operate free of any errors, other than those caused by third-party software, for a period of one year from the date of purchase; (8) the contract Pennybakers lost with the Greater Atlanta Garfield Fan Club would have netted Pennybakers a profit of at least $25,000; and (9) the MicroSpaz 3000GT and the new graphics software have been glitch-free.

141. Assuming that UCC Article 2 governs this dispute, does Pennybakers have a viable claim against S&C for breach of an express warranty or the implied warranty of merchantability with regard to the GR8 computer?

    (A) Pennybakers has a viable claim against S&C for breaching the express warranty (set forth on the warranty card) and the implied warranty of merchantability.

    (B) Pennybakers has a viable claim against S&C for breaching the express warranty, but not the implied warranty of merchantability.

    (C) Pennybakers has a viable claim against S&C for breaching the implied warranty of merchantability, but not the express warranty.

    (D) Pennybakers does not have a viable claim against S&C for breaching either the express warranty or the implied warranty of merchantability.

142. Assuming that UCC Article 2 governs this dispute, does Pennybakers have a viable claim against S&C for breach of the implied warranty of fitness for a particular purpose with regard to the GR8 computer?

(A) Yes, because S&C is a merchant dealing in goods of the kind.

(B) Yes, because S&C knew or had reason to know the purpose for which Pennybakers wanted a computer.

(C) Yes, because S&C knew or had reason to know the purpose for which Pennybakers wanted a computer, and Pennybakers foreseeably relied on S&C to select the right computer for that purpose.

(D) No, because Pennybakers' purpose for purchasing the GR8 computer was not sufficiently particular to give rise to a UCC § 2-315 warranty.

143. Assuming that Article 2 governs this dispute, does Pennybakers have a viable claim against S&C for breach of one or more implied warranties with regard to the software?

ANSWER:

On March 1, 2003, Whit and Suzy Sample placed a "For Sale" sign in the front yard of the house in Paradise that they bought two years earlier from its builder, Thomas Homes. The very same day, the Burgers, who were on a house hunting trip from Tennessee where they were then living, saw the "For Sale" sign and offered the Samples $150,000 for the house, which the Samples accepted. No realtor represented either party. The Burgers and the Samples sat down in the living room and prepared a contract by copying paragraphs from a standard-form real estate contract that Suzy borrowed from the local library, making certain changes and additions agreed to by both the Samples and the Burgers.

The contract that the Burgers and the Samples signed contains the following language:

1. Hamilton ("Ham") and Patty Burger (collectively "Buyers") agree to purchase from Whitman ("Whit") and Suzy Sample (collectively "Sellers"), and Sellers agree to sell to Buyers, all right and title to Sellers' house and real property located at 425 Mesquite Lane, Paradise City, Paradise, for the purchase price of $150,000, to be paid by Buyers to Sellers on May 31, 2003 (the "closing date"), at which time Sellers will convey to Buyers an unencumbered deed and clear title to said house and real property.

. . . .

16. Sellers make no warranty, other than those required by law, about the condition of the house. Buyers agree to assume responsibility for any defects not discovered by Buyers prior to the closing date. Sellers agree to make the house available for one or more inspection(s), arranged and paid for by Buyers, prior to the closing date.

. . . .

20. This contract constitutes the entire agreement between the Buyers and the Sellers with respect to the purchase and sale of the aforementioned house and related real and personal property, and the parties hereby agree that any prior drafts of, or discussions relating to, this contract will have no legal effect.

Three days after they moved into the house, Patty noticed some cracking in the ceilings of two of the downstairs rooms. These cracks were barely visible, but the Burgers were concerned that the ceiling cracks were evidence of foundation problems. Ham had a structural engineer friend look at the cracks. The friend told Ham that the foundation of the house might need repair because the cracks suggested that it was not correctly built. When asked, the Samples truthfully said that they had never noticed the ceiling cracks.

144. Assuming that the ceiling cracks evidence that the house's foundation needs repair, would the fact that the house has a faulty foundation have violated any actual or implied term of the contract between the Samples and the Burgers?

ANSWER:

Romeo had been courting Juliet for several years. Finally, he decided to propose marriage. Romeo shopped around to find the best deal on the right ring. Romeo found the ring he sought at Old Will's Jewelers for $10,000. Romeo was unable to pay the entire purchase price immediately. Old Will, the sole proprietor of Old Will's Jewelers, agreed to sell Romeo the ring for $2,500 down and $7,500 to be paid in 10 equal monthly installments. Romeo asked Old Will to hold the ring for him and promised to return the next day with the down payment.

When Old Will subsequently questioned Romeo's creditworthiness and demanded that Romeo pay the full purchase price in cash or the deal was off, Romeo bought a ring of comparable size and quality from another jeweler, Fennyman's Fine Jewelry, for $12,500, proposed to Juliet, she accepted, and they lived happily ever after (at least, so far). Romeo then sued Old Will's Jewelers to recover the difference between the price of the replacement ring and the price of the ring that Old Will had promised to sell Romeo.

Shortly after Romeo filed his suit, Juliet accidentally broke one of the prongs on the replacement ring Romeo gave her. Wanting to get the ring fixed without telling Romeo, and unaware that he had ever considered purchasing a different ring for her (much less that he was involved in litigation over it), Juliet stopped during lunch at the jeweler's store just around the corner from her office — the aforementioned Old Will's Jewelers — to have the ring repaired. The clerk, Henslowe, who took the ring told her it would be ready for her to pick up after 5:00 p.m. He then tagged the ring and left it on the repair box. Old Will, who was handling repairs that afternoon, read the name on the repair tag, put two and two together, and realized whose ring it was that had been left for him to fix. Steaming over Romeo's suit, Old Will fixed the prong and then put the ring in a display case, at a bargain price, hoping some lucky soul would come along and buy it. Before that could happen, however, one of Old Will's customers, Rosaline, saw the ring and recognized it as one of several that had been stolen from her house several months earlier. Further investigation revealed that the thief had pawned the ring at Fennyman's Friendly Pawn Shop, which had then "sold" it to its more respectable sister, Fennyman's Fine Jewelry, which, in turn, sold it to Romeo, who gave it to Juliet.

145. Assuming that the ring was stolen from Rosaline, can Romeo sue Fennyman's Fine Jewelry for breaching the implied warranty of good title?

(A) No, because Fennyman's Fine Jewelry did not know the ring was stolen.

(B) No, because Fennyman's Friendly Pawn Shop took voidable title in the ring, and Fennyman's Fine Jewelry, a good faith purchaser for value, could transfer good title to Romeo as a buyer in the ordinary course of business.

(C) No, because Fennyman's Fine Jewelry had voidable title in the ring, and could transfer good title to Romeo as a buyer in the ordinary course of business.

(D) Yes, because one who takes possession of a stolen item can never pass anything but void title; and, therefore, Fennyman's Fine Jewelry sold Romeo a ring in which Fennyman's could not give Romeo good title.

Suppose, instead, that the ring was not stolen from Rosaline or anyone else, and was sitting in the display case where Old Will had maliciously put it when Thomas Kent wandered into the store, looking for an engagement ring for his beloved, Violet. Kent saw Juliet's ring in the display case and purchased it from another sales clerk, Webster, who was unaware that the ring was not part of the store's inventory. When Juliet returned to the store to reclaim her ring, she discovered that Webster had inadvertently sold it to Kent, who took it with him.

146. Can Juliet reclaim her ring from Kent, given that she did not authorize Old Will to sell it?

ANSWER:

On May 1, 2002, Shaggy agreed to purchase Morbid Manor from Fred for $50,000. Shaggy and Fred further agreed that Shaggy would pay Fred the full $50,000 purchase price on or before July 1st, and that Fred would transfer title to Morbid Manor to Shaggy, upon receipt of the full purchase price.

147. Assuming that Fred and Shaggy formed an enforceable contract, which of the following statements by Shaggy on June 1st would have constituted an anticipatory repudiation of that contract?

   (A) Shaggy told Fred, "I recently lost my job at The Malt Shoppe, and I am not sure I'll be able to pay you the entire $50,000 by July 1st."

   (B) Shaggy told his friend Velma, "I know Fred is planning to use the money I promised to pay him for Morbid Manor to travel to Europe with Daphne. I'm sick and tired of him ending up with the girl and me ending up with the dog. I'm not going to pay him anything. Morbid Manor is nothing but a rickety old house anyway."

   (C) Shaggy told Fred, "I have thought this over, and I am not going to pay you the money I promised you. How about a 'Scooby Snack' instead?"

   (D) Shaggy told Fred, "The more I think about it, the more I am convinced that you are asking too much for Morbid Manor. Would you agree to sell it to me for $45,000, instead of $50,000?"

148. Assuming that Shaggy's statement constituted an anticipatory repudiation, which of the following would Fred have been entitled to do in response to Shaggy's repudiation?

   (A) Do nothing, hoping that Shaggy would, in fact, perform as and when promised.

   (B) Cancel the contract and retain Morbid Manor.

   (C) Sell Morbid Manor to Mr. Greeley for $45,000 and sue Shaggy for the $5,000 difference between the contract and resale prices, plus whatever other damages Fred incurs.

   (D) All of the above.

Suppose that, faced with Shaggy's repudiation, Fred chose to do nothing, hoping Shaggy would, in fact, perform as and when promised. Suppose, further, that Shaggy called Fred the next day and said, "I was just kidding the other day. I fully intend to keep my promise and pay you $50,000 for Morbid Manor on or before July 1st."

149. Would Fred still have been entitled to cancel the contract, sell Morbid Manor to Mr. Greeley, or sue Shaggy for damages?

(A) Yes, because Fred did not seek Shaggy's retraction.

(B) Yes, because Shaggy's repudiation preceded Fred's sale of Morbid Manor to Mr. Greeley.

(C) No, because Shaggy retracted his repudiation before July 1st.

(D) No, because Shaggy retracted his repudiation before Fred acted in reliance on Shaggy's repudiation.

Suppose, instead, that Fred sold Morbid Manor to Mr. Greeley on June 24th, and that Shaggy called Fred on June 25th and said, "I was just kidding earlier. I fully intend to keep my promise and pay you $50,000 for Morbid Manor on or before July 1st."

150. Did Fred breach his contract with Shaggy by selling Morbid Manor to Mr. Greeley?

(A) Yes, because Shaggy effectively retracted his repudiation before the time his performance was due.

(B) Yes, because Fred sold Morbid Manor to Mr. Greeley before the date he had set for Shaggy to perform.

(C) Yes, because Fred failed to seek adequate assurances from Shaggy before selling Morbid Manor to Mr. Greeley.

(D) No. Shaggy's repudiation entitled Fred to sell Morbid Manor to Mr. Greeley, even if Fred chose to do so before the date he had previously agreed to close the sale to Shaggy.

Returning to the facts of Questions 147 and 148, suppose that, in order to sell Morbid Manor to Shaggy "free and clear" of any liens or other impediments of title, Fred had to pay the last $5,000 he owed Gomez and Morticia, from whom Fred bought Morbid Manor 18 months earlier, and to obtain and record a release of lien from Gomez and Morticia.

151. In light of Shaggy's repudiation, did Fred have to pay off the loan prior to July 1st if the remaining $5,000 was not otherwise due until December 31st?

ANSWER:

152. Suppose, instead, that Morbid Manor burned to the ground on June 15th. If Shaggy anticipatorily repudiated and Fred had not already sold Morbid Manor to a third party or otherwise acted in reliance on Shaggy's repudiation before Morbid Manor was destroyed by fire, would Shaggy be liable to Fred for the agreed purchase price?

(A)   Yes, because Shaggy assumed the risk of loss to Morbid Manor once he agreed to purchase it from Fred.

(B)   Yes, because Shaggy's repudiation shifted the risk of loss to Morbid Manor to Shaggy until Fred sold it to someone else or resolved to keep it for himself.

(C)   No, because the destruction of Morbid Manor made Shaggy's performance impossible or impracticable or frustrated his purpose for agreeing to purchase Morbid Manor from Fred.

(D)   Yes, because the destruction of Morbid Manor effectively unjustly enriched Shaggy, who would otherwise have been liable to Fred for the purchase price.

153.   Return to the facts of Questions 147 and 148. Assuming that Fred had reasonable grounds to demand adequate assurances from Shaggy that he would purchase Morbid Manor as and when promised, which of the following statements is true?

(A)   Fred was required to demand assurances from Shaggy and to make his demand in writing.

(B)   Fred was entitled to demand assurances from Shaggy; but, if he chose to do so, Fred was required to make his demand in writing.

(C)   Fred was required to demand assurances from Shaggy, and could make his demand by any reasonable means.

(D)   Fred was entitled to demand assurances from Shaggy; and, if he chose to do so, Fred could make his demand by any reasonable means.

Returning to the facts of Questions 147 and 148, assume that (1) Shaggy's June 1st statement was not, in and of itself, an anticipatory repudiation; (2) Fred had reasonable grounds to demand adequate assurances from Shaggy that he would perform as and when promised; and (3) Fred's June 3, 2002, phone call constituted a proper request for assurances.

154.   If Fred telephoned Shaggy on June 3rd and asked for assurances, no later than June 10th, that Shaggy would have the $50,000 to purchase Morbid Manor by July 1st, which of the following statements or acts by Shaggy would have satisfied Fred's request?

(A)   Shaggy told Fred on June 3rd, "I'll do everything I can to make sure that I have the money by July 1st."

(B)   On June 10th, Fred received a letter from First National Bank of Squaresville informing Fred that the Bank would guarantee Shaggy's promise to pay Fred $50,000 on or before July 1st, to purchase Morbid Manor.

(C)   On June 14th, Shaggy called Fred to tell him: "I just got off the phone with my financial adviser, who was on vacation all of last week, and I told her to sell some of the stocks I bought with the money I inherited from Uncle Bob. She said it would take a couple of days to get me a check, but I will have your $50,000 before July 1st."

(D)   On June 30th, Shaggy showed up at Fred's house with $50,000 in cash to purchase Morbid Manor.

155.   Assuming that Shaggy adequately assured Fred that he would perform as and when promised, would Fred have been entitled to sell Morbid Manor to a third party or otherwise dispose of it prior to July 1st because of Shaggy's prior repudiation?

ANSWER:

156.   If Shaggy failed to timely satisfy Fred's reasonable request for adequate assurances of performance, which of the following would Fred have been entitled to do?

(A)   Urge Shaggy to reconsider and perform as and when promised.

(B)   Cancel the contract and retain Morbid Manor.

(C)   Sell Morbid Manor on June 24th to Mr. Greeley for $45,000 and sue Shaggy for $5,000, plus any incidental and consequential damages Shaggy's repudiation caused Fred.

(D)   All of the above.

Romeo had been courting Juliet for several years. Finally, he decided to propose marriage. Romeo shopped around to find the best deal on the right ring. Romeo found the ring he sought at Old Will's Jewelers for $10,000. Romeo was unable to pay the entire purchase price immediately. Old Will, the sole proprietor of Old Will's Jewelers, agreed to sell Romeo the ring for $2,500 down and $7,500 to be paid in 10 equal monthly installments. Romeo asked Old Will to hold the ring for him and promised to return the next day with the down payment.

Romeo returned to Old Will's the next afternoon with a check for $2,500, drawn on Romeo's account at Padua Bank & Trust ("PB&T"). Old Will agreed to hold Romeo's check until Romeo picked up the ring the following morning. Later that afternoon, however, Old Will called PB&T to confirm that Romeo's account contained sufficient funds to cover the check. PB&T informed Old Will that the account balance was currently "less than $500," and that, "over the past year, the balance in this account has averaged less than $1,000." Old Will then called the local credit bureau, which characterized Romeo as "a questionable credit risk" for any amount greater than $500.

Old Will promptly called Romeo, chastised him for writing "a rubber check," and demanded that Romeo pay the entire purchase price in cash. Romeo told Old Will that he had transferred funds into his PB&T account to cover the check, but that, because he had done so after 3:00 p.m., his account balance would not reflect the additional funds until tomorrow. Romeo offered to bring $2,500 cash when he came to pick up the ring. Old Will would not budge. He insisted that Romeo pay the full price in cash or the deal was off. Romeo refused, bought a ring of comparable size and quality from another jeweler for $12,500, and proposed to Juliet. She accepted, and they lived happily ever after (at least, so far).

Assume that Romeo and Old Will had an enforceable contract, and that Romeo transferred sufficient funds into his PB&T account in time to cover the check if Old Will had deposited it the same day that Romeo was to pick up the ring.

157. Did Romeo anticipatorily repudiate his contract with Old Will by writing a check for more than the then-current balance in his checking account?

   (A) No, because Old Will promised to hold the check until the next day, by which time Romeo's account *could* have had sufficient funds in it.

   (B) No, because Old Will promised to hold the check until the next day, by which time Romeo's account *would* have had sufficient funds in it.

   (C) Yes, because Romeo should have accounted for the possibility that Old Will would at least inquire about the current balance in Romeo's bank account and might become reasonably insecure after discovering what the account balance was and what it had been.

   (D) Yes, because writing an insufficient funds check is illegal, and any illegal behavior in preparing to perform, or in the course of performing, a contract is an anticipatory repudiation, as a matter of law.

158. Did Old Will anticipatorily repudiate Old Will's Jewelers' contract with Romeo?

   (A) No, because Old Will had reasonable grounds for insecurity and, therefore, was free to demand assurances of due performance.

   (B) No, because Romeo failed to adequately respond to Old Will's reasonable demand for assurances.

   (C) Yes, because Old Will failed to properly demand assurances from Romeo.

   (D) Yes, because Old Will was estopped from demanding assurances or refusing to perform because he had already accepted Romeo's down payment.

Returning to the facts of Question 157, suppose that Romeo, while watching the local news after returning home from dropping the check off with Old Will (the day before Romeo was to pick up the ring), saw a story on the local news about the allegedly fraudulent practices of several local jewelers. The news story reported that confidential sources claiming to have first-hand knowledge said that, after the customers had inspected their diamonds, the jewelers were replacing the diamonds with artificial diamonds worth less than 10% of the genuine articles. The story went on to report that Old Will's Jewelers was named in one complaint filed several months earlier with the district attorney's office and that the DA's office had investigated the complaint but found insufficient evidence to bring criminal charges.

159. Would the news report have given Romeo reasonable grounds for insecurity, entitling him to demand assurances from Old Will, suspend his own performance until Old Will adequately assured him, and avoid the contract if Old Will did not seasonably provide Romeo adequate assurances?

(A) No, because you cannot always believe what you see and hear on the news.

(B) No, because the single allegation about Old Will was made several months ago and, as yet, the district attorney's office had not pursued it.

(C) No, because Romeo planned to propose to Juliet in a couple of days and could not give Old Will the statutory 30 days to respond to a demand for adequate assurances.

(D) Yes, because a reasonable person in Romeo's position would, based on the third-party information, have grounds to be insecure about Old Will performing as promised.

160. Assuming that Romeo had reasonable grounds for insecurity, how might Old Will have gone about adequately assuring Romeo that he was selling him the same diamond ring Romeo agreed to buy?

ANSWER:

Returning to the facts of Question 157, suppose that Old Will's Jewelers is in San Diego, California and Padua Bank & Trust is in Padua, Italy. Suspending disbelief, for the purpose of keeping this fact pattern short, further suppose that: (1) Old Will would take a personal check drawn on a foreign bank; (2) Romeo could write a check on his PB&T account for dollars; and (3) Old Will could gather the same information about Romeo's PB&T account and his general creditworthiness as he could if this were a local transaction.

161. If Romeo wanted to purchase the ring from Old Will to add it to the inventory of his own jewelry store in Padua (rather than to give as a gift to his intended bride), what did the CISG require or entitle Old Will to do once he became reasonably insecure about Romeo's ability to perform as and when promised?

(A) Old Will was required to demand assurances from Romeo and to make his demand in writing.

(B) Old Will was entitled to demand assurances from Romeo; but, if he chose to do so, Old Will was required to make his demand in writing.

(C) Old Will was required to demand assurances from Romeo, and could make his demand by any reasonable means.

(D) Old Will was entitled to demand assurances from Romeo; and, if he chose to do so, Old Will could make his demand by any reasonable means.

On March 1, 2003, Gwyneth and Russell agreed that Gwyneth would pay Russell $100 each for two tickets to the March 15th New York premiere of *The Orange Pumpernickel*. They further agreed that Russell would deliver the tickets to Gwyneth no later than March 14th. The New York premiere of Cameron Ridley's new movie, *The Orange Pumpernickel*, was scheduled for March 15th at the Radikal City Musik Hall. That same night, the 41st Street Playhouse scheduled the premiere of a stage production of *The Orange Pumpernickel*, directed by David Marmoset.

On March 2nd, Russell purchased two tickets from the 41st Street Playhouse for $75 each. On March 14th, when Russell delivered the tickets to Gwyneth, she refused to pay, claiming that Russell had agreed to sell her tickets to the movie, not the play. Russell did not have any tickets to the movie, and none were commercially available at that late date. Russell tried unsuccessfully to find another buyer for the play tickets and to obtain a refund from the Playhouse. Unable to use them himself, he left the tickets with Gwyneth in case she changed her mind.

Gwyneth sued Russell for failing to provide her with the movie tickets. Russell countersued Gwyneth for failing to pay for the tickets he delivered to her.

162. Assuming that Russell knew that Gwyneth wanted tickets to the movie premiere, rather than tickets to the play premiere, but Russell bought her play tickets anyway, did Russell breach their contract, entitling Gwyneth to refuse to pay Russell?

   (A) No, because Gwyneth was not sufficiently specific when she agreed to pay Russell $200 for two tickets to the premiere of *The Orange Pumpernickel*.

   (B) No, because Russell's performance, defective though it may have been, would unjustly enrich Gwyneth if she is excused from paying Russell for the tickets.

   (C) No, because Russell substantially performed, entitling Gwyneth to sue Russell for damages, but not discharging Gwyneth's obligation to perform her part of the bargain.

   (D) Yes, because Russell's breach was material and total, discharging Gwyneth's duty to pay Russell for the tickets.

Suppose, instead, that Russell delivered the play tickets to Gwyneth on March 4th, rather than March 14th. Gwyneth refused to pay for them and informed Russell that he had purchased the wrong tickets. Russell apologized profusely and said he would return with tickets to the movie premiere.

163. Would Gwyneth have been entitled to cancel her contract with Russell?

(A)   No, because Gwyneth was not sufficiently specific when she agreed to pay Russell $200 for two tickets to the premiere of *The Orange Pumpernickel*.

(B)   No, because Russell substantially performed, entitling Gwyneth to sue Russell for damages, but not discharging her obligation to perform her part of the bargain.

(C)   No, because Russell's breach, while material, was only partial, entitling him to cure the breach at any time up to and including March 14th.

(D)   Yes, because Russell's breach was material and total, discharging Gwyneth's duty to pay Russell for the tickets.

Returning to the facts of Question 163, suppose that, after Gwyneth refused to pay for the tickets Russell delivered to her on March 4th and informed him that he had purchased the wrong tickets, Russell replied, "Sorry, love. You said two tickets to *The Orange Pumpernickel*, and I bought two tickets to *The Orange Pumpernickel*. If you want tickets other than these, get them yourself."

164.   Would Gwyneth have been entitled to cancel her contract with Russell?

(A)   No, because Gwyneth was not sufficiently specific when she agreed to pay Russell $200 for two tickets to the premiere of *The Orange Pumpernickel*.

(B)   No, because Russell's breach, while material, was only partial, entitling him to cure the breach at any time up to and including March 14th (the date his performance was due under the contract).

(C)   Yes, because Russell's breach was material and total, discharging Gwyneth's duty to pay Russell for the tickets.

(D)   Yes, because Russell accompanied his partial breach with a repudiation, relieving Gwyneth of any obligation to give Russell a chance to cure his partial breach.

Returning to the facts of Question 162, suppose that Russell bought two tickets to the movie premiere for $75 each. When Russell attempted to deliver the tickets to Gwyneth on March 14th as called for by their contract, she was not home, so he slipped the tickets through her mail slot with a note saying "You can pay me tomorrow." Gwyneth hoped to star in the much-anticipated sequel to *Titanic* and planned to schmooze its director, Cameron, while at the movie premiere. Unbeknownst to Russell, Gwyneth heard later that day on *Entertainment This Night* that Cameron had suddenly become ill and would not be coming to New York for the premiere. Gwyneth decided not to attend the premiere and returned the tickets to Russell the next day. Russell demanded to be paid for the tickets. Gwyneth refused. Due to circumstances beyond his control, Russell was unable to use, sell, or return the tickets.

165.   Without delving into the details of remedies just yet, which of the following statements best represents Russell's legal posture?

(A)   Gwyneth's breach was partial and material, not relieving Russell of any obligation to perform, but entitling Russell to sue Gwyneth for damages.

(B)   Gwyneth's breach was total and material, not relieving Russell of any obligation to perform, but entitling Russell to sue Gwyneth for damages.

(C)   Gwyneth's breach was partial and material, relieving Russell of any obligation to perform and entitling Russell to sue Gwyneth for damages.

(D)   Gwyneth's breach was total and material, relieving Russell of any obligation to perform and entitling Russell to sue Gwyneth for damages.

LeJames Brown, a rising basketball star, just signed a multi-year endorsement contract with Swoop Shoes ("Swoop"), which promises to pay Brown at least $2,000,000 per year. Swoop uses a distinctive logo on all of its trademarked shoes, hats, shirts, and other apparel and accessories. Brown's contract with Swoop requires him to be seen in public — on and off the basketball court — only in Swoop shoes, "unless the occasion requires wearing a style of shoe that Swoop does not make, such as hiking boots, swim fins, dress shoes, or loafers." Brown's contract with Swoop requires him to forfeit $10,000 for every exhibition, regular season, or post-season game, and $5,000 for every practice that is open to the public, in which he is seen wearing non-Swoop shoes. The contract also specifies fines for being photographed, filmed, or seen in public wearing non-Swoop shoes (subject to the exceptions mentioned above). Swoop also expressly reserves the right to unilaterally cancel its contract with Brown and cease making monthly payments to Brown, if Brown repeatedly violates the terms of his contract with Swoop, or if Brown is indicted or convicted of a felony or other crime that would harm Swoop's image.

The Muncie Maulers of the National Basketball League recently made Brown their first round draft pick. Muncie has an exclusive, pre-existing arrangement with Swoop's archrival in the court sport shoe market: Springbok. Springbok pays Muncie $1,000,000 per year for Muncie's players to wear Springbok shoes during all exhibition, regular season, and post-season games, although the contract is silent as to what shoes a Maulers player may wear otherwise. According to Muncie's contract with Springbok, Muncie must forfeit $5,000 per player, per game for each instance that any Maulers player wears non-Springbok shoes, $10,000 if the game is nationally televised. So, for instance, if two Maulers wore non-Springbok shoes during a nationally-televised game, Muncie would lose $20,000. Brown's $3,000,000 per year contract with Muncie includes a clause requiring him to wear only "team-approved" shoes during all exhibition, regular season, and post-season games. If Brown wears shoes that are not team-approved during any exhibition, regular season, or post-season game, he is subject to a team fine of up to $5,000. If Brown repeatedly violates the "team-approved" shoe clause of his contract, Muncie may, at its discretion, suspend him for up to the same number of games in which he has already worn unapproved shoes.

166.   If Brown were to wear Swoop shoes during pre-game warm-ups that are open to the public, which of the following would be true?

(A)   Brown would be in breach of his Swoop contract, and Muncie would be in breach of its Springbok contract.

(B)   Brown would be in breach of his Swoop contract, but Muncie would not be in breach of its Springbok contract.

(C) Brown would not be in breach of his Swoop contract, but Muncie would be in breach of its Springbok contract.

(D) Brown would not be in breach of his Swoop contract, and Muncie would not be in breach of its Springbok contract.

167. If Brown were to wear Swoop shoes during games, which of the following would be true?

(A) Brown would be in breach of his Swoop contract, and Muncie would be in breach of its Springbok contract.

(B) Brown would be in breach of his Swoop contract, but Muncie would not be in breach of its Springbok contract.

(C) Brown would not be in breach of his Swoop contract, but Muncie would be in breach of its Springbok contract.

(D) Brown would not be in breach of his Swoop contract, and Muncie would not be in breach of its Springbok contract.

Assume that (1) Brown's playing (as opposed to sitting on the bench or being suspended by the team) generates, or is reasonably expected to generate, more than $5,000 of additional ticket revenues for Muncie per game; (2) the cost to Brown of Swoop terminating their contract is substantially greater than the cost to Muncie of Springbok terminating their contract; (3) the likelihood of Swoop terminating its contract with Brown if he fails to play in their shoes is substantially greater than the likelihood of Springbok terminating its contract with Muncie because Brown fails to wear Springbok shoes during games; (4) Muncie neither can, nor does it want to, trade Brown to another team; and (5) both Springbok and Swoop have highly effective means in place to monitor Muncie's and Brown's respective compliance with their contracts.

168. If Brown and Muncie are both rational actors, and Springbok and Swoop are immovable, what is the most efficient arrangement Brown and Muncie can make to enable both to keep their respective contracts with Swoop and Springbok to the greatest extent possible and to minimize the fines and risk of termination each faces for not fully complying with their contracts?

ANSWER:

On February 15, 2002, Wallace Williams and Bruce Roberts entered into a written contract whereby Wallace, a professional entertainer, would perform at Bruce's resort hotel the weeks of July 1-7, August 26-September 1, and October 14-20, 2002. Wallace agreed to perform eight shows (two on each Saturday) each of the three weeks. Bruce agreed to pay Wallace $40,000 per week, plus 5% of net ticket sales per show. After a successful first week at Bruce's resort in the Berkshires, Wallace traveled to Vail, Colorado, where he was scheduled to perform several shows over the next six weeks at various locations in and around Vail. As his stay in Vail was reaching its end, Wallace was seriously injured in a freak hot tub accident. He required multiple surgeries to repair the damage and was put in traction for a minimum of six weeks. Wallace's agent, Angus "Catfish Buck" McKinney, called Bruce with the bad news: Wallace would still be in traction, and therefore unable to perform at Bruce's resort, during the week of August 26-September 1, although he was expected to fully recover in time for his scheduled October 14-20 performances.

169. After receiving the bad news from Angus, if Bruce booked a replacement act for the week of August 26-September 1, did he breach his contract with Wallace?

   (A) Yes, because Wallace could have recovered more quickly than anticipated, and Bruce must have allowed for that possibility by keeping Wallace's performance slot open for him.

   (B) Yes, because Wallace had already substantially performed.

   (C) No, because the contract between Wallace and Bruce was divisible.

   (D) No, because Wallace had not yet substantially performed.

170. Could Bruce have cancelled the remainder of his contract with Wallace, based on the information Angus gave him, without subjecting himself to a breach of contract claim by Wallace?

   (A) No, because Wallace could have recovered more quickly than anticipated, and Bruce must have allowed for that possibility by keeping Wallace's performance slot open for him.

   (B) No, because Wallace had already substantially performed.

   (C) Yes, because the contract between Wallace and Bruce was divisible.

   (D) Yes, because Wallace had not yet substantially performed.

Suppose that Bruce decided to keep the week of October 14-20 open for Wallace, who was, in fact, able to perform that week at Bruce's resort in the Berkshires. However, as a result of his weakened condition following his accident, surgeries, and lengthy recovery, Wallace was unable to perform more than one show per day. He gave Bruce the option to choose between the early and late shows on Saturday. Bruce preferred that Wallace perform the later of the two scheduled shows, which he did.

171. Was Wallace's failure to perform the early show Saturday a material breach of his contract with Bruce?

ANSWER:

Despite his accident, Wallace enjoyed his stay in the Vail area and decided to build a vacation home there. Wallace's friend, Nester, fancied himself quite the architect. Wallace asked Nester to design the house for him, select the materials to be used building and finishing out the house, hire a general contractor to build the house, and supervise construction from start to finish. Wallace agreed to pay Nester $30,000 for his design and supervision services, plus room and board in a comfortable bed and breakfast located near the land that Wallace purchased for his new home. Wallace told Nester he wanted to be able to spend the week of New Year's entertaining friends in his new vacation home, so time was of the essence both with regard to Nester's design and selection of materials and the general contractor's completion of the house. Based on Nester's rough design, the general contractor he hired, Boulder Builders, estimated the house would take three months to build. Both Nester and Boulder's president, Rockhead, knew that general contractors typically overestimate the time of completion in order to avoid disappointing the client and incurring delay penalties, which are a standard feature of custom home contracts. To allow Boulder the full 12 weeks it had estimated to complete the house (including holidays off for Boulder's workers and subcontractors) in time to furnish and prepare it for Wallace and his friends to use the house by the weekend before New Year's, Boulder needed Nester's final plans and material requirements by September 15th.

172.   If Nester failed to deliver the final plans and materials requirements to Boulder until October 1st, did Wallace, through his agent Nester, materially breach his contract with Boulder, allowing Boulder to quit the project rather than face an unhappy client when Boulder proved unable to complete the house in the time left?

ANSWER:

Assume that the parties decided to go forward with Boulder's construction of Wallace's new vacation home, notwithstanding Nester's tardiness. Nester's materials specifications indicated that Boulder was to use exclusively "Acme Brick No. 63" in constructing the circular fireplace, hearth, and chimney that dominate the large downstairs common room. When Rockhead called Acme Brick to order the needed bricks, Acme's sales manager, Wiley, told Rockhead that he did not have a sufficient inventory of No. 63 bricks to fill the order, but agreed to sell Boulder Acme's remaining stock of No. 63 bricks and to notify Boulder if additional supplies became available in the coming weeks. Rockhead, unwilling to risk Acme not locating or producing sufficient additional No. 63 bricks, consulted the *Sweets Building Products Directory* and found another style of brick, Brown Bricks No. F-17, which appeared to be identical in every respect to Acme No. 63 bricks, except that they had "Brown," rather than "Acme," molded into the face of each brick. Because Rockhead intended to install the bricks so that the "logoed" side of the bricks was not showing anyway, he ordered a sufficient supply of Brown No. F-17 bricks to complete the job.

173.   Did Boulder materially breach its contract with Wallace by using Brown No. F-17 bricks where Nester specified Acme No. 63 bricks?

    (A)   Yes, because Boulder's use of Brown Bricks, rather than Acme Bricks, substantially deprived Wallace of the benefit of his bargain.

(B) Yes, because Boulder cannot adequately compensate Wallace for any diminution in the value of the house to Wallace as a result of Boulder's use of Brown Bricks rather than Acme Bricks.

(C) Yes, because Boulder's substitution of Brown Bricks for Acme Bricks was inconsistent with Boulder's duty of good faith and fair dealing.

(D) No, because Boulder's use of Brown Bricks when Acme Bricks proved to be unavailable in adequate quantities did not substantially deprive Wallace of the benefit of his bargain and was consistent with Boulder's duty of good faith and fair dealing, and Boulder can adequately compensate Wallace for any diminution in the value of the house to Wallace as a result of Boulder's use of Brown Bricks rather than Acme Bricks when the supply of Acme No. 63 bricks ran out.

Suppose that Nester specified that the "Acme" label face out on every third brick because he planned to let *Architectural Monthly* shoot a photo spread of the new house before Wallace occupied it, and he knew that Acme would be very generous to any designer who featured its product so favorably. Unfortunately, Boulder was unable to acquire a sufficient supply of Acme bricks to satisfy that specification.

174. If Boulder laid, or instructed its masonry subcontractor to lay, all of the hearth, fireplace, and chimney bricks "face in" — so that the appearance of the brick would be uniform, rather than having bricks stamped "Acme" and bricks stamped "Brown" showing, which of the following would be true?

(A) Boulder materially breached its contract with Wallace.

(B) Wallace's duty to pay Boulder upon completion of the house would be suspended until Boulder cured the nonconformity by dismantling and relaying the brick hearth, fireplace, and chimney.

(C) Wallace's duty to pay Boulder upon completion of the house would be discharged because of Boulder's uncured, material breach.

(D) Boulder's sole liability to Wallace would be for any diminution in the value of the house to Wallace as a result of Boulder's use of Brown Bricks rather than Acme Bricks when the supply of Acme No. 63 bricks ran out.

Mercury Rising ("Mercury") is an Illinois manufacturer of indoor and outdoor thermometers. Tubular Glass ("Tubular") is a Michigan manufacturer of precision glass tubing. On March 14, 2003, following telephone negotiations between the two, Will Bruce, Mercury's purchasing agent, faxed a purchase order to Tubular for 5,000 one-foot lengths of glass tubing, at a price of $5.00 per foot, to be delivered to Mercury's plant no later than May 1st. Later that same day, Tubular faxed a written acknowledgment, agreeing to manufacture and deliver 5,000 one-foot lengths of glass tubing, at a price of $5.00 per foot, to Mercury's plant no later than May 1st. The terms of Tubular's acknowledgment also (1) disclaimed of all implied warranties, and (2) required Mercury to pay the full contract price, including the cost of shipping the tubing from Tubular's plant to Mercury's plant, when Mercury received the tubing. The parties did not correspond further.

Before the goods reached Mercury, Mercury found another seller, Glaz Emporium ("Glaz"), who offered to provide the same quantity and quality of glass tubing, no later than May 2nd, at a price of $4.50 per foot. Mercury agreed on April 15th to purchase the tubing from Glaz, and refused to receive the shipment from Tubular when it arrived on May 1st. Tubular wants to sue Mercury for breach of contract.

175.   Assuming that Tubular and Mercury had an enforceable contract, did Mercury breach its contract with Tubular by refusing to accept Tubular's May 1st shipment?

ANSWER:

Returning to the facts in the first paragraph of Question 175, suppose that Mercury received Tubular's May 1st shipment and paid the carrier $25,500 (including $500 for transportation). Shortly thereafter, however, Mercury determined that 80% of the tubing Tubular supplied was of inferior quality and unfit for the use for which Mercury bought it.

176.   Assuming that Tubular and Mercury had an enforceable contract, and no contrary agreement between the parties, what recourse would UCC Article 2 have afford Mercury with respect to inferior tubing it discovered before accepting the goods?

   (A)   Mercury could have rejected the entire shipment, including the conforming tubing, and sued Tubular for any damages resulting from Tubular's delivery of nonconforming tubing.

   (B)   Mercury could have accepted the entire shipment, including the nonconforming tubing, seasonably notified Tubular of the nonconformity, and sued Tubular for any damages resulting from Tubular's delivery of nonconforming tubing.

   (C)   Mercury could have accepted the conforming tubing, rejected the nonconforming tubing, and sued Tubular for any damages resulting from Tubular's delivery of nonconforming tubing.

   (D)   None, because Mercury waived any nonconformities by paying the carrier in full upon receipt of the goods.

177.   Absent a contrary agreement between the parties, what rights UCC Article 2 have afford Mercury with respect to the nonconforming tubing if Mercury did not discover the nonconformity until after it had already accepted the tubing?

   (A)   Mercury could have rejected the nonconforming tubing, seasonably notified Tubular of the nonconformity, and sued Tubular for any damages resulting from Tubular's delivery of nonconforming tubing.

(B)   Mercury could have revoked its acceptance of the nonconforming tubing promptly after discovering the nonconformity, seasonably notified Tubular of the nonconformity, and sued Tubular for any damages resulting from Tubular's delivery of nonconforming tubing.

(C)   Mercury could have revoked its acceptance of the nonconforming tubing promptly after discovering the nonconformity, provided that it failed to reject the nonconforming tubing upon receipt because the nonconformity was not readily apparent, seasonably notified Tubular of the nonconformity, and sued Tubular for any damages resulting from Tubular's delivery of nonconforming tubing.

(D)   Mercury could have revoked its acceptance of the nonconforming tubing promptly after discovering the nonconformity, provided that it failed to reject the nonconforming tubing upon receipt because the nonconformity was not readily apparent, seasonably notified Tubular of the nonconformity, allowed Tubular a reasonable opportunity to cure the nonconformity, and sued Tubular for any damages resulting from Tubular's delivery of nonconforming tubing and Tubular's delay in curing, or inability to cure, the nonconformity.

Returning to the facts of the first paragraph of Question 175 and of Question 176, suppose that, rather than purchasing the glass tubing from the Michigan-based Tubular Glass, Mercury purchased it from Windsor, Ontario-based Philippe Glass ("PG"). Otherwise, the essential facts are the same: PG shipped the tubing to arrive at Mercury's plant no later than May 1, 2003; Mercury received Tubular's May 1, 2003 shipment, and paid the carrier $25,500 (including $500 for transportation); and, shortly thereafter, Mercury determined that 80% of the tubing PG supplied was of inferior quality and unfit for the use for which Mercury bought it.

178.   Assuming that Mercury and PG had an enforceable contract governed by the CISG, what recourse would Mercury have with respect to the inferior tubing?

ANSWER:

Tiffani wanted to lease space for her growing law practice in a building owned by Colt. However, Tiffani could not afford to pay rent on two places. On July 1, 2002, she signed a contract to lease 3,000 square feet of office space in Colt's building, for $9.00 per sq. ft. per month, all utilities included, commencing September 1, 2002, subject to (1) Tiffani being released from her current lease by her current landlord LexCentre, or (2) Tiffani's lease with LexCentre expiring on December 31, 2002, whichever occurred first. Tiffani's lease contract with Colt also provided Tiffani an option to lease up to an additional 5,000 square feet, subject to availability, provided that she exercises that option, if at all, within one year of occupying the original 3,000 square feet. If she leases a total of 5,000 square feet or more, her monthly rent will fall to $8.00 per square foot.

179. September 1st came and went without any word from Tiffani that she was ready to move in. Could Colt begin charging Tiffani rent as of September 1, 2002?

    (A)   Yes, because Tiffani promised to pay rent to Colt starting September 1st.

    (B)   Yes, because Tiffani promised to induce LexCentre to release her from her present lease and she has failed to do so.

    (C)   Yes, because otherwise Colt, who could not arrange to lease the space to someone else if Tiffani was unable to move in by or shortly after September 1st, would suffer a forfeiture if the space went unleased until January 1, 2003.

    (D)   No, because Tiffani's obligation to move in at any time prior to January 1, 2003 was conditioned on LexCentre releasing her from her current lease — an event the occurrence of which she could not meaningfully control.

Suppose that, concerned that Tiffani might not be able to get out of her current lease until January 1, 2003, Colt leased the space that Tiffani wanted to the law firm of David & Galati, for $9.50 per sq. ft. monthly rent, from July 1, 2002 to December 31, 2002. Colt's lease agreement with David & Galati included an option to renew for up two years, but it required both David & Galati's and Colt's consent to effectuate the renewal. It also contained a provision allowing either party to terminate the lease on 30 days notice, with the terminating party liable to the other for one month's rent if they terminated the lease before December 31, 2002.

180. If Tiffani successfully obtained a release from her LexCentre lease prior to December 31, 2002, could she have demand that Colt order David & Galati to vacate and, if they failed to do so, could she have sued Colt for breach of contract?

    (A)   No, because Colt was not obligated to lease the space to Tiffani before January 1, 2003.

(B)   No, because Colt could claim temporary impracticability, suspending his obligation to lease space to Tiffani until January 1, 2003, or until David & Galati vacated the premises, whichever occurred first.

(C)   Yes, because Colt promised to make the space available for Tiffani at any time on or after September 1st, provided she took the space no later than January 1, 2003.

(D)   Yes, but only if David & Galati refused to vacate the space within 30 days of Tiffani's demand.

Suppose that, unknown to Tiffani, Colt was on intimate terms with Sherry, LexCentre's property manager. Over dinner on September 2nd, Colt told Sherry that Tiffani was trying to move from LexCentre to Colt's building; but, because Tiffani appeared to be bound through the end of the year to her LexCentre lease, Colt had rented the space Tiffani wanted to David & Galati on more favorable terms. Colt still wanted Tiffani to move to his building on or after January 1, 2003, but he also wanted to continue to receive David & Galati's higher rent payment through December 31st. Colt asked Sherry whether she could "stall" Tiffani and not agree to release her early from her lease. Sherry agreed to do so.

181.   If Colt sued Tiffani for unpaid rent after September 1st, could Tiffani avoid liability for the unpaid rent?

ANSWER:

Returning to the facts of Question 179, suppose, instead, that shortly after she reached her agreement with Colt, Tiffani became involved in a very complex, document-intensive, and time-consuming case. As September 1st approached, Tiffani had not yet spoken to Sherry or anyone else in LexCentre's property management office, and the thought of packing and moving the mass of documents Tiffani had sorted through and was still sorting through was completely unappealing to her. The case continued for several months before eventually settling in mid-November. When Tiffani then asked Sherry to let her out of her LexCentre lease, Sherry responded that, with the end of the year approaching so soon anyway, and given the requirement in LexCentre's lease that Tiffani give 30 days notice of intent to vacate, whether before, at, or after, the lease's expiration date, LexCentre would not agree to release Tiffani from the remainder of her lease.

182.   Could Tiffani successfully use LexCentre's refusal to release her from their lease agreement as a defense to any claim brought by Colt for unpaid rent beginning September 1st?

(A)   Yes, because she was not obligated to begin performing her lease agreement with Colt until January 1, 2003, unless LexCentre allowed her to terminate her lease with LexCentre before December 31, 2002.

(B)   Yes, because moving in the midst of her massive case would have been impracticable for Tiffani.

(C)   Yes, because LexCentre refused her request to terminate her lease before December 31, 2002.

(D)   All of the above.

Bamm Bamm, age 25, lived with his parents, Barney and Betty, in a nice neighborhood in Bedrock. Bamm Bamm had his own bedroom, but wanted a place to play his drums. He contacted Slate Construction Company ("Slate") to get an estimate on adding a music room to the house. His parents had no particular need for the additional room, but they wanted to support his musical interests and preferred that he not play the drums in his bedroom.

Fred, one of Slate's supervisors, came to the house and met with Bamm Bamm to discuss the addition. Fred had Bamm Bamm fill out a credit application and explained that Slate would only agree to perform the work on credit if Bamm Bamm's credit rating was satisfactory. Fred also gave Bamm Bamm a written "offer" detailing the specifics of the project, the expected cost and time of completion, and the payment schedule. The "offer" clearly indicated that it was conditional on Bamm Bamm having satisfactory credit. It also stated: "This agreement shall become binding only upon written acceptance by Slate Construction Company or upon commencing performance of the work." The total cost was to be $10,000.

After a few weeks passed without word from Slate, Bamm Bamm assumed that his credit rating had proved unacceptable. (He was rather destructive, at times, and had promised to make amends to several neighbors and area businesses, but he was not always able to do so in a timely manner.) Bamm Bamm wrote to Fred: "I have changed my mind and no longer want the construction work done which we discussed." Slate never received the letter. Bamm Bamm sold his drums and took up power lifting at the local gym — a hobby that did not require adding on to his parents' house.

A month or so later, while Barney and Betty were vacationing at Yellowrock Park and Bamm Bamm was out of town at a power lifting competition, a Slate crew quickly (but in a workmanlike manner) built the addition, leaving behind an invoice billing Bamm Bamm for the work. When Barney, Betty, and Bamm Bamm returned to Bedrock, they discovered the new music room and the bill from Slate, with the first payment due in one month.

No longer needing the room, and unable to pay for the work (having squandered his meager savings on steroids and baby oil), Bamm Bamm telephoned Fred. Fred referred the call to in-house counsel, Stonewall, who replied: "Sorry, we did not receive your letter. According to our agreement, we were to perform the work once your credit check was approved. It was. We did. You owe us $10,000.00." Stonewall subsequently sent Bamm Bamm several letters demanding payment, and then threatening suit for nonpayment, but Bamm Bamm could not pay.

Betty eventually met with Stonewall and asked her to stop harassing Bamm Bamm. When Stonewall insisted that *someone* pay Slate for the work it performed, Betty orally agreed to pay

Slate the remaining balance due ($10,000 plus interest), in 12 monthly installments of $950 each, if Slate would stop all efforts to collect from Bamm Bamm. Stonewall agreed, on Slate's behalf, not to pursue Bamm Bamm any further. Betty made only three payments. Bamm Bamm fled the jurisdiction and was last seen working in a circus side show in a distant land.

183.   Which of the following terms best describes Betty's agreement with Slate?

(A)   Illusory promise.

(B)   Modification.

(C)   Novation.

(D)   Substituted agreement.

184.   Assuming that Betty's contract with Slate satisfied all applicable requisites to enforceability, could Slate still enforce its agreement with Bamm Bamm as well?

ANSWER:

Suppose that the original contract between Bamm Bamm and Slate had been for the purchase of a custom-made pool table and accessories for $10,000, payable in monthly installments, and that Betty and Slate orally agreed that Betty would assume responsibility for the unpaid installments on the pool table.

185.   Should a court enforce Betty's agreement with Slate?

(A)   No, because Betty did not enter into it of her free will.

(B)   No, because Betty's agreement was not supported by separate consideration.

(C)   No, because Betty did not sign any writing evidencing her agreement with Slate.

(D)   No, because forcing Betty to answer for Bamm Bamm's debt would be unconscionable.

All Things Greene ("ATG") is a commercial landscaper, doing business in Iowa City, Iowa. Its business was doing so well that its owner, Tom Greene, decided earlier this year to expand ATG's operations to neighboring states and to open up retail outlets in Iowa City, Peoria (Illinois), and Madison (Wisconsin), each of which will operate under the name "The Greene Thumb," but will be a subsidiary of ATG. Seeking to stock inventory for the new stores and obtain equipment needed for his landscaping operation, ATG mailed Basin Iron & Steel ("Basin"), a Missouri manufacturer of cast iron products, a written order for 20,000 hoedad collars. (A hoedad is a tool used for planting seedling trees. The hoedad collar secures the metal blade to a wooden handle.) ATG's order form stated that the hoedad collars were to be delivered in installments by the dates stipulated in the purchase order. It also stated: "No modification of this contract shall be binding upon Buyer unless made in writing and signed by Buyer's authorized representative. Buyer shall have the right to make changes in the Order by a notice, in writing, to Seller." Basin accepted the purchase order in a written acknowledgment and commenced to manufacture the hoedad collars.

Basin was consistently late in tendering delivery. ATG, however, accepted the late deliveries without declaring a breach or invoking the written modification condition. However, after accepting 15,000 hoedad collars, ATG invoked the delivery schedule in the purchase order, cancelled the contract, and sued Basin for breach of contract for damages.

186. Assuming the "no modification" provision in ATG's purchase order is valid, is ATG foreclosed from suing Basin for breach because ATG previously accepted late deliveries?

  (A) No, the "no modification" clause should be taken at face value, such that ATG's prior failures to demand strict performance do not evidence his willingness to modify the terms of the contract.

  (B) No, Basin is in breach of contract, and the parties have not explicitly agreed to waive each other's breaches of the contract.

  (C) No, because ATG's contract with Basin required a writing to satisfy the statute of frauds; therefore, any attempt to modify the contract must also satisfy the statute of frauds.

  (D) Yes, because, despite the lack of a writing satisfying the statute of frauds, ATG implicitly agreed to modify the contract by waiving Basin's prior failure to timely deliver.

187. Would your answer to Question 186 change if Basin were located in Canada, rather than in Missouri?

ANSWER:

Greene wants to offer the finest in garden gnomes to ATG's landscaping clients and The Greene Thumb's retail customers, so ATG entered into a contract with Gromit's Gnomes, whose place of business is in Shropshire, England. England is not a party to the CISG. Therefore, ATG and Gromit's Gnomes agreed that Iowa law would govern their contract. Gromit's imports certain materials essential to its gnome manufacturing operations from Luxembourg. When Luxembourg suddenly, and without apparent provocation, declared war on and embargoed all imports from and exports to Great Britain (of which England is a part), Gromit's found itself without a reliable supply of several key ingredients for making its world-famous garden gnomes. Gromit's sales chief, Shaun, telephoned ATG to explain that Gromit's would be unable, due to the embargo, to fill ATG's recent order of 500 gnomes, which Shaun had confirmed by fax only a few days earlier.

188. Assuming the embargo was not reasonably foreseeable, and therefore not implicitly accounted for in the parties' contract, to what extent will the doctrine of commercial impracticability under UCC § 2-615 insulate Gromit's from liability to ATG?

   (A) None, because the parties chose to make their contract subject to Iowa law, not the UCC.

   (B) It will excuse Gromit's from performing its contract with ATG.

   (C) It will suspend Gromit's duty to perform its contract with ATG for the duration of the embargo or until ATG cancels its order, whichever occurs first.

   (D) It will suspend Gromit's duty to perform its contract with ATG for the duration of the embargo or until ATG cancels its order, whichever occurs first, but only if Gromit's provides prompt and adequate notice to ATG of the cause of its inability to perform as promised.

189. What options does Article 2 afford ATG once it received notice from Shaun that Gromit's could not perform its contract with ATG for the duration of the embargo?

ANSWER:

On March 1, 2003, Gwyneth and Russell agreed that Gwyneth would pay Russell $100 each for two tickets to the March 15th New York premiere of *The Orange Pumpernickel*. They further agreed that Russell would deliver the tickets to Gwyneth no later than March 14th. The New York premiere of Cameron Ridley's new movie, *The Orange Pumpernickel*, was scheduled for March 15th at the Radikal City Musik Hall. That same night, the 41st Street Playhouse scheduled the premiere of a stage production of *The Orange Pumpernickel*, directed by David Marmoset.

On March 2nd, Russell purchased two tickets from the 41st Street Playhouse for $75 each. On March 14th, when Russell delivered the tickets to Gwyneth, she refused to pay, claiming that Russell had agreed to sell her tickets to the movie, not the play. Russell did not have any tickets to the movie, and none were commercially available at that late date. Russell tried unsuccessfully to find another buyer for the play tickets and to obtain a refund from the Playhouse. Unable to use them himself, he left the tickets with Gwyneth in case she changed her mind. Gwyneth sued Russell for failing to provide her with tickets to the movie premiere.

190. If Russell bought Gwyneth tickets to the play because, despite his best efforts, he was unable to obtain any tickets to the movie premiere at any price, would he have a viable defense to Gwyneth's breach of contract claim?

   (A) Yes, Russell could defend on the grounds of failure of a condition precedent.

   (B) Yes, Russell could defend on the grounds of frustration of purpose.

   (C) Yes, Russell could defend on the grounds of impracticability.

(D)   No, Russell has no defense to his failure to purchase the tickets he promised Gwyneth.

191.   If, despite his best efforts, Russell could not obtain any movie tickets for less than $500 per ticket — a price he considered to be "too high" in light of Gwyneth's promise to pay him only $100 per ticket — would he have a viable defense to Gwyneth's breach of contract claim?

ANSWER:

Suppose that, while trying to find tickets for Gwyneth, Russell was run over by a runaway hansom cab and was in the hospital recovering from his injuries until after March 14th.

192.   Would Russell have a viable defense to Gwyneth's suit for breach of contract?

ANSWER:

Suppose, instead, that Russell bought two tickets to the movie premiere for $75 per ticket. Their "fair market value" on March 2nd was $125. (Russell got them at a discount because the ticket broker recognized him from his last movie.) By March 14th, the "fair market value" of the movie premiere tickets had risen to $175. Gwyneth hoped to star in the much-anticipated sequel to *Titanic* and planned to schmooze its director, Cameron, while at the movie premiere. When Russell attempted to deliver the tickets to Gwyneth on March 14th, as called for by their contract, she was not home, so he slipped them through her mail slot with a note saying "You can pay me tomorrow." Unbeknownst to Russell, Gwyneth heard later that day on *Entertainment This Night* that Cameron had suddenly become ill and would not be coming to New York for the premiere. Gwyneth decided not to attend the premiere and returned the tickets to Russell the next day. Russell demanded to be paid for the tickets. Gwyneth refused. On March 15th, the "fair market value" of the movie premiere tickets had fallen slightly to $150, due to the now-publicized non-appearance of Cameron. However, due to circumstances beyond his control, Russell was unable to use, sell, or return the tickets.

193.   On what basis could Gwyneth defend Russell's claim for breach of contract?

(A)   Failure of a condition precedent.

(B)   Frustration of purpose.

(C)   Impracticability.

(D)   None of the above.

On March 1, 2003, Gwyneth and Russell agreed that Gwyneth would pay Russell $100 each for two tickets to the March 15th New York premiere of *The Orange Pumpernickel*. They further agreed that Russell would deliver the tickets to Gwyneth no later than March 14th. The New York premiere of Cameron Ridley's new movie, *The Orange Pumpernickel*, was scheduled for March 15th at the Radikal City Musik Hall. That same night, the 41st Street Playhouse scheduled the premiere of a stage production of *The Orange Pumpernickel*, directed by David Marmoset.

On March 2nd, Russell purchased two tickets from the 41st Street Playhouse for $75 each. On March 14th, when Russell attempted to deliver the tickets to Gwyneth, as agreed, she was not home. Russell, who had to catch a flight to London that evening, slipped them through her mail slot with a note saying, "Here are the tickets you wanted, Gwyn. You can pay me when I get back." By the day of the sold out premieres, the going price for a ticket to the play was $125. No tickets to the movie were available.

Gwyneth, who hoped to star in the much-anticipated sequel to *Titanic* and planned to schmooze its director, Cameron, at the movie premiere, was shattered when she opened Russell's envelope and found that he had purchased tickets to the wrong *The Orange Pumpernickel*. She was not at home when Russell delivered the tickets because she had been shopping for a dress and accessories for the occasion. Not wanting to appear as if she was "trying too hard," she bought a modest, off-the-rack Vergauche dress (which she had altered at the store) and matching shoes for $5,000, borrowed a $25,000 Winny Hairston necklace and matching earrings for a nonrefundable 10% deposit, and booked a limousine and driver for the evening for $350. She also made an appointment at her salon for the morning of the premiere to have her hair, face, and nails done. Working on relatively short notice, she had to guarantee the $500 fee in order to book the appointment.

Gwyneth was unable to obtain tickets to the movie premiere from any other source. During the post-premiere coverage on *Entertainment This Night*, Cameron announced that he had decided to cast Belle Harry as the female lead in *Titanic 2: Jack is Back*. Hollywood newspaper *Hush-Hush* reported in its next issue that Belle will be paid $15 million for her performance in *T2:JiB*.

Gwyneth sued Russell for failing to provide her with the movie tickets. Russell countersued Gwyneth for failing to pay for the tickets he delivered to her.

194. If Russell did not know about the movie premiere when he bought the play tickets, and Gwyneth did not know about the play premiere when she agreed to pay Russell for tickets, what remedy may Russell be entitled to recover for Gwyneth's failure to pay for the tickets?

   (A) $200, the measure of Russell's expectation damages.

(B) $150, the measure of Russell's reliance damages.

(C) $250, the measure of Russell's restitutionary damages.

(D) $0, because he bought the wrong tickets.

195.   What if, despite the fact that the play tickets were not what she wanted, and despite not having paid Russell for them, Gwyneth used the play tickets. What remedy would Russell most likely recover?

(A) $200, the measure of Russell's expectation damages.

(B) $150, the measure of Russell's reliance damages.

(C) $250, the measure of Russell's restitutionary damages.

(D)   Nothing. Russell purchased the wrong tickets. Gwyneth was simply mitigating her damages when she decided to use the tickets rather than sit at home and watch *Gladiator* for the 53rd time.

Suppose, instead, that Russell knew all along that Gwyneth wanted tickets to the movie premiere and, despite that knowledge, Russell provided her with tickets to the play.

196.   Assuming that Gwyneth was unable to find other tickets to the movie premiere, unable to find a purchaser for the play tickets, and did not attend the play, what would be the measure of her expectation damages?

(A) $14,999,800, the salary awarded Belle for the role Gwyneth sought, less the unpaid price of the tickets.

(B) $8,350, the cost of her dress, accessories, personal care, and limousine and driver.

(C)   She would owe Russell $200.

(D)   None of the above.

197.   What other remedy could Gwyneth elect, in lieu of expectation damages?

(A)   Rescission.

(B)   Reliance damages.

(C)   Restitutionary damages.

(D)   Specific performance.

Returning to the facts of Question 194, suppose that Gwyneth used the tickets to attend the play, where she met Sam Quentin, who offered her the lead in his live-action adaptation of *Fritz the Cat*. Sam does not have Cameron's bankroll, but he assured Gwyneth that he would pay her at least $500,000 for the role, even if he has to give her part of his salary.

198. Assuming that Gwyneth had not yet paid him for the play tickets, to what remedy might Russell be entitled for Gwyneth's use of the play tickets, before any offset he owes Gwyneth for his breach of their contract for movie premiere tickets?

    (A) $200, the measure of Russell's expectation damages.

    (B) $150, the measure of Russell's reliance damages.

    (C) $500,250, the measure of Russell's restitutionary damages.

    (D) $0, because he bought the wrong tickets.

Returning to the facts of Question 196, suppose that Gwyneth purchased tickets to the movie premiere at the last minute for $500 each (including the ticket broker's fee), and that she sold the play tickets to her neighbor, Kate, for $150. Gwyneth had a wonderful time at the movie premiere, but she did not meet Cameron, who had to cancel at the last minute due to a sudden illness.

199. Assuming the parties concede the existence of a contract and that Gwyneth has not yet paid Russell for the play tickets, what is the proper measure of Gwyneth's expectation damages?

    (A) $1,000, the price Gwyneth paid for tickets to the movie premiere.

    (B) $800, measuring the difference between the price Gwyneth paid for the tickets to the movie premiere ($1,000) and the price she expected to pay had Russell performed as promised ($200).

    (C) $700, measuring the difference between the price Gwyneth paid for the tickets to the movie premiere ($1,000) and the price Russell paid for the play tickets ($150), less the $150 that Kate paid her for the play tickets.

    (D) $650, measuring the difference between the price Gwyneth paid for the tickets to the movie premiere ($1,000) and the price she expected to pay had Russell performed as promised ($200), less the $150 that Kate paid her for the play tickets.

200. Same facts as Question 199, except that Gwyneth gave the play tickets to Kate rather then selling them to her. What damages would Gwyneth be entitled to recover from Russell?

ANSWER:

Returning to the facts of Question 196, suppose that Gwyneth had the chance to purchase tickets to the movie premiere at the last minute for $500 each, but she chose not to do so.

201. Assuming that Gwyneth did not pay Russell for the play tickets, to what remedy or remedies might Gwyneth be entitled?

ANSWER:

Returning to the facts of Question 196, suppose that, when Gwyneth attempted to return the necklace and earrings to Winny Hairston, the store manager refused to accept them, claiming that the necklace had been damaged while in her care. Because the necklace and earrings are a unique matched set, he would not accept the earrings, which appear undamaged. Instead, he handed Gwyneth a receipt for $22,500, which he had billed to the credit card she gave him to charge the non-refundable deposit.

202.   Assuming that Russell breached their contract, could Gwyneth recover the cost of the jewelry from Russell?

   (A)   Yes. But for Russell's promise to acquire two tickets to the movie premiere for her, Gwyneth would not have borrowed the jewelry from Winny Hairston, and it would not have been damaged while in her care.

   (B)   No, because Russell would not be liable for Gwyneth's failure to take proper care of the jewelry she borrowed.

   (C)   No, because the jewelry was leased goods subject to Article 2A of the New York Uniform Commercial Code, and Winny Hairston bore the risk of any loss of or damage to the jewelry while it was in Gwyneth's possession.

   (D)   No, because it was not reasonably foreseeable to Russell that Gwyneth, who owns thousands of dollars worth of jewelry, would feel compelled to purchase or lease additional jewelry to attend the movie premiere.

Returning to the facts of Question 196, suppose that, instead of buying two tickets to the play premiere, on March 2nd Russell bought two tickets to the movie premiere for $75 per ticket. Their "fair market value" on March 2nd was $125. (Russell got them at a discount because the ticket broker recognized him from his last movie.) By March 14th, the "fair market value" of the movie premiere tickets had risen to $175. When Russell attempted to deliver the tickets to Gwyneth on March 14th, as called for by their contract, she was not home. Russell, who had to catch a flight to London that evening, slipped them through her mail slot with a note saying, "Here are the tickets you wanted, Gwyn. You can pay me when I get back." Unbeknownst to Russell, Gwyneth heard later that day on *Entertainment This Night* that Cameron had suddenly become ill and would not be coming to New York for the premiere. Gwyneth decided not to attend the premiere and returned the tickets to Russell the next day. Russell demanded to be paid for the tickets. Gwyneth refused. On March 15th, the "fair market value" of the movie premiere tickets had fallen slightly to $150, due to the now-publicized non-appearance of Cameron. However, because he was out of the country, Russell was unable to use, sell, or return the tickets.

203.   If Russell sued Gwyneth, what damages should he recover?

   (A) $200, the measure of Russell's expectation damages.

(B) $150, the measure of Russell's reliance damages.

(C)   Restitutionary damages in the amount of $300.

(D)   Restitutionary damages in the amount of $350.

In early June 2002, Rochelle Payne, the Dean of Missy's College of Law, located in the state of Magnolia, telephoned Hilda Rodriguez, a resident of South Mesquite (located in another state several hundred miles away from Magnolia), and offered her a two-year appointment as a visiting professor of law at an annual salary of $50,000, plus certain expenses, provided that Hilda could move to Magnolia in time to begin the Fall 2002 semester. Rochelle mentioned a remote possibility that the visiting position might become permanent, but she cautioned Hilda against considering that possibility when deciding whether to accept the visiting offer. Hilda accepted, quit her lucrative private practice in South Mesquite, sold her home in South Mesquite, and moved herself, her hubby, Biff, and their adorable child, Lars, to Magnolia.

When she left private practice, Hilda was earning an annual salary of $100,000 plus certain expenses. She and her husband sold their house for $175,000, before closing costs and fees. They had paid $150,000 for the house three years earlier. Immediately before its sale, the house appraised for $200,000. However, due to the urgency of the move to Magnolia, the Rodriguezes accepted the best offer they received within the time available. At the time they sold the house, the Rodriguezes owed $125,000 on the mortgage loan. After realtors' commissions, closing costs, etc., the Rodriguezes received $160,000 on the sale, which, after paying off their mortgage loan, "netted" them $35,000. Concerned about a negative tax outcome if they did not roll the $35,000 into the purchase of a new home within 12 months, the Rodriguezes purchased a home in Magnolia for $135,000 ($35,000 cash down + $100,000 mortgage loan), including all closing costs and fees. And, while Missy's did contribute $2,500 to their moving expenses, the Rodriguezes paid another $5,000 out of their own pockets.

During the spring semester of her first year, Rochelle informed Hilda that the spring semester would likely be her last. While Hilda's job performance was satisfactory, former Supreme Court Justice Brilliant Foote, a Magnolia native, had inquired about teaching part-time at Missy's while he worked on his memoirs, and Rochelle decided to use the funds set aside for Hilda's salary to pay Foote.

Despite the fact that Rochelle orally offered Hilda a two-year appointment, Hilda's written employment agreement with Missy's was for the 2002-03 academic year only. The employment agreement provided, in its entirety:

> Subject to the approval of the Board of Trustees, Missy's College of Law hereby agrees to employ Hilda Rodriguez as a Visiting Assistant Professor of Law, for the nine-month academic year beginning on or about August 19, 2002, and ending on or about May 16, 2003, at a salary of $50,000 for said nine-month term. Said person shall be afforded all of the benefits and privileges of a permanent faculty member of the same rank (Assistant Professor of Law), and will be expected to perform his/her teaching,

administrative, and other job functions in accordance with the Policy & Procedures Manual in effect at all relevant times.

Hilda and Rochelle, on behalf of Missy's, both signed the employment agreement, which said nothing, one way or the other, about whether it would, would not, might, or might not, be renewed for the 2003-04 academic year. The only apparently applicable provision of the Policy & Procedures Manual states:

> 15.5. Reappointment of Visiting Faculty. Reappointment of visiting faculty for an additional academic semester or year, up to a total appointment of two full academic years, shall be at the discretion of the Dean of the Law School, subject to approval by the School's Board of Trustees. If the Dean wishes to reappoint a visiting faculty member for an academic semester or year, the completion of which would give the visiting faculty member more than two full academic years of service at the Law School, the Dean must first seek and receive consent from a two-thirds majority of the tenured and tenure-track faculty.

That notwithstanding, Hilda insists that Rochelle offered her a two-year appointment and that she would never have quit her practice, sold her house, and moved her family to Magnolia had she known it would only be for a one-year visitorship.

Immediately upon learning of her impending termination, Hilda began searching for a new job. She uncovered three prospects.

The only other law teaching job she has been able to find on such short notice is at the Sunrise Law School ("SLS"), which is located in Orange and is not yet accredited by the American Bar Association. SLS's dean offered Hilda a one-year contract, teaching the same courses she taught in 2002-03 at Missy's, at a salary of $55,000 per year. The cost of living in Orange is approximately 10 percent higher than in Magnolia, so the salary is roughly comparable. Because it is offering her only a one-year contract, SLS will only pay $1,000 toward Hilda's relocation expenses. She estimates that it will cost another $8,000 to pack up herself, Biff, Lars, and all their stuff and move to Orange. She also anticipates that she will lose about $10,000 on the sale of the house in Magnolia once all commissions, fees, etc. are paid. Given the relatively higher cost of living, Hilda believes that a house comparable to the one she now owns in Magnolia will cost at least $150,000 in Orange. However, she should be able to rent a house comparable to the one she now owns for about what her current mortgage payments are on the house she and Biff own in Magnolia.

Hilda has also received an offer from the Valet Rain law firm in Magnolia to pay her $60,000 per year to serve as "of counsel" to the firm. (Because Hilda is not yet licensed in Magnolia, the firm will not hire her as a partner, despite her experience and expertise.)

Finally, Hilda has been invited to return to South Mesquite and join a newly-formed firm, Spit & Polish, L.L.P. ("S&P"), that split from her old firm, Lock, Stock, Block & Barrell, P.C. ("LSBB"). S&P would pay her an annual salary of $75,000, with the understanding that, as the firm got on better financial footing, and she reestablished herself with clients, her salary would be adjusted accordingly. S&P is not in a position to pay Hilda on expenses. LSBB is unable to offer her a position at this time.

While the offers from both law firms are more financially lucrative than either her current teaching position or the position SLS has offered her, Hilda derives tremendous satisfaction from teaching. Moreover, she obviously did not accept the job at Missy's for financial reasons, given that she took a 50% gross pay cut to enter the teaching profession. Hilda, Biff, and Lars have made many new friends in Magnolia and enjoy the somewhat slower pace of life there, and their "quality of life" would suffer some if they had to move either to Orange or back to South Mesquite.

Hilda has come to talk to you shortly before the end of the Spring 2003 semester. As far as Hilda knows, Missy's has not yet finalized any employment agreement with Justice Foote, who may not join the faculty. Rochelle, concerned that there will be no one to teach first-year Civil Procedure if Justice Foote decides not to join the faculty, has hinted to other faculty members, some of whom have relayed it to Hilda, that it would not be a terrible thing for Missy's if Hilda did not take a job elsewhere just yet. Other than her initial expression of surprise and disappointment when Rochelle first notified her of her impending termination, Hilda has not spoken with either Rochelle about her future plans.

204. Assuming that Hilda has a viable breach of contract claim against Missy's for terminating her without cause before the end of the second year of her two-year contract, which of the following jobs should Hilda accept in order to mitigate her damages?

    (A) The teaching position at SLS in Orange.

    (B) The position at Valet Rain in Magnolia.

    (C) The position with S&P in South Mesquite.

    (D) Whichever of the above Hilda prefers.

205. Assuming that Hilda has a viable breach of contract claim against Missy's for terminating her without cause before the end of the second year of her two-year contract, if she accepts the teaching job at SLS, what would be the measure of Hilda's expectation damages?

    (A) $3,000.

    (B) $8,000.

    (C) $13,000.

    (D) $28,000.

206. Assuming that Hilda has a viable breach of contract claim against Missy's for terminating her without cause before the end of the second year of her two-year

contract, which of the following would be the best measure of Hilda's reliance damages?

(A) $30,000.

(B) $50,000.

(C) $80,000.

(D) $130,000.

207. Assuming that Hilda *does not* have a viable breach of contract claim against Missy's, due to her failure to get Missy's promise to employ her for two years in writing, if Hilda has a viable claim based on promissory estoppel, which of the following remedies available to Hilda would provide her the greatest relief if she prevailed?

(A) Expectation damages.

(B) Reliance damages.

(C) Restitutionary damages.

(D) Specific performance.

Suppose that Joaquin contracts to build a building for Estrella on Estrella's land for $100,000. Joaquin's expected cost to complete the project is $90,000. Estrella repudiates the contract after Joaquin has spent $60,000. Estrella has not yet paid Joaquin anything, and Joaquin cannot salvage any value from the money spent. The value to Estrella of the partially completed building is $40,000.

208. Assuming that Joaquin and Estrella had an enforceable contract, and that Estrella breached that contract by repudiating it, calculate Joaquin's expectation damages, reliance damages, and restitutionary damages.

ANSWER:

Sally Rich, age 22, told her parents that she would have their dining room wallpapered while they were on vacation. Sally hired Wally Hanger to put wallpaper on the walls in Sally's parents' house. When Sally hired Wally, the walls were unpapered, but tastefully painted.

Their written contract provided, in relevant part:

Hanger agrees to paper the walls of Mr. & Mrs. Rich's dining room to Sally Rich's satisfaction, using any paper Sally Rich selects from Hanger's sample book, for a total price of $1,000.

In the event that the quality of Hanger's work does not meet Sally Rich's satisfaction, Hanger agrees, at its election, (i) to repair any defective paper and/or defectively installed paper at Hanger's own expense; (ii) to remove the defective paper and/or defectively installed paper and refinish and paint the walls, as they were prior to Hanger's work, at Hanger's own expense; or (iii) to refund the contract price, less the cost of all nondefective paper and other materials. Alternatively, Sally Rich may demand that Hanger pay her liquidated damages in the amount of $500, the payment of which by Hanger will discharge Hanger of any further liability.

Sally selected wallpaper with a rustic scene with dancing nymphs and satyrs. Wally promptly papered the dining room with paper like the sample. The paper and materials expended cost Wally $900. There were no visible defects in any of the installed wallpaper.

When the room was done, Sally showed it to her father, who was shocked at the nude nymphs and satyrs. Sally then wrote to Wally, stating:

I am not satisfied with the wallpaper because it shocks my father and because some of the paper panels are out of alignment. I will not pay your bill unless and until you repaper the dining room to my satisfaction and at your expense.

In fact, some panels were out of alignment, but the problem could only be seen with a magnifying glass. It would cost Wally (1) $500 to remove the "nymph and satyrs" wallpaper, (2) $1,000 to install new wallpaper (which can be installed over the existing paper), (3) $300 to refinish and repaint the walls the way they were once the wallpaper was removed, and (4) $250 to repair those panels that are out of alignment. Uncertain whether Wally would comply with her demand, Sally solicited bids from other wallpaper companies to repaper the dining room and, in the alternative, to remove the paper and repaint the room as it was. The lowest bids she received from a reputable company were from WallCo, which bid (1) $1,250 to remove the "nymph and satyrs" wallpaper and install replacement wallpaper and (2) $900 to remove the "nymph and satyrs" wallpaper, then refinish and repaint the walls.

The market value of the house would be unchanged if the "nymph and satyrs" wallpaper remained, if it was replaced with new wallpaper, or if it was removed and the room repainted. It is clear that Mr. & Mrs. Rich's "enjoyment value" of the house will be less with the "nymph and satyrs" wallpaper than without it; however, it is not clear whether their "enjoyment value" will be any different depending on whether the walls are refinished and repainted or covered with different wallpaper.

209. Assuming that (1) Sally and Wally had an enforceable contract, (2) Sally was honestly or reasonably dissatisfied, and (3) Sally and Wally are rational actors, what amount of damages would Sally most likely recover if Wally refused Sally's demand to repaper the dining room to Sally's satisfaction at Wally's expense?

(A) $250.

(B) $350.

(C) $500.

(D) $1,250.

Romeo had been courting Juliet for several years. Finally, he decided to propose marriage. But how? After consulting his friends and 1-800-Dial-A-Psychic, he decided to fly himself, Juliet, and several close friends and relatives to Maui, at his own expense, and propose to Juliet during a private luau to the strains of the ukulele.

Having the heart of a true romantic, Romeo disclosed his plans to Juliet's parents and asked (and received) their permission to marry their daughter. Having the limited means of a true romantic, Romeo shopped around to find the best deal on the right engagement ring. After lots of shopping, a week before leaving for Maui, Romeo found the ring (and the price) he was looking for at Old Will's Jewelers for $10,000. Romeo was unable to pay the entire purchase price immediately. He wanted to pay $2,500 prior to taking delivery and the remaining $7,500 in 10 monthly installments of $750 each. Old Will, the proprietor, suggested that Romeo consider a less expensive ring — one that he could pay for all at once — but Romeo insisted that his Juliet have the best. Old Will was willing to sell on installments, but wanted to add a $50 interest charge to each of the monthly installments. Romeo refused to pay interest, and Old Will gave in, agreeing to sell Romeo the ring for $2,500 down and $7,500 to be paid in 10 equal monthly installments. Romeo asked Old Will to hold the ring for him and promised to return the next day with the down payment.

Romeo returned to Old Will's the next afternoon with a check for $2,500, drawn on Romeo's account at Padua Bank & Trust ("PB&T"). Old Will agreed to hold Romeo's check until Romeo picked up the ring the following morning. Later that afternoon, however, Old Will called PB&T to confirm that Romeo's account contained sufficient funds to cover the check. PB&T informed Old Will that the account balance was currently "less than $500," and that, "over the past year, the balance in this account has averaged less than $1,000." Old Will then called the local credit bureau, which characterized Romeo as "a questionable credit risk" for any amount greater than $500.

Old Will promptly called Romeo and chastised him for writing "a rubber check" and demanded that Romeo pay the entire purchase price in cash before Old Will would give him the ring. Romeo told Old Will that he had transferred funds into his PB&T account to cover the check, but that, because he had done so after 3:00 p.m., the additional funds would not show up in his account balance until tomorrow. Romeo offered to bring $2,500 cash the next day when he came to pick up the ring. Old Will would not budge. He insisted that Romeo pay the full price in cash or the deal was off. Romeo told Old Will that his stubbornness would cost Romeo dearly, because he did not have time to find a replacement ring before leaving for Maui.

Unable to find a replacement ring or to change travel plans (the airline tickets were non-refundable), Romeo went to Maui without the ring (though not without Juliet and entourage). Without the ring, Romeo felt he could not propose. The trip was, in his words, "a flop," costing him $15,000 in airfare, hotel, and related expenses.

When Romeo returned to town, he received a call from Marlowe, the new owner of Old Will's. (Old Will lost the store to Marlowe in a card game. But, because the shop's name was well known in the community and Old Will still owed Marlowe unpaid gambling debts, Marlowe kept the name and left Old Will in charge of the store so that he could work off his debt to Marlowe.) Marlowe expressed his regret at the misunderstanding between Romeo and Old Will and offered to sell the Romeo the identical ring for $7,500. Romeo refused Marlowe's offer, saying that he was unwilling to purchase the ring because of Old Will's conduct and because he feared that post-sales service might be inadequate. Romeo, instead, bought a ring of comparable size and quality from another jeweler for $12,000, proposed to Juliet, she accepted, and they lived happily ever after (so far, at least).

Romeo has sued Old Will's Jewelers for breach of contract. Old Will's Jewelers has answered with the defense of anticipatory repudiation. Assume that (1) each action taken and each statement by Old Will and Marlowe are attributable to Old Will's; (2) Romeo did transfer the $2,500 into his PB&T account in time to cover the check if Old Will had deposited it the same day that Romeo was to pick up the ring; (3) the replacement ring was indeed of comparable size and quality to the original ring; and (4) the market value of the ring Romeo agreed to buy from Old Will was $11,000 on the day that Romeo delivered the $2,500 check to Old Will's Jewelers.

210. Assuming that Romeo had an enforceable contract to purchase the ring from Old Will's Jewelers for $2,500 plus 10 monthly installments of $750 each, and that Old Will's Jewelers breached its contract with Romeo in a way that could give rise to a compensable claim by Romeo, what actual damages would UCC Article 2 entitle Romeo to recover?

    (A) $2,000, the difference between the price Romeo agreed to pay Old Will for the original ring and the price he paid for the replacement ring.

    (B) $1,000, the difference between the fair market value of the ring Romeo agreed to buy from Old Will and the price he paid for the replacement ring.

    (C) Nothing, because Romeo refused Marlowe's offer to sell him for $7,500 the same ring Romeo had previously agreed to purchase for $10,000.

    (D) $2,500, the difference between the price Romeo originally agreed to pay Old Will and the price at which Marlowe offered to sell the same ring to Romeo.

211. Could Romeo recover some or all of the cost of his Maui trip as consequential damages?

    (A) No, because Article 2 categorically denies aggrieved parties their consequential damages.

    (B) No. While Article 2 does permit aggrieved sellers to recover consequential damages, it does not permit aggrieved buyers to recover consequential damages.

    (C) No, because Old Will could not reasonably foresee Romeo's consequential damages.

    (D) No. Even if Article 2 permits aggrieved buyers to recover consequential damages, Romeo did not suffer any compensable consequential damages.

Mercury Rising ("Mercury") is an Illinois manufacturer of indoor and outdoor thermometers. Tubular Glass ("Tubular") is a Michigan manufacturer of precision glass tubing. On March 14, 2003, following telephone negotiations between the two, Will Bruce, Mercury's purchasing agent, faxed a purchase order to Tubular for 5,000 one-foot lengths of glass tubing, at a price of $5.00 per foot, to be delivered to Mercury's plant no later than May 1st. Later that same day, Tubular faxed a written acknowledgment, agreeing to manufacture and deliver 5,000 one-foot lengths of glass tubing, at a price of $5.00 per foot, to Mercury's plant no later than May 1st. The terms of Tubular's acknowledgment also (1) disclaimed of all implied warranties, and (2) required Mercury to pay the full contract price, including the cost of shipping the tubing from Tubular's plant to Mercury's plant, when Mercury received the tubing. The parties did not correspond further.

Before the goods reached Mercury, Mercury found another seller, Glaz Emporium ("Glaz"), who offered to provide the same quantity and quality of glass tubing, no later than May 2nd, at a price of $4.50 per foot. Mercury agreed on April 15th to purchase the tubing from Glaz, and refused to receive the shipment from Tubular when it arrived on May 1st.

Assume that:

1. Tubular and Mercury had an enforceable contract;

2. Mercury's refusal to accept the shipment from Tubular constituted a breach of Mercury's contract with Tubular;

3. on May 15th, Tubular entered into a contract to sell 4,000 feet of the glass tubing originally destined for Mercury to another customer, Video Matrix, for $6.00 per foot, which Video Matrix agreed to transport at its own expense from Tubular's plant to Video Matrix's Wisconsin factory no sooner than June 2nd;

4. Tubular did not notify Mercury of its post-breach sale to Video Matrix;

5. the market price of the glass tubing on April 2nd was $5.25 per foot;

6. the market price of the glass tubing on April 15th was $5.00 per foot;

7. the market price of the glass tubing on May 1st was $5.50 per foot;

8. the market price of the glass tubing on May 15th was $6.00 per foot;

9. the transportation cost between any two locations involved in this Question is $100 per 1,000 feet;

10. the storage cost is $0.05 per foot per month; and

11. Tubular's cost of manufacturing the tubing ordered by Mercury was $4.50 per foot.

212. What remedies does Article 2 afford Tubular against Mercury?

ANSWER:

213. What resale damages could Tubular recover under UCC § 2-706, as of June 2, 2003, taking into account Tubular's new contract with Video Matrix?

    (A) $0.

    (B) $1,500.

    (C) $1,750.

    (D) $2,150.

214. Assuming that Tubular is entitled to recover contract-market differential damages under UCC § 2-708(1), what is the measure of those damages?

    (A) $0.

    (B) $500.

    (C) $750.

    (D) $3,250.

215. Is Tubular eligible to recover lost profit damages under UCC § 2-708(2)?
ANSWER:

216. Regardless of your answer to Question 215, assuming that Tubular is entitled to recover lost profit damages under UCC § 2-708(2), what was the measure of those damages as of June 2, 2003?

    (A) $0.

    (B) $1,250.

    (C) $2,500.

    (D) $3,250.

217. Assuming that Tubular is entitled to sue for price under UCC § 2-709, what is the measure of those damages?

    (A) $1,800.

    (B) $5,000.

    (C) $5,800.

(D) $25,800.

On July 14, 2003, Monica, a fruit merchant, mailed Chandler, a fruit stand operator, a written offer to sell up to 500 crates of mangoes (30 per crate) for $6.00 per crate. By the terms of Monica's offer, Chandler had the exclusive right to accept or decline the offer until July 25th at 5:00 p.m. Chandler received Monica's written offer at 2:00 p.m. on July 16th.

On July 17th, Monica wrote to Chandler revoking the offer. Monica promptly placed the letter in the mail, properly addressed and with adequate postage. Later that same day, Monica sold all 500 crates of mangoes to Phoebe, a mango-loving vegetarian (or should it be "fruititarian"?), at a price of $6.50 per crate.

On July 19th, Chandler wrote to Monica stating that he would purchase 100 crates of mangoes from Monica for $6.00 per crate, provided that Monica deliver the mangoes no later than September 1st.

Monica received Chandler's letter on July 21st. Monica immediately sent a fax to Chandler informing him that she had revoked her offer and sold the mangoes to Phoebe. Chandler received Monica's July 17th letter a few hours after receiving Monica's fax.

Assume that:

1.   Monica's sale to Phoebe was a breach of her contract with Chandler;

2.   Monica could acquire another 100 crates of mangoes in time to deliver them to Chandler by September 8th;

3.   Chandler could purchase replacement mangoes for delivery on or before September 1st from another seller, Ross, for $7.00 per crate (including delivery);

4.   the market price of mangoes on July 21st was $6.50 per crate;

5.   the market price of mangoes on September 1st was $7.00 per crate; and

6.   Chandler sells 50 crates of mangoes per week to his customers at a price of 3 mangoes for $1.

218.   If Chandler sued on or after September 1st, what UCC Article 2 remedy would afford Chandler the most complete recovery against Monica?

(A)   Cover damages under UCC § 2-712.

(B)   Contract-market differential damages under UCC § 2-713.

(C)   Damages for nonconformity under UCC § 2-714.

(D)   Specific performance under UCC § 2-716.

Pennybakers is a small, but successful, interior design business located in Athens, Georgia. Wanting to expand into graphic design and advertising, Pennybakers' principal, Petunia Pennybaker, contracted with an upstart computer engineering firm, Scott & Co. ("S&C"), to design customized graphics software. S&C's chief engineer, Adam Scott — who Petunia met on a flight from Atlanta to San Jose, California (where S&C is headquartered) — promptly designed and tested the software. Claiming that he was dissatisfied with the software's performance on Pennybakers' existing computers, Adam suggested that Pennybakers buy a new computer specially designed for graphics software, the Scott GR8 ("GR8"), to run the new software. S&C manufactures the GR8. Delighted with Adam's demonstration of the custom software using the GR8, Petunia willingly agreed to buy the GR8 to run the software. The parties amended their contract to include Pennybakers' purchase and S&C's delivery of the GR8.

Less than two weeks after taking delivery of the software and the GR8, Petunia began to notice a recurrent glitch that caused a small, bespectacled dog to appear randomly in the graphical layouts she designed using the GR8. Acting on a hunch, Petunia discovered the same glitch while running other software that had been installed on the GR8. When she called S&C to complain, her call was directed to S&C's customer service specialist, Bob, who was unable to solve Petunia's problem. The problem persisted, causing Pennybakers to lose a lucrative advertising contract for the Greater Atlanta Garfield Fan Club. Finally fed up with it all, and wanting to prevent any further loss of business, Pennybakers purchased a MicroSpaz 3000GT computer for $3,000 and new graphics software for $2,000. Pennybakers also filed suit against S&C, alleging breach of any and all applicable express or implied warranties.

The parties' pleadings and discovery reveal, in addition to the foregoing, that: (1) Pennybakers paid S&C $25,000 to design the custom software; (2) Pennybakers paid S&C $2,500 for the GR8 computer; (3) Pennybakers paid S&C the entire $27,500 prior to taking delivery of the software and the GR8; (4) the parties agree that any glitch is a "hardware" problem with the GR8, not a "software" problem; (5) Pennybakers' expert witness has opined that the software designed by S&C would have performed as well or better on any number of other commercially-available computers as it did on the GR8 before the glitch appeared; (6) Petunia's assistant, Cleo, loaded the software onto another computer and ran it for several weeks without ever encountering the glitch; (7) the warranty card that accompanied the GR8 computer did not disclaim any implied warranties and expressly warranted that the computer would operate free of any errors, other than those caused by third-party software, for a period of one year from the date of purchase; (8) the contract Pennybakers lost with the Greater Atlanta Garfield Fan Club would have netted Pennybakers a profit of at least $25,000; and (9) the MicroSpaz 3000GT and the new graphics software have been glitch-free.

219. Assuming that UCC Article 2 governs this transaction and that S&C breached one or more Article 2 warranties, what damages might Pennybakers be entitled to recover?

ANSWER:

220.   Assume, instead, that S&C's place of business is Cabo San Lucas, Mexico, this
       transaction is governed by the CISG, and that S&C breached one or more warranties
       recognized by the CISG. What remedy or remedies would the CISG afford Pennybakers
       against S&C?

ANSWER:

Methuselah was getting along in years and wanted to ensure that the chinchilla ranch he had inherited from his father, who had inherited it from *his* father, would stay in the family for many years to come. Methuselah's eldest son, Lamech, predeceased him, leaving Lamech's son (Methuselah's grandson) Noah next in line to inherit the ranch. (Methuselah, being about as "old school" as one could possibly be, strongly believed in primogeniture.) Noah, who was only 16 years old at the time, had never done well in school, but he seemed to enjoy spending his free time at the ranch, helping out however he could. Methuselah was concerned that, while Noah might *want* to run the ranch when Methuselah retired or died, Noah might not be *able* to handle the ranch's business affairs.

Desiring to provide Noah with training that would enable him to take over the business, Methuselah entered into a contract with Adam Keynes, a business consultant who lived in a nearby city and had particular expertise in farm and ranch finances and management. The contract provided that Keynes would meet with Noah one afternoon a week during the school year, and twice a week during the summer, to tutor Noah in accounting, economics, finance, and management, for three years or until Noah took over day-to-day management of the ranch, whichever occurred first. The contract further provided that, when Noah assumed the reins of the family business, Keynes would make himself available, up to 10 hours per week for the first two years, to consult with Noah on matters related to the family's business and the family's and Noah's personal finances. Methuselah agreed to pay Keynes an annual retainer of $10,000, plus $100 per hour until Noah's 19th birthday, and $200 per hour thereafter. Methuselah and Keynes put the essential terms of the contract in writing and signed it, and Methuselah paid Keynes one-half ($5,000) of the first year's retainer, with a promise to pay the other $5,000 within 90 days.

221. Assuming that Methuselah and Keynes formed an enforceable contract, what is Noah's status with respect to that contract?

   (A) Noah is an incidental creditor beneficiary.

   (B) Noah is an intended creditor beneficiary.

   (C) Noah is an incidental donee beneficiary.

   (D) Noah is an intended donee beneficiary.

222. Assuming no additional facts other than that Keynes appeared at the family homestead the following week, as promised, and commenced tutoring Noah, as promised, at what point in time did Noah's rights as a third party beneficiary of the contract between Methuselah and Keynes vest (*i.e.*, become enforceable)?

   (A) When Methuselah and Keynes signed the contract.

(B)   When Methuselah paid Keynes $5,000 toward his first year's retainer.

(C)   When Keynes appeared at Methuselah's door to begin tutoring Noah.

(D)   When Keynes began tutoring Noah.

Suppose that, after several months of (remarkably successful) weekly tutoring, Keynes received an offer to join the faculty of Truly Impressive State University ("TISU"), located in New Ivy — half a continent away from Methuselah's spread. Keynes informed Methuselah and Noah that he had been offered the job he had been waiting for his whole life, and that he would be moving to New Ivy in about three months. Keynes offered to continue tutoring Noah until the time came for him to move, and reminded Noah that he would always be "only a phone call away."

223.   Assuming that Keynes's quitting his tutoring job and moving to New Ivy was a breach of his contract with Methuselah, who could bring suit against Keynes?

(A)   Only Methuselah, because he was the one with whom Keynes exchanged promises and who was paying Keynes in exchange for Keynes's services.

(B)   Only Noah, because he was the intended recipient of Keynes's services and the only one who will be worse off for Keyness departure.

(C)   Either Methuselah or Noah (or both), because both had vested rights in the contract entitling them to sue to enforce the contract.

(D)   Neither Methuselah nor Noah, because continuing to perform his tutoring contract was impracticable for Keynes, which would excuse him from any liability on the contract.

Returning to the facts of Questions 221, suppose that, rather than terminating the tutoring contract to accept the teaching position at TISU, Keynes terminated the tutoring contract because Methuselah stopped paying for his services.

224.   Would Noah have a cause of action against Methuselah for breaching his contract with Keynes?

ANSWER:

In addition to providing for Noah's preparation for assuming control of the family business, Methuselah also wanted to make some provision for the rest of his children and grandchildren. Methuselah telephoned Jimmy Mack, the local agent for Good Hands Insurance ("GHI"), and discussed life insurance and other estate planning options. He then called Doc Epstein who (his nickname notwithstanding) had provided legal advice and representation to Methuselah for many years, to get Doc's counsel on the various options Methuselah had discussed with Mack. A couple of days later, Methuselah met with Jimmy Mack and purchased four $500,000 term life insurance policies. Each policy named one of his daughters — Esther, Ruth, Susanna, and Judith — as the primary beneficiary of 50% of the face value of the policy, and each daughter's children as the primary beneficiaries of equal shares of the other 50% of each policy and secondary beneficiaries of their respective mother's 50%. When Methuselah purchased the policies, Esther had two children (Samuel and Micah), Ruth had three (Jonah, Joel, and Sarah), and Judith had two (Daniel and Mary). Susanna was six months pregnant with her first child, Adam, who was born, as was his younger sister, Eve, before Methuselah died. The beneficiary designations on each life insurance policy listed Methuselah's daughter by name, but identified each daughter's children as, simply, "her natural or adopted children."

Suppose that Methuselah and Susanna had a falling out several months before he died, and Methuselah stopped paying the monthly premiums on the insurance policy of which she and her children were the beneficiaries. After Methuselah died, GHI refused to pay Susanna and her children the proceeds of that policy. Shortly thereafter, Susanna, whose grief following her father's death was compounded when she learned that he had left her nothing to provide for herself or her children, took her own life.

225. If Adam and Eve (through their legal guardian) sued GHI to recover the proceeds of the policy naming Susanna and her natural or adopted children as the beneficiaries, which of the following defenses could GHI successfully assert to avoid liability?

   (A) Adam and Eve were not intended beneficiaries of the policy because they were unborn when Methuselah purchased the policy.

   (B) Methuselah and GHI mutually rescinded the policy when Methuselah ceased making premium payments.

   (C) Methuselah's failure to make premium payments when due was a breach of the policy terms, relieving GHI from any obligation to pay benefits on Methuselah's death.

   (D) Susanna's suicide voided GHI's obligation to pay Adam and Eve the 50% of the policy benefits on which Susanna was designated as the primary beneficiary and "her natural or adopted children" as secondary beneficiaries.

Returning to the facts of Questions 221 and 222, suppose that Noah, try as he might, simply could not follow most of Keynes's tutoring and grew increasingly disenchanted with the idea of taking over the family ranching business. One weekend, Noah and some friends went to a concert featuring rising celtic-techno-goth sensation Wallace Williams. Five minutes in, Noah was hooked. When he returned home, he told his grandfather that he wanted to become a musician. After some lengthy conversations, Methuselah saw that Noah would not be swayed. Noah and Methuselah then talked with Esther's eldest son, Samuel, who was delighted to be offered the opportunity to be groomed to take over the family business from his grandfather.

226. If Noah transferred his rights to receive the benefit of Keynes's tutoring and, eventually, consulting expertise, to Samuel, would Keynes be obligated to perform his contract with Methuselah for Samuel's benefit?

    (A)   No, Keynes's contract only obligated him to tutor and consult with Noah. If Samuel wanted the benefit of Keynes's expertise, Methuselah or Samuel would have to make a new contract with Keynes for Samuel's benefit.

    (B)   Yes, provided that Noah first notified Keynes that he was assigning his rights under the contract to Samuel.

    (C)   Yes, if Keynes consented to Noah assigning his rights to Samuel.

    (D)   Yes, as long as nothing in Keynes's contract with Methuselah restricted Noah's ability to assign his rights to Samuel.

Regardless of your answer to Question 226, assume that Noah could and did assign his rights under the contract to Samuel.

    227.   What rights, if any, would Noah retain under the contract until Keynes received notice of the assignment or actually began to perform for Samuel's benefit?

ANSWER:

Returning to the facts of Questions 221-223, suppose that, after receiving the teaching offer from TISU, Keynes spoke with David Malthus, a colleague of his, about taking over the responsibility of tutoring and consulting for Noah. Malthus was intrigued, and agreed to assume Keynes's duties under the contract between Keynes and Methuselah.

    228.   Were Methuselah and Noah obliged to accept Keynes's delegation of his duties to Malthus?

ANSWER:

Regardless of your answer to Question 228, assume that Noah and Methuselah were bound to accept Keynes's delegation to Malthus or that, even though they were not so bound, they consented to the delegation.

    229.   If Malthus failed to perform adequately, who could Noah and Methuselah sue for breach?

    (A)   Only Malthus, because they accepted or were otherwise bound by Keynes's delegation.

    (B)   Only Keynes, because he repudiated his duty to perform for Noah's benefit, and his decision to let Malthus perform for him did not relieve Keynes of liability for his repudiation.

(C) Either Malthus or Keynes (or both), because Keynes's delegation to Malthus did not relieve Keynes of liability, but Malthus's acceptance of Keynes's delegation subjected Malthus to liability, as well.

(D) Neither Malthus nor Keynes, because only Keynes was liable on the contract and his liability was discharged by the impracticability of simultaneously performing his duties to Noah and his duties at TISU.

Return to the facts of Questions 221 and 222. One of the many pieces of machinery Methuselah has on the farm is a riding mower. One day, while walking from his car to Methuselah's front door, moments before a scheduled tutoring session with Noah, Keynes was stopped in his tracks by a loud thump. When he turned to see what it was, Keynes saw a large, jagged rock that had been kicked up by the riding mower (which was being operated by local handyman Enos Slater) crashing into and through the windshield of his car, knocking off the rear view mirror, and imbedding itself in the leather upholstery of the driver's seat. The riding mower was manufactured by Yubotah, and Methuselah had purchased it fairly recently from Jared's Lawn & Garden, which is a "certified Yubotah dealer." Assume that (1) Methuselah's chinchilla ranch is located in a state that has adopted UCC § 2-318 (Alternative C), (2) the damage to Keynes's car was due to a defect in the mower that pre-dated Methuselah's purchase of it, and (3) the manufacturer's warranty that came with the riding mower (a) disclaims all implied warranties in favor of the express warranty and (b) disclaims liability to persons other than the purchaser of the riding mower for anything other than personal injury.

230. Against whom could Keynes bring a colorable claim for breach of warranty under UCC Article 2?

(A) Only Yubotah, because Jared cannot be held liable for defective products that he does not manufacture.

(B) Only Jared, because Methuselah purchased the riding mower from Jared, not from Yubotah.

(C) Either Yubotah or Jared (or both), because a manufacturer is liable for its defective products regardless of whether it sells them directly to the consumer or through a retailer (as in this case), and a seller is liable for any defective product it sells, whether it manufactured the product or not.

(D) Neither Yubotah nor Jared, because the only injury Keynes suffered was to his property, not his person, and the manufacturer's warranty disclaimed liability for non-personal injury to third parties.

PRACTICE FINAL EXAM: QUESTIONS

Tempus Fugit ("Tempus") manufactures wall clocks in its factory in Tempe, Arizona. Frank's Cranks ("FC") manufactures precision gear works in its factory in Nuevo Laredo, Mexico. GEARZ, FC's authorized dealer for Arizona and New Mexico, has its place of business in Albuquerque, New Mexico. On March 1, 2003, Tempus' purchasing manager telephoned GEARZ and, after discussing Tempus' particular needs, faxed a purchase order for 1,000 sets of precision gear works, at a price of $50.00 per set, to be delivered to Tempus no later than April 15th. Tempus' purchase order stated, *inter alia*: "All disputes will be governed by Arizona law." Later that same day, FC faxed Tempus an acknowledgment from Nuevo Laredo, agreeing to manufacture for and sell to Tempus 1,000 sets of gear works satisfying Tempus' specifications, at a price of $50.00 per set, and to deliver them to Tempus no later than April 15th. FC's acknowledgment also contained a provision requiring Tempus to pay the full contract price, including transportation costs, upon receipt of the gears. FC's acknowledgment neither repeated nor disputed Tempus' choice-of-law provision. There was no further correspondence between the parties. The goods left FC's factory in Nuevo Laredo on or about April 5th, and arrived at Tempus' factory in Tempe on April 12th. Upon receipt of the goods, Tempus paid the carrier $52,500, representing the full contract price, plus $2,500 for transportation.

231. Given the contractual choice of law provision, what body of law primarily governs the agreement between Tempus and FC?

   (A) Arizona common law.

   (B) The Arizona Uniform Commercial Code (UCC).

   (C) The U.N. Convention on Contracts for the International Sale of Goods (CISG).

   (D) The Uniform Electronic Transactions Act (UETA).

Pennybakers is a small, but successful, interior design business located in Athens, Georgia. Wanting to expand into graphic design and advertising, Pennybakers' principal, Petunia Pennybaker, contracted with an upstart computer engineering firm, Scott & Co. ("S& C"), to design customized graphics software. S& C's chief engineer, Adam Scott — who Petunia met on a flight from Atlanta to San Jose, California (where S& C is headquartered) — promptly designed and tested the software. Claiming that he was dissatisfied with the software's performance on Pennybakers' existing computers, Adam suggested that Pennybakers buy a new

131

computer specially designed for graphics software, the Scott GR8 ("GR8"), to run the new software. S& C manufactures the GR8. Delighted with Adam's demonstration of the custom software using the GR8, Petunia willingly agreed to buy the GR8 to run the software. The parties amended their contract to include Pennybakers' purchase and S& C's delivery of the GR8.

Less than two weeks after taking delivery of the software and the GR8, Petunia began to notice a recurrent glitch that caused a small, bespectacled dog to appear randomly in the graphical layouts she designed using the GR8. Acting on a hunch, Petunia discovered the same glitch while running other software that had been installed on the GR8. When she called S& C to complain, her call was directed to S& C's customer service specialist, Bob, who was unable to solve Petunia's problem. The problem persisted, causing Pennybakers to lose a lucrative advertising contract for the Greater Atlanta Garfield Fan Club. Finally fed up with it all, and wanting to prevent any further loss of business, Pennybakers purchased a MicroSpaz 3000GT computer for $3,000 and new graphics software for $2,000. Pennybakers also filed suit against S& C, alleging breach of any and all applicable express or implied warranties.

The parties' pleadings and discovery reveal, in addition to the foregoing, that: (1) Pennybakers paid S& C $25,000 to design the custom software; (2) Pennybakers paid S& C $2,500 for the GR8 computer; (3) Pennybakers paid S& C the entire $27,500 prior to taking delivery of the software and the GR8; (4) the parties agree that any glitch is a "hardware" problem with the GR8, not a "software" problem; (5) Pennybakers' expert witness has opined that the software designed by S& C would have performed as well or better on any number of other commercially-available computers as it did on the GR8 before the glitch appeared; (6) Petunia's assistant, Cleo, loaded the software onto another computer and ran it for several weeks without ever encountering the glitch; (7) the warranty card that accompanied the GR8 computer did not disclaim any implied warranties and expressly warranted that the computer would operate free of any errors, other than those caused by third-party software, for a period of one year from the date of purchase; (8) the contract Pennybakers lost with the Greater Atlanta Garfield Fan Club would have netted Pennybakers a profit of at least $25,000; and (9) the MicroSpaz 3000GT and the new graphics software have been glitch-free.

232.   Assuming that the courts in the jurisdiction whose law governs this dispute (1) have held that customized software is not a good and (2) follow the majority rule with respect to mixed contracts, should UCC Article 2 govern Pennybakers' claims against S& C in this lawsuit?

(A)   Yes, because the predominant purpose of Pennybakers' contract with S& C was to purchase the GR8 computer.

(B)   No, because the predominant purpose of Pennybakers' contract with S& C was to pay S& C to design customized graphics software.

(C)   Yes, because the gravamen of Pennybakers' complaint is that the GR8 computer failed to perform as promised.

(D)   No, because the gravamen of Pennybakers' complaint is that the customized graphics software failed to perform as promised.

Beauford wrote to Sanjay on March 1, 2003 offering to purchase Sanjay's house for $200,000. Beauford's letter stated that his offer would expire "if I do not receive a written reply from you on or before April 1, 2003." On March 5th, Sanjay telephoned Beauford to confirm his acceptance of Beauford's offer. On March 10th, Sanjay wrote a letter accepting Beauford's offer, properly addressed it, and mailed it to Beauford, who never received the letter. Not having received any response to his acceptance, Sanjay telephoned Beauford on March 31st to confirm his acceptance of Beauford's offer. Beauford replied that he had not yet received Sanjay's letter. Sanjay reaffirmed his desire to sell Beauford his house for $200,000 and promised to fax Beauford a copy of the March 10th acceptance letter the next day. On April 1st, Sanjay faxed a copy of his March 10th letter to Beauford, who received the fax moments later.

233. At what point in time, if ever, did Sanjay form an agreement with Beauford by accepting Beauford's offer at a time and in a manner invited by the offer?

   (A) When Sanjay telephoned his acceptance to Beauford on March 5th.

   (B) When Sanjay sent his acceptance letter on March 10th.

   (C) When Sanjay telephoned Beauford on March 31st.

   (D) When Sanjay faxed a copy of his March 10th letter to Beauford on April 1st.

234. Suppose that, when Sanjay called Beauford on March 31st, Beauford said, "I revoke my offer." Was Beauford's revocation effective?

   (A) No, because Sanjay had already accepted by means of his March 5th telephone call.

   (B) No, because Sanjay had already accepted by means of his March 10th letter.

   (C) Yes, but only if Beauford said, "I revoke my offer" before Sanjay said, "I accept" or, "I confirm my acceptance."

   (D) Yes, because Sanjay had not accepted Beauford's offer on its terms prior to Beauford telling Sanjay, "I revoke my offer."

On July 1, 2003, Ross, a Galveston, Texas-based seafood merchant, mailed Joey, a buyer for several independently-owned grocery stores located in Arkansas and Oklahoma, a written offer to sell up to 1,000 pounds of Ecuadorian pygmy shrimp for $10.00 per pound, shipping and handling included. By the terms of Ross' offer, Joey had the exclusive right to accept or decline the offer until July 14th at 5:00 p.m. Joey received Ross' written offer on July 5th at 2:00 p.m. At 3:00 p.m. on July 5th, Joey mailed a letter to Ross stating that he would purchase 500 pounds of Ecuadorian pygmy shrimp for $8.00 per pound, provided that Ross could deliver the shrimp no later than August 1st. Joey properly addressed the letter and affixed adequate postage.

On July 7th, Ross wrote to Joey revoking the offer. Ross promptly placed the letter in the mail, properly addressed, and with adequate postage. Later that same day, Ross sold all 1,000 pounds of shrimp to Rachel for $12.00 per pound.

On July 8th, Joey learned that a hurricane had wiped out a substantial part of the Ecuadorian shrimping fleet and washed tons of pygmy shrimp ashore, where they perished before they could be preserved. Experts predicted that a shortage of Ecuadorian pygmy shrimp was imminent and that the market price would likely increase by more than 100% during the next several weeks. Not knowing whether Ross had already received his July 5th letter (he had not), and having no knowledge of Ross' transaction with Rachel, Joey immediately faxed a letter to Ross asking him to "disregard my earlier letter" and stating that Joey would purchase 500 pounds of Ecuadorian pygmy shrimp from Ross for $10.00 per pound, provided that Ross deliver the shrimp no later than August 1st.

Ross received Joey's July 8th fax at noon on July 8th. Ross immediately sent a return fax to Joey informing him that he had revoked his offer and, regrettably, had already sold all 1,000 pounds of Ecuadorian pygmy shrimp to Rachel. Joey received Ross' July 7th letter at 3:00 p.m. on July 8th. Ross received Joey's July 5th letter at 4:00 p.m. on July 8th.

235.   Did Joey and Ross form a contract, obligating Ross to sell Joey 500 pounds of Ecuadorian pygmy shrimp for delivery by August 1st?

(A)   No, because Ross sent Joey notice of his revocation before Joey sent Ross his July 8th fax.

(B)   Yes, because Ross made a firm offer that he could not revoke prior to 5:00 p.m. on July 14th, unless Joey rejected or counteroffered before then, and Ross received Joey's July 8th fax prior to 5:00 p.m. on July 14th and prior to receiving Joey's July 5th letter.

(C)   Yes, because Ross received Joey's July 8th acceptance before he received Joey's July 5th letter.

(D)   Yes, because Joey accepted Ross' offer before Ross sold the Ecuadorian pygmy shrimp to Rachel and attempted to revoke his offer to Joey.

236.   If Joey can prove that he and Ross formed a contract for the purchase and sale, respectively, of 500 pounds of Ecuadorian pygmy shrimp, was that contract subject to a statute of frauds?

(A)   No, because the contract between Ross and Joey was one to be fully performed in less than one year; therefore, it was outside the scope of *Restatement (Second)* § 110(1)(e).

(B)   No, because Ecuador and the United States are both parties to the CISG and Joey was not purchasing the shrimp for personal, family, or household use; therefore, the contract is governed by the CISG, which has no statute of frauds.

(C)   Yes, because the contract between Ross and Joey was for the sale of personal property for $5,000 or more; therefore, the contract is governed by UCC § 1-206.

(D)   Yes, because the contract between Ross and Joey was for the sale of goods for $500 (or $5,000, if applying Revised Article 2) or more; therefore, the contract is governed by UCC § 2-201.

237. Assuming that the contract between Ross and Joey was subject to a statute of frauds, can Joey satisfy the applicable statute of frauds based on the foregoing facts?

ANSWER:

The Yucca Museum of Art, located in a suburb of Las Vegas, decided the time had come to build a new wing onto its existing building in order to house its growing collection of fine origami (works of art made with folded paper). The Museum announced a $25 million fundraising campaign. The Museum's fundraising brochure stated that $20 million would be used to pay for the new wing. The brochure also stated that the Museum would name the new wing after the first donor to pledge $5 million, or the largest single donor if no one pledged $5 million. At the bottom of the brochure appeared the following language:

> *This new wing cannot become a reality unless we receive sufficient pledges to pay for it. We will not begin construction on the new wing until we have at least $10 million in total pledges toward the cost of the new wing or at least one "keystone" pledge toward the cost of the new wing in excess of $5 million.*

Museum policy requires the Museum to apply all undesignated (non-"earmarked") pledges to its general purpose fund until the general purpose portion of any particular fundraising campaign (here, $5,000,000) is satisfied, at which time any remaining undesignated funds may be used for a particular purpose (here, the new wing).

The Museum mailed its fundraising brochure on September 1, 2002. On September 20th, noted philanthropists Roy and Bai Golly pledged $750,000 to the Museum. The Gollys did not designate a particular use for their gift. On September 30th, Dr. Edwina Splunk, chief of medicine at Yucca Medical College and successful investor, pledged $2 million, with the notation that her funds were to be used only for the new wing. On October 15th, Dave & Aimee Flockenstein pledged $4,250,000 to the Museum's fundraising drive. The Flockensteins did not designate a specific use for their gift. As of October 15th, the Museum had received a number of smaller (less than $50,000 each) pledges totaling $500,000.

On November 1st, Leopard Tree, a world-famous professional ping-pong player, pledged $4,500,000 on the condition that her funds were to be used only for the new wing. A few days later, on November 5th, Mary O'Mary sent the Museum her pledge card, having written on it "$4,750,000, on the condition that the funds may be used only for the new wing." On November 6th, Museum officials approved a set of plans that had been prepared by a prominent local architect and hired a general contractor to oversee construction on the new wing. Ground was broken on December 1st, and construction was well under way by March 1, 2003.

By December 31, 2002, the Museum had received three more large ($50,000 or more each) pledges and dozens of additional small pledges totaling $9,000,000. None of these large pledges specified the use to which the donor's money must be put. Having exceeded its goal for both the total campaign and the new wing, the Museum stopped soliciting funds for the new wing.

A few days later, the Flockensteins offered to increase their total pledge to $5,000,000 if the Museum would name its new wing in their honor. Museum officials thanked the Flockensteins for their generosity, but explained that, under the terms of the campaign brochure, the "naming rights" belonged to Mary O'Mary, who had made the largest pledge to the new wing. The Flockensteins then "renewed" their original, undesignated pledge of $4,250,000.

Museum policy required that all pledges be paid no later than 120 days after the Museum received the pledge, with the exception that pledges in excess of $50,000 could be paid in up to five equal installments, the first of which had to be made within 120 days after the Museum received the pledge. On March 1, 2003, the Museum sent Mary a reminder that she had pledged to pay no less than $950,000 (one-fifth of $4,750,000) on or before April 6th. On March 15th, Mary wrote to the Museum's board of directors, notifying them that, due to huge losses suffered speculating on Ecuadorian pygmy shrimp futures, she would be unable to make the $950,000 payment due by April 6th, and "canceling" her entire pledge of $4,750,000. Museum officials, finding their project now under-funded by $4,500,000, want to know their legal options.

238. Leaving aside for the moment whether the Museum might have other claims against Mary, which of the following statements is clearly *untrue*?

   (A) The Museum offered naming rights to the first person to pledge at least $5,000,000 for the new wing or, lacking any such bid, to the largest single pledge toward the new wing.

   (B) Mary accepted the Museum's offer by making the largest pledge earmarked for the new wing.

   (C) Mary's promise to pay was consideration exchanged for the Museum's promise of naming rights to the first person to pledge at least $5,000,000 for the new wing or, lacking any such bid, to the largest single pledge toward the new wing.

   (D) Mary's agreement with the Museum satisfies any relevant statute of frauds.

Callie painted Dionne's house, after which Dionne promised to pay Callie $500 for the materials and labor Callie expended. Dionne did not pay.

239. Does Callie have a viable equitable claim against Dionne?

   (A) Yes, based on promissory estoppel.

   (B) Yes, based on promissory restitution.

   (C) Yes, based on unjust enrichment.

   (D) No.

Suppose that, as she began to paint Dionne's house, Callie noticed smoke coming from the attached garage. Callie climbed down her ladder, ran to her truck, grabbed her fire extinguisher and her cell phone, found the garage entry door unlocked, and entered and extinguished the fire.

240. If Dionne promised, after the fact, to pay Callie $500 for Callie's efforts to save Dionne's house from burning down, would Callie have a viable equitable claim against Dionne if Dionne failed to pay as promised?

ANSWER:

On March 1, 2003, Whit and Suzy Sample placed a "For Sale" sign in the front yard of the house in Paradise that they bought two years earlier from its builder, Thomas Homes. The very same day, the Burgers, who were on a house hunting trip from Tennessee where they were then living, saw the "For Sale" sign and offered the Samples $150,000 for the house, which the Samples accepted. No realtor represented either party. The Burgers and the Samples sat down in the living room and prepared a contract by copying paragraphs from a standard-form real estate contract that Suzy borrowed from the local library, making certain changes and additions agreed to by both the Samples and the Burgers.

The contract that the Burgers and the Samples signed contains the following language:

1. Hamilton ("Ham") and Patty Burger (collectively "Buyers") agree to purchase from Whitman ("Whit") and Suzy Sample (collectively "Sellers"), and Sellers agree to sell to Buyers, all right and title to Sellers' house and real property located at 425 Mesquite Lane, Paradise City, Paradise, for the purchase price of $150,000, to be paid by Buyers to Sellers on May 31, 2003 (the "closing date"), at which time Sellers will convey to Buyers an unencumbered deed and clear title to said house and real property.

2. Sellers further agree that Buyers may occupy said house up to one month prior to the closing date, in which event Buyers will pay Sellers on the closing date, in addition to the aforementioned purchase price, a rental fee of $1,500 for the month or $50 per day, if Buyers do not occupy the house prior to May 15th.

3. Buyers agree to pay Sellers on the execution of this contract a nonrefundable deposit of $5,000, which will be credited against the amount due from Buyers on the closing date, provided that Buyers pay the balance of the purchase price and any other amounts due on said closing date.

. . . .

8. Sellers agree to transfer the following personal property to Buyers along with the house: (1) all window treatments; (2) all appliances, including the oven, stove, refrigerator/freezer, and dishwasher; (3) the furniture in the upstairs game room; and (4) all lawn and patio furniture.

. . . .

16. Sellers make no warranty, other than those required by law, about the condition of the house. Buyers agree to assume responsibility for any defects not discovered by Buyers prior to the closing date. Sellers agree to make the house available for one or more inspection(s), arranged and paid for by Buyers, prior to the closing date.

. . . .

20. This contract constitutes the entire agreement between the Buyers and the Sellers with respect to the purchase and sale of the aforementioned house and related real and personal property, and the parties hereby agree that any prior drafts of, or discussions relating to, this contract will have no legal effect.

Notwithstanding paragraph 20, the Burgers claim the Samples agreed to make the Burgers' obligation to complete the purchase conditional on Ham's mother selling her house in Tennessee. (His mother was then to move into Ham and Patty's old home and assume the mortgage payments on it.) When asked, the Samples say they never agreed to such a condition.

When the Burgers moved into the house on May 1st, Patty noticed that the Samples had taken the eight exterior solar window screens that Whit had told Patty he had custom-made for the house, as well as the washer and dryer that Suzy told Patty were only a few months old. The next day, the Burgers learned from one of their new neighbors that the owners of the house at 429 Mesquite Lane (two houses north of the Burgers' new home) puts on an enormous Christmas light display that paralyzes traffic for one square mile for more than a month. The light from the millions of lights in the display turns night into day and makes sleeping very difficult. The display and the complaints of the neighbors have been reported in the local newspaper more than once.

On May 4th, three days after they moved into the house, Patty noticed some cracking in the ceilings of two of the downstairs rooms. These cracks were barely visible, but the Burgers were concerned that the ceiling cracks were evidence of foundation problems. Ham had a structural engineer friend look at the cracks. The friend told Ham that the foundation of the house might need repair because the cracks suggested that it was not correctly built. When asked, the Samples truthfully said that they had never noticed the ceiling cracks.

241. Which of the following facts, if true, should entitle the Burgers to rescind their contract with the Samples?

(A) Ham's mother has been unable to sell her house in Tennessee; therefore, a condition precedent to the contract has failed.

(B) The ceiling cracks evidence a breach of the implied warranty of habitability, the implied warranty of workmanlike performance, or both.

(C) The Samples breached the contract when they removed the solar window screens and the washer and dryer from the house.

(D) The Samples failed to disclose their neighbor's holiday lights festival and its effects on those living in nearby houses, including the house the uninformed Burgers agreed to purchase from the uninformative Samples.

On February 15, 2002, Wallace Williams and Bruce Roberts entered into a written contract whereby Wallace, a professional entertainer, agreed to perform at Bruce's resort hotel in the Berkshires for the week of July 1-7, 2002 and Bruce agreed to pay Wallace $25,000 for performing. In early May, Wallace had a hit single that, virtually overnight, made him a star who could command at least $75,000 for a one-week engagement. On June 1st, Wallace telephoned Bruce demanding $75,000 for his July 1-7 performances. Bruce told Wallace that "a deal is a deal" and would not agree to pay Wallace more than $25,000.

242. In light of Bruce's unwillingness to renegotiate the contract, would Wallace have been justified in refusing to perform?

ANSWER:

Suppose that, after Bruce told Wallace that "a deal is a deal," Wallace told Bruce: "Then find yourself another act, Laddie, because I don't sing for $25,000 anymore." Bruce called his booking agent and located a replacement act, Gem, who agreed to perform at Bruce's hotel July 1-7 for $35,000. On July 1st, Wallace appeared at Bruce's hotel to perform. Upon being told that Bruce had booked a replacement act, Wallace called his lawyer and instructed him to sue.

243. Who anticipatorily repudiated the contract between Wallace and Bruce?

(A) Bruce, when he refused to discuss paying Wallace more than the agreed price.

(B) Wallace, when he told Bruce he would not perform as scheduled for the agreed price.

(C) Bruce, when he booked Gem to replace Wallace, without trying to convince Wallace to perform as promised.

(D) Bruce, when he refused to allow Wallace to perform on July 1st as agreed.

Suppose, instead, after initially refusing to renegotiate, Bruce relented when Wallace said he would not appear unless Bruce agreed to pay him more. After several discussions, including a lengthy face-to-face discussion the morning of June 8th, Bruce dictated a new contract to his secretary, in the exact words of the first contract and running for the same period with Wallace's compensation changed from $25,000 to $50,000. Wallace and Bruce signed the new contract and tore up the old one. Thereafter, Wallace performed as agreed, but Bruce refused to pay Wallace more than $25,000.

244. Did Bruce breach his contract with Wallace by refusing to pay Wallace more than $25,000?

ANSWER:

Jenny Beasley wants to sue her former employer, Owl's Nest, for breaching its promise to award a new Mitsubishi to the winner of a March 2003 sales contest. Jenny claims that her manager,

Jason Boone, told her and the other waitresses at the Paradise Road Owl's Nest that whoever sold the most margaritas at each participating Owl's Nest location during March 2003 would have her name entered in a drawing, and that the winner of the drawing would receive a new Mitsubishi. As the contest progressed, Jason told the waitresses that he did not know whether the winner would receive a Mitsubishi car, truck, or SUV, but that the winner would have to pay any registration fees on the vehicle. On or about April 8th, Jason informed Jenny that she had sold more margaritas during March than any other waitress at the Paradise Road Owl's Nest, and that he had submitted her name for the drawing. Two weeks later, Jason informed Jenny that she had won the drawing. He proceeded to blindfold her and lead her to the parking lot outside the restaurant. Waiting for her there was not a Mitsubishi car, truck, or SUV, however, but a plastic model of a Mitsubishi Zero, a World War II Japanese fighter airplane. Jason was laughing. Jenny was not.

Owl's Nest pays its waitresses $5.00 per hour for each hour they work, and allows them to keep 75% of their tips. The restaurant keeps the other 25%. Waitresses are scheduled to work between 35 and 40 hours per week. They can work extra shifts when another waitress wants or needs time off, but are not allowed to work more than 50 hours per week. In the three months prior to March 2003, Jenny worked an average of 40 hours per week, and earned an average of $1,600 per month in tips ($1,200 of which she kept). During March 2003, Jenny worked an average of 50 hours per week, and earned $2,000 in tips ($1,500 of which she kept). In order to work the extra hours during March, Jenny had to pay a babysitter $7.00 per hour to stay with her daughter, Evelyn.

Owl's Nest waitresses are at-will employees, who work without written employment contracts. The company's policy manual requires any employee to give two weeks notice prior to terminating her employment, and requires Owl's Nest to give any employee two weeks notice prior to terminating her employment, unless Owl's Nest is terminating the employee for cause. Every employee receives a copy of the policy manual when she is hired. Jenny received a copy of the policy manual when she began working at Owl's Nest in January 2002.

Assume for purposes of the following questions that Jason acted with apparent, if not actual, authority; therefore, his words and actions are attributable to Owl's Nest.

245. Can Owl's Nest successfully defend Jenny's breach of contract claim by arguing that Jason's promise of "a new Mitsubishi" was too ambiguous to obligate Owl's Nest to give Jenny the keys to a new Mitsubishi car, truck, or van?

　　(A)　Yes, because Mitsubishi is one of the world's largest manufacturing concerns, which makes hundreds, if not thousands, of different products.

　　(B)　No, because Jason's subsequent statements that the winner "would receive a Mitsubishi car, truck, or SUV," and that "the winner would have to pay any registration fees on the vehicle" sufficiently clarified that Jason meant a Mitsubishi car, truck, or SUV.

　　(C)　Yes, because the parol evidence rule will bar any attempt by Jenny to present evidence regarding Jason's subsequent statements.

(D)   No, because the parol evidence rule does not bar the admission of evidence regarding statements made after the parties entered into their agreement.

246.   Assuming Jenny has a viable breach of contract claim against Owl's Nest, which of the following remedies available to Jenny would provide her the greatest relief if she prevailed?

(A)   Expectation damages.

(B)   Reliance damages.

(C)   Restitutionary damages.

(D)   Specific performance.

During a morning broadcast on May 1, 2002, Chicago disc jockey Ben Boulder announced that his station, KOOK, would provide backstage passes and concert tickets for the May 4th Ozzy Lavigne concert to the first 20 people who presented themselves at KOOK's booth outside the concert venue with a temporary "KOOK Rock" tattoo on their forehead. He further said that KOOK would pay $30,000 a year for five years to anyone who got the station's logo permanently tattooed on his or her forehead and then notified KOOK. Loyal KOOK listeners Lloyd Christmas and Harry Dunne heard Boulder's show, almost immediately called the radio station to confirm that the promotion was legitimate, then drove to the station later that morning to talk to station officials in person for further confirmation. Station management assured them both over the phone and in person that it was a legitimate promotion. On the morning of May 2, Lloyd and Harry went to The Skorpion's Sting tattoo parlor and had the "KOOK Rock" logo tattooed on their foreheads. They then drove together to the station, where KOOK personnel took photos of their new tattoos and posted them to the station's web site (http://www.kookrock.net) under the heading "And The Winners Are:" Assume that Boulder was an authorized agent of KOOK, and therefore KOOK is liable for anything Boulder said or did during any of his shows broadcast by KOOK.

247.   Leaving aside for the moment whether Harry and Lloyd might have other claims against KOOK, which of the following statements is clearly untrue?

(A)   KOOK made a valid offer to pay $30,000 per year for five years to anyone who would have the station's logo permanently tattooed to his or her forehead.

(B)   Lloyd and Harry accepted KOOK's offer by getting the station's logo permanently tattooed to their forehead and then notifying the station of their acceptance-by-performance.

(C)   KOOK's promise to pay them $30,000 per year for five years for having the station's logo permanently tattooed to their foreheads was consideration for Lloyd and Harry having the station's logo permanently tattooed to their forehead; and having the station's logo permanently tattooed to their forehead and the attendant publicity it generated for KOOK was consideration for KOOK's promise to pay Lloyd and Harry $30,000 per year each for five years.

(D)   Harry's and Lloyd's agreements with KOOK satisfied the relevant statute of frauds.

248.   Would Lloyd and Harry have viable promissory estoppel claims against KOOK?
ANSWER:

Returning to the facts of Question 247, assume that KOOK failed to pay either Lloyd or Harry any of the $150,000 each thought they had coming to them, and that both men were fired from their jobs on May 3rd for "looking ridiculous."

At the time he was fired, Lloyd worked as a local sales agent for a medical supply company, earning $48,000 per year, plus expenses. After being unable to find work for six months, Lloyd paid a local cosmetic surgeon $6,000 to have the tattoo removed and the appearance of his forehead restored. Shortly thereafter, Lloyd was rehired by his former employer (who had told its customers on Lloyd's route that he was on medical leave) at the same salary and with the same benefits as before. However, his employer refused to reimburse him for the cost of the cosmetic surgery or any unpaid salary.

At the time he was fired, Harry was earning $500 per week as an orderly at a local nursing home. Harry lacked the financial resources to have cosmetic surgery to remove the tattoo, and has been unable to find work — other than a few odd jobs like those he occasionally did during his spare time when he worked at the nursing home. Furthermore, Harry became so upset over what a foolish thing he had done and how badly the radio station had treated him that he tried to hang himself, after which his housemates decided to help him out by beating him with a baseball bat, breaking several bones and causing him other serious physical injuries, until police intervened. Harry incurred $10,000 worth of (uninsured) medical expenses as a result of his injury, for which he is suing his housemates. However, because his housemates were just scraping by before they were arrested, and have lost their jobs while in jail awaiting trial on both criminal and civil charges, Harry figures he is unlikely to get any money out of them, and their renter's insurance did not cover intentional assault or battery or attempted suicide.

249.   Which of the following remedies is unavailable to Harry and Lloyd, assuming they can prove a promissory estoppel claim against KOOK?

(A)   Expectation damages.

(B)   Reliance damages.

(C)   Restitutionary damages.

(D)   Specific performance.

Monica agreed on May 1, 2003 to deliver to Chandler's warehouse, on or before July 1st, 10 crates of rare Moroccan kumquats. Chandler agreed to pay Monica $100 per crate within seven days after receipt, and sent Monica a written confirmation to that effect, satisfying UCC § 2-201(2). Monica delivered the kumquats on July 1st, and Chandler accepted them. However, Chandler wrongfully refused to make payment within seven days. Meanwhile, the bottom fell out of the kumquat market. The market price on May 1st, when Monica and Chandler made their contract, was $90 per crate. The market price on July 1st, when Monica delivered her kumquats to Chandler, was $40 per crate. The market price on July 8th, when Chandler refused to pay as promised, was $30 per crate. As the market began to rebound, Monica, in a good faith effort to limit her losses, located a third party who bought the kumquats on July 15th for $50 per crate (a $25 per crate loss to Monica, who had paid her Moroccan supplier $75 per crate).

250. What measure of damages available to Monica should result in the greatest award of damages against Chandler if Monica prevailed?

   (A) Contract-resale differential damages under UCC § 2-706.

   (B) Contract-market differential damages under UCC § 2-708(1).

   (C) Lost profits under UCC § 2-708(2).

   (D) Action for price under UCC § 2-709.

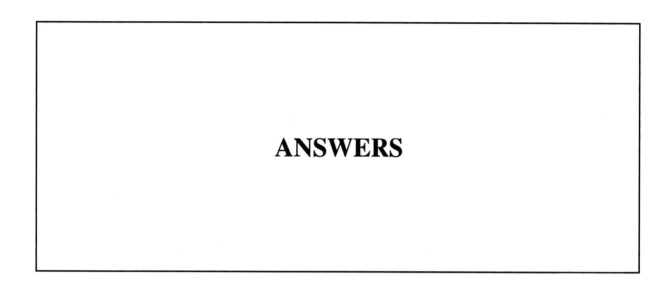

ANSWERS

1. **Answer (B) is correct**. Absent a contrary agreement between the parties, UCC Article 2 governs the transaction between ATG and JJ, because the juniper saplings were goods when ATG and JJ entered into the contract.

    While it is true that common law generally governs contracts involving real property, UCC § 2-105(1) defines "goods" to include "growing crops and other identified things attached to realty as described in the section on goods to be severed from realty (Section 2-107)." UCC § 2-107(2), in turn, provides that "[a] contract for the sale apart from the land of growing crops or other things attached to realty and capable of severance without material harm thereto . . . or of timber to be cut is a contract for the sale of goods within [Article 2]." Therefore, even if the saplings were growing on real property, Article 2 would govern this sale. If the saplings were growing in movable planters, then we would not even need to look at UCC § 2-107 to decide that the saplings were goods. Either way, **Answer (D) is incorrect**.

    Two of the most common mistakes students make concerning the scope of Article 2 are believing that Article 2 applies only to goods for which the contract price is $500 or more (or $5,000 or more, if applying Revised Article 2) and believing that Article 2 applies only to merchants. Both beliefs are unfounded. Article 2 applies to *all* contracts for the sale of goods, regardless of their price. *See* UCC § 2-102. The $500 (or $5,000) threshold only dictates which contracts for the sale of goods require some writing in order to satisfy the statute of frauds. *See* UCC § 2-201. Therefore, **Answer (C) is incorrect**.

    Article 2 applies different, and typically less forgiving, standards for the behavior of merchants, as compared to non-merchants, *see* UCC § 2-104 cmt. 2 and sections cited therein, but Article 2 applies to *all* contracts for the sale of goods, regardless of whether the contracting parties are merchants or non-merchants, *see* UCC § 2-104 cmt. 1. Therefore, **Answer (A) is incorrect**.

    Revised Article 2 does not materially change current UCC §§ 2-102, 2-104, 2-105, or 2-107.

2. **Answer (D) is the best answer**. UETA, where enacted, applies to "electronic records and electronic signatures relating to a transaction" governed, *inter alia*, by UCC Article 2. UETA § 3(a) & (b)(2). Both Iowa and Colorado have enacted UETA (and, in any event, the Question instructed you to assume they had). However, UETA applies only to transactions "between parties each of which has agreed to conduct transactions by electronic means." UETA § 5(b). UETA defines "electronic" to mean "relating to technology having electrical, digital, magnetic, wireless, optical, electromagnetic, or similar capabilities." UETA § 2(5). Here, JJ has clearly consented to transact by

electronic means by faxing its acceptance to ATG. Whether ATG consented to transact electronically by placing its order via telephone is a bit trickier. On the one hand, a telephone seems to fit within UETA's definition of "electronic." *See id.* On the other hand, a telephone call, unlike e-mail or a fax, does not leave behind an "electronic record," as UETA defines that term, *see* UETA § 2(7) & (13), unless some kind of recording is made of the call, *see* UETA § 2 cmt. 6. If no such recording is made, then no "electronic record" exists, and a court may well find that ATG has not consented to transact electronically. Without ATG's consent, UETA does not apply. Therefore, **Answer (C) is not the best answer**.

Answer (A) is incorrect because UETA, by its terms, applies to contracts governed by Article 2. *See supra.* **Answer (B) is incorrect** because, despite the fact that it is a federal statute, E-SIGN explicitly yields to UETA. *See* 15 U.S.C. § 7002(a)(1).

3. **Answer (C) is the best answer.** The mere fact that Cindy was purchasing goods as part of the contract is not, in and of itself, sufficient to invoke Article 2, provided that the contract also involved the purchase of non-goods. Thus, **Answer (A) is incorrect**.

The fact that the goods Cindy was purchasing would become sufficiently attached to real property to become "fixtures" does not keep them from being treated as goods for purposes of deciding whether Article 2 governs the transaction. *See* UCC § 2-105(1) (defining "goods" based on their function "at the time of identification to the contract for sale"). Thus, **Answer (D) is incorrect**.

The choice between Answer (B) and Answer (C) boils down to whether the contract was for the sale of goods or for services. Courts faced with this issue have recognized two distinct tests. The "majority" rule is the "predominant purpose" test, which asks whether the plaintiff's predominant purpose in entering into the transaction as a whole was to purchase or sell goods or services. If the plaintiff's predominant purpose was to purchase or sell goods, then Article 2 applies to the whole transaction (including the service part of it); if the plaintiff's predominant purpose was to purchase or sell services, then Article 2 does not apply to any part of the transaction (not even the goods). *See, e.g., Advent Systems v. Unisys*, 925 F.2d 670 (3d Cir. 1991); *Coakley & Williams v. Shatterproof Glass*, 778 F.2d 196 (4th Cir. 1985); *In re Trailer & Plumbing Supplies*, 578 A.2d 343 (N.H. 1990). The "minority" rule is the "gravamen of the action" test, which focuses on what part of the transaction gave rise to the plaintiff's claim. If the plaintiff's claim arose from the goods component of the transaction, then Article 2 would apply to the complaint, even if the predominant purpose of the transaction was to sell or buy services. If the plaintiff's claim arose from the service component of the transaction, then Article 2 would not apply, even if the predominant purpose of the transaction was to sell or buy goods. *See, e.g., Anthony Pools v. Sheehan*, 455 A.2d 434 (Md. 1983).

It appears that Cindy's predominant purpose in this transaction (as evidenced by the fact that 80% of the total contract price, including the landscaping plan fee, was for labor and other services) was to purchase ATG's landscaping services. While the relative cost of the goods and services is not outcome-determinative, Cindy probably could have purchased a similar gazebo at a local home improvement store and installed it herself or paid someone else to do so, whereas she specifically sought out ATG's landscaping expertise to design and execute a landscaping plan for her backyard. Assuming that Iowa courts follow the majority rule and apply the predominant purpose test (Iowa's appellate courts do not appear to have chosen between the two, although the Eighth Circuit has applied the predominant purpose test to claims governed by Minnesota and Missouri law, *see AKA Distributing Co. v. Whirlpool Corp.*, 137 F.3d 1083 (8th Cir. 1998), and *Vess Beverages, Inc. v. Paddington Corp.*, 886 F.2d 208 (8th Cir. 1989), respectively), if Cindy's predominant purpose was to purchase ATG's services, then Article 2 would not apply to the transaction, despite the fact that ATG's services included installing a number of goods (including the gazebo). Therefore, **Answer (C) is better than Answer (B)**.

4. **Answer (D) is the best answer**. If Iowa courts apply the "gravamen of the action" test (discussed in the answer to Question 3), Article 2 might appear to govern the transaction because the gazebo was a tangible, movable object "at the time of [its] identification to the contract for sale." UCC § 2-105(1). However, a careful reading of Question 4 reveals that the issue is not the gazebo itself, but the quality of ATG's workmanship in *installing* it. (Imagine that Cindy had contracted with Vincent to paint her house. Obviously, painting Cindy's house requires paint, and paint is a good. Paint, however, does not apply itself. So, painting Cindy's house also requires the services of one or more painter(s) — here, Vincent. Assuming that Vincent both purchased the paint and painted the house, if the gravamen of Cindy's complaint was the quality of the paint, the complaint would be governed by Article 2; if the gravamen of Cindy's complaint was the quality of Vincent's painting, the complaint would be governed by common law.) Because installation is a service, and the gravamen of Cindy's action is ATG's performance of that service, her dispute with ATG over its installation of the gazebo would be governed by common law — even if the predominant purpose of the entire transaction was the purchase of goods.

Answers (A) and (C) are incorrect because the gravamen of the action test only addresses what law governs an action brought on a contract, not what law governs the entire contract. **Answer (B) is incorrect** not because it overstates the scope of the gravamen of the action test, but because it misstates the gravamen of Cindy's action.

5. **Answer (B) is the best answer**. Now, the gravamen of Cindy's complaint is goods, not services. If Iowa courts apply the gravamen of the action test, and the problem with the gazebo is that the wood ATG used to build it was inferior, then Article 2 would govern Cindy's complaint, and **Answers (C) and (D) are incorrect** because they conclude that common law applies. **Answer (A) is incorrect** because it overstates the scope of the gravamen of the action test (see the answer to Question 4).

6. **Answer (C) is the best answer**. Absent a contrary agreement between the parties, the CISG governs ATG's contract with McKenzie for the trees because they were goods sold by a Canadian seller to a U.S. buyer, both Canada and the U.S. have ratified or

otherwise adopted the CISG, and ATG did not buy the trees for its own personal, family, or household use.

Article 1(1)(a) provides that the CISG applies to contracts for the sale of goods between parties whose places of business are in different countries, *each* of which has ratified or otherwise adopted the CISG (called "Contracting States"). Unless the parties agree otherwise, the CISG will not govern a contract if one party's place of business is in a Contracting State and the other party's place of business is in a different country that is not a Contracting State. Therefore, **Answer (A) is incomplete**. The U.S. and Canada are different countries, both of which are signatories to the CISG. Therefore, this transaction *could* be governed by the CISG. However, despite the fact that both the U.S. and Canada are Contracting States, certain contracts for the sale of goods between parties whose places of business are in different Contracting States are not governed by the CISG. Therefore, **Answer (B) is also incomplete**. Articles 1(2), 2, 3(2), and 6 set forth several exceptions to the general rule of Article 1(1)(a). The two relevant exceptions in this case are Article 1(2), which provides that the CISG does not govern international sales of goods when "[t]he fact that the parties have their places of business in different States . . . does not appear either from the contract or from any dealings between, or information disclosed by, the parties at any time before or at the conclusion of the contract," and Article 2(a), which states that the CISG does not apply to international sales of goods for "personal, family or household use." Here, ATG knew it was dealing with a Canadian seller and McKenzie knew it was dealing with a U.S. buyer. Therefore, Article 1(2) does not apply, and **Answer (D) is incorrect**. As for Article 2(a), while RBA may well have intended to give the trees it was purchasing from ATG to its clients and staff for their personal, family, or household use, RBA was not buying the trees for its personal, family or household use. And, more to the point, ATG — the party who had the contract with McKenzie — was not buying the trees for *its* personal, family or household use. Consequently, Answer (C) is the best answer.

7. **Answer (A) is the best answer** for the same reasons given in the answer to Question 6.

Article 3(2) provides that the CISG "does not apply to contracts in which the preponderant part of the obligations of the party who furnishes the goods consists in the supply of labour or other services." One might think that this exception would exclude the custom-made, blown-glass, hand-painted Christmas ornaments from the scope of the CISG. However, Article 3(1) prefaces the Article 3(2) exception by stating: "Contracts for the supply of goods to be manufactured or produced are to be considered sales unless the party who orders the goods undertakes to supply a substantial part of the materials necessary for such manufacture or production." Reading the two provisions together, had ATG purchased the ornaments from another source, and then sent them to McKenzie to have RBA's logo hand-painted onto each ornament, the contract would fall outside the scope of the CISG. However, the mere fact that McKenzie was selling custom-made — rather than "ready-made" — goods is not enough to take a contract that is otherwise within the scope of the CISG outside its scope. *See* Secretariat's Commentary on the Draft Convention on Contracts for the International Sale of Goods, March 14, 1979, U.N. Doc. A/CONF.97/5, art. 3 cmt. 4, *available at* http://www.cisg.law.pace.edu/cisg/text/ secomm/secomm-03.html. This is consistent with the position taken by UCC § 2-105(1), which includes "specially-manufactured goods" in the definition of "goods" for purposes of, *inter alia*, determining Article 2's scope. Therefore, **Answer (D) is incorrect**.

Answer (C) is incorrect because, as discussed in the answer to Question 3, Article 2 does not govern contracts for which the predominant purpose is the purchase of services.

Answer (B) is incorrect because the CISG makes no provision (nor does Article 2, for that matter) for looking beyond the purpose of the actual purchaser to the purpose of the actual purchaser's customers — be they known or unknown.

8. **Answer (D) is the best answer**. Absent a contrary agreement between the parties, ATG's contract with Rita will be governed by common law because ATG's contract with Rita was for Rita's personal services. While it is true that Rita, if successful, was to arrange for ATG to purchase real property from the owner of the lot in question, Rita was not selling the real property to ATG. Therefore, **Answer (C) is incorrect**.

Article 2 has nothing to do with ATG's agreement with Rita, nor will it have anything to do with ATG's purchase of the real property, if consummated. Article 2 does not apply to contracts for the purchase of real property. Nor could Rita or ATG be merchants, as Article 2 uses that term, in real property, because Article 2 defines a "merchant" only with respect to goods. *See* UCC § 2-104(1). Besides, as discussed in the answer to Question 1, Article 2 applies or not because goods are involved, not because one or both parties to the transaction are merchants. Therefore, **Answers (A) and (B) are incorrect**.

9. This contract for the purchase of real property is governed by common law or by jurisdiction-specific statutory law governing real property transfers. In any event, it is outside the scope of Article 2.

10. It should not. While the personal property situated on the realty might be goods, *see* UCC §§ 2-105(1) & 2-107, ATG's predominant purpose was to purchase the real property, not the personal property. Common law, or jurisdiction-specific statutory law governing real property transfers, should govern this contract, rather than Article 2.

11. **Answer (B) is the best answer**. Article 2 should govern ATG's contract with BRU because the buildings were goods when ATG and BRU contracted for ATG's purchase and BRU's sale, delivery, and installation of the buildings. *See* UCC § 2-105(1).

The buildings clearly are "movable" personal property — otherwise BRU would not be able to prefabricate them or keep them in stock and then deliver them to the location designated by ATG. Therefore, **Answer (A) is incorrect**. The fact that the buildings will become improvements to real property after they are installed does not affect their status as goods "at the time of identification to the contract for sale." Therefore (as was the case with the gazebo in the answer to Question 3), **Answer (C) is incorrect**.

Answer (D) is tempting because there would certainly be considerable labor and other services involved in fabricating, delivering, and installing the buildings. Avoid this particular temptation. First, the text of the Question describes the buildings as prefabricated; therefore BRU will be selling pre-manufactured (or "ready-made") goods. Second, recall that Article 2 defines "goods" to include specially-manufactured goods. UCC § 2-105(1). Therefore, even if BRU was fabricating the buildings for ATG, that fact would not keep the buildings from being goods. Third, while a reasonable person might consider the delivery and installation of the prefabricated buildings to be the predominant purpose of ATG's contract with BRU, because Answer (D) includes an untrue statement, an intelligent law student (which you obviously are, or you would not have had the good sense to consult — and, hopefully, purchase — this study guide) should never consider an answer containing an untrue statement to be a correct answer. Therefore, **Answer (D) is incorrect**.

12.   **Answer (B) is correct**. UCC Article 2A governs any non-sale transaction, regardless of form, that transfers the rights to possess and use goods for a period of time in return for consideration. *See* UCC §§ 2A-102 & 2A-103(1)(j). Article 2A defines "goods" in much the same way as Article 2. *See* UCC § 2A-103(1)(h). As such, the bulldozer is a good. Because all four possible answers assume that the bulldozer is a good, that revelation does not get us any closer to a solution.

For the same reasons discussed in the answer to Question 1, neither the merchant status of one or both parties nor the amount of the lease payments dictate whether the contract is governed by Article 2A. Article 2A applies to all contracts for the lease of goods, regardless of the amount of the lease payments. The $1,000 (or $10,000, under Revised Article 2A) threshold only dictates which contracts for the lease of goods require some writing in order to satisfy the applicable statute of frauds. UCC § 2A-201. Therefore, **Answer (C) is incorrect**. While merchant status may subject a party to a different, and typically less forgiving, standard for the behavior, as compared to non-merchants, *see, e.g.*, UCC §§ 2A-205, 2A-212 & 2A-511, Article 2A applies to all contracts for the lease of goods, regardless of whether the contracting parties are merchants or non-merchants. Therefore, **Answer (A) is incorrect**.

The tricky question with leases typically revolves around whether the lease agreement is a "true lease" or a "disguised sale." To answer that question, one must often delve into the bowels of the most vexing provision in the UCC: Section 1-201(37). The good news is that the agreement in this Question is sufficiently straightforward that we need not dwell on the vagaries of UCC § 1-201(37). Because ATG may terminate the lease at any time without penalty (other than the "unearned" remainder of one week's rent payment if ATG returns the bulldozer before the end of the week) and because ATG's right to renew the lease is not for little or no additional consideration, this lease is a "true lease." Therefore, **Answer (B) is correct** and **Answer (D) is incorrect**.

Revised § 1-203 replaces current UCC § 1-201(37). Alas, Revised § 1-203 improves only the structure of current UCC § 1-201(37), leaving its content essentially unchanged.

13. No. This is a case in the classic mold of *Raffles v. Wichelhaus*, 159 Eng. Rep. 375 (Ex. 1864) (per curiam). As in *Raffles*, there was never any "meeting of the minds" between Russell and Gwyneth; therefore, under classical contract theory, no contract was ever formed. Applying the more modern test of R2 § 201, "[w]here the parties have attached different meanings to a promise or agreement or a term thereof, . . . neither party is bound by the meaning attached by the other, even though the result may be a failure of mutual assent." R2 § 201(2)-(3). Absent mutual assent, there is no contract for Gwyneth to enforce against Russell or vice versa. R2 § 17(1).

14. **Answer (D) is the best answer.** Owl's Nest will argue that Jason was joking when he made the "offer"; therefore, he did not intend to form a contract. An offer made in jest might prevent a sincere acceptance from forming a binding contract. An acceptance made in jest might not form a binding contract when made in response to a sincere offer. An ostensible offer *and* acceptance, both made in jest, almost certainly will not form a binding contract, even though a reasonable, disinterested third party might understand the parties' words or actions to form a binding contract. *See, e.g., McClurg v. Terry*, 21 N.J. Eq. 225 (N.J. Ch. 1870). On the other hand, an ostensible offer *or* acceptance, made in jest without the other party's knowledge, almost certainly will form a binding contract, *see, e.g., Lucy v. Zehmer*, 84 S.E.2d 516 (Va. 1954), unless a reasonable, disinterested third party *would* understand the party's words or actions to be in jest, *see, e.g., Leonard v. Pepsico, Inc.*, 88 F. Supp. 2d 116 (S.D.N.Y. 1999), *aff'd*, 210 F.3d 88 (2d Cir. 2000). *See generally You Asked For It, You Got It . . . Toy Yoda: Practical Jokes, Prizes, and Contract Law*, 3 Nev. L.J. 526 (2003). Thus, for this argument to relieve Owl's Nest of liability, either (1) Jenny must have also thought Jason was not serious, *see, e.g., Keller v. Holderman*, 11 Mich. 248 (1863), or (2) a reasonable person in Jenny's position would have had to think that Jason was not serious, *see, e.g., Theiss v. Weiss*, 31 A. 63 (Pa. 1895). Employers hold sales contests all the time, often offering lavish prizes that far exceed the value of the winner's performance (but not, if the employer is savvy, the value of all the contestants' collective performance). *See, e.g., Mears v. Nationwide Mutual Insurance Co.*, 91 F.3d 1118 (8th Cir. 1996) (offering his and her Mercedes to the claims representative who submitted the winning "theme" for an upcoming convention). The facts do not suggest that either Jenny or a disinterested third party would have thought that Jason did not intend to make an offer. Therefore, **Answers (A) and (C) are incorrect.**

Owl's Nest will also argue that Jason's statement about the contest was not an offer, with respect to the Mitsubishi, because Jenny was unable to conclude a contract for the Mitsubishi by her assent. All she could accomplish by her assent was to make herself eligible for the drawing. However, just because the offer is conditional (*e.g.,*

I will pay you $500 *if* you win the race) does not prevent it from being an offer. The fact that winning the Mitsubishi required the occurrence of two conditions — Jenny winning the sales contest at her restaurant and then winning the drawing — should not make Jason's offer any less enforceable than if all Jenny had to do was win the contest. Therefore, **Answer (B) is incorrect.**

Jason offered Jenny the chance at a prize if she sold the most margaritas during the contest. R2 § 24. None of the foregoing excuses for why Owl's Nest should not be bound hold water. Consequently, **Answer (D) is the best answer.**

15.   **Answer (D) is the best answer.** Jason did not need notice of Jenny's acceptance of his offer. He was the on-site Owl's Nest manager. He knew or should have known the hours the waitresses were working and the sales and tips they were reporting. (For once, Uncle Sam may have gotten his "fair share" of the waitress' tip income.) Moreover, he did not invite the waitresses to accept his offer by promising to perform or performing — only their performance would suffice. Therefore, this contract did not trigger the notice requirement of R2 § 54, making **Answer (A) incorrect.** Because Jason sought performance rather than a promise, **Answer (B) is incorrect,** as well.

Jason offered Jenny the chance at a prize if she sold the most margaritas during the contest. R2 § 24. Jenny accepted the offer by (1) continuing to work at Owl's Nest for the duration of the contest, despite being free to leave at any time with two weeks notice, and (2) working more hours, selling more margaritas, and earning more tip income for Owl's Nest than she typically did in the average month prior to the contest period. R2 § 30. **Answer (C) tells half the story,** but **Answer (D) is the best answer.**

16.   **Answer (B) is the best answer** because Neumann failed to accept Smith's offer by calling during the live broadcast.

An offer is the "manifestation of willingness to enter into a bargain, so made as to justify another person in understanding that his assent to that bargain is invited and will conclude it." R2 § 24. Smith's statement on *Mary Prince Live!* that he would pay $100,000 to anyone who called the show and cited any section of the Internal Revenue Code "that says an individual is required to file a tax return" constituted a valid offer. See *Carlill v. Carbolic Smoke Ball Co.,* [1893] 1 Q.B. 256 (C.A. 1892), and the discussion of reward cases in *Leonard v. Pepsico, Inc.,* 88 F. Supp. 2d 116 (S.D.N.Y. 1999), *aff'd,* 210 F.3d 88 (2d Cir. 2000). *See generally* Rowley, *supra,* at 548-52. If anyone had called the show and cited the Code sections that Neumann produced, a contract would have been formed and Smith would have been obligated to pay the $100,000 reward, for his bluff would have been properly called. Therefore, **Answer (A) is incorrect.** Nothing in the facts indicates that Smith reserved the right to refuse to pay even if a caller cited Code provisions that disproved his position. Therefore, **Answer (C) is incorrect.** Likewise, nothing in the facts indicates that the terms of Smith's challenge or the manner in which he made it belied his sincerity to the point that a reasonable person could not believe he was in earnest. Therefore, **Answer (D) is incorrect.**

Neumann, however, did not see the *Mary Prince Live!* program upon which Smith appeared. Neumann saw the *DMM Wakeup News* rebroadcast of Smith's *Mary Prince Live!* appearance. Smith was not available and the *DMM Wakeup News* was not prepared to take telephone calls about Smith's offer during the rebroadcast. An offeror is the master of his offer, and Smith clearly limited his offer in such a way that it would remain open only until the conclusion of the live *Mary Prince Live!* broadcast. Moreover, even if a reasonable person in Neumann's position could have misunderstood the nature of the rebroadcast and assumed that the offer was still "alive" at the time of the rebroadcast, Neumann did not call the show to accept. Rather, she wrote to the show. So, even if Smith had not clearly limited the time for accepting his offer, Neumann failed to accept in the manner dictated. Therefore, no contract was formed unless Smith elected to honor Neumann's invalid acceptance — something Smith clearly did not do — making **Answer (B) the best answer**.

17. Sandra's June 30th fax certainly appears to have been an offer (as defined in the answer to Question 16). Sandra was not merely advertising the land's availability for sale; she solicited Bosworth's purchase of the land. Her fax used the word "offer" three times. Although that is not dispositive, it is indicative of her intent and of Bosworth's understanding. Sandra also indicated that she was only offering the land to Bosworth for a stated time (whether, in fact, she was or not), further reinforcing the conclusion that Sandra's fax was an offer to sell 100 acres of undeveloped land for $1,000 per acre and that Bosworth could have concluded the agreement by accepting the offer.

18. **Answer (D) is the best answer**. As a general rule, an offeror may revoke her offer at any time prior to the offeree's acceptance, notwithstanding seemingly contrary language in the offer. R2 §§ 36(1)(c), 42 & 43. Therefore, **Answer (A) is incorrect**. Two exceptions to the general rule are binding options (*see* R2 § 87(1)(a)) and statutory firm offers (*see* UCC § 2-205 and R2 § 87(1)(b)). Sandra's offer was neither a binding option nor a statutory firm offer. The firm offer rule applies only to offers by merchants to buy or sell *goods*. Land is not a good, so the firm offer rule does not apply. Therefore, **Answer (B) is incorrect**. Sandra might have created an option in favor of Bosworth. But, because the option was not supported by separate consideration, Sandra was free to ignore the option and sell to a third party, R2 § 87(1)(a) — subject to the risk that Bosworth had already accepted without Sandra's knowledge. Therefore, **Answer (C) is incorrect**, leaving Answer (D) as the best answer.

19. Yes. The "mirror image rule" requires a purported acceptance to contain precisely the same terms as the offer — no more, no less. R2 § 58. The common law considers a purported acceptance not satisfying the "mirror image rule" to be a counteroffer. R2 § 59. The object, quantity, and price terms of Bosworth's e-mail mirrored those of Sandra's fax. The only term missing from his e-mail related to the time within which Bosworth was required to accept, but he accepted within the time allotted. As such, the e-mail satisfied the "mirror image rule," and was an acceptance per R2 § 50(1).

20. Probably not. Unless the terms of the offer stated otherwise, Sandra's offer was personal and terminated on either Sandra's or Bosworth's death or incapacity. R2 §§ 36(1)(d)

& 48; *see, e.g., Heideman v. Northwestern National Life Insurance Co.*, 546 N.W.2d 760 (Minn. Ct. App. 1996). On the other hand, if Bosworth had died after timely and validly accepting Sandra's offer, Rochester could insist that Sandra perform the contract that was formed before Bosworth died. *See, e.g., In re Beier*, 137 A.2d 617 (N.J. Super Ct. Ch. Div. 1958).

21. **Answer (D) is correct.** As a general rule, an offeree may accept an offer by any reasonable means. However, if an offer prescribes the time, place, or manner of acceptance, the offeree must strictly comply with those requirements to create a contract. R2 § 60. On the other hand, if the offer merely *suggests* a particular time, place, or manner of acceptance, the offeree is not precluded from accepting in a different time, place, or manner. *Id.* Here, Sandra's offer did not merely suggest that Bosworth accept in writing, it required that Bosworth accept in writing. Therefore, **Answer (C) is incorrect**.

Is an e-mail "written"? The *Restatement* does not tell us. By analogy, the UCC defines "writing" to include "printing, typewriting or any other intentional reduction to tangible form." UCC § 1-201(46). (*Revised § 1-201(43) adopts current UCC § 1-201(46)'s definition for both "writing" and "written."*) The UCC does not say "means," it says "includes." Therefore, this is a non-exclusive list. A growing number of jurisdictions have recognized e-mailed "documents" as satisfying the "writing" requirement of the statute of frauds. *See, e.g., Cloud Corp. v. Hasbro, Inc.*, 314 F.3d 289 (7th Cir. 2002); *Roger Edwards, LLC v. Fiddes & Son, Ltd.*, 245 F. Supp. 2d 251 (D. Me. 2003). In those jurisdictions, anyway, we could make a strong argument that e-mail is also a "writing" for purposes of accepting an offer "in writing." Fortunately, Sandra and Bosworth each consented — Sandra by sending her offer in the form of a fax, and Bosworth by responding with an e-mail — to transact electronically. As such, this transaction falls within the scope of UETA. UETA § 5(b) (UETA "applies only to transactions between parties each of which has agreed to conduct transactions by electronic means"). UETA § 7(a) provides that an electronic writing or signature may not be denied legal effect or enforceability. UETA § 7(c) provides that "[i]f a law requires a record to be in writing, an electronic record satisfies the law." R2 § 60 requires Bosworth to have accepted Sandra's offer in writing. UETA § 7 (with apologies to Jean-Luc Picard) makes it so. Therefore, **Answer (D) is correct** and **Answer (B) is incorrect**.

Answer (A) is incorrect. As explained in the answer to Question 19, the mirror image rule requires that the terms of Bosworth's acceptance mirror those in Sandra's offer. The mirror image rule says nothing about the manner in which Bosworth may or must make his acceptance.

22. **Answer (D) is the best answer.** As explained in the answer to Question 18, because Sandra's offer was neither a firm offer nor a binding option, she was free to revoke it at any time before Bosworth accepted it. Therefore, **Answer (B) is not the best answer.** A revocation is effective upon receipt by the offeree. R2 § 42. An offeree receives a written revocation when it (1) comes into the offeree's possession, (2) comes

into the possession of an agent the offeree authorized to receive it, or (3) is deposited in some place which the offeree has authorized as the place where such communications should be deposited. R2 § 68; *see also* UETA § 15(b)(1) ("Unless otherwise agreed between a sender and the recipient, an electronic record is received when . . . it enters an information processing system that the recipient has designated or uses for the purpose of receiving electronic records or information of the type sent and from which the recipient is able to retrieve the electronic record; and (2) it is in a form capable of being processed by that system."). Because the facts of this Question do not indicate that Sandra sent, much less that Bosworth received, a revocation prior to Bosworth's acceptance, we can assume that Bosworth accepted Sandra's offer before she terminated his power to accept by revoking the offer. Moreover, because an acceptance given "by telephone or other medium of substantially instantaneous two-way communication" is treated as if it was given face-to-face, we can assume that Sandra received Bosworth's 1:00 p.m. e-mailed acceptance prior to Sandra's 5:00 p.m. deadline. R2 § 64; *see also* UETA § 15(a) ("Unless otherwise agreed between the sender and the recipient, an electronic record is sent when it: (1) is addressed properly or otherwise directed properly to an information processing system that the recipient has designated or uses for the purpose of receiving electronic records or information of the type sent and from which the recipient is able to retrieve the electronic record; (2) is in a form capable of being processed by that system; and (3) enters an information processing system outside the control of the sender or of a person that sent the electronic record on behalf of the sender or enters a region of the information processing system designated or used by the recipient which is under the control of the recipient."). Therefore, **Answer (D) is the best answer**.

Because Sandra's offer stated that it would expire on its own terms unless she *received* Bosworth's written acceptance prior to 5:00 p.m. on Thursday, July 3rd, the mere fact that Bosworth sent his acceptance to Sandra before the deadline — even if she had not revoked the offer prior to that time — was insufficient to accept Sandra's offer. Therefore, **Answers (A) and (C) are incorrect**.

23. **Answer (D) is the best answer**. As explained in the answer to Question 18, Sandra was free to revoke her offer to Bosworth at any time prior to Bosworth's acceptance. The "mailbox rule" provides Bosworth's acceptance was effective once he dispatched it properly. R2 §§ 63(a) & 66. Sandra's revocation, on the other hand, was only effective when Bosworth received it. R2 § 42; see also UETA § 15(b). (See the answer to Question 22 for further discussion of these Restatement and UETA provisions.) Here, Bosworth e-mailed his acceptance to Sandra at 1:00 p.m. on July 3rd. Bosworth sent the e-mail to the address indicated on Sandra's letterhead. Bosworth's message was received by Sandra's inbox within seconds of when he sent it. Sandra did not e-mail her revocation to Bosworth until two hours later. He received it shortly thereafter. Bosworth accepted before Sandra revoked. Sandra's requirement that she receive Bosworth's acceptance by 5:00 p.m. on July 3rd does not affect the working of the mailbox rule as long as Sandra did, in fact, receive Bosworth's acceptance by the deadline — which she did. While either Answer (C) or Answer (D) is acceptable,

Answer (D) is the best answer because it correctly ties the effectiveness of Sandra's revocation to Bosworth receiving it, rather than Sandra sending it. By the same token, **Answer (C) is not the best answer** because it incorrectly ties the effectiveness of Sandra's revocation to Sandra sending it, rather than Bosworth receiving it.

Answer (B) is not the best answer because, while true, it is incomplete. Regardless of when Bosworth sent his acceptance, if Sandra did not receive it by 5:00 p.m. (PST) on July 3rd, her offer would have expired by its own terms, and she would not have needed to revoke it in order to terminate Bosworth's power to accept.

Answer (A) is incorrect. As explained in the answer to Question 22, because Sandra's offer required that she *receive* Bosworth's written acceptance prior to 5:00 p.m. on Thursday, July 3rd, or the offer would expire on its own terms, the mere fact that Bosworth sent his acceptance to Sandra before the deadline — even if she had not revoked her offer prior to that time — is insufficient to accept Sandra's offer.

24. Sandra's revocation should have been effective. As explained in the answer to Question 18, Sandra was free to revoke her offer to Bosworth at any time prior to Bosworth's acceptance. A revocation is effective when, *inter alia*, the offeror deposits it in some place that the offeree has authorized as a place to deposit such communications. R2 §§ 42 & 68; *see also* UETA § 15(b) (quoted in the answer to Question 22). So, if Bosworth's office is an authorized place to receive this type of correspondence, Bosworth may be deemed to have "received" Sandra's revocation as soon as the fax was "deposited" at his office — probably within seconds of when Sandra sent it by fax at 12:00 p.m. on July 3rd. Given that Bosworth received Sandra's initial offer by fax at his office, and that he did not tell Sandra to direct future correspondence elsewhere, there is no reason to believe that Bosworth's office was not an authorized place to receive Sandra's fax. Because Bosworth received Sandra's revocation before he dispatched his acceptance (albeit from a different location) at 1:00 p.m. the same day, Sandra's revocation would have terminated Bosworth's power to accept.

25. **Answer (D) is correct**. The "mailbox rule" provides that an acceptance is generally effective once the offeree dispatches it, R2 § 63(a), provided that he dispatches it properly, R2 § 66. However, if the offer contains an acceptance deadline, the offeree's failure to accept before or by that deadline terminates the offeree's power to accept; otherwise, an offer terminates if the offeree does not accept it within a "reasonable" period of time. R2 §§ 36(1)(b) & 41(1). While an acceptance given "by telephone or other medium of substantially instantaneous two-way communication" is generally treated as if it was given face-to-face for purposes of the mailbox rule, R2 § 64; *see also* UETA § 15(a) (both discussed in the answer to Question 22), because Sandra's offer specified that she had to *receive* Bosworth's written acceptance by 5:00 p.m. on July 3rd, and because she did not receive it until after that time, Bosworth's acceptance was legally ineffective. Sandra could have elected to honor Bosworth's late acceptance, R2 § 70, but she was not obligated to do so. Therefore, **Answer (D) is correct**, and **Answers (B) and (C) are incorrect**.

Answer (A) is incorrect because it ties the effectiveness of Bosworth's acceptance to his sending it, rather than Sandra receiving it — which runs afoul of the clear language of Sandra's offer requiring that she receive Bosworth's acceptance by the stated deadline.

26.   **Answer (C) is the best answer**. Because Sandra and Bosworth had each consented to transact electronically, *see* UETA § 5(b), Sandra "received" Bosworth's acceptance when Bosworth properly dispatched it via e-mail — and, therefore, before the offer expired by its own terms. UETA § 15(b); *see also* R2 § 64. UETA § 15(b)(1) deems an electronic record "received when it enters an information processing system that the recipient has designated or uses for the purpose of receiving electronic records or information of the type sent and from which the recipient is able to retrieve the electronic record." Therefore, **Answer (A) is incorrect**. And, because Sandra consented to transact electronically, she accepted UETA's rules of offer and acceptance, including the risk that she would be deemed to have received a communication from Bosworth that she had not physically received. Therefore, **Answer (B) is incorrect. Answer (D) is not the best answer** because, while true, it ignores the possibility that Sandra could simply have allowed her offer to expire by its own terms. If she did not receive Bosworth's acceptance prior to 5:00 p.m. on July 3rd, it would not matter when thereafter she received it — unless *she* chose to treat it as an acceptance despite the fact that her offer had already expired.

27.   **Answer (C) is the best answer**. The key issue here is the timeliness of Bosworth's July 3rd acceptance. As a general rule, an acceptance is effective once the offeree properly dispatches it, R2 §§ 63(a) & 66, while an offeree's rejection is only effective when the offeror receives it, R2 § 40. The mere fact that Bosworth had dispatched a rejection did not terminate his power to accept. Therefore, **Answer (A) is incorrect**.

However, having dispatched a rejection before dispatching his acceptance, Bosworth's later-dispatched acceptance would only be effective if Sandra *received* it prior to receiving the rejection; otherwise, the earlier-dispatched rejection terminated Bosworth's power to accept, and the later-dispatched acceptance was either a counteroffer or Bosworth's offer for a new contract on the same terms. R2 § 40. Therefore, **Answer (D) is incorrect**. Here, Bosworth mailed Sandra a rejection on July 1st. Bosworth then e-mailed Sandra an acceptance on July 3rd. Sandra received Bosworth's e-mail acceptance almost instantaneously. *See* R2 § 64 & UETA § 15(a) (both discussed in the answer to Question 22). So, Sandra received the acceptance at or about 1:00 p.m. on July 3rd, and the earlier-dispatched rejection at 4:00 p.m. on July 3rd. Bosworth's acceptance took precedence over his rejection because Sandra received Bosworth's acceptance before she received his rejection. (If Sandra had effectively revoked the offer before she received Bosworth's acceptance, the acceptance would not revive the properly revoked offer, even if the revocation occurred after Bosworth dispatched his acceptance, as long as his rejection or counteroffer pre-dated his acceptance.) Therefore, **Answer (C) is the best answer**; whereas, **Answer (B) is correct, but incomplete**.

28.   **Answer (C) is the best answer.** As with Question 27, the key issue here is whether Bosworth's July 3rd acceptance "trumped" his July 1st counteroffer. As is true for a rejection, while an offeree who makes a counteroffer forfeits the power to accept the original offer unless the offeror or offeree clearly manifests a contrary intent, R2 §§ 36(1)(a) & 39, a counteroffer is only effective when the offeror receives it, R2 § 40. As is also true for a rejection, once an offeree dispatches a counteroffer, a later-dispatched acceptance will be effective only if the offeror *receives* the later-dispatched acceptance before receiving the earlier-dispatched counteroffer. R2 § 40. Therefore, for precisely the same reasons given in the answer to Question 27 (substituting the word "counteroffer" for "rejection"), Answer (C) is the best answer; **Answer (B) is correct, but incomplete**; and "**Answers (A) and (D) are incorrect**"

29.   Probably not. Sandra's fax appears to be merely an invitation to offer, which Sandra made to 30 persons including Bosworth. This is not exactly a newspaper ad or a "For Sale" sign, as Sandra did not make her invitation to the public at large. On the other hand, it is neither a "reward" offer, *see, e.g., Carlill v. Carbolic Smoke Ball Co.*, [1893] 1 Q.B. 256 (C.A. 1892), nor a "first come, first served" offer, *see, e.g., Lefkowitz v. Great Minneapolis Surplus Store, Inc.*, 86 N.W.2d 689 (Minn. 1957). A court will most likely deem Bosworth's June 30th fax to be an offer to purchase 100 of the 500 acres advertised at the price stated in Sandra's fax. Because Sandra has yet to accept Bosworth's offer, no contract has been formed. On the other hand, if a court were to find that Sandra's fax was an offer, then — provided that Sandra had not already received other acceptances exhausting her 500 acres — Bosworth accepted that offer, forming an enforceable contract as discussed above.

30.   **Answer (D) is the best answer.** Because Bosworth and Sandra are residents of different countries both of which are parties to the CISG, the Corvettes are goods whether they are purchased for use or for resale, and Sandra and Bosworth must have both been aware from the information contained in Sandra's fax and on the cover sheet that Sandra was sending the fax from her U.S. place of business to Bosworth's Canadian place of business, this transaction appears to be governed by the CISG. *See* CISG arts. 1(1)(a) & 1(2). Whether that appearance proves true or false depends on whether Bosworth was purchasing one or more of the Corvettes for personal, family, or household use, which would take the transaction — at least with respect to any cars bought for Bosworth's personal, family, or household use — outside the scope of the CISG, unless Sandra neither knew nor should have known that Bosworth would so use the cars. *See* CISG art. 2(a). Notice how the exception is phrased: the CISG does not apply to sales of goods for personal, family, or household use, unless the seller had no reason to know that the buyer was purchasing the goods for personal, family, or household use. *See* Secretariat's Commentary on the Draft Convention on Contracts for the International Sale of Goods, March 14, 1979, U.N. Doc. A/CONF.97/5, art. 2 cmt. 2 (commenting that a dealer's purchase of a single automobile for resale would be within the scope of the CISG, provided that the CISG otherwise applies), *available at* http://www.cisg.law.pace.edu/ cisg/text/secomm/secomm-02.html. So, if Sandra did not know or have reason to know at any time prior to, or at the conclusion of, the

transaction that vintage automobile dealer Bosworth was purchasing one or more vintage Corvettes for personal, family, or household use, rather than for resale, the transaction would be governed by the CISG, making the UCC's and the common law's treatment of Sandra's fax irrelevant unless the CISG defers or defaults to Article 2 or to common law. *See Filanto, S.p.A. v. Chilewich International Corp.*, 789 F. Supp. 1229 (S.D.N.Y. 1992) (holding that the CISG "trumps" Article 2 in cases where the CISG applies), *appeal dismissed*, 984 F.2d 58 (2d Cir. 1993).

Article 14(1) of the CISG states: "A proposal for concluding a contract addressed to one or more specific persons constitutes an offer if it . . . indicates the intention of the offeror to be bound in case of acceptance [and] . . . indicates the goods and expressly or implicitly fixes or makes provision for determining the quantity and the price." Sandra addressed her fax to 30 specific persons, including Bosworth. Her fax indicated her intention to sell the cars to the first five or fewer recipients willing to meet her terms, including the stated sales price. Her fax also set an upper limit on quantity — five — and provided that she would sell the cars first-come, first-served. So, at any point in time after receiving the fax, Bosworth could have found out how many cars Sandra was offering by finding out how many of the five she had already sold. Therefore, Sandra's fax should be considered an offer under CISG art. 14(1), making Answer (D) the best answer and **Answer (C) incorrect**.

Because the CISG does not explicitly defer to domestic law on this issue, nor does it default to domestic law by not addressing whether Sandra's fax is an offer, **Answer (A) and Answer (B) are irrelevant** under the facts given.

31. **Answer (D) is the best answer**. As previously discussed, the common law "mirror image rule" requires that a purported acceptance contain precisely the same terms as the offer — no more, no less. R2 § 58. The common law considers a purported acceptance not satisfying the "mirror image rule" to be a counteroffer. R2 § 59. This contract, however, is for the sale of goods. Therefore, it is governed by UCC Article 2, which rejects the common law "mirror image rule." Under UCC § 2-207(1) a contract is formed, even though the acceptance contains additional or different terms, if the offeree definitely expresses its intent to accept the offer and does not expressly condition its acceptance on the offeror's assent to the additional or different terms. Here, Tubular surely intended to accept Mercury's offer, despite tacking onto its acceptance what was likely "boilerplate" language. Thus, Tubular's acknowledgment was an acceptance, not a counteroffer.

Mercury's purchase order constituted an offer. Tubular's acknowledgment was an acceptance, despite the additional terms, because it was not made expressly conditional on Mercury's agreement to the additional terms. Therefore, **Answer (A) is incorrect**.

While Article 2 permits an acceptance to contain additional terms without transforming it into a counteroffer, if Tubular expressly conditioned its acceptance of Mercury's offer on Mercury's assent to the additional terms, then Tubular's acknowledgment would be a counteroffer. UCC § 2-207(1). Here, there was no language in Tubular's acknowledgment expressly conditioning its acceptance on Mercury's assent to the additional terms. Therefore, Tubular's acknowledgment was an acceptance, not a counteroffer, making Answer (D) the best answer and **Answer (C) incorrect**.

Section 2-207 further provides that, had Tubular expressly conditioned its acceptance on Mercury's assent to the additional terms, making Tubular's acknowledgment a counteroffer, Tubular and Mercury could still have formed a contract by their actions — here, Tubular by shipping and Mercury by receiving and paying for the goods. UCC § 2-207(3). However, UCC § 2-207(3) only applies if the parties did not form a contract by their exchange of correspondence. Because Tubular's acknowledgment was an acceptance despite its additional terms, the parties *did* form a contract by their exchange of correspondence, taking UCC § 2-207(3) out of play. Therefore, **Answer (B) is incorrect**.

Revised Article 2 moves current UCC § 2-207(1) to Revised § 2-206(3), leaving it essentially unchanged for the purposes of this Question, but eliminating the "expressly conditioned" language hinted at in the prior paragraph, and explored more fully in the answer to Question 33.

32. **Answer (D) is the best answer** for the reasons given in the answer to Question 31. Because Article 2 rejects the common law "mirror image rule," **Answer (A) is incorrect**. Because conflicting terms in an acceptance of an offer to buy or sell goods will not transform it into a counteroffer, unless the offeree expressly conditions its acceptance on the offeror's assent to the conflicting terms, **Answer (B) is incorrect**. Here, there was no language in Tubular's acknowledgment expressly conditioning its acceptance on Mercury's assent to the additional terms. Therefore, Tubular's acknowledgment was an acceptance, not a counteroffer, making Answer (D) the best answer and **Answer (C) incorrect**.

33. **Answer (C) is the best answer**. Tubular's acknowledgment disclaimed all implied warranties. Tubular's acknowledgment also expressly conditioned its acceptance on Mercury's assent to Tubular's new terms. As a consequence, Tubular's acknowledgment was a counteroffer. UCC § 2-207(1). However, as discussed in the answer to Question 31, the mere fact that Tubular's acknowledgment was a counteroffer did not put it out of the parties' power to form a contract. Therefore, **Answer (A) is incorrect**. Mercury and Tubular may have formed a contract by their actions, rather than their correspondence. UCC § 2-207(3). Tubular shipped the tubing without having received either an assent or objection from Mercury, and Mercury took delivery of and paid for the tubing, despite being aware of Tubular's warranty disclaimer. These actions are "[c]onduct by both parties which recognizes the existence of a contract . . . although the writings of the parties do not otherwise establish a contract." UCC § 2-207(3). Therefore, the parties did form a contract — not because Mercury accepted Tubular's additional terms, rather because Mercury took delivery of and paid for Tubular's goods.

As we will explore more thoroughly in *Topic 7: Terms of the Agreement*, the contract so formed will be made up of the terms on which the parties' writings agreed, plus any UCC "gap fillers" needed to perform or enforce the contract. The additional terms contained in Tubular's acknowledgment do not become part of the contract. Therefore, **Answers (B) and (D) are incorrect**.

Revised Article 2 no longer deems "expressly conditioned" acceptances to be counteroffers; however, given that Revised § 2-207 dictates the same scheme for determining a contract's terms whether the contract is formed by written offer and acceptance, by performance, or by oral agreement followed by a written confirmation, it is not clear that eliminating the "counteroffer" distinction has any significance. We will have to await the Official Comments to Revised Article 2, which have not been finalized as of this writing, to see whether the drafters intend otherwise. Revised § 2-207 continues to recognize that contracts may be formed by performance, and retains the current UCC § 2-207(3) scheme for discerning the terms of contracts formed by performance (as well as, it seems, the terms of all other contracts). See Revised § 2-207.

34. **Answer (D) is the best answer** because, unlike UCC § 2-207, the CISG *does* apply the "last shot rule," binding the party who indicates its assent by performance to the terms of the last writing exchanged prior to that performance — here, binding Mercury to the terms of PG's acknowledgment, because Mercury accepted and paid for the goods without objecting to the terms of PG's counteroffer.

Under the CISG, a contract would have formed, even though PG's acknowledgment contained additional or different terms, if (1) the additional or different terms did not materially alter the terms of Mercury's offer and (2) Mercury did not object in writing to any discrepancy between the terms of the purchase order and the acknowledgment. CISG art. 19(2). Therefore, **Answer (A) is not the best answer** because it assumes that the CISG applies the "mirror image rule," which it does not.

If the additional or different terms in PG's acknowledgment materially altered the terms of Mercury's offer, or if Mercury timely and properly objected to the discrepancy, then the CISG would deem PG's acknowledgment to be a rejection and counteroffer. *See* CISG art. 19(1). Therefore, **Answer (C) is not the best answer** because it mistakenly assumes that the CISG treats a counteroffer containing materially different terms as an acceptance if the offeror (Mercury) fails to object to those terms.

PG's C.O.D. payment term and warranty disclaimer each appear to have materially altered Mercury's offer. *See* CISG art. 19(3) ("Additional or different terms relating . . . to . . . payment . . . [or the] extent of one party's liability to the other . . . are considered to alter the terms of the offer materially."). Therefore, under CISG art. 19, unlike UCC § 2-207(1), the parties did not form a contract based on their writings. However, because the CISG deems PG's acknowledgment to be a counteroffer, Mercury could form a contract by accepting the goods delivered pursuant to that counteroffer. CISG art. 18(1). Therefore, **Answer (B) is not the best answer** because it mistakenly assumes that the CISG will not find a contract formed by conduct in the absence of writings whose terms conform to one another.

35. **Answer (D) is the best answer**. The first issue this Question raises is whether Bobbie offered Pablo a unilateral or a bilateral contract. A unilateral contract is one in which one party makes a promise in exchange for specified performance by the other. A bilateral contract is one in which each party makes a promise in exchange for a promise made by the other. The facts do not indicate that Bobbie sought Pablo's promise to do the work; rather, the facts indicate that Bobbie sought Pablo's performance. Therefore, Bobbie offered Pablo a unilateral contract, and **Answer (B) is incorrect**.

So, what is the rule for revoking unilateral contracts? The prevailing view for many years was that a person in Bobbie's position could revoke her offer to Pablo at any time prior to Pablo's acceptance by *complete* performance. This is the classic "Brooklyn Bridge" hypothetical: A offers to pay B some sum of money if B will walk across the Brooklyn Bridge. One step shy of completing the walk, A calls out to B, "I revoke my offer." Because B did not complete the requested performance prior to A's revocation, A and B have no contract. *See* I. Maurice Wormser, *The True Conception of Unilateral Contracts*, 26 YALE L.J. 136, 136-38 (1916). Section 45 of the first *Restatement* changed the common law rule by providing that, unless the terms of the offer manifest the offeror's intent to reserve the right to revoke once the offeree begins to perform, where an offer invites an offeree to accept by rendering a performance and does not invite a promissory acceptance, an option contract arises when the offeree tenders or begins the invited performance or tenders a beginning of it. The *Restatement (Second)* perpetuates this sea change in the law of unilateral contracts. *See* R2 § 45 & cmt. b. Therefore, **Answer (A) is incorrect**.

While it is generally true that an offeree can accept a unilateral contract by merely performing the act requested, if the offeree (1) is given the choice between accepting by promise and accepting by performance, (2) elects to accept by performance, and (3) has reason to know that the offeror has no adequate means of learning of the offeree's performance with reasonable promptness and certainty, then the offeror's obligation will be discharged <u>unless</u> (a) the offeree exercises *reasonable diligence* to notify the offeror of her performance, (b) the offeror *otherwise learns* of the offeree's performance within a reasonable time, or (c) the offer itself indicates that the offeree *need not notify* the offeror. R2 § 54(2)(a)-(c). Here, Pablo did not give notice, despite the fact that he knew that Bobbie was more than a thousand miles away, would have no way of knowing that Pablo had begun the work, and would have no way of knowing that Pablo finished the work until she received his bill or returned to the house the following summer. At first glance, then, it appears that Pablo may have been required to give Bobbie notice under R2 § 54(2). However, nothing in the Question indicates that Bobbie gave Pablo the option of promissory acceptance; therefore, R2 § 54(2) does not apply. Unless Bobbie requested Pablo to notify her when he began work — and there is nothing in the Question to indicate that she did — Pablo was not required to give Bobbie notice in order to accept her offer. R2 § 54(1). Therefore, **Answer (C) is incorrect**.

Lacking a contractual or legal notice requirement, if the performance contemplated by the offer must be done over a period of time, once the offeree begins to substantially perform, the offeror can no longer revoke the offer. R2 § 45(1). Here, Pablo's work on Bobbie's house was obviously going to take several weeks. Therefore, once he began to substantially perform that work, Bobbie lost her right to revoke, making Answer (D) the best answer. In any event, Pablo must *actually begin* to perform. Merely preparing to perform will not be enough to prevent Bobbie from revoking.

36. While she could no longer revoke, Bobbie would not be bound to pay Pablo the $20,000 contract price until Pablo *completed* the requested performance, unless Bobbie caused Pablo's failure to complete the requested performance by prevention, waiver, or repudiation. R2 § 45(2).

37. **Answer (C) is the best answer.** This is a contract for the sale of goods, governed by Article 2. UCC § 2-206(1)(b) provides that "an order or other offer to buy goods for prompt or current shipment shall be construed as inviting acceptance either by a prompt promise to ship or by the prompt or current shipment of conforming goods." ATG ordered 500 juniper saplings for delivery in one month or less. ATG did not specify how Uncle Buck should accept ATG's order. As such, Uncle Buck could accept either by notifying ATG that it would ship the requested saplings or by shipping the requested saplings. Uncle Buck chose the latter.

The only possible hitch for Uncle Buck is UCC § 2-206(2), which states: "Where the beginning of a requested performance is a reasonable mode of acceptance, an offeror who is not notified of acceptance within a reasonable time may treat the offer as having lapsed before acceptance." While 46 days (or 45, if you count like most courts) may seem a long time for Uncle Buck to remain silent, the fact that ATG set June 15th as the delivery deadline suggests that notification of acceptance any time before the deadline would be "within a reasonable time." Moreover, while UCC § 2-206(2) *might* have allowed ATG, after hearing nothing from Uncle Buck for some period of time, to make other arrangements, effectively revoking its offer to Uncle Buck, the facts do not indicate that ATG did so. Uncle Buck's truck was sitting on ATG's doorstep, so to speak. ATG, not yet having revoked, should not be allowed to do so once the conforming goods await its acceptance. Therefore, **Answer (A) is not the best answer.**

Because ATG made an offer for a unilateral contract, such that Uncle Buck was expected to "accept" the offer by delivering the trees at the stated price, ATG could revoke at any time prior to Uncle Buck's delivery. Like the unfortunate offeree in *Petterson v. Pattberg*, 161 N.E. 428 (N.Y. 1928), whose attempt to accept the offer in that case was thwarted when the offeror met him at the door and revoked the offer before the offeree could open his mouth to say, "I accept," Uncle Buck here would have been susceptible, under pre-*Restatement* common law, to ATG revoking its offer at any time before Uncle Buck delivered the trees. However, as discussed in the answer to Question 35, R2 § 45 now prevents an offeror from revoking once the offeree has begun to perform. Depending on how one defines "delivery," Uncle Buck may have fully performed by arriving at ATG's lot prior to the delivery deadline with the trees on the truck. If so, then ATG could not revoke its offer of a unilateral contract even under pre-*Restatement* law. On the other hand, if the trees had to be unloaded or paid for before "delivery" was complete, then ATG could still revoke under *Petterson*, but not under R2 § 45, because Uncle Buck had clearly begun to perform before ATG attempted to revoke (and ATG knew that Uncle Buck had begun to perform, because Uncle Buck's truck was at ATG's lot awaiting unloading). Therefore, **Answer (B) is incorrect**.

Answer (D) is incorrect because nothing in the language of ATG's offer suggested it was irrevocable. Yes, ATG is a merchant. Yes, ATG made the offer in writing. No, the delivery deadline for Uncle Buck is not a term that "gives assurance that [ATG's offer] will be held open . . . during the time stated or if no time is stated for a reasonable time." UCC § 2-205. ATG's offer to Uncle Buck was not a firm offer.

Revised Article 2 does not change current UCC § 2-205, except to expressly allow for electronic records in lieu of a writing, nor does it change current UCC § 2-206 other than to renumber a modified version of current UCC § 2-207(1) as Revised § 2-206(3).

38.   Chandler's offer to buy additional mangoes at the contract price was not a counteroffer. It was merely an offer to modify the quantity term in the existing contract or to form a new contract on the same terms as the existing one, except for additional mangoes. Unless accepted by Monica, it would not have affected the contract formed by Monica's July 14th letter and Chandler's July 19th fax. There is no evidence that Monica accepted the Chandler's offer to purchase additional mangoes for $6.00 per crate.

39.   **Answer (D) is the best answer**. Now Chandler's contract with Monica rests on the fact that Monica's original offer was a firm offer subject to UCC § 2-205, because (1) Monica is a merchant, (2) she made the offer in writing, and (3) the written offer contained language of non-revocability. Therefore, Monica could not revoke the offer prior to 5:00 p.m. on July 25th. So, even if Chandler had received Monica's revocation before Chandler accepted, Chandler's acceptance would still be effective as long as Monica received the acceptance prior to 5:00 p.m. on July 25th.

Answer (A) is incorrect because, even if Monica's offer was not a firm offer, Answer (A) misstates the common law "mailbox rule," R2 § 63, which is incorporated into Article 2 via UCC § 1-103.

Chandler received Monica's revocation before he sent his acceptance. Under the common law, Chandler's receipt of Monica's revocation before sending his acceptance would have terminated his ability to accept her offer. R2 §§ 35(2) & 36(1)(c). However, this was a contract for the sale of goods, Monica is a merchant dealing in goods of the kind at issue, and she made a written, firm offer. As such, UCC § 2-205 trumps the common law. Therefore, **Answer (B) is not the best answer**.

Answer (C) is correct, but incomplete. Chandler's acceptance was effective, and he sent it to Monica before her July 25th deadline. However, Chandler's acceptance was not effective *because* he sent it to Monica before her July 25th deadline. Had Monica not made a firm offer subject to UCC § 2-205, Chandler's timely acceptance would have been for naught. Monica would have revoked her offer before Chandler accepted it.

40. **Answer (B) is the best answer**. According to the common law "mailbox rule," R2 § 63, which is incorporated into Article 2 via UCC § 1-103, an acceptance is effective as soon as the offeree dispatches it to the offeror, whereas a revocation is only effective when the offeree receives it. Here, Chandler sent his acceptance before he received Monica's revocation; therefore, his acceptance was effective and her revocation was not. **Answer (A) is incorrect** because it misstates the "mailbox rule."

Answer (C) is correct, but incomplete. Chandler's acceptance was effective, and he did send it to Monica before her July 25th deadline. However, Chandler's acceptance was not effective *because* he sent it to Monica before her July 25th deadline. Chandler's acceptance was effective because he sent it to Monica before he received her revocation. Had the chronology been as it was in Question 39, the mere fact that Chandler sent his acceptance before Monica's deadline would not have kept Chandler's acceptance from being nullified by Monica's prior revocation.

Answer (D) is incorrect because, even though Monica's offer contained the same language that made it irrevocable in the answer to Question 39, because Monica is not a merchant in this Question, her offer was not a firm offer under UCC § 2-205.

41. **Answer (D) is the best answer**. Generally speaking, the law does not consider an offeree's mere silence or inaction as constituting an acceptance *that is binding against the offeree. See, e.g., Hansen v. Transworld Wireless TV-Spokane, Inc.*, 44 P.3d 929 (Wash. Ct. App. 2002). However, an offeree's mere silence or inaction may constitute an acceptance if, *inter alia*, "the offeror has stated or given the offeree reason to understand that assent may be manifested by silence or inaction, and the offeree in remaining silent and inactive intends to accept the offer." R2 § 69(1)(b); *see, e.g., Eimco Division, Envirotech Corp. v. United Pacific Insurance Co.*, 710 P.2d 672 (Idaho Ct. App. 1985). Here, Home Video Outlet's letter told Verbal that, in order to cancel his pre-approved subscription, he should return the letter, with the word "CANCEL" written on it, in the enclosed self-addressed, postage-paid envelope. That takes care of the future installments. However, Verbal still has the first tape, for which he may be billed $4.95 despite complying with the cancellation instructions in the letter. So, to avoid liability, Verbal should also return the tape. Therefore, **Answers (B) and (C) are incomplete**.

Answer (A) is incorrect, at least as a matter of contract law. Verbal may live in a jurisdiction that has enacted one or more consumer protection statutes that protect consumers from unsolicited mailings like this. And, as a practical matter, Home Video Outlet is not going to sue him to recover the $4.95, either based on the contract that he may have formed by not returning the tape or on a theory of unjust enrichment. Nonetheless, it is important to see that, in some cases, silence or inaction can be deemed an acceptance. Here, Home Video Outlet's letter told Verbal that, if he wanted to accept their offer, he should do nothing. That is exactly what he did.

42. As a rule, contract law does not consider an offeree's silence to bind the offeree as an acceptance. However, mere silence or inaction may constitute acceptance if "an offeree takes the benefit of offered services with reasonable opportunity to reject them and reason to know they were offered with the expectation of compensation." R2 § 69(1)(a). Because Edie informed Verbal, at the end of the first session, what her fee was for lessons, and because Verbal took the benefit of Edie's services for several weeks, Verbal's actions would have constituted an acceptance of Edie's offer, binding Verbal to pay her fee.

43. **Answer (C) is the best answer.** While Methuselah may have offered the ranch to Noah, and Noah may have accepted it — though the former is certainly questionable — there was no consideration to support any promise Methuselah may have made to Noah.

At pre-*Restatement* common law, consideration was defined as a benefit to the offeror or a detriment to the offeree. *See* R2 § 79 cmt. b. Because Methuselah would not benefit (in this lifetime, at least) from willing the chinchilla ranch to Noah, nor would Noah have to suffer any detriment in order to get the ranch, Methuselah's promise was not supported by consideration and Noah had no contractual right to the ranch under pre-*Restatement* law. The *Restatement (Second)* dispenses with the requirement that, to be consideration, something must be a benefit to the offeror, a detriment to the offeree, or both. *See* R2 § 79(a). Therefore, **Answer (A) is incorrect** both because it relies upon an outdated concept of consideration and because it misstates the concept as requiring a detriment to the offeror, when in fact it required a detriment to the offeree.

The *Restatement* also disavows the pre-*Restatement* views that the consideration must have induced the offeror to make the offer and that the offer must have induced the offeree to give the consideration. *See* R2 § 81. Therefore, **Answer (B) is incorrect**.

The *Restatement* focuses more on process than substance, defining consideration as a return promise or performance *sought by the offeror* in exchange for his or her offer and *given by the offeree* in exchange for (but not necessarily as an inducement for) the offeror's offer. R2 § 71(2). Performance, in turn, may take the form of (1) engaging in some act other than making a promise, including paying money or other value, (2) forbearing from acting in a way that is otherwise legally permissible, or (3) creating, modifying, or destroying a legal relation. *See* R2 § 71(3). Noah neither promised, acted, refrained from acting, created, modified, or destroyed a legal relation, nor paid his grandfather any money in exchange for Methuselah's promise, nor did Methuselah seek any of the foregoing from Noah. Therefore, there was no "bargained for" consideration, and Noah had no contractual right to the ranch under the *Restatement* approach.

While a number of scholars and a handful of contemporary courts have advocated a "moral obligation" theory of enforcing promises that are otherwise unenforceable for lack of consideration, the *Restatement* clearly rejects the idea that a moral obligation to honor one's promises, without more, suffices for, or dispenses with, the need for consideration. *See, e.g., Estate of Graham v. Morrison*, 576 S.E.2d 355 (N.C. Ct. App. 2003). *See generally* Jean Fleming Powers, *Rethinking Moral Obligation as a Basis for Contract Recovery*, 54 ME. L. REV. 1 (2002). Therefore, **Answer (D) is not the best answer.**

44. **Answer (D) is the best answer**. The question is not whether Noah's promise to refrain from drinking and gambling and to avoid speeding tickets for the rest of Methuselah's life would have been valuable consideration *per se*. As discussed in the answer to Question 43, consideration may take the form of a return promise, R2 §§ 71 & 75, provided that what is promised would itself be consideration, *see* R2 § 75. The question is whether Methuselah bargained for Noah's return promise. Methuselah did not ask Noah to promise to refrain from the specified vices for the remainder of Methuselah's life. Methuselah asked Noah to actually refrain from those vices. Noah's promise was not consideration because Methuselah did not seek it in exchange for his promise to will the chinchilla ranch to Noah. *See* R2 § 71(2). Therefore, **Answer (D) is the best answer**, and **Answer (B) is incorrect**.

As discussed in the answer to Question 43, the *Restatement* has replaced the old "benefit-detriment" test with the concept of "bargained for" consideration. Therefore, although they state the old test correctly, unlike their counterpart in Question 43, **Answers (A) and (C) are incorrect**.

45. **Answer (C) is the best answer** because Noah actually refrained from the specified vices for the remainder of Methuselah's life, which *was* what Methuselah bargained for. As discussed in the answer to Question 44, Methuselah did not ask Noah to *promise* to refrain from the specified vices for the remainder of Methuselah's life; Methuselah asked Noah to *actually refrain* from those vices. Noah's promise to do so was not consideration because Methuselah did not seek it in exchange for his promise to will the chinchilla ranch to Noah. *See* R2 § 71(2). Therefore, **Answer (B) is incorrect**.

As discussed in the answer to Question 43, the *Restatement* has replaced the old "benefit-detriment" test with the concept of "bargained for" consideration. Therefore, although they state the old test correctly, unlike their counterpart in Question 43, **Answers (A) and (D) are incorrect**.

46. **Answer (A) is the correct answer**. Unlike Question 44, where Methuselah sought Noah's performance, not his promise, this Question states that Methuselah sought Noah's promise to refrain from the specified vices. Therefore, Methuselah got exactly what he asked for, and Noah's promise was the "bargained for" consideration for Methuselah's promise. R2 §§ 71 & 75.

As discussed in the answer to Question 43, the *Restatement* has replaced the old "benefit-detriment" test with the concept of "bargained for" consideration. Therefore, although they state the old test correctly, unlike their counterpart in Question 43, **Answers (B) and (C) are incorrect**.

As explored more fully in *Topic 4: Formation Defenses*, a minor may, until reaching the age of majority (and typically for some short period thereafter), avoid a contract he or she entered into while a minor. *See* R2 § 14. However, R2 § 78 states that "[t]he fact that a rule of law renders a promise voidable or unenforceable does not prevent it from being consideration." So, Methuselah's estate could not use the fact that Noah could have avoided the contract as an excuse to keep from honoring the contract if it was otherwise enforceable and survived Methuselah's death. Therefore, **Answer (D) is incorrect**.

47. Perhaps. The fact that the promise permitted Methuselah to choose between two possible considerations is okay, as long as each of the choices, standing alone, would be valid consideration. R2 § 77(a). That said, there are two potential stumbling blocks here. First, what is "suitable" housing? If the determination of whether accommodations were "suitable" was left up to Methuselah, his promise to provide Shem's family with "suitable" rent-free housing may have been illusory. *See* R2 § 77 cmt. a. Second, even if the "suitable" term did not make the promise illusory, the provision that Methuselah would house Shem's family "for as long as Shem tends Methuselah's herd" could run afoul of R2 § 76 if the promise to house was deemed to be conditional on Shem's continued service and the court were to find that Methuselah had sufficient control over Shem's continued service as to prevent the condition from occurring. On the other hand, as discussed later in *Topic 8: Terms Implied by Law*, once they formed their contract, Methuselah owed Shem a duty of good faith and fair dealing, *see* R2 § 205, which may have obliged Methuselah to provide Shem and his family, at a minimum, housing that a reasonable, disinterested third party would deem "suitable," and to not act or fail to act in such a way as to affect the occurrence of the condition.

48. Almost certainly. Now both alternatives that Methuselah offers would, standing alone, each be consideration for Shem's promise to tend Methuselah's chinchilla herd for six months. R2 § 77(a). Admittedly, the promise was worded so that it appeared that Methuselah, rather than Shem, would be the one who got to choose between the options. But, as long as either option, standing alone, was sufficient consideration to form a valid contract, and Shem was willing to leave the choice to Methuselah (and accept the risk that Methuselah will choose a different option than Shem), then the fact that Methuselah had the right to choose would not prevent contract formation. Moreover, as discussed in the answer to Question 47, Methuselah owed Shem a duty of good faith and fair dealing, which may have obliged Methuselah to provide Shem and his family with objectively "suitable" housing.

49. **Answer (A) is the correct answer**. Jared sought Methuselah's promise to trade him a breeding pair of chinchillas in exchange for Jared's promise to provide Methuselah the lumber and other materials he needed. Therefore, Methuselah's promise was the consideration that Jared bargained for.

The fact that the chinchillas were worth so much less than the fencing materials is irrelevant if the chinchillas were what Jared wanted. *See* R2 § 79(b) & cmt. c. Therefore, **Answer (B) is incorrect**.

The chinchillas, like the fencing materials, are goods, *see* UCC § 2-105(1); therefore, Article 2 governs this contract, *see* UCC § 2-102. However, Article 2 does not specifically address the issue of consideration. To determine whether Methuselah gave consideration for Jared's promise, we must refer back to common law. *See* UCC §§ 1-103, 1-201(11) & 2-106(1) (*Revised §§ 1-103(b), 1-201(12) & 2-106(1), respectively*).

Because Methuselah's promise was valid consideration at common law, it was also valid consideration for purposes of Article 2. Therefore, **Answer (C) is incorrect**.

The fact that the contract between Methuselah and Jared might have triggered the Article 2 statute of frauds — UCC § 2-201 — would not prevent Methuselah's promise from being consideration to support Jared's promise. (As explored more fully in *Topic 5: Statutes of Frauds*, triggering, but not satisfying, the Article 2 statute of frauds may prevent either Methuselah or Jared from enforcing their contract against the other in the absence of any signed writing evidencing the contract.) Therefore, **Answer (D) is incorrect**.

50.   On the one hand, the fact that Methuselah's promise to provide Jared the chinchillas was conditional would not keep the promise from being consideration — provided that Methuselah did not have the legal right to prevent the condition from occurring. *See* R2 § 76 & cmt. d. On the other hand, Methuselah's imposition of the condition transformed his promise from an acceptance of Jared's offer to a counteroffer, which Jared subsequently accepted. Therefore, Methuselah's conditional promise was consideration for both Jared's promise to provide the lumber and other materials and Jared's promise to not operate a competing chinchilla ranch within 100 miles of Methuselah's ranch.

51.   No. As explained in the answer to Question 49, the fact that one party's promise or performance is significantly more or less valuable (to a disinterested third party) than the other party's promise or performance does not keep the first party's promise or performance from being consideration for the second party's promise or performance, as long as each party bargained for the other party's promise or performance in exchange for their own promise or performance. Methuselah asked Enos to make repairs. Enos agreed to do so, on Methuselah's schedule, provided that Methuselah agreed to pay Enos double his usual hourly rate. Methuselah promised to pay Enos the higher rate in exchange for Enos's making the repairs as soon as Jared delivered the necessary materials to Methuselah's ranch. Therefore, Enos did exactly what Methuselah bargained for, at the price Methuselah bargained for.

52.   **Answer (D) is the correct answer**. Benedict promised to repaint Arnold's car in exchange for Arnold's promise to pay Benedict the $500. Therefore, Arnold's promise is what Benedict bargained for. While that normally would be sufficient to make Arnold's promise consideration, Arnold already owed Benedict a duty to pay him the $500. Arnold's promise to perform an existing legal duty Arnold owed to Benedict was not valid consideration, unless the obligation was doubtful or the amount owed was subject to a good faith dispute. R2 § 73. The facts of this Question deny any such doubt or dispute. Therefore, **Answer (A) is incorrect**. The fact that Arnold had, up to this point, failed to pay Benedict the $500 does not change this. Therefore, **Answer (C) is incorrect**.

Just as Methuselah's promising Jared something worth substantially less than what Jared promised Methuselah in Question 49 did not affect whether Methuselah's promise was adequate consideration for Jared's promise and Methuselah's promise to pay Enos twice the "going rate" for his work in Question 51 did not affect whether Enos's performance was adequate consideration for Methuselah's promise to pay him, the fact that Arnold promised to pay Benedict twice the "going rate" for Benedict's promise to repaint his car does not transform Arnold's legally inadequate consideration into adequate consideration. Therefore, **Answer (B) is incorrect**.

53. **Answer (D) is the correct answer** because Arnold offered Benedict consideration over and above the $500 already owed. Arnold's promise to perform an existing legal duty owed to Benedict would not be valid consideration, as discussed in the answer to Question 52, unless the obligation was doubtful or the amount owed was subject to a good faith dispute. R2 § 73. In this Question, Arnold offered consideration that "differs from what was required by the duty in a way which reflects more than a pretense of a bargain." R2 § 73. If the parties bargained for this consideration, and Benedict was willing to paint Arnold's car for the $750, then a court will not inquire into the adequacy of the consideration. Therefore, **Answer (A) is incorrect**.

The fact that Arnold had, up to this point, failed to pay Benedict the $500 he owed him does not change the analysis. Arnold's offer to pay Benedict $750 to paint his car is or is not adequate consideration standing alone, unless the amount of the prior debt or Arnold's obligation to pay it were the subject of an honest dispute. The facts deny such a dispute. Therefore, **Answer (B) is incorrect**.

For the same reasons discussed in the answer to Question 52, the fact that Arnold promised to pay Benedict three times the "going rate" for Benedict's promise to repaint his car would not transform Arnold's otherwise legally inadequate consideration into adequate consideration. Therefore, **Answer (C) is incorrect**.

54. **Answer (B) is the best answer**. Sandra's promise to sell Bosworth 100 acres of undeveloped land for $1,000 per acre was supported by consideration. Sandra "bargained for" Bosworth's promise to pay because she sought it in exchange for her promise to sell and Bosworth gave it in exchange for Sandra's promise to sell. R2 § 71(1)-(2). Sandra made it clear that she wanted Bosworth's promise to pay $100,000 in exchange for her land and Bosworth made it clear that he was promising to do so. Consideration may take the form of a return promise, if the promised performance would, itself, be consideration. R2 § 75. Because paying $100,000 to Sandra would be consideration to support her promise to sell the acreage, promising to pay Sandra $100,000 would also be consideration to support her promise to sell her acreage. Therefore, Answer (B) is the best answer and **Answer (A) is incorrect**.

Answers (C) and (D) deal with whether Bosworth's e-mail was sufficient to accept Sandra's offer, not with the adequacy of consideration. As discussed in the answers to Questions 21 and 22, Bosworth's e-mail was sufficient to accept Sandra's offer under the facts of this Question. Therefore, **Answers (C) and (D) are incorrect**.

55. **Answer (C) is correct**. Slate's construction work could not serve as consideration for Betty's promise because Slate had completed its work before Betty made her promise.

Past acts do not constitute consideration. *See, e.g., Lantec, Inc. v. Novell, Inc.*, 306 F.3d 1003 (10th Cir. 2002); *Pfeiff v. Kelly*, 623 N.Y.S.2d 965 (N.Y. App. Div. 1995). Therefore, **Answer (B) is incorrect**.

Answer (A) is incorrect because Betty did not assume Bamm Bamm's debt. Instead, she made a new promise to pay Bamm Bamm's debt. If there was consideration to support Betty's new promise, the promise formed a contract. *See* R2 §§ 279-280.

While Betty and Barney's failure to authorize the work might be a successful defense to paying Slate for the work Slate performed, it has nothing to do with whether the improvements are consideration for Betty's subsequent promise to pay Slate the debt that Bamm Bamm incurred. Therefore, **Answer (D) is incorrect**.

56.   Probably so. Stonewall promised to stop pursuing Bamm Bamm for the prior debt; and, in fact, she ceased trying to collect from Bamm Bamm, which at that time she (on Slate's behalf) had a legal right to do. If Betty sought that forbearance when she promised to pay Slate, and if Stonewall forbore because of Betty's promise to pay Slate, then the R2 § 71 test should be satisfied. *See, e.g., Jabour v. Calleja*, 731 So. 2d 792 (Fla. Dist. Ct. App. 1999). Although Betty did not recite that she was giving her promise in order to keep Slate from suing Bamm Bamm for the outstanding debt, Betty's request to "take it easy" on Bamm Bamm indicates that was her motivation. There is, then, a reasonable argument that Betty's promise was supported by Slate's forbearance.

57.   **Answer (D) is the best answer.** Jason sought Jenny's continued employment and hard work in exchange for his promise to enter her name in the drawing if she sold the most margaritas during the contest, and Jenny gave the additional effort (and, perhaps, stayed on at Owl's Nest longer than she would have) in exchange for Jason's promise. R2 § 71(2). Owl's Nest will likely argue that Jenny was already contractually obligated to work as hard as she could while she was on duty. Therefore, she did not give any consideration that was not already due. This argument fails for several reasons.

First, because Jenny was an at-will employee, she could have quit at any time with two weeks notice. Foregoing her right to quit given in exchange for Jason's offer was consideration to support it. *See, e.g., Olsen v. Bondurant & Co.*, 759 P.2d 861 (Colo. Ct. App. 1988). Therefore, **Answer (A) is correct**.

Second, Jenny worked more hours, earning more "tip tax" and sales revenues for Owl's Nest, during the contest period than before the contest period. Her extra effort, not otherwise due, given in exchange for Jason's offer was consideration to support it. *See, e.g., Leone v. Precision Plumbing & Heating of Southern Arizona, Inc.*, 591 P.2d 1002 (Ariz. Ct. App. 1979). Therefore, **Answer (B) is correct**.

Third, Jenny sold more margaritas, again earning more "tip tax" and sales revenues for Owl's Nest, during the contest period than before the contest period. Again, her extra effort, not otherwise due, given in exchange for Jason's offer was consideration to support it. *See, e.g., Holland v. Earl G. Graves Publishing Co.*, 46 F. Supp. 2d 681 (E.D. Mich. 1998). Therefore, **Answer (C) is correct**.

Because Answers (A), (B), and (C) are all true statements, **Answer (D) is the best answer** because it encompasses all three. *See generally* Keith A. Rowley, *You Asked For It, You Got It . . . Toy Yoda: Practical Jokes, Prizes, and Contract Law*, 3 NEV. L.J. 526, 552-55 (2003).

58. **Answer (D) is the best answer.** Valid consideration may be given to a third party. R2 § 71(4). Therefore, **Answer (C) is incorrect**. The issue is whether Jason sought that consideration when he offered Jenny the chance to win the Mitsubishi. As discussed in the answer to Question 57, Jason sought Jenny's continued employment and hard work in exchange for his promise to enter her name in the drawing if she sold the most margaritas during the contest, he did not seek her employment of a babysitter. While the latter may have been a necessary condition to Jenny, it was neither a necessary condition to the Owl's Nest nor, based on the facts stated, a foreseeable one. Therefore, **Answers (A) and (B) are not the best answers**. Jason wanted Jenny to continue working at Owl's Nest and to sell additional margaritas. Circumstances not of Owl's Nest's making dictated that, in order to sell more margaritas, Jenny felt she needed to work additional hours; and, in order to work the additional hours, Jenny had to pay for a babysitter. She may have also burned extra gasoline, if she worked shifts she otherwise would not have. Are those expenses consideration? Probably not.

59. Perhaps. The key to this Question is whether Dawson owed Carol a pre-existing duty to replace the tires on the minivan. If he did, his promise to perform a duty he was already bound to perform is not consideration to bind Carol to her promise to let Dawson take the kids to the game. R2 § 73. If he did not, then his promise to replace the tires on the minivan, coupled with his performance in the form of reimbursing Carol for the price of the new tires and installation, is consideration to bind Carol to her promise to let Dawson take the kids to the game. R2 §§ 71 & 73. Would replacing the tires on the minivan fall within Dawson's pre-existing duty under the divorce decree and property settlement agreement to pay "such other sums as may be required to keep the minivan safely operational?" Perhaps. Would it matter if the tires Carol replaced were in satisfactory condition and would not need to be replaced for safety reasons for many months? Perhaps not. If Dawson had disputed his responsibility to replace the tires before agreeing to do so, this Question might fall under the exception in the second clause of R2 § 73. Dawson did not do so.

60. **Answer (C) is the best answer.** Now Carol clearly asked for more than Dawson was bound by the terms of the divorce decree and settlement agreement to provide. Adding a DVD system could hardly be considered "upkeep" — although, if the minivan already had a DVD systems and the issue was repairing or replacing it, one could argue that would be upkeep. Here, there is no evidence of a pre-existing DVD system. Therefore, **Answer (A) is incorrect**.

While it is true that R2 § 191 deems promises "affecting the right of custody of a minor child" as unenforceable on grounds of public policy "unless . . . consistent with the best interest of the child," the comments to R2 § 191 clearly contemplate something more than permitting the non-custodial parent to take the children to a sporting event on a non-visitation weekend. *See, e.g., Combs v. Sherry-Combs*, 865 P.2d 50 (Wyo. 1993) (citing R2 § 191 as grounds for invalidating a marital settlement agreement provision awarding custody to the parent of the same gender as a particular child). Therefore, **Answer (B) is not the best answer**.

And, while it is true that consideration must generally be bargained for to be valid, and Carol did bargain for Dawson's promise to pay for a new DVD system, she also bargained for Dawson's promise in Question 59 to install new tires. Yet, to the extent that Dawson was already bound to provide the new tires under the facts of Question 59, his promise to do so, though "bargained for" by Carol, was not consideration. Therefore, **Answer (D) is not the best answer**.

61. **Answer (C) is the best answer.** "Void" contracts are unenforceable as a matter of law — that is to say, neither party can say or do anything that will make the contract enforceable. For example, a contract to murder someone is a void contract because it is illegal. Contract law affords no remedy for the breach of such a contract. Contracts entered into by minors are not void, though they may be *voidable* at the minor's option. *See Zelnick v. Adams*, 561 S.E.2d 711 (Va. 2002). Therefore, **Answer (A) is incorrect**.

A "voidable" contract is one that a party may avoid for one of several reasons. *See* R2 § 7. One reason for avoiding a contract is that the party seeking to avoid it was a minor when he entered into the contract. Minors are permitted to enter into any contract an adult can, provided that the contract is not one the law prohibits for minors (*e.g.*, an agreement to purchase cigarettes or alcohol). Subject to certain limitations (three of which are discussed in the next three paragraphs), a minor has the right before or shortly after achieving the age of majority to avoid a contract he entered into as a minor. *See* R2 § 14; *see, e.g.*, *Nicholas v. People*, 973 P.2d 1213 (Colo. 1999). However, a minor may not avoid contracts that fall within one of the exceptions. Therefore, **Answer (B) is not the best answer**.

In order for a minor to avoid a contract, he need only manifest his intention not to be bound by it. The minor may manifest his intent to avoid (or "disaffirm") the contract by words or actions. Generally speaking, a minor may disaffirm a contract at any time during his minority or for a reasonable time after he reaches the age of majority. A minor who fails to timely disaffirm will have constructively affirmed the contract. *See, e.g.*, *Dixon v. American Buildings Co.*, 379 S.E.2d 533 (Ga. Ct. App. 1989). A minor may also reaffirm or ratify a contract he would otherwise be able to avoid. *See, e.g.*, *Fletcher v. Marshall*, 632 N.E.2d 1105 (Ill. Ct. App. 1994). Because disaffirmance may be implicit, as well as explicit, Wallace's insistence on a new agreement, within a week of turning age 18, could be seen as an implicit disaffirmance of the earlier contract. Therefore, **Answer (D) is incorrect**.

A minor who enters into a contract to purchase food, shelter, clothing, medical attention, or other goods or services necessary to maintain his well-being may, technically speaking, avoid the contract, but he will generally be liable for the reasonable value of those goods and services. *See* R2 § 12 cmt. f; *see, e.g.*, *Williams v. Buckler*, 264 S.W.2d 279 (Ky. 1954); *Zelnick v Adams, supra*. Wallace's contract with Bruce was not for food, shelter, clothing, medical attention, or other goods or services necessary to maintain his well-being.

A minor who affirmatively misrepresents his age when he enters into a contract may not be able to avoid the contract, depending on the law of the state whose law governs the contract. Some states permit disaffirmance even if the minor misrepresented his age when entering into the agreement. *See, e.g., Gillis v. Whitley's Discount Auto Sales, Inc.*, 319 S.E.2d 661 (N.C. Ct. App. 1984). Some states prohibit disaffirmance in all cases where the minor misrepresented his age. *See, e.g., Youngblood v. State*, 658 S.W.2d 598 (Tex. Crim. App. 1983). Some states prohibit disaffirmance in cases where the minor has engaged in business as an adult. *See, e.g., Martin v. Stewart Motor Sales*, 73 N.W.2d 1 (Iowa 1955). Some states permit disaffirmance, but subject the minor to tort liability for his misrepresentation. *See, e.g., Kiefer v. Fred Howe Motors, Inc.*, 158 N.W.2d 288 (Wis. 1968). There are no facts in this Question suggesting that Wallace affirmatively misrepresented his age to Bruce.

Because he lacked the capacity to be bound by the February 15th contract at the time, and because the February 15th contract was not for food, clothing, shelter, medical attention, or other goods or services necessary to maintain his well-being, Wallace was entitled, at his discretion, to disaffirm it before or shortly after reaching the age of majority. As long as Wallace did not affirmatively deceive Bruce about his age when they signed the February 15th agreement, Wallace should not be bound by it. Therefore, **Answer (C) is the best answer**.

62.   **Answer (D) is the best answer.** A promisor may avoid a contract, on the ground of duress, if his assent was induced by an *improper threat* that left him with *no reasonable alternative* but to assent. *See, e.g., Totem Marine Tug & Barge, Inc. v. Alyeska Pipeline Service Co.*, 584 P.2d 15 (Alaska 1978). Certain threats are improper *per se*: (1) a threat of crime or tort, including a threat that would itself be a crime or tort; (2) a threat of criminal prosecution; (3) a threat to bring a civil suit in bad faith; or (4) a threat that breaches the duty of good faith and fair dealing owed to the promisor. R2 § 176(1). Other threats are improper when coupled with an exchange on unfair terms, R2 § 176(2), but none of those apply here because Wallace was only seeking to modify the contract to better reflect his current market value. The compensation he sought was not an exchange on unfair terms. Nor would Wallace's threat not to perform unless Bruce agreed to pay him more money fall within any of the categories identified by R2 § 176(1). The only possibility is "a threat that breaches the duty of good faith and fair dealing owed to the victim," but these facts do not fit that claim because Wallace was not demanding more money "without legitimate commercial reason." R2 § 176 cmt. e. Wallace's star was on the rise. He was no more guilty of breaching the duty of good faith and fair dealing than an athlete who demands more money or a trade despite having a contract in place. Therefore, **Answer (A) is incorrect**.

Undue influence involves taking unfair advantage of another's weakness of mind or taking an oppressive and unfair advantage of another's necessity or distress. *See, e.g., Odorizzi v. Bloomfield School District*, 54 Cal. Rptr. 533 (Cal. Dist. Ct. App. 1966). Like duress, undue influence involves coercing a promisor into acting against his free will. Unlike duress, undue influence requires no threat, nor does it require that the party exercising the influence left the promisor with no other reasonable alternative than that sought. *See* R2 § 177. There is no evidence that Wallace attempted to exercise any undue influence over Bruce or that Bruce was susceptible to undue influence. Therefore, **Answer (B) is incorrect**.

Unconscionability can arise where disparate bargaining power between the parties to an agreement (1) deprives the party asserting unconscionability of any meaningful choice as to the terms of the agreement (procedural unconscionability) or (2) results in one or more terms that are so one-sided, under the circumstances existing at the time of the making of the contract, as to be oppressive or manifestly unfair (substantive unconscionability). R2 § 208. Some courts seem willing to find a term unconscionable when only the substantive prong of the test has been satisfied. *See, e.g., Donovan v. RRL Corp.*, 27 P.3d 702 (Cal. 2001). Most courts, however, will require a showing of both procedural and substantive unconscionability. *See, e.g., Williams v. Walker-Thomas Furniture Co.*, 350 F.2d 445 (D.C. Cir. 1965). The facts of this Question do not suggest that Bruce lacked bargaining power. Indeed, even having consented to forming a new contract, Bruce still signed Wallace for considerably less than his going value. Nor are the terms of the deal so unfair as to deprive Bruce of the benefit of his bargain. Therefore, **Answer (C) is incorrect**.

Answers (A), (B), and (C) all being incorrect, Answer (D) is the best answer.

63. **Answer (A) is the best answer**. Unlike in Question 62, now Bruce should be able to shield himself from liability by claiming duress. As explained in the previous answer, R2 § 175 allows Bruce to avoid a contract if his assent was induced by, *inter alia*, a threat of crime or tort, including a threat that would itself be a crime or tort. R2 § 176(1)(a). Brandishing a gun is both a crime and a tort and a threat of a greater crime or tort. The fact that the threat was made by someone other than Wallace does not prevent Bruce from avoiding the contract unless, *inter alia*, Wallace had no reason to know of the threat. Wallace was in the room at the time. So, even if he did not know that the threat would be made, he did know that the threat was made. As such, he should not be able to profit from it by holding Bruce to the contract that Bruce consented to only after the threat.

    Answers (B) and (C) are not the best answers for the same reasons discussed in the answer to Question 62. **Answer (D) is not the best answer** because Answer (A) is correct.

64. **Answer (B) is the best answer**. If Bruce was so drunk as to be legally incapable of forming a contract, then he may be excused from performing the June 8th contract. "Mere mental weakness" is not enough to excuse Bruce on the ground of incapacity. *Estate of McGovern v. State Employees' Retirement Board*, 517 A.2d 523 (Pa. 1986). On the other hand, if Bruce was unable, when he entered into the June 8th agreement, to understand in a reasonable manner the nature and consequences of the transaction, or to act in a reasonable manner in relation to the transaction, and Wallace had reason to know of Bruce's condition, then Bruce may avoid the contract *even if his intoxication was purely voluntary*. R2 § 16. Therefore, **Answer (A) is incorrect**.

    A person lacking contractual capacity when he formed a contract may, upon (re)gaining the necessary capacity to do so, impliedly ratify the contract he made while lacking capacity by acting in a manner that is clearly inconsistent with disaffirmance or avoidance. Because Wallace would have been bound to perform from July 1-7 under either the first contract or the second one, the fact that Bruce allowed him to perform was not necessarily a ratification of the second contract. Therefore, **Answer (C) is incorrect**.

The facts suggest that Bruce, while perhaps under the influence of alcohol, was not so drunk as to be incapacitated. First, he negotiated Wallace down from his initial demand of $75,000 to $50,000. Second, he dictated the terms of the new contract to his secretary. Third, he signed the new contract, and had the presence of mind to have Wallace sign, too (in the event that the latter might try to bail out despite the increased compensation). Fourth, he tore up the original contract, suggesting that he understood that the new deal replaced the old deal. *Compare, e.g., Lucy v. Zehmer*, 84 S.E.2d 516 (Va. 1954). Therefore, **Answer (D) is incorrect** and Answer (B) is the best answer.

Even if the court were to find Bruce was incapacitated, R2 § 15(2) precludes Bruce from avoiding the contract "to the extent that the contract has been so performed in whole or in part or the circumstances have so changed that avoidance would be unjust. In such a case a court may grant relief as justice requires." Wallace, believing that he had a contract to perform at Bruce's hotel for $50,000, did so, only to learn after the fact that Bruce did not intend to pay him more than $25,000. Wallace has fully performed. Bruce has only paid $25,000 of the $50,000 he promised to pay. If the court finds that Bruce was incapacitated, it should exercise its equitable powers to decide what award — between $0 and $25,000 — would constitute "justice" for Wallace.

65.   **Answers (A) and (B) are incorrect** for the same reasons given in the answer to Question 61. Answer (C) looks tempting, again, but we should not be premature.

That brings us to Answer (D). Bob Dylan (born Robert Zimmerman), at one time, the most famous living American musician, and still a legend in folk and rock music circles, entered into a recording contract with Columbia Records when he was 20 years old. At the time, the age of majority in New York (whose law governed the contract) was 21. When Dylan sought to disaffirm the contract shortly after turning 21, Columbia was able to thwart him because he had used Columbia's studio six or seven times after his 21st birthday. Thus, like Dylan, Wallace should be barred from disaffirming his contract with Vestal because he used Vestal's studio and equipment after reaching the age of majority. Therefore, while it would be the correct answer but for Wallace's reaffirmance, **Answer (C) is incorrect**, and **Answer (D) is the best answer**.

66.   **Answer (C) is correct**. The facts of the question indicate that Wallace purchased the apartment after he performed at Bruce's hotel. That means it was at least July 8th. The facts also talk about his having concluded a summer tour; so, in all likelihood, Wallace purchased the apartment in August or September. In any event, it was after June 1st, which (recall from the facts of Question 61) was when Wallace reached the age of majority. There is nothing in the facts of this Question to suggest that he was intoxicated or mentally incompetent when he signed the installment purchase contract. Therefore, **Answer (A) is incorrect**.

At the risk of jumping ahead a bit, the implied duty of good faith and fair dealing (explored more in *Topic 8: Terms Implied by Law*) only applies to the performance and enforcement of a contract, not to its formation. Therefore, **Answer (B) is incorrect**.

The choice between Answers (C) and (D) boils down to whether Sharman could lie about having or being able to convey good title without ever actually saying that he had, or could convey, good title. The *Restatement* takes the position that Sharman's non-disclosure of a fact known to him is the equivalent of an affirmative misrepresentation if it concerns a material fact and if disclosing the material fact would correct a mistaken belief Wallace had about a basic assumption on which Wallace was making the contract. *See* R2 §§ 159, 161-162. Whether or not a buyer of realty will receive clean title to the realty after satisfying the purchase contract is certainly a material fact, and Wallace's assumption that Sharman had good title to convey was a basic assumption on which Wallace made the contract. As such, Wallace was entitled, *inter alia*, to avoid his contract with Sharman, cease making payments under the contract, and recover any monies paid to Sharman (although he may owe Owen for the use of the apartment during the time he occupied it). Therefore, **Answer (C) is correct** and **Answer (D) is incorrect**.

67. **Answer (A) is the best answer**. The interest rate provided in the contract was usurious — and, therefore, illegal. A contract made illegally, or for an illegal purpose, is void. Under applicable New York law, any rate of interest over 16% is usurious, *see* N.Y. BANKING LAW § 14-a (McKinney 2001), and any loan charging a usurious rate of interest is void, regardless of whether the lender knew or intended that the interest rate was usurious, *see, e.g., Babcock v. Berlin*, 475 N.Y.S.2d 212 (N.Y. Sup. Ct. 1984). If, however, the 18% were only a "penalty" rate — applicable to past due amounts — and the base rate was less than 16%, the loan would not be usurious. *See, e.g., Hicki v. Choice Capital Corp.*, 694 N.Y.S.2d 750 (N.Y. App. Div. 1999).

While the interest term *might* be substantively unconscionable, there are no facts to suggest procedural unconscionability. (See the answer to Question 62 for more discussion of unconscionability.) Because most courts require both procedural and substantive unconscionability to void a contract, **Answer (B) is not the best answer**.

As discussed in the answer to Question 66, and in greater depth in *Topic 8: Terms Implied by Law*, the implied duty of good faith and fair dealing only applies to the performance and enforcement of a contract, not to its formation. Therefore, **Answer (C) is incorrect**.

Answer (D) is not the best answer because there is no evidence that Sharman affirmatively misrepresented — knowingly (fraud) or not (negligent misrepresentation) — the contract interest rate or its legality. And, absent some duty to speak, Sharman's silence was not a misrepresentation. Generally, neither party to a contract has a duty to volunteer information unless the other party asks. The facts do not indicate that Wallace asked Sharman about the contract interest rate. Nor do the facts clearly raise one of the exceptions, discussed in greater detail in the answer to Question 241, in which common or statutory law would have required Sharman to disclose in the absence of a question by Wallace.

68. Wallace may be able to avoid the contract as unconscionable. As discussed in the answer to Question 62, unconscionability can arise where (1) the party asserting unconscionability is deprived of any meaningful choice as to the terms of the agreement (procedural unconscionability) or (2) one or more terms that are so one-sided, under the circumstances existing at the time of the making of the contract, as to be oppressive or manifestly unfair (substantive unconscionability). R2 § 208. Here, Wallace signed a document without having the chance to read it, much less bargain over its terms, and the agreement purported to require him to pay Sonya potentially millions of dollars over five years in exchange for weekly housecleaning. The latter surely satisfies the substantive unconscionability prong. The harder issue for Wallace is whether he could have reasonably relied on the seeming innocuousness of Sonya's request rather than looking more carefully at the document before he signed it. The facts that he may have been in a hurry or caught off guard by Sonya's request may not be enough to satisfy the procedural unconscionability prong. If a New York court would find a contract unconscionable solely on the basis of substantive unconscionability, or if they use a "sliding scale" approach whereby the magnitude of the contract's substantive unconscionability will require very little procedural unconscionability to satisfy the court that it should not enforce the contract, Wallace should prevail. On the other hand, if New York courts consider procedural and substantive unconscionability as equally important and inquire into each prong without regard for their findings regarding the other, Wallace may have to find another defense — such as fraud or unilateral mistake — to avoid sharing his royalties with Sonya.

What *is* New York law on this issue? *See Gillman v. Chase Manhattan Bank, N.A.*, 534 N.E.2d 824, 839 (N.Y. 1988) ("While determinations of unconscionability are ordinarily based on the court's conclusion that both the procedural and substantive components are present, there have been exceptional cases where a provision of the contract is so outrageous as to warrant holding it unenforceable on the ground of substantive unconscionability alone." [citations omitted]).

69. **Answer (C) is the best answer.** R2 § 152(1) provides that, "[w]here a mistake of both parties at the time a contract was made as to a basic assumption on which the contract was made has a material effect on the agreed exchange of performances, the contract is voidable by the adversely affected party unless he bears the risk under the rule stated in R2 § 154." Gwyneth was the party most adversely affected by her and Russell's mutual mistake regarding which *The Orange Pumpernickel* she wanted to attend. If a court enforced the agreement, Russell would be paid, as expected, but Gwyneth would not get what she bargained for. Thus, Gwyneth should be able to avoid the contract under R2 § 152(1). R2 § 154(b) appears to reinforce this result. Russell seems to have impliedly assumed the risk that he would purchase the tickets for the wrong event because he did not bother to ask Gwyneth which *The Orange Pumpernickel* she meant. Given the vast number of performance venues and nightly performances in New York, Russell would not seem to be able to invoke R2 § 152 to relieve

himself of liability. Therefore **Answer (A) is not the best answer**. If the option to avoid the contract under R2 § 152 rests solely with Gwyneth, and she refuses to avoid the contract (which, presumably, she would do if she was suing Russell for breach), Russell's best bet appears to be R2 § 201.

R2 § 153 appears to be even less help to Russell than R2 § 152. (This should not be surprising, as contract law has always been more sympathetic toward mutual mistakes than unilateral ones.) Working our way up from the bottom of R2 § 153, Gwyneth did not have reason to know that Russell meant a different *The Orange Pumpernickel* than she did, nor did she cause the misunderstanding (*e.g.*, by saying "You know, the one with Ford Prefect in it."), nor would enforcing the contract against Russell be unconscionable. R2 § 153(a)-(b). Because he volunteered to perform a service without finding out everything he needed to know to perform it as Gwyneth desired, it is difficult to imagine that holding Russell to his promise would shock a court's conscience (assuming the court first found mutual assent — which it should not do, as explained below). With neither R2 § 153(a) nor R2 § 153 (b) seeming to apply, Russell should find no relief in the body of R2 § 153 either. Therefore, **Answer (B) is incorrect**.

Ultimately, this Question strongly resembles *Raffles v. Wichelhaus*, 159 Eng. Rep. 375 (Ex. 1864) (per curiam). As in *Raffles*, there was never any "meeting of the minds" between Russell and Gwyneth; therefore, under classical contract theory, no contract was ever formed. Applying the more modern tests of R2 §§ 20(1) & 201, "[t]here is no manifestation of mutual assent . . . if the parties attach materially different meanings to their manifestations and neither party knows or has reason to know the meaning attached by the other"; therefore, "neither party is bound by the meaning attached by the other, even though the result may be a failure of mutual assent." Absent mutual assent, there is no contract for Gwyneth to enforce against Russell or vice versa. R2 § 17(1). Therefore, **Answer (C) is the best answer**. The difference between this case and *Raffles* is that the thwarted cotton sellers in *Raffles* still had a valuable supply of cotton they could sell to someone else. Russell has two tickets to something that has already occurred. He "wins," because he does not owe Gwyneth damages. But, it is a Pyrrhic victory, because he is still out the cost of the tickets.

While Russell's implied assumption of the risk for purposes of unilateral and mutual mistake precludes him from finding shelter in those defenses, his failure to inquire further which *The Orange Pumpernickel* Gwyneth meant, given that he did not know there was more than one, should not cause mutual assent where it is otherwise lacking. Therefore, because the absence of mutual assent obviates Russell's need for a defense to a non-existent contract, **Answer (D) is not the best answer**.

70. No. Owl's Nest will argue that Jason and Jenny understood "a new Mitsubishi" to mean different things; both parties were mistaken about the other party's meaning; neither party assumed the risk of the other's misunderstanding; and, the meaning of "a new Mitsubishi" was material to the agreed exchange of performances, thereby making the contract voidable by Owl's Nest. R2 § 152. Unlike Russell (in Question

69), who had no reason to know that Gwyneth meant anything different than he did, Jason had every reason to know Jenny and the other waitresses attributed a very different meaning to "Mitsubishi" than he did. As such, Owl's Nest cannot take refuge in R2 §§ 20(1)(a) & 201(3). Rather, it will be bound by Jenny's objectively reasonable understanding that the drawing was for a Mitsubishi car, truck, or SUV. *See, e.g., Spence v. Superintendent, Great Meadow Correctional Facility*, 219 F.3d 162 (2d Cir. 2000); *Harris Corp. v. Giesting & Associates, Inc.*, 297 F.3d 1270 (11th Cir. 2002).

71. **Answer (D) is the best answer.** The fact that Hilda might have become unable or unwilling to perform the contract during the first year does not change the fact that this was a contract for services not to be fully performed within one year. R2 § 110(1)(e) requires that a writing signed by the party against whom enforcement is sought evidence such a contract. There is no such writing, so Hilda cannot enforce the contract against Missy's. Therefore, **Answer (C) is incorrect.**

While Hilda may have been paid on an annual basis, she and Rochelle agreed on a two-year contract. Therefore, **Answer (A) is incorrect.** While Hilda's detrimental reliance may (as we will explore in more depth in *Topic 6: Equitable Claims*) allow her to enforce Missy's promise *despite* the fact that Hilda can produce no writing that satisfies the statute of frauds, her detrimental reliance would not, by itself, satisfy the statute of frauds. Therefore, **Answer (B) is incorrect.**

72. **Answer (D) is the correct answer.** The payroll record "reasonably identifies the subject matter of the contract," R2 § 131(a) — namely, Hilda's employment by Missy's. It "is sufficient to indicate that a contract with respect thereto has been made between the parties," R2 § 131(b) — why else is Missy's putting Hilda on the payroll? It "states with reasonable certainty the essential terms of the unperformed promises in the contract," R2 § 131(c) — the document, at a minimum, indicates the position to which Rochelle appointed her, the amount and frequency of her pay, and the term of her appointment. And, Rochelle signed it, on behalf of Missy's, which is the "party to be charged."

A common misconception about statutes of frauds is that they require written contracts. While that may have been true historically, the statutes of frauds you are most likely to encounter in first-year Contracts or on a bar exam do not require a written contract. Rather, R2 § 110, UCC § 2-201, and UCC § 1-206 require only a signed writing that (1) satisfies one or more specified content requirements, and (2) evidences that the parties formed a contract relating to the subject matter of their actual agreement. *See* R2 § 131 & cmt. d; UCC §§ 1-206(1) & 2-201(1). Therefore, **Answer (A) is incorrect.**

Another common misconception about statutes of frauds is that they require that all parties to the contract sign the writing. Again, while that may have been true historically, neither R2 § 110, UCC § 2-201, nor UCC § 1-206 require the signatures of all parties to the contract. Instead, they only require the signature of "the party against whom enforcement is sought," UCC §§ 1-206(1) & 2-201(1), or "the party to be charged," R2 § 131. The trick, of course, is that the parties generally do not know, when they enter into a contract, which one of them is going to need to seek legal recourse to enforce the contract against the other at some future date; so, the parties often will insist that everyone sign the writing. However, the statutes of frauds themselves include no such requirement. Therefore, **Answer (B) is incorrect**.

A less common misconception — but a misconception, nonetheless — is that, for purposes of the statute of frauds, time stops at the moment the contract is formed (*i.e.*, if there is no writing in existence at that time, no subsequent writing can satisfy the statute of frauds). R2 § 136 states: "A memorandum sufficient to satisfy the Statute may be made or signed at any time before or after the formation of the contract." Moreover, there is an abundance of case law finding documents created after the formation of an oral contract to be sufficient to satisfy (retroactively) the statute of frauds when suit is later brought on the contract. *See, e.g., Bazak International Corp. v. Mast Industries, Inc.*, 535 N.E.2d 633 (N.Y. 1989); *Crabtree v. Elizabeth Arden Sales Corp.*, 110 N.E.2d 551 (N.Y. 1953); *see also In re McAllister*, 211 B.R. 976 (Bankr. N.D. Ala. 1997) (collecting cases). Therefore, **Answer (C) is incorrect**.

Revised Article 1 deletes current UCC § 1-206 and narrows the scope of Article 1 so that it applies only to transactions governed by another UCC Article. Revised Article 2 increases the triggering amount from $500 in current UCC § 2-201(1) to $5,000 in Revised § 2-201(1), but makes no other changes of particular consequence to § 2-201.

73. **Answer (D) is the best answer**. Hilda could have fully performed this contract within one year, because she could have died, become disabled, or voluntarily retired in that time. As such, R2 § 110(1)(e) does not require a signed writing to evidence the contract.

While it is true that the parties may have *expected* Hilda to work for Missy's for two years or more, it is also true that Hilda could fully perform the contract by dying, becoming disabled, or voluntarily retiring prior to the commencement of the contract's second year. Because the contract provides that it would terminate when the first of these events occurred, it could be fully performed in less than one year. Therefore, **Answer (A) is incorrect**.

While giving Hilda the option to voluntarily retire might make *her* promise to teach at Missy's for two years or until she retires illusory, it does not make *Missy's* promise to employ Hilda for two years or until she retires illusory. And, in any event, lack of consideration is not a factor in deciding whether a contract, if one exists, satisfies the statute of frauds. Therefore, **Answer (B) is incorrect**.

Whether a contract satisfies the "one-year provision" of the statute of frauds depends on the state of affairs when the parties formed the contract, not on what happens thereafter. So, this contract does or does not satisfy the statute of frauds irrespective of what happened to Hilda after the contract formed. Therefore, **Answer (C) is incorrect**.

74. **Answer (D) is the best answer**. While it is true that Hilda could have fully performed this contract by working for two years, it is also true that Hilda could have fully

performed by dying, becoming disabled, or voluntarily retiring prior to the commencement of the contract's second year. Because the contract provides that it would terminate when the first of these events occurred, it could be fully performed in less than one year. As such, R2 § 110(1)(e) does not require a signed writing to evidence the contract. Therefore, **Answer (D) is correct** and **Answer (A) is incorrect**.

Answers (B) and (C) are incorrect for the same reasons discussed in the answer to Question 73.

75. **Answer (C) is the best answer.** The agreement between Bosworth and Sandra, as represented by Sandra's June 30th offer and Bosworth's July 3rd acceptance, should satisfy the statute of frauds. The statute of frauds is implicated because this is a contract for the sale of an interest in real property. R2 §§ 110(1)(d) & 125(1). The statute requires one or more writings, signed by the party against whom enforcement is sought, that (1) reasonably identify the subject matter of the contract, (2) indicate that the parties have made a contract with respect to the subject matter or that the signer has offered a contract to the other party, and (3) state with reasonable certainty the essential terms of the unperformed promises in the contract. R2 § 131. Here, Bosworth is trying to enforce the contract against Sandra, so he needs a writing signed by Sandra that evidences the contract Bosworth seeks to enforce.

Sandra wrote the June 30th offer. The written offer states the quantity of land to be sold (100 acres) and the price ($1,000.00 per acre). Even if Sandra did not sign it in the traditional sense of the word, she sent the letter on her letterhead, and it likely bears a fax "banner," both of which will attribute it to Sandra. But, does it "indicate that a contract for sale *has been made* between the parties"? Not by itself. Therefore, **Answer (A) is incorrect**.

While factually true, **Answer (B) is not the best answer** because it ignores the "composite document rule." *See* R2 § 132. The composite document rule — in either its "strong" (no evidence permitted other than the documents themselves) or "weak" (oral testimony may tie the documents together) form — will allow Bosworth to introduce his e-mailed acceptance of Sandra's offer, and the two taken together will indicate that a contract for sale has been made between the parties for 100 acres of undeveloped land situated at the intersection of Wyld Stallyns Drive and No Way. R2 § 132; see also UETA § 7. Therefore, **Answer (C) is the best answer**.

Only in contracts between merchants for the sale of goods will a statute of frauds permit one contracting party to attribute its signature to the other contracting party. *See* UCC § 2-201(2). This is not a contract for the sale of goods, nor does anything in the facts suggest that Sandra and Bosworth are merchants in goods. Therefore, **Answer (D) is incorrect**.

76. R2 § 110(1)(e) requires that a writing, signed by the party against whom enforcement is sought, evidence any contract to employ someone for a period of more than one year. Therefore, assuming that Lewis was less than 64 years old when MEC allegedly promised to employ him until age 65, there must be a writing signed by MEC (or

its agent) that is sufficient to evidence MEC's alleged promise. Lewis and MEC allegedly executed the handwritten December 15, 1992 amendment to the September 1, 1987 contract. If MEC or its agent signed the December 15, 1992 amendment, then the statute of frauds would be satisfied. If not, the only writings sufficient to bind MEC are the September 1, 1987 contract and the October 1, 1989 amendment to, and reaffirmation of, the September 1, 1987 contract — each of which recited or incorporated recitals that Lewis'ss employment was "at-will." These writings are sufficient to satisfy the statute of frauds that a contract of employment existed, but not that the parties had agreed to anything other than an at-will term.

77. **Answer (C) is the best answer**. Betty has agreed to make 12 monthly payments, with the first one due by the end of month during which she made the agreement and the other 11 due by the end of each succeeding month. Twelve months make a year; 11 months and change are less than one year. Thus, R2 § 110(1)(e) does not require a writing signed by Betty (and, even if it did, Betty's partial performance may bar her from denying the contract at least to the extent of her performance).

This is not a contract for goods or other personal property, so the UCC statutes of frauds do not apply. What about R2 § 110? The *Restatement* requires a writing evidencing the contract and signed by the party against whom enforcement is sought in five cases: (1) a contract of an executor or administrator to answer for a duty of its decedent, R2 § 110(1)(a); (2) a contract to answer for the duty of another, R2 § 110(1)(b); (3) a contract made upon consideration of marriage, R2 § 110(1)(c); (4) a contract for the transfer of an interest in land, R2 § 110(1)(d); and (5) a contract that cannot be fully performed within one year from the date of making, R2 § 110(1)(e).

If this qualifies as a contract of suretyship, Slate will need a qualifying writing. Fortunately for Slate, Betty did not promise to pay *if* Bamm Bamm did not; rather, Betty promised to pay *because* Bamm Bamm had not. As such, it is not a surety contract, and R2 § 110(1)(b) is not implicated. Therefore, **Answer (B) is incorrect**. Nor is this a contract to transfer an interest in land. Betty did not agreed to pay Slate for the addition to her and Barney's house (which may, under Bedrock law, be treated as a part of the realty), she promised to pay Slate for forbearing debt collection efforts against her son. Therefore, **Answer (A) is incorrect**.

Answer (D) may be correct, depending on what Betty (or Slate) wrote on her checks. But, because no writing was required, and because we do not know whether Betty (or Slate) wrote anything on the checks other than the date, payee's name, amount, Betty's signature, and Slate's indorsement, **Answer (D) is not the best answer**.

78. **Answer (C) is the best answer**. While there is no specific provision in the *Restatement* requiring a writing, or dispensing with the writing requirement, for pledges to make charitable contributions, some charitable pledges contemplate giving for more than one year. As such, R2 § 110(1)(e) generally governs whether a writing must evidence a charitable pledge. It is also possible that a charitable pledge might be the subject of

a contract made by an executor or administrator on behalf of an estate (*e.g.*, to fulfill the decedent's wish that some charity or charities receive a part of the decedent's estate), R2 § 110(1)(a), or a contract to transfer an interest in land (*e.g.*, a benefactor gives a parcel of land to a local charity), R2 § 110(1)(d). Therefore, **Answer (A) is incorrect**.

The facts do not tell us over what time period the Museum expects Mary to make the five equal installments. But that does not matter, because Mary could have paid the entire $4.75 million in one lump sum or paid all five installments within one year of her pledge, if she so chose. The Museum did not require her to pay it in five installments; it simply allowed her to, on the condition that she pay the first installment within 120 days. Thus, Mary's pledge is not a contract that cannot be fully performed within one year. On the other hand, a contract that can be fully performed within one year may be subject to another statute of frauds. For example, a contract that can be fully performed within one year might be the subject of a contract made by an executor or administrator on behalf of an estate, R2 § 110(1)(a), a contract for the transfer of an interest in land, R2 § 110(1)(d), or a contract for the sale of goods for $500 (or $5,000, if applying Revised Article 2) or more. Therefore, **Answer (B) is not the best answer**.

Mary's March 15th letter and her pledge card each evidence a contract between Mary and the Museum (even though the purpose of the March 15th agreement was to avoid the contract). If the pledge card were not enough standing alone (it probably is), the letter and the pledge card, read together, would satisfy the statute of frauds. Therefore, **Answer (C) is the best answer**, and **Answer (D) is incorrect**.

79. No. Jenny was to perform the services that were the subject of the contract over a period of one month, commencing shortly after Jason made the offer. Therefore, the contract did not need to be evidenced by a writing to be enforceable. R2 § 110(1)(e).

80. **Answer (C) is the best answer**, at the time of this writing, outside of Texas and Virginia.

Buffy's list was intangible personal property. Its value lay not with the physical list itself, but with the information contained in that list. It was not a good subject to the Article 2 statute of frauds. *See* UCC §§ 2-105 & 2-201. Therefore, **Answer (A) is incorrect**.

While Buffy may well have spent considerable time and energy compiling the list, she may also have bought it or received it as a gift from someone else. There is no way, based on the facts of the Question, for us to know. Fortunately, it does not matter. Unlike an artist who is hired to paint a portrait, and whose contract is almost certainly predominated by the artist's rendering her artistic services, an artist who sells an already-painted painting is selling goods. Here, Buffy sold the list, not her (or whomever's) services compiling the list. Therefore, **Answer (D) is incorrect**.

Therefore, we must look to pre-Revised Article 1, which governs sales of personal property to the extent that other Articles of the UCC do not provide more specific rules. Unlike its counterparts in Article 2 and common law, both of which render a contract unenforceable in its entirety if it is subject to and fails to satisfy the applicable statute of frauds, UCC § 1-206 does not defeat the enforceability of the contract; rather, it limits a non-complying contract's enforceability to $5,000 "in amount or value of remedy." So, in this case, Buffy could enforce the oral agreement to sell her address and phone list to Spike up to $5,000 in amount or value of remedy. Therefore, **Answer (C) is correct** and **Answer (B) is incorrect**.

Recall that Revised Article 1 deletes current UCC § 1-206 and narrows the scope of Article 1 so that it applies only to transactions governed by another UCC Article. In the absence of a state-specific amendment to Revised Article 1 or another statute governing personal property transactions not within the scope of any other Article of the UCC, Buffy and Spike's contract would appear to be governed by common law. And, because the common law statute of frauds does not require a writing for the type of contract at issue, Buffy should be able to fully enforce the contract against Spike.

81. **Answer (C) is the best answer.** This was a contract for the sale of goods. As such, Article 2 governs it. Because this contract was for the sale of goods in an amount greater than $500, there must have been one or more writings, signed by Tubular (the party against whom enforcement is sought), evidencing the contract, identifying the goods, and stating the quantity to be sold. UCC § 2-201. Here, Tubular does not appear to have signed any writing accepting or acknowledging Mercury's order. However, because both parties were merchants per UCC § 2-104(1), and because Mercury's purchase order was a written confirmation to which Tubular did not timely object in writing, UCC § 2-201(2), Mercury's purchase order would satisfy UCC § 2-201 if it contained the information required by UCC § 2-201(1). We know that it identified the goods to be sold as one foot lengths of glass tubing, and that it stated a quantity of 5,000 and a price of $5.00 per foot. "Signed" for purposes of UCC § 2-201 includes most things that identify the sender. Therefore, if the purchase order had Mercury's name and address on it, or was on Mercury's letterhead or a Mercury form, or was accompanied by a fax cover sheet with Mercury's name on it, or it displayed Mercury's name on the "banner" at the top or bottom of each faxed page, it should satisfy UCC § 2-201(1). Thus, **Answer (B) is incorrect**.

Answer (A) is incorrect. Even though Mercury's confirmation contained terms in addition to or different from those to which the parties orally agreed, a contract was formed because Mercury did not make its confirmation expressly conditional on Tubular's agreement to the additional terms. UCC § 2-207(1).

The fact that Tubular told Mercury it had to specially manufacture the glass tubing to meet Mercury's specifications might seem to trigger the "specially-manufactured goods" exception to the Article 2 statute of frauds. UCC § 2-201(3)(a). It does not. The question is not whether Mercury's specifications were different from those typically adhered to by Tubular. The question is whether glass tubing made to Mercury's specifications was "not suitable for sale to others in the ordinary course of [Tubular]'s business." If so, the exception would apply, because Tubular had obviously "made either a substantial beginning of [the tubing's] manufacture" at the time of Tubular's breach, given that the tubing was rerouted to another buyer. The reason the exception would not apply, however, is precisely that: Tubular was able to find another purchaser for the tubing; therefore, the tubing obviously *was* "suitable for sale to others in the ordinary course of [Tubular]'s business." Moreover, while UCC § 2-201(3)(a) and the comments to UCC § 2-201 never come right out and say that this exception exists only for the use of the seller (Tubular) against a repudiating buyer (Mercury), a careful reading of the language of UCC § 2-201(3)(a) reveals that the exception is triggered only if the seller has done certain things prior to *receiving* notice of repudiation. A seller would not "receive" notice of its own repudiation. It could only "receive" notice of the buyer's repudiation. Therefore, even if the tubing ordered by Mercury qualified as "specially-manufactured," Tubular's repudiation should not trigger the UCC § 2-201(3)(a) exception. Consequently, **Answer (D) is incorrect**.

82. For the reasons discussed in the answers to Questions 6 and 7, Mercury's contract with PG would be governed by the CISG. The CISG has no statute of frauds. CISG art. 11. Therefore, neither Mercury nor PG would need to produce a writing signed by the other in order to enforce this contract.

83. **Answer (A) is the best answer if this is a "true lease"; Answer (C) is the best answer if this is a "disguised sale."**

   This is a lease for 10 months. If Dharma and Greg decide to exercise the purchase option and keep the leased goods, they will have them for more than 10 months, but the goods will no longer be subject to the lease contract. The fact that the parties can fully perform the contract within one year means that this contract does not trigger the one-year provision in R2 § 110(1)(e). As discussed in the answer to Question 78, however, the contract may be subject to another statute of frauds. Therefore, **Answer (D) is not the best answer**.

   UCC § 2A-201 only requires a writing when total lease payments, *excluding* any renewal or purchase option fee, equal or exceed $1,000. Because the amount of the purchase option does not figure into calculating the total lease payments due, this contract does not trigger UCC § 2A-201. Therefore, **Answer (B) is incorrect**.

   If this is a lease of goods for a period of 10 months, with lease payments totaling $990, then the lease falls outside of UCC § 2A-201 and need not be evidenced by a signed writing. If this is a sale of goods for $1,015 (the sum of the 10 lease payments plus the purchase option), then Dharma and Greg will need a writing signed by Drew in order to enforce their agreement against Drew. UCC § 2-201(1). With these facts, it is not manifestly clear one way or the other whether the transaction is a "true lease" or a "disguised sale." The facts that the total monthly payments are almost double the fair market value of the equipment and that Dharma and Greg have the option to purchase the equipment at the end of the lease term for much less than its expected fair market value weigh in favor of this being a "disguised sale." *See* UCC § 1-201(37)

(*Revised § 1-203*). On the other hand, the fact that the equipment will still have significant economic value at the end of the 10-month term weighs in favor of the transaction being a "true lease." *See id.* Under current law, **if this is a "disguised sale," Answer (C) is the best answer; if it is a "true lease," Answer (A) is the best answer**.

Recall that Revised Article 2 raises the threshold price for § 2-201 from $500 to $5,000. Therefore, if Revised Article 2 governed this Question, Answer (C) would be incorrect, leaving us to decide whether this is a "true lease" — making Answer (A) correct — or a "disguised sale" — in which case all four alternatives would be incorrect.

84. **Answer (C) is the correct answer**. UCC § 2-201(1) requires that one or more writings signed by the party against whom enforcement is sought — ATG — evidencing a contract for the sale of goods for $500 or more. Here, no such writing is a part of, or results from, the telephone conversation between Greene and Russell on May 1st. Therefore, their contract, if they even had one, did not satisfy the statute of frauds.

    The juniper saplings are goods. UCC Article 2 is the governing law. Because Article 2 has its own statute of frauds, UCC § 1-206 does not apply. Therefore, **Answer (A) is incorrect**.

    While UCC § 2-201(1) requires that the writing specify or provide a means for determining (without further agreement) the quantity of goods at issue, whether the writing states price is irrelevant for purposes of UCC § 2-201(1) — and, indeed, for purposes of forming a contract under Article 2, *see* UCC § 2-305(1) — except to the extent that the total price of the goods determines whether the contract must satisfy UCC § 2-201(1). Therefore, **Answer (B) is incorrect**.

    The fact that ATG and Uncle Buck are both merchants — which they clearly are, as both deal in goods of this kind as a vocation, rather than a hobby or avocation, *see* UCC § 2-104(1) & cmt. 2 — only changes UCC § 2-201's requirements in one way: If one merchant sends a written confirmation to another merchant, and the receiving merchant does not object to the contents of the confirmation within 10 days of receipt, the sending merchant's signature will satisfy the requirement that the receiving merchant sign the writing in order to enforce the contract so memorialized against the receiving merchant. UCC § 2-201(2). Because there was no writing of any kind signed by either party in this Question, UCC § 2-201(2) is inapplicable despite the fact that ATG and Uncle Buck are both merchants. Therefore, **Answer (D) is incorrect**.

    Recall that Revised Article 1 no longer includes a "default" statute of frauds. So, if this dispute were governed by the law of a jurisdiction that has adopted Revised Article 1, Answer (A) would be non sequitur.

85. **Answer (D) is the correct answer**. As discussed in the answer to Question 84, UCC § 2-201(1) requires that ATG have signed one or more writings evidencing a contract for a specified or determinable quantity of juniper saplings. Here, in order to satisfy

that writing requirement, Uncle Buck will have to avail itself of the composite document rule. However, once it does so, Uncle Buck will have satisfied UCC § 2-201(1), and ATG's statute of frauds defense will be for naught.

Uncle Buck's June 2nd confirming fax evidences that the parties had formed a contract ("confirming your agreement"). Therefore, **Answer (A) is incorrect**. Moreover, Uncle Buck's June 2nd confirming fax is valid against ATG, even though only Uncle Buck signed it, because ATG failed to object in writing to the confirming fax within 10 days of receipt. UCC § 2-201(2). Therefore, **Answer (B) is incorrect**, though factually true.

UCC § 2-201(1) requires that the writings state the quantity of goods to be sold. UCC § 2-201(1) & cmt. 1. Uncle Buck's June 2nd fax included no quantity term. However, Uncle Buck may satisfy the quantity requirement by adding to the June 2nd fax (1) its June 14th invoice for 250 saplings at $15 per sapling plus delivery costs of $50; (2) ATG's check written on June 14th for $3,800 — the amount of Uncle Buck's June 14th invoice; (3) its July 16th invoice for 250 saplings at $18 per sapling plus delivery costs of $50; (4) ATG's notation on the July 16th invoice accepting 250 trees at $15 each "per June 2nd agreement"; and (5) ATG's check written on July 16th for $3,800 — $15 per tree plus $50 delivery fees. Therefore, **Answer (C) is not the best answer**, because the June 2nd fax is not the only writing with which Uncle Buck can satisfy the statute of frauds.

86. Yes. Even if the writings discussed in the answer to Question 85, taken together, did not satisfy the statute of frauds, two other exceptions apply to this case: the partial performance exception, UCC § 2-201(3)(c), and the judicial admission exception, UCC § 2-201(3)(b). ATG received and accepted 500 juniper saplings. Therefore, UCC § 2-201(3)(c) will permit Uncle Buck to enforce the contract against ATG as to those 500 juniper saplings. Moreover, ATG has admitted in its pleadings the existence of the contract for 500 juniper saplings, and that it owed (and paid) Uncle Buck "$7,500, plus shipping" under the contract. Therefore, UCC § 2-201(3)(b) will permit Uncle Buck to enforce the contract against ATG for 500 juniper saplings, at a price the finder of fact will determine based on the evidence.

Revised § 2-201 retains all of the statute of frauds exceptions included in current UCC § 2-201.

87. **Answer (D) is the best answer.** The Museum should have a promissory estoppel claim under R2 § 90(1) & (2). R2 § 90(1) requires proof of (1) a promise, (2) that the promisor could reasonably foresee would induce action or forbearance by the promisee, (3) which does induce such action or forbearance, (4) as a result of which injustice can be avoided only by enforcing the promise. Many courts add that the promisee's reliance must be reasonable. *See, e.g., Chrysler Corp. v. Chaplake Holdings, Ltd.*, 822 A.2d 1024 (Del. 2003); *First National Bank of Logansport v. Logan Manufacturing Co.*, 577 N.E.2d 949 (Ind. 1991); *Pop's Cones, Inc. v. Resorts International Hotel, Inc.*, 704 A.2d 1321 (N.J. Super. Ct. App. Div. 1998); *Karnes v. Doctors Hospital*, 555 N.E.2d 280 (Ohio 1990); *Durkee v. Van Well*, 654 N.W.2d 807 (S.D. 2002). The biggest stumbling block in most charitable subscription cases is for the charity to prove that it reasonably relied to its detriment on the promise and that its reasonable reliance was foreseeable. R2 § 90(2) eliminates the element of reliance (and, hence, foreseeable reliance) from charitable subscription cases. Therefore, **Answers (A) and (B) are incorrect**. That does not end the inquiry, however.

The issue on which this dispute should turn is whether a court must enforce Mary's promise to avoid injustice. The Museum would have continued seeking donations had Mary not made her pledge. The Museum also would have accepted the Flockensteins' offer to increase their pledge from $4,250,000 to $5,000,000 and named the new wing after them or their designee (which could have led to additional future donations from them, their family, and friends). And, as things currently stand, the Museum cannot build the new wing without the money Mary pledged. The "$64,000 question" — or, in this case, the $4,000,000 question — is whether the Museum can find one or more donors to make pledges to the campaign or pledge additional amounts to make up for the loss of Mary's money. If so, then Mary may be off the hook. If not, then injustice will certainly result if a court does not enforce Mary's promise. Courts are hesitant to assume that there is a bottomless pit of charitable money out there that fundraisers can tap at will. The drafters of the *Restatement (Second)* seem to agree. Illustration 17 to Section 90 finds an enforceable promise arising from a donor's pledge of $100,000 to a university, payable in five annual installments, and confirmed in writing by the donor's agent. Section 139, which complements Section 90, *see* R2 § 139 cmt. a, explores the concept of avoiding injustice in more depth than does Section 90, and several of the factors listed in R2 § 139(2) as signals of injustice are present in this Question. Therefore, **Answer (D) appears to be a better answer that Answer (C)**, though the result of any court's analysis of the injustice issue is difficult to predict.

88. **Answer (D) is the best answer.** The Museum need only have given consideration if it was trying to enforce Mary's pledge as a contract, rather than a promise. Therefore, **Answer (A) is incorrect**.

Many jurisdictions have either not adopted R2 § 90(2) or specifically rejected it. *See, e.g., Arrowsmith v. Mercantile-Safe Deposit & Trust Co.*, 545 A.2d 674 (Md. 1988); *Congregation Kadimah Toras-Moshe v. DeLeo*, 540 N.E.2d 691 (Mass. 1989). In those jurisdictions, the primary factor courts use to decide whether to enforce charitable pledges seems to be whether the pledge was for a sufficiently specific purpose — and, in some cases, of sufficiently significant value — to presume foreseeable reliance by the charity, *see, e.g., King v. Trustees of Boston University*, 647 N.E.2d 1196 (Mass. 1995) (upholding university's right to maintain papers given it by Dr. Martin Luther King, Jr. based on the many years that the university had maintained, catalogued, stored, and made the papers available for research) or whether it was a general pledge on the basis of which the pledgor could not reasonably foresee specific, detrimental reliance by the charity, *see, e.g., Maryland National Bank v. United Jewish Appeal Federation of Greater Washington, Inc.*, 407 A.2d 1130 (Md. 1979) (denying charity the right to enforce a pledge made to its general purpose fund against the estate of the pledgor). Because Mary's pledge was for the specific purpose of building the new wing, and because Mary knew or should have known that her pledge accounted for nearly 25% of the fundraising goal for the new wing, her pledge was both specific enough and significant enough to make the Museum's detrimental reliance reasonable and reasonably foreseeable. Therefore, **Answer (B) is incorrect**.

The Museum did, in fact, detrimentally (as it turns out) rely on Mary's pledge when it shut down its fundraising campaign early — something it would not have done but for Mary's substantial pledge. Therefore, **Answer (C) is incorrect**.

89. **Answer (B) is the best answer**. The primary issues in a non-R2 § 90(2) jurisdiction are the specificity of the pledge and its size relative to the total effort. While the Gollys' $750,000 pledge is certainly hefty, it was not specifically directed to the new wing. And, given the size of the overall campaign and the explanation of how funds were to be allocated, the Museum would be hard-pressed to argue that it reasonably relied to its detriment on the Gollys' pledge with regard to the new wing. If this were a R2 § 90(2) jurisdiction, the Museum would probably have a claim, but under *Maryland National Bank* it appears to be out of luck.

For reasons explained in the answer to Question 88, consideration is a moot point. Therefore, **Answer (A) is incorrect**. The facts do not support a finding that the Museum detrimentally relied on the Gollys' pledge, as it continued the fundraising campaign for several months after receiving the Gollys' pledge, until the total amount of pledges exceeded the goal by $750,000 — serendipitously the precise amount of the Gollys' pledge. Thus, the Gollys could have retracted their pledge and the campaign still would have reached its goal. Without actual reliance, **Answers (C) and (D) are incorrect**.

90. **Answer (C) is the best answer**. *Restatement of Restitution* § 117 would afford Glenn and his mates a claim against Nick if (1) they acted lawfully and without owing Nick any pre-existing duty as a result of their relationship to him or their own acts or omissions; (2) they acted without Nick's permission out of necessity; (3) they had no reason to believe that Nick would not consent if asked; (4) they intended to be

compensated for their efforts; and (5) Nick accepted the boat when they returned it to him. The sticking point here is that there is nothing to suggest that Glenn, Will, and Jean-Luc had money on their mind when they went after Nick's boat. Like good samaritans who stop to aid fellow motorists in distress, they acted gratuitously and had no reliance interest to protect. **Answers (A), (B), and (D), while all true, are insufficient to afford Glenn, Will, and Jean-Luc a claim against Nick**.

91.   **Answer (B) is the best answer.** In *Glenn v. Savage*, 13 P. 442 (Or. 1887), the court held that, in order for Glenn to recover for rescuing Savage's lumber from the river, Savage must have either asked for Glenn's assistance or, after learning of Glenn's actions, promised to pay Glenn after the fact. This latter notion of "promissory restitution" is now embodied in R2 § 86, which provides that a promise, made in recognition of a benefit already received, is binding to the extent necessary to prevent injustice, if (1) the promisee did not render the benefit as a gift, (2) not enforcing the promise would unjustly enrich the promisor, and (3) the promise is not disproportionate to the benefit the promisor received.

Nick made his promise after the fact. Therefore, Glenn, Will, and Jean-Luc could not have relied on his promise in rescuing the boat, making **Answer (A) incorrect**. As more fully explored in the answer to Question 90, Glenn, Will, and Jean-Luc would be denied recovery under *Restatement of Restitution* § 117 because they did not act with the intent to be paid. Therefore, **Answer (C) is incorrect**. Nor is this the type of case in which courts have implied a quasi-contract in order to keep Nick from being unjustly enriched. He was not, in fact, enriched. Instead, Glenn, Will, and Jean-Luc simply helped preserve the value of his property. Therefore, **Answer (D) is incorrect**.

92.   **Answer (D) is the best answer.** Glenn appears to have two claims against Nick: breach of a unilateral contract and promissory estoppel. Promissory restitution applies only where the promise to pay comes after the service was rendered, which is not the case here. Therefore, **Answer (B) is incorrect**. Section 117 of the *Restatement of Restitution* only applies in situations where a party is forced by circumstances not of his own making to act without the owner's permission. Here Nick asked for Glenn's help. Therefore, **Answer (C) is incorrect**.

In order to prevail on a claim that Nick breached his unilateral contract with Glenn, Glenn must establish offer ("If you fetch my boat and bring it back to me, I'll pay you $100."), acceptance-by-performance (Glenn's retrieval of the boat), and consideration (Nick sought Glenn's performance in exchange for his promise and Glenn performed in exchange for Nick's promise to pay him). There is no statute of frauds issue because the contract is for services to be fully performed in less than one year. Therefore, Glenn has a viable breach of contract claim against Nick. OK. What does that have to do with the viability of any equitable claim Glenn might have? One of the elements Glenn must establish in order to recover in promissory estoppel is that the court can prevent injustice only by enforcing Nick's promise. In determining whether only enforcing a promise can prevent injustice, the *Restatement (Second)* points courts to the unavailability of any other remedy. *See* R2 § 139(2)(a). If Glenn can recover for breach of contract, the court need not consider his equitable claim. Therefore, **Answer (D) is the best answer**. **Answer (A) is the second-best answer** because Glenn's promissory estoppel claim should yield to his claim based on the contract formed by Nick's offer and Glenn's acceptance-by-performance. But, if the court were to find no contract, Glenn appears to have a valid promissory estoppel claim.

93.   **Answer (D) the best answer**. Lestrade cannot claim promissory estoppel because Holmes's promise did not cause Lestrade to detrimentally rely by agreeing to pay for Watson's care up to the date of Holmes's visit. Lestrade had already agreed to do that. R2 § 90(1). Therefore, **Answer (A) is incorrect**.

As discussed in the answer to Question 91, R2 § 86 provides that a promise, made in recognition of a benefit already received, is binding to the extent necessary to prevent injustice, as long as (1) the promisee did not render the benefit gratuitously, (2) not enforcing the promise would unjustly enrich the promisor, and (3) the promise is not disproportionate to the benefit the promisor received. *Restatement of Restitution* § 116 permits recovery for services rendered to prevent (or treat) serious bodily harm or pain (or death), undertaken without the beneficiary's knowledge or consent, if (1) the benefactor acted unofficiously and with intent to charge for the services, (2) the benefactor had no reason to know the beneficiary would not consent to the services if asked, and (3) the beneficiary's condition prevented consent. Lestrade's problem with both provisions is that he clearly did not act with the expectation of being compensated for his services and he may well have considered his intercession on Watson's behalf a gift. So, as to the pre-visit expenses, Lestrade seems to be out of luck. Moreover, *Restatement of Restitution* § 116 only authorizes recovery from the beneficiary of the services. Under these facts, that would be Watson or Watson's estate, but not Holmes or Holmes's estate. Therefore, **Answers (B) and (C) are incorrect**.

94.   **Answer (A) is the best answer, unless Lestrade can prove breach of contract, in which case Answer (D) is the best answer**. Lestrade clearly has a promissory estoppel claim for post-visit expenses because he agreed to continue to pay for Watson's care only after Holmes promised to reimburse him. Holmes's promise clearly induced Lestrade to reasonably and foreseeably rely to his detriment, and Lestrade would suffer an injustice if Holmes were not held to his promise — unless Lestrade and Holmes had an enforceable contract. If they did, then avoiding injustice would not require the court to enforce Holmes's promise using the rubric of promissory estoppel. Lestrade could be made whole by awarding him damages for breach of contract.

Whether Lestrade and Holmes had an enforceable contract is unclear because Holmes's promise might fall under the category of a contract "to answer for the duty of another"; and, therefore, require a signed writing under R2 § 110(1)(b). The comments to R2 § 112 are somewhat more helpful:

> The word "duty" is used here as a substitute for the words "debt, default or miscarriages" used in the English statute to describe the principal obligation. Those words and corresponding words in American statutes include all kinds

of duties recognized by law, *whether or not contractual* and whether already incurred or to be incurred in the future. The person owing the duty is called the principal debtor or obligor. The duty may be conditional, voidable or unenforceable; but if there is no duty at all, the Statute does not apply.

R2 § 112 cmt. b (emphasis added). However, having said that the duty need not be contractual in nature, the *Restatement* proceeds to offer 11 illustrations to R2 § 112 — all of which presume either (1) a pre-existing contract between the party for whose duty the promisor is agreeing to answer (the "principal debtor or obligor" to use the terminology of R2 § 112 cmt. b) and the obligee, or (2) that the promisor has been given separate consideration for his promise to answer for the principal debtor/obligor. Neither of those presumptions holds true in this Question. In the words of one commentator, "The second *Restatement*, by speaking in terms of a contract to answer for another's duty, suggests that the origins of the obligation must be in the contract. The meaning of an agreement to answer for another's duty often engenders confusion." HOWARD O. HUNTER, MODERN LAW OF CONTRACTS § 7:24 (rev. ed. 1999) (footnote omitted). Professor Hunter then discusses the case of *Lawrence v. Anderson*, 184 A. 689 (Vt. 1936),

> in which a doctor came upon an accident and stopped to help. The injured man's daughter assured the doctor that she would pay for his services. When the doctor later requested payment, first from the man's estate and then from the daughter, the Vermont court refused to enforce the daughter's promise. The doctor indicated that the decedent was the original obligor when he sued the estate. The daughter's promise made her a surety and her promise was unenforceable because it was not in writing.

Whether *Lawrence*, decided more than 40 years prior to the publication of the *Restatement (Second)*, remains good law in the latter's wake is unclear. Holmes signed no writing. If a writing was required, Lestrade would have to fall back on promissory estoppel. *See* R2 § 139. If no writing was required, Lestrade should have a good breach of contract claim because (1) Holmes offered to reimburse Lestrade for Watson's care; (2) Lestrade accepted by agreeing to pay Watson's bill; and (3) Holmes's promise to repay Lestrade whatever he paid on Watson's behalf was consideration for Lestrade's promise to the hospital to pay Watson's expenses. *See* R2 §§ 71 & 75.

Answer (B) is incorrect because promissory restitution addresses promises made after the promisee has performed, but this Question asks about Holmes's liability for expenses incurred following (rather than preceding) his promise.

Answer (C) is not the best answer because, while Holmes's promise would have given Lestrade grounds to expect to be compensated (unlike the facts of Question 93), *Restatement of Restitution* § 116 authorizes a claim only against Watson or his estate.

95. Probably not. As for the pre-visit expenses, the hospital seems, unlike Lestrade, to have a claim under *Restatement of Restitution* § 116, because it would reasonably have expected to be paid for the life-sustaining services its doctors and nurses provided.

The problem is that *Restatement of Restitution* § 116 entitles the hospital to restitution from the beneficiary (or his estate). Based on our facts, Holmes is neither. As for promissory restitution (R2 § 86), the hospital satisfies the first requirement — it did not render the services gratuitously. The problem is the second requirement — not enforcing the promise would unjustly enrich Holmes. It is not all that clear how Holmes, or Holmes's estate, would be unjustly enriched by not having to pay for the unsuccessful care rendered to Watson.

96. **Answer (D) is the best answer.** Without a promise of any sort from Holmes, Lestrade cannot recover for either breach of contract or promissory estoppel. Therefore, **Answers (A) and (B) are incorrect**. Without a promise, his only avenue is *Restatement of Restitution* § 116, which is foreclosed because, as discussed in the answer to Question 93, Lestrade did not act expecting compensation. Therefore, **Answer (C) is incorrect**.

97. **Answer (C) is the best answer.** Without a promise from Holmes, the hospital cannot recover for either breach of contract or promissory estoppel. Therefore, **Answers (A) and (B) are incorrect**. However, unlike Lestrade, the hospital can recover both pre-and post-visit expenses under *Restatement of Restitution* § 116, because it acted with the reasonable expectation of being compensated; and here, unlike Question 95, Holmes and his estate are deemed to be beneficiaries of the hospital's care for Watson. Therefore, **Answer (D) is incorrect**.

98. If Lewis's breach of contract claim fails because of the statute of frauds, then Lewis may seek to recover under R2 § 139, which would require him to prove that (1) MEC should reasonably have expected Lewis to act or forbear based on MEC's promise of continued employment; (2) Lewis did, in fact, act or forbear based on the promise; (3) Lewis suffered a detriment because of his reliance on MEC's promise; and (4) injustice can be prevented only by enforcing MEC's promise, notwithstanding the statute of frauds, because (a) Lewis has no other remedy; (b) Lewis's action or forbearance — not quitting MEC and finding a job elsewhere — was "definite and substantial"; (c) Lewis's action or forbearance was a reasonable response to MEC's promise; and (d) Lewis's action or forbearance was a reasonably foreseeable response to MEC's promise. Thus, if Lewis is unable to produce the handwritten December 15, 1992 amendment signed by MEC, he should be able to recover under R2 § 139 for MEC's breach of its promise to retain him until age 65.

99. **Answer (D) is the best answer.** Slate is not trying to use Betty's promise as the basis for recovering the cost of constructing the addition to the Rubbles' house. Slate is past that now. Rather, Slate is trying to use Betty's promise as the basis for recovering the balance of the debt Betty promised to pay in exchange for Slate's promise to cease collection efforts against Bamm Bamm. Therefore, **Answers (A) and (B) are both factually true but legally inaccurate**.

Answer (C) is correct, but incomplete. Betty clearly promised to pay Slate the balance due, and Betty could foresee Slate relying on her promise by forbearing collection efforts against Bamm Bamm. Slate did, in fact, forbear. The real question is whether avoiding injustice requires enforcing Betty's promise. Because Bamm Bamm has fled the jurisdiction, and because, unlike most contemporary American jurisdictions, Bedrock does not recognize statutory liens for repairs and improvements to realty, Slate's only possible recovery is from Betty, so the promise should be enforced. (Indeed, given the timing of events here, perhaps Bamm Bamm and Betty intended to delay Slate from suing until Bamm Bamm had fled the jurisdiction. If so, then Slate should have a rock-solid promissory estoppel claim.)

100. **Answer (D) is the best answer.** As discussed in the answer to Question 91, R2 § 86 provides that a promise, made in recognition of a benefit already received, is binding to the extent necessary to prevent injustice, if (1) the promisee did not render the benefit gratuitously, (2) not enforcing the promise would unjustly enrich the promisor, and (3) the promise is not disproportionate to the benefit the promisor received. The facts are clear that Betty made her promise after Slate completed its work. Therefore, **Answer (A) is incorrect.** Slate did not undertake the work gratuitously — it intended to be paid. Therefore, **Answer (B) is incorrect.** Betty promised to pay Slate only the outstanding balance of Bamm Bamm's debt plus interest, making the promise proportionate to the value given. Therefore, **Answer (C) is incorrect.** Betty will argue that she and Barney neither wanted nor needed the music room addition; and, therefore, they have not been unjustly enriched. However, Slate's $10,000 worth of work surely increased the value of Betty and Barney's home — even if Betty and Barney would not have engaged Slate to do the work in the first place.

101. **Answer (C) is the best answer.** Because Betty owns property that has substantially benefited from Slate's work, Slate can argue that Betty will be unjustly enriched if she is allowed to retain the benefit without further payment. It is true that Slate has received $2,850 so far, but that is well below the value of the addition. In *Commerce Partnership 8098 L.P. v. Equity Contracting Co.*, 695 So. 2d 383 (Fla. Dist. Ct. App. 1997), for example, a subcontractor was allowed to seek recovery in restitution from the owner of an office building, even though the subcontractor did not have a contract with the owner, because the owner had received and retained the value of the subcontractor's stucco and surfacing work without paying for it — and, thus, had been unjustly enriched. Betty will argue that she and Barney neither wanted nor needed the music room addition; and, therefore, they have not been unjustly enriched. However, because the addition, assuming it was competently constructed, undoubtedly added value to the Rubbles' home — even if only in terms of greater resale value — **Answer (D) is not the best answer.**

Webb v. McGowin, 168 So. 196 (Ala. Ct. App. 1935), with its discussion of the "material benefit rule," is not really on point. On the facts of this Question, there was ample time for Slate to have requested Betty's permission before beginning work; and unlike the plaintiff in *Webb*, Slate has not suffered substantial bodily injuries. Therefore, **Answer (A) is not the best answer.** Nor does *Restatement of Restitution* § 117 help Slate, because its actions were not to protect Betty's property from damage. Therefore, **Answer (B) is not the best answer.**

102. **Answer (A) is the best answer**. The primary goal of contract construction and interpretation is to give effect to the parties' intent, manifested when they entered into the contract, in light of the circumstances surrounding its formation. *See* R2 § 212(1). A court must give effect to the objective intent of the parties, as it is expressed or apparent in writing, as opposed to the subjective intent of parties who failed to fully capture their intent when they wrote the contract in question. *See* R2 §§ 200 cmt. b & 212 cmt. a.

While subjective intent may be relevant when both parties share the same subjective intent, even though a disinterested third party might think they meant otherwise, *see* R2 § 201(1), courts generally concern themselves with the parties' objective manifestations of their intent, rather than their hidden agendas. Therefore, **neither Answer (B) nor Answer (D) is the best answer**.

Answer (C) is not the best answer because, while parties can form many types of contracts without a writing, when the parties do commit some or all of the terms of their agreement to writing, a court should begin its analysis with the writing.

103. **Answer (D) is the best answer**. A *fully integrated* written agreement discharges *all* prior or contemporaneous oral agreements and prior written agreements relating to the same subject matter as the fully integrated written contract. *See* R2 § 213(2). While the parol evidence rule is not, itself, a rule of evidence, it does have evidentiary consequences. Courts will generally not permit the trier of fact to hear evidence of prior agreements, negotiations, or representations superceded by a fully integrated writing. However, if an integrated term or agreement is susceptible to more than one reasonable meaning (*i.e.*, *ambiguous*), the trier of fact may consider extrinsic evidence, even if the writing is fully integrated, to determine which of the possible meanings the parties must have objectively intended when they entered into their contract. *See* R2 § 212.

A contract is integrated if it represents the final agreement of the parties as to one or more written terms. R2 § 209(1). A contract is *fully integrated* if it represents the full and final agreement of the parties as to *all* terms related to the contract's subject matter. R2 § 210(1). A contract is *partially integrated* if it is final as to some or all of the terms contained in the writing, but not as to all terms relevant to the subject matter. R2 § 210(2). Two factors courts consider when deciding whether and to what extent a written agreement is integrated are the presence (or lack thereof) of a "merger" or "integration" clause and the presence (or lack thereof) of one or more "open" terms. If the written agreement contains a clause stating that it "constitutes the entire agreement of the parties" regarding the subject matter of the contract, that clause evidences integration. On the other hand, when one or more terms are left for future determination, or if one or more key terms are obviously missing from the written agreement, the missing or open term is evidence rebutting integration. A third factor courts consider when determining the degree to which a writing is integrated is the extent of the negotiations between the parties leading up to the written agreement. The more the parties discussed the terms of the deal before executing the written agreement, the more likely a court will find the writing to be integrated. Courts may also consider the sophistication of the parties, the presence of waivers or disclaimers of implied warranties and other statutory remedies, and whether the terms proffered by the party trying to establish non-integration are ones that the parties "would certainly have included in the document had it been part of their agreement." *Betaco, Inc. v. Cessna Aircraft Co.*, 32 F.3d 1126, 1132 (7th Cir. 1994).

A partially integrated agreement discharges prior or contemporaneous oral agreements and prior written agreements *to the extent they are inconsistent* with one or more integrated terms. R2 § 213(a). **Answers (A) and (B) are incorrect** because, if a writing is only partially integrated, the trial court should permit the trier of fact to consider extrinsic evidence to ascertain the presence and meaning of unintegrated terms of the agreement.

Answer (C) is not the best answer because it ignores the possibility that, while a fully integrated writing is the full and final expression of the terms of the parties' agreement, one or more terms in the fully integrated writing may be reasonably susceptible to more than one interpretation. If that is the case, the trial court should permit the trier of fact to consider extrinsic evidence to resolve that ambiguity.

104.   **Answer (B) is the best answer**. *See* R2 §§ 209(2) & 212(2). **Answer (A) is not the best answer**, tempting though it may be. Even though the trial judge will almost certainly have to consider facts in making her threshold determinations on the extent of integration and the presence of ambiguity, her findings are treated as findings of law, rather than findings of fact. *See* R2 § 212(2) & cmt. d. Therefore, Answer (A) is an inferior choice to Answer (B).

Answers (C) and (D) are incorrect. If the trial judge decides, as a threshold matter, that a written agreement is less-than-fully integrated or is not unambiguous, then the judge may ask the jury to find, as matters of fact, what additional terms the parties consented to, the meaning of any terms whose meanings the parties dispute, or both. However, until the trial judge makes her threshold determinations on the extent of integration and the presence of ambiguity, the jury is out of the equation.

105.   **Answer (B) is the best answer**. In a "four corners" jurisdiction (*e.g.*, Mississippi), a trial judge should not look beyond the written agreement, and any other documents incorporated therein by reference, until she has decided that the written agreement plus any documents incorporated therein by reference do not constitute the entire agreement of the parties, are ambiguous as to one or more terms, or both. *See, e.g., Pursue Energy Corp. v. Perkins*, 558 So. 2d 349 (Miss. 1990). The judge is not, as the descriptive

term suggests, limited to only what is within the "four corners" of the written agreement itself. Therefore, **Answer (A) is not the best answer** because it is underinclusive.

Answers (C) and (D) are incorrect because they are overinclusive. One of the principal distinctions between the way that courts in "four corners" jurisdictions construe and interpret written agreements and the way their counterparts in *Restatement* or "modified objectivist" jurisdictions (*e.g.*, Texas) do so is the universe of evidence a trial judge may consider in making her threshold determinations regarding integration and ambiguity. In a "four corners" jurisdiction, that universe is limited to the evidence described in Answer (B), as explained above. In a "modified objectivist" jurisdiction, the universe is much larger, including evidence of other documents that appear to relate to the agreement and any other evidence a party wishes to proffer regarding the circumstances surrounding the contract's formation, *see, e.g.*, *Lenape Resources Corp. v. Tennessee Gas Pipeline Co.*, 925 S.W.2d 565 (Tex. 1996) — evidence of which lies beyond the limits of the universe known to a "four corners" judge.

The other key distinctions between the "four corners" and "modified objectivist" approach to construing and interpreting contracts rest on whether and to what extent a court will presume that a contract is integrated simply because it is written and the weight a court will give to a merger or integration clause. Unless something on the face of the written agreement compels a contrary finding, "four corners" judges presume that (1) a written agreement is integrated as to the terms contained therein, *see, e.g.*, Bank of Lena v. Slay, 170 So. 635 (Miss. 1936), and (2) a written agreement containing a merger or integration clause is fully integrated, *see, e.g.*, *Stribling Brothers Machinery Co. v. Girod Co.*, 124 So. 2d 289 (Miss. 1960). "Modified objectivist" judges, on the other hand, neither presume that an agreement is integrated simply because the parties wrote it out, *see* § R2 210 cmt. b ("[A] writing cannot of itself prove its own completeness, and wide latitude must be allowed for inquiry into circumstances bearing on the intention of the parties."), nor afford great weight to the fact that the writing includes a merger or integration clause (particularly if the writing is a form contract and the merger or integration clause is part of the form, rather than a separately negotiated or separately written provision), *see* R2 § 216 cmt. e ("Written agreements often contain clauses stating that there are no representations, promises or agreements between the parties except those found in the writing. . . . But such a clause does not control the question whether the writing was assented to as an integrated agreement. . . .").

106.   **Answer (D) is the best answer** for the reasons explained in the answer to the Question 105. **Answers (A), (B), and (C) are not the best answers** because, as explained in the answer to Question 105, they are underinclusive.

107.   **Answer (A) is the best answer**. An instrument is ambiguous if one or more terms or provisions are susceptible to more than one reasonable meaning. *See, e.g.*, *Lenape Resources Corp. v. Tennessee Gas Pipeline Co.*, 925 S.W.2d 565 (Tex. 1996).

Because, as discussed previously, the primary goal of construing and interpreting contracts is to give effect to the objective intent of the parties when they entered into the contract, the best time to test ambiguity is when the parties formed the contract. A strong argument may also be made for testing ambiguity when a party's performance is due. However, ambiguity that did not exist prior to the time of trial should not influence the trial court. Therefore, **Answer (B) is not the best answer**.

Mere disagreement between the parties about the meaning of a provision of a contract is not enough to make the contract ambiguous. This is particularly true when the disagreement arises at or after the time one party believes the other to be in breach. Therefore, **Answer (D) is incorrect**. This is also true if the parties disagreed when they formed the contract, and each party knew that the other party assigned a different meaning to a particular term. *See* R2 § 201(2). On the other hand, if the parties disagreed when they formed the contract, but neither party knew that the other disagreed with his own understanding of the terms, one of two results will follow: (1) the court will find that the parties disagreed so fundamentally that there was no mutual assent, and therefore no contract, *see* R2 §§ 20(1) & 201(3); or (2) the court will find that there was mutual assent, but the meaning of the disputed term is ambiguous, so neither party will be bound to the meaning subscribed to it by the other, unless that meaning coincides with what the court (with or without the aid of the jury) finds to be the reasonable, objective interpretation of the term, *see* R2 § 201(3). Therefore, because we are not told the extent of either party's knowledge of the other party's intent when they entered into the contract, **Answer (C) is not the best answer** (though it could be under a particular set of facts not described in this Question).

108. **Answer (A) is the best answer**. Ambiguity may be *patent* — appearing on the face of the contract — or *latent* — arising from words the meaning of which are uncertain when applied to the subject matter of the contract. Here, two different provisions on the face of the policy indicate coverage for one year and coverage for three years. Bruce need not proffer any extrinsic evidence to establish that the policy is ambiguous. It is facially ambiguous. Therefore, **Answer (B) is not the best answer**. Reasonable minds could differ whether GHI had agreed to insure Bruce for one year or three years. Therefore, **Answer (C) is incorrect**.

While the policy as a whole may be either fully or partially integrated, focusing on the duration of coverage, there is nothing in the facts to indicate that the parties did not intend one or both conflicting statements in the policy to be their final agreement as to the duration of the policy. A typographical error need not affect the extent of a contract's integration, though it will quite likely introduce ambiguity where there may not have been any otherwise. Therefore, **Answer (D) is incorrect**.

109. **Answer (B) is the best answer**. Nothing in the facts suggests that the application and the binder were incorporated by reference into the insurance policy. Therefore, any ambiguity they introduce would be *latent*, rather than patent. Here, the face of the policy indicates coverage for one year. Bruce must proffer extrinsic evidence of three years' coverage to establish the ambiguity of the policy. Therefore, **Answer (A) is not the best answer**.

Taking the policy, the application, and the binder together, reasonable minds could differ whether GHI had agreed to insure Bruce for one year or three years. Therefore, **Answer (C) is incorrect**. **Answer (D) is incorrect** for the same reasons discussed in the answer to Question 108.

110. **Answer (C) is the best answer.** Because the policy refers to the versions of Attachments A and B in effect at the time of loss, there was no way for Bruce to tell, either when he entered into his contract with GHI (most likely, when Simms issued the binder) or when he first received the policy, what property was covered and what perils were excluded because he did not know when a loss would occur, if at all.

   Answer (A) is incorrect because the policy refers on its face to documents that may not be in existence when the policy was issued. **Answer (D) is incorrect** because at least one of the terms of the policy is final: the Insured's identity. Therefore, the policy is not wholly unintegrated.

   Answer (B) is trickier. If neither Attachment A nor Attachment B changed in any respect from when Bruce received his policy and when a loss occurred, if ever, GHI could make a viable argument that the policy was integrated with respect to covered premises and excluded perils. However, the policy makes it clear that Attachment A and Attachment B *could* change after Bruce received his policy and before a loss occurred. Perhaps a better argument for GHI is that the policy is integrated with respect to those premises covered in the original Attachment A that remained covered at all relevant times and those perils excluded in the original Attachment B that remained excluded at all relevant times, but not integrated with respect to additional premises or additional perils. That argument probably passes the "blush test" (*i.e.*, a lawyer could make the argument in court without blushing from embarrassment), but it would not make Answer (B) correct, even so, because neither Attachment A nor Attachment B would be final for as long as GHI reserved the right to modify the premises covered or the perils excluded. Therefore, **Answer (B) is not the best answer**.

111. **Answer (D) is the best answer.** As previously discussed in the answer to Question 105, one of the principal distinctions between the "four corners" approach to construing and interpreting contracts and the "modified objectivist" approach is the presumption that courts make about the significance of a merger or integration clause. "Modified objectivist" judges do not afford great weight to the fact that the writing includes a merger or integration clause — particularly if the writing is a form contract and the merger or integration clause is part of the form, rather than a separately negotiated or separately written provision.

   Answer (B) states the basic approach of "four corners" jurisdictions, as discussed more fully in the answer to Question 105. Therefore, **Answer (B) is incorrect**. Answer (A) takes the "four corners" approach to an extreme that only a handful of cases have contemplated: It is written, therefore it is fully integrated, all evidence to the contrary notwithstanding. Therefore, **Answer (A) is incorrect**.

Answer (C) presents a tempting alternative to Answer (D), and there are certainly courts who purport to adhere to the *Restatement* approach that, nonetheless, view a merger clause as creating a rebuttable presumption in favor of full integration. *See, e.g., Advertising & Policy Committee of the Avis Rent A Car System v. Avis Rent A Car System*, 780 S.W.2d 391 (Tex. App. 1989), *vacated on other grounds*, 796 S.W.2d 707 (Tex. 1990). That is not the position the *Restatement* takes. So, for our purposes, **Answer (C) is not the best answer**. That said, before you make the transition from answering hypothetical questions in a law school study aid to answering real questions from live clients, check the decisions of the courts in the jurisdiction whose law governs your dispute to see whether they fall closer to Answer (C) or Answer (D).

112. **Answer (B) is the best answer.** The fact that Falcon Crest, on behalf of Global, saw it necessary to issue a change order amending the contract suggests that the written contract was not the full and final agreement of the parties with respect to the subject matter — *i.e.*, B&S' construction of the refinery for Global. The parties may have *intended* the written contract to be the full and final agreement as of the date the signed it; but, by the time B&S' performance was due, the parties realized that the written agreement was not the full and final expression of their agreement. Thus, Falcon Crest, acting as Global's agent, amended the original written agreement.

Answers (A) and (C) are both tempting, but they go more to the issue of ambiguity than integration. Answer (A) is, essentially, evidence of a trade usage that may help B&S explain why it understood "Osaka steel" to mean "steel of the same type or grade as Osaka steel." Answer (C) reinforces the trade usage, providing evidence that Falcon Crest, who issued the specifications for Global and who was responsible for overseeing the construction project for Global, also considered "Osaka steel" to mean "steel of the same type or grade as Osaka steel." Neither of these pieces of evidence, however, goes to the extent to which the written agreement was integrated. Therefore, **Answers (A) and (C) are not the best answers**, also making **Answer (D) not the best answer**.

113. **Answer (D) is the best answer.** Now we are in the realm of ambiguity. Therefore, evidence of a trade usage (Answer (A)), prior dealings between the same parties on other projects (Answer (C)), and the parties' own construction of this agreement (Answer (B)) are all relevant to determining whether the written agreement is ambiguous and to resolving any ambiguity. Therefore, **Answers (A), (B), and (C) are all correct, but underinclusive**.

114. **Answer (D) is the best answer.** The exceptions to the common law parol evidence rule — *e.g.*, fraud, mistake, incapacity, duress, scrivener's error — are equally applicable to the Article 2 parol evidence rule. *See, e.g., Franklin v. Lovitt Equipment Co.*, 420 So. 2d 1370 (Miss. 1982).

Answer (C) is not the best answer because a term relating to the nature of the steel AmeriSteel was selling B&S would not satisfy the test for "consistent additional term" in UCC § 2-202 cmt. 3. So, even though it reaches the correct conclusion, Answer (C) does so by incorrect means.

Answers (A) and (B) are incorrect because both incorrectly assume that the Article 2 parol evidence rule is not subject to any exceptions other than those expressly stated in UCC § 2-202. Even if the contract between B&S and AmeriSteel was fully integrated, B&S would not be barred from presenting extrinsic evidence that fit within an exception to the rule stated in UCC § 2-202. *See, e.g., SMR Technologies, Inc. v. Aircraft Parts International Combs, Inc.*, 141 F. Supp. 2d 923 (W.D. Tenn. 2001).

Revised Article 2 leaves current UCC § 2-202 essentially unchanged, except that it moves part of current Official Comment 1 into the text as Revised § 2-202(2).

115. No. "Where the parties have attached different meanings to a promise or agreement or a term thereof, it is interpreted in accordance with the meaning attached by one of them if at the time of the agreement that party did not know of any different meaning attached by the other, and the other knew [or had reason to know] the meaning attached by the first party." R2 § 201(2)(a). Thus, Russell agreed to provide Gwyneth with two tickets to *The Orange Pumpernickel* movie premiere for $200. The fact that there was another *The Orange Pumpernickel* premiering that same night did not make Russell's promise to Gwyneth ambiguous because he knew which show she meant and she did not know that Russell might mean a different show.

116. No. "Where the parties have attached the same meaning to a promise or agreement or a term thereof, it is interpreted in accordance with that meaning." R2 § 201(1). While a disinterested third party may not have known which *The Orange Pumpernickel* Gwyneth meant when she agreed to pay Russell for two tickets to the show's premiere or which *The Orange Pumpernickel* Russell meant when he agreed to provide Gwyneth with two tickets to the show's premiere, because Gwyneth and Russell both meant the movie premiere, Gwyneth cannot now avoid the Russell's attempt to enforce the contract by arguing that the terms of their agreement were ambiguous.

117. **Answer (A) is the correct answer**. UCC § 2-202(b) permits the finder of fact to consider evidence of consistent additional terms to explain or supplement a *partially* integrated written agreement, but keeps such evidence from the trier of fact if the written agreement is *fully* integrated.

A "usage of trade" is "any practice or method of dealing having such regularity of observance in a place, vocation or trade so as to justify an expectation that it will be observed with respect to the transaction in question." UCC § 1-205(2). A "course of dealing" is "a sequence of previous conduct between the parties to a particular transaction which is fairly to be regarded as establishing a common basis of understanding for interpreting their expressions and other conduct." UCC § 1-205(1). "Where the contract for sale involves repeated occasions for performance by either party with knowledge of the nature of the performance and opportunity for objection to it by the other, any *course of performance* accepted or acquiesced in without objection shall be relevant to determine the meaning of the agreement." UCC § 2-208. A "consistent additional term" is one that, though agreed upon by the parties, would not necessarily have been included in the writing. UCC § 2-202 cmt. 3.

UCC § 2-202(a) *always* permits consideration of (1) trade usage, (2) course of dealing, and (3) course of performance to explain or supplement even a fully integrated written agreement. Therefore, **Answers (B), (C), and (D) are incorrect**.

Revised Articles 1 and 2 consolidate current UCC §§ 1-205 & 2-208 into Revised § 1-303, but make no substantive change to the definitions or legal consequences of trade usages, courses of dealing, and courses of performance.

118. **Answer (B) is the best answer** because there is no writing that was intended by *both* Justin and Belinda to be a final expression of their agreement, even with respect to the terms included therein. Belinda's confirmation was a writing, therefore **Answer (A) is incorrect**, but there are no facts that suggest Justin intended Belinda's confirmation to be a final expression of Justin's agreement with respect to anything. And, because Justin is not a merchant (*see* UCC § 2-104 cmt. 2), he is not bound by Belinda's written "confirmation" due to his failure to timely object in writing to the terms thereof. Therefore, **Answer (D) is incorrect**.

Answer (C) raises an interesting point about the Article 2 parol evidence rule: the text of UCC § 2-202 is silent regarding the effect of ambiguity. Unlike the common law parol evidence rule, UCC § 2-202 appears to say (by not saying to the contrary) that ambiguity alone will not permit the court to consider evidence other than trade usage, course of dealing, and course of performance if the contract for the sale of goods is fully integrated, or those three plus consistent additional terms if the contract is only partially integrated. Indeed, UCC § 2-202 cmt. 1(c) "definitely rejects . . . [t]he requirement that a condition precedent to the admissibility of the type of evidence specified in [§ 2-202(a)] is an original determination by the court that the language used is ambiguous." Therefore, Answer (C) is technically incorrect. As a practical matter, courts generally will consider extrinsic evidence other than the kinds expressly permitted by UCC § 2-202 if it finds one or more terms of the sales contract ambiguous. *See, e.g., Random House, Inc. v. Rosetta Books LLC*, 150 F. Supp. 2d 613 (S.D.N.Y. 2001), *aff'd*, 283 F.3d 490 (2d Cir. 2002); *Quaker Alloy Casting Co. v. Gulfco Industries, Inc.*, 686 F. Supp. 1319 (N.D. Ill. 1988). Doing so seems to be consistent with the broad language of UCC § 1-103, which permits courts to incorporate common law and equity to decide issues not explicitly resolved by the language of Article 2 or the official comments. All that said, we need not trouble the court in this case with grappling with Answer (C), because Answer (B) being true opens the flood gates to extrinsic evidence. Moreover, as an important matter of form, a court wishing to import ambiguity analysis into this Article 2 dispute should also import the requirement that the court find ambiguity *before* permitting the jury to hear extrinsic evidence. Thus, **Answer (C) is not the best answer**.

119. **Answer (C) is the best answer**. Under UCC § 2-207, different terms in a single confirmation to an already concluded oral agreement should not become part of the agreement unless the other party expressly agreed to them. If the rule were otherwise, then a party would be able to unilaterally change the terms of an already concluded agreement. Using the standard approach to different terms in a single confirmation,

then the price of each Beetle should be $5,000, not $7,500. Therefore, **Answers (B) and (D) are incorrect**.

The standard approach to different terms in a single confirmation breaks down, however, when the different term is quantity. We cannot decide the terms of a contract until we first establish that we have an enforceable contract. Because UCC § 2-201 deals with enforceability, its requirements will supersede those of UCC § 2-207. (UCC § 2-207 cmt. 6 tells us that "[t]he written confirmation is also subject to Section 2-201.") UCC § 2-201(1) provides, in part: "A writing is not insufficient because it omits or incorrectly states a term agreed upon but the contract is not enforceable under this paragraph beyond the quantity of goods shown in such writing." In this case, then, Justin would not be able to enforce a contract with Belinda beyond the two cars mentioned in Belinda's signed letter to Justin. That letter will qualify as the writing Justin needs to enforce the contract under UCC § 2-201(1), because Belinda — the party to be charged — signed it, it is sufficient to indicate Justin and Belinda made a contract for sale, and it states a quantity. Because he must rely on that letter as the basis for enforcing the contract, Justin will be stuck under UCC § 2-201(1) to no more than two cars. Therefore, **Answer (A) is incorrect and Answer (B) is incorrect again**.

120. Justin and Belinda have their places of business in, respectively, Mexico and the United States, both of which are Contracting States to the CISG. Justin wanted to purchase the Beetles for resale, not for personal, family, or household use, and the parties did not expressly opt out of the CISG. Therefore, this contract is governed by the CISG. *See* CISG arts. 1(1)(a), 2(a) & 6. The CISG has no statute of frauds and no parol evidence rule. *See* CISG art. 11 ("A contract of sale need not be concluded in or evidenced by writing and . . . may be proved by any means, including witnesses."). As such, Justin and Magda should be allowed to testify that Belinda agreed to sell Justin four Beetles for $5,000 each, and Justin should not be limited to the number of Beetles stated in Belinda's letter. Article 19 — the CISG's counterpart to much of UCC § 2-207 — should not apply here, because the parties had already formed their contract before Belinda sent her letter. Therefore, the letter should be treated as a proposal, which Justin was free to decline, to modify the already-formed agreement.

121. **Answer (D) is the best answer**. Because both parties are merchants, UCC § 2-207(1) & (2) determines the terms of the contract. All agreed terms are in. So, we know quantity (5,000 feet), price ($5.00 per foot), and the delivery deadline (May 1, 2003). What about the additional terms in Tubular's acknowledgment? If they "materially alter" the offer, they will not become part of the contract. UCC § 2-207(2)(b) & cmt. 3. If they do not "materially alter" the original bargain, then they will become part of the contract unless (1) Mercury's offer expressly limited Tubular's acceptance to the terms of the offer, UCC § 2-207(2)(a), which it did not; or (2) Mercury objected to the additional terms within a reasonable time, UCC § 2-207(2)(c), which it did not. Tubular's acknowledgment contained three new terms: (1) a disclaimer of all implied warranties, (2) a provision requiring Mercury to pay the cost of shipping the tubing from Tubular's factory to Mercury's, and (3) a provision requiring Mercury to pay

the full contract price, including transportation costs, upon receipt of the tubing (*i.e.*, "C.O.D."). The disclaimer of warranties — which may not have ultimately been effective under UCC § 2-316 — materially altered the terms of Mercury's offer, UCC § 2-207 cmt. 4; therefore, **Answer (C) is incorrect**, and the disclaimer is not part of the parties' contract. The other two terms do not appear to materially alter the original bargain, unless there is some prior course of dealing between these parties or some trade usage or custom that is so contrary to these terms as to make these terms "result in surprise or hardship if incorporated without [Mercury's] express awareness." UCC § 2-207 cmt. 4. Any other terms necessary to complete the contract will be supplied by UCC "gap-fillers." Therefore, with Tubular's warranty disclaimer negated, Mercury would be free to sue Tubular under one or more Article 2 implied warranties.

Answer (A) is incorrect because it presumes that Article 2 applies the common law "last shot rule." However, the comments to UCC § 2-207 make it clear that Article 2 abandons the "last shot rule" (along with the "mirror image" rule) in favor of a scheme designed to more easily find contracts and to make it more difficult for one party to control the terms of those contracts.

Answer (B) is incorrect because UCC § 2-207(1) would deem Tubular's acknowledgment to be a counteroffer *only* if Tubular expressly conditioned its acceptance of Mercury's offer on Mercury's assent to the additional terms in Tubular's acknowledgment. Tubular did not expressly condition its acceptance; therefore, Tubular's acknowledgment was not a counteroffer.

Revised Article 2 dispenses with current UCC § 2-207(2) and the concept of "material alteration." Any additional or different term to which both parties do not (eventually) agree is "knocked-out" under Revised § 2-207, and replaced with the relevant "gap filler."

122.   **Answer (D) is the best answer**. Tubular's acknowledgment disclaimed all implied warranties. Mercury's purchase order claimed all implied warranties. Therefore, the "knockout rule" eliminates both Tubular's terms and Mercury's term and substitutes the UCC "gap-filler" — which, in this case, is the implied warranty of merchantability: UCC § 2-314. *See* Melvin Aron Eisenberg, *The Limits of Cognition and the Limits of Contract*, 47 STAN. L. REV. 211 (1995) ("[U]nder the 'knockout rule,' when a contract is formed under [UCC § 2-207(1)] by an exchange of forms, and the preprinted terms of the forms differ, all conflicting preprinted terms, whether or not clear and conspicuous, drop out, and the contract consists only of the terms on which the forms agree . . . and terms implied by law."); *see, e.g.,Daitom, Inc. v. Pennwalt Corp.*, 741 F.2d 1569 (10th Cir. 1984); *Westinghouse Electric Corp. v. Nielsons, Inc.*, 647 F. Supp. 896 (D. Colo. 1986).

Answer (A) is not the best answer because, while factually correct in this Question, because of the operation of the "knockout rule" explained in the previous paragraph, it will not always be the case that an offeror's reservation will be given effect.

Answers (B) and (C) are incorrect because they ignore the fact that UCC § 2-207(2) abandoned the "last shot rule."

123. **Answer (D) is the best answer.** Because Tubular's acknowledgment expressly conditioned its acceptance of Mercury's offer on Mercury's assent to Tubular's new terms, Tubular's acknowledgment was a counteroffer. UCC § 2-207(1). Because Mercury did not expressly assent to Tubular's new terms, the parties did not form a contract by their exchange of writings. That means we must find that the parties' actions, rather than their correspondence, formed a contract under UCC § 2-207(3). Here, Tubular shipped the tubing without having received either an assent or objection from Mercury, and Mercury took delivery of and paid for the tubing, despite being aware of Tubular's warranty disclaimer. These actions are "[c]onduct by both parties which recognizes the existence of a contract . . . although the writings of the parties do not otherwise establish a contract." UCC § 2-207(3). Therefore, the terms of the contract are those on which the writings agree — here, price, quantity, identity of the goods, and delivery deadline — plus any necessary UCC "gap-fillers." One such gap-filler is the implied warranty of merchantability.

     Answer (A) is incorrect because, given Mercury's failure to assent or object in writing to Tubular's new terms, the "knockout rule" discussed in the answer to Question 122 would not apply. **Answers (B) and (C) are incorrect** because they presume that Article 2 applies the common law "last shot rule." But, as discussed in the answer to Question 121, Article 2 abandoned the "last shot rule."

124. In the absence of material alteration, the terms would be those contained in Mercury's offer, plus the additional terms contained in Tubular's reply. CISG art. 19(2). However, Tubular's reply did materially alter Mercury's offer, CISG arts. 19(1) & (3); so, no help there. Mercury's receipt of and payment in full for the tubing constituted an acceptance of Tubular's counteroffer, under CISG arts. 18(1) & (3). So, the terms would be those contained in Tubular's counteroffer — including the warranty disclaimer. Here, unlike UCC § 2-207, the "last shot rule" prevails.

125. **Answer (B) is the best answer.** The fact that the Samples agreed to let the Burgers occupy the house prior to closing and the inclusion of paragraph 8, conveying particular items of personal property, strongly suggest that this writing was the product of the parties' negotiation, and not simply some boilerplate form (although it may have started as one). Paragraph 20, while no more than evidence of integration (as discussed in the answer to Question 111), is still that: evidence of integration. Taken together, the length of the contract, the non-standard terms, and the merger clause all suggest some degree of integration. Therefore, **Answer (A) is incorrect**. However, the references in paragraph 8 to matters outside the four corners of the document — "furniture in the upstairs game room," "lawn and patio furniture," and, to a lesser extent, "window treatments" and "appliances" — point away from full integration and toward partial integration. Therefore, **Answer (C) is incorrect**. While Answer (D) is conceptually true — under the "modified objectivist" approach, a writing cannot prove its own integration — here, there seems to be ample evidence on the face of the writing to presume partial integration, subject to proof to the contrary from sources outside the four corners of the contract of conveyance. Because this Question limits itself to the facial quality of the contract, **Answer (D) is not the best answer.**

126. **Answer (D) is the best answer**. If such a condition existed, and if the Burgers can prove it, they will be excused from performing the contract to purchase the Samples' house due to failure of a condition precedent. R2 § 225(1). The parol evidence rule will not exclude extrinsic evidence of the condition precedent — despite it not being mentioned in the written contract — even if the writing is fully integrated (and here the explicit reference to facts outside the agreement, *i.e.*, "the furniture in the upstairs game room," belies the meaningfulness of the integration clause in paragraph 20), because the parol evidence rule does not exclude extrinsic evidence of a condition precedent even to an otherwise fully integrated, unambiguous agreement. *See* R2 § 217. Therefore, **Answer (B) is incorrect**.

While a writing must evidence a contract for the sale or other transfer of an interest in real property in order to satisfy the statute of frauds, R2 §§ 110(1)(d) & 125, that writing need not contain every term of the contract. Therefore, **Answer (A) is incorrect**.

Answer (C) is not the best answer because, while it leads to the correct result, it takes an illogical route to get there. If anything, the fact that the parties discussed something and then left it out of the writing generally evidences that the parties did not agree on that term.

127. Whether the solar screens were part of the sale will depend on how the court construes the phrase "window treatments" in paragraph 8 of the contract. The facts do not indicate that the parties defined the term in their written agreement, and it is easy enough to see that "window treatments" can mean more than one thing: exterior screens, storm windows, awnings, canopies, glazing, UV film, blinds, drapes, shutters, roller shades, etc. If the Burgers and the Samples attributed different meanings to the phrase, R2 § 201(1) is inapplicable. If there is no evidence that the Samples knew or had reason to know that the Burgers meant "window treatments" to include the solar screens or that the Burgers knew or had reason to know that the Samples meant "window treatments" to exclude the solar screens, R2 § 201(2) would, likewise, be inapplicable. Therefore, the written agreement, even if fully integrated, is not unambiguous, and the court should permit extrinsic evidence, at a minimum, to explain the meaning of "window treatments." The problem is that there is no extrinsic evidence in the facts that will help the Burgers. So, absent a shared understanding of the parties that will bring R2 § 201(1) back into play, or knowledge on the Samples' part that the Burgers considered "window treatments" to include the solar screens and no knowledge on the Burgers' part that the Samples thought otherwise, bringing R2 § 201(2) back into play, or a trade usage, a deed restriction requiring solar screens, or some other evidence beyond that presented in the facts, the Samples ought not be bound to the Burgers' definition of "window treatments." R2 § 201(3).

128. **Answer (D) is the best answer**. The principle *noscitur a sociis* instructs a court to construe or interpret a word in the context of the terms immediately preceding and following it. *See* Edwin W. Patterson, *The Interpretation and Construction of Contracts*, 64 COLUM. L. REV. 833, 853 (1964) ("The meaning of a word in a series may

be affected by the others in the same series; or, a word may be affected by its immediate context."). The fact that the custom-made exterior solar screens were the only interior or exterior window treatment the Burgers ever saw on or in the Samples' house has absolutely nothing to do with the meaning of the words immediately preceding or following "window treatments" in paragraph 8 of the contract.

On the other hand, the fact that the custom-made exterior solar screens were the only interior or exterior window treatment the Burgers ever saw on or in the Samples' house would certainly figure into a court's attempt to consider the circumstances surrounding the contract's formation. *See* R2 § 202(1) ("Words and other conduct are interpreted in the light of all the circumstances. . . ."); R2 § 209 cmt. a ("[B]oth integrated and unintegrated agreements are to be read in the light of the circumstances. . . ."); R2 § 201 cmt. b ("Uncertainties in the meaning of words are ordinarily greatly reduced by the context in which they are used. . . . In general, the context relevant to interpretation of a bargain is the context common to both parties."). In accounting for the circumstances surrounding the contract's formation, "the court should place itself, as near as possible, in the exact situation of the parties when they executed the instrument, so as to determine their intentions, the objects to be accomplished, obligations created, time of performance, duration, mutuality, and other essential features." Keith A. Rowley, *Contract Construction and Interpretation: From the "Four Corners" to Parol Evidence (and Everything in Between)*, 69 Miss. L.J. 73, 140 (1999); *see also* R2 § 202 cmt. b ("When the parties have adopted a writing as a final expression of their agreement, interpretation is directed to the meaning of that writing in the light of the circumstances. The circumstances for this purpose *include the entire situation, as it appeared to the parties*, and in appropriate cases may include facts known to one party of which the other had reason to know." [emphasis added]). Thus, **Answer (A) is not the best answer**.

While courts should make every effort to construe the express terms of the agreement so that they are in harmony with the parties' conduct, *see* R2 § 202(5), when the express terms and the parties' conduct are not consistent, the express terms control, *see* R2 § 203(a). *See* Mark K. Glasser & Keith A. Rowley, *On Parol: The Construction and Interpretation of Written Agreements and the Role of Extrinsic Evidence in Contract Litigation*, 49 Baylor L. Rev. 657, 676-77 (1997). Paragraph 8 says "*all* window treatments" (emphasis added). The solar screens were the *only* window treatments. For the Samples to argue that they did not consider the solar screens to be "window treatments," as evidenced by their having removed them in good faith, marginalizes the express term. As such, **Answer (B) is not the best answer**.

Courts should construe contractual provisions, if possible, in such a way as to give each provision meaning and purpose — or, in other words, so that no provision is rendered meaningless or moot. *See* Glasser & Rowley, *supra*, at 671; *see, e.g., Lenape Resources Corp. v. Tennessee Gas Pipeline Co.*, 925 S.W.2d 565 (Tex. 1996). Because the custom-made exterior solar screens were the only interior or exterior window treatment the Burgers ever saw on or in the Samples' house, the term "window treatments" in paragraph 8 either meant (1) the custom-made exterior solar screens or (2) nothing. If a contract or contractual provision is susceptible to two reasonable constructions, one of which would render it meaningful and the other moot, the construction making the contract or provision meaningful must prevail. *See* Glasser & Rowley, *supra*, at 671-72; *see, e.g.*, *Harris v. Rowe*, 593 S.W.2d 303 (Tex. 1979). Therefore, **Answer (C) is not the best answer**.

129.   **Answer (B) is the best answer**. When applying the primary rules of construction and interpretation fails to resolve an ambiguity, the court should construe the ambiguous term against the party responsible for drafting it. *See* R2 § 206; Glasser & Rowley, *supra*, at 683-87. The presumption against the drafter should be less pronounced when the other party has taken an active role in the drafting process or is particularly knowledgeable, *see* R2 § 206 reporter's note and cases cited therein, and should be nonexistent when both parties actively participate in drafting the contract. Thus, *contra proferentem* would have no place given the original facts of Question 125, where the Samples and Burgers drafted the contract together. But this Question says the Samples were solely responsible for drafting the agreement; therefore, *contra proferentem* would be available to the trial court to resolve an otherwise unresolved ambiguity.

A court construing an ambiguity against the drafters *because* they were the drafters should have already considered the circumstances surrounding the contract's formation, tried to give each provision of the contract meaning and purpose, and still have found the meaning of "window treatments" reasonably susceptible to more than one meaning. *See* Glasser & Rowley, *supra*, at 683. As the Michigan Supreme Court recently explained:

> The rule of *contra proferentem* is a rule of last resort because [t]he primary goal in the construction or interpretation of any contract is to honor the intent of the parties, and the rule of *contra proferentem* does not aid in determining the parties' intent. Instead, . . . [i]t is a rule of legal effect. . . . [I]ts purpose is not to render more accurate or more perfect a jury's understanding of the meaning of the contract, but is merely to ascertain the winner and the loser in connection with a contract whose meaning has eluded the jury despite all efforts to apply conventional rules of interpretation.

Klapp v. United Insurance Group Agency, Inc., 663 N.W.2d 447, 456 (Mich. 2003) (quotation and citations omitted). Therefore, **neither Answer (A) nor Answer (C) is the best answer**.

As for *noscitur a sociis*, it is as unhelpful here as it was under the facts of Question 128. The difference is that Question 128 asked for the *least* helpful rule, making *noscitur a sociis* the best answer, because the words immediately surrounding "all window treatments" could have in no way aided the court's resolution of the meaning of "all window treatments." Here, the court has chosen to construe the ambiguity against the drafter, without regard for what the words surrounding the ambiguous term might have to say. Therefore, **Answer (D) is incorrect**.

130.   **Answer (B) is the best answer**, provided that a court will find a washer and dryer to belong to the same "genus" as an oven, stove, refrigerator/freezer, and dishwasher.

As with the solar screens, the court should begin its analysis with R2 § 201(1) & (2). However, if the court were unable to find a common understanding between the parties or that the Samples knew what the Burgers meant and the Burgers did not know or have reason to know that the Samples meant otherwise, the court could seek refuge in the rules of construction and interpretation.

While the Burgers can certainly make a "plain language" argument, like that in Answer (A), that a washer and a dryer are "appliances," the Samples can counter that the "plain language of the contract expressly indicates which items are included in 'appliances,'" and that the washer and dryer are not. Therefore, **Answer (A) is not the best answer**. Similarly, while the Samples can argue that their performance — their "practical construction" — clearly indicates that they did not consider the washer and dryer to be included in the items to be conveyed under paragraph 8, that assumes too much. Such an argument would essentially mean that any breach could be explained away as one party's practical construction of the contract. Therefore, **Answer (D) is not the best answer**.

That leaves us with two "secondary" rules of construction: *ejusdem generis* and *expressio unius est exclusio alterius*. When an enumeration of specific things is followed by some more general word or phrase, then the general word or phrase will usually be construed to refer only to things of the same general nature or class as those specifically enumerated. *See* Patterson, *supra*, at 853 ("A general term joined with a specific term will be deemed to include only things that are like (of the same genus as) the specific one. . . . *E.g.*, *S* contracts to sell *B* his farm together with the 'cattle, hogs, and other animals.' This would probably not include *S*'s favorite house-dog, but might include a few sheep that *S* was raising for the market."). On the other hand, when some more general word or phrase does not follow or accompany an enumeration of specific things, then things of the same kind or species as those specifically enumerated are deemed to be excluded. *See id.* at 853 ("If one or more specific terms are listed, without any general or inclusive terms, other items although similar in kind are excluded. *E.g.*, *S* contracts to sell *B* his farm together with the 'cattle and hogs on the farm.' This language would be interpreted to exclude the sheep and *S*'s favorite house-dog."). Here, the list of specified items — "oven, stove, refrigerator/freezer, and dishwasher" — is accompanied by a more general word or phrase — "all appliances, including. . ." Therefore, **Answer (C) is not the best answer**.

131. Yes. Even if the trial court finds the contract to be unambiguous and fully integrated as a matter of law, there are numerous parol evidence rule exceptions that might permit the admission of Leon's oral assurance to Paola that the property was zoned outside of the 50-year flood plain. At least five might apply in this case. First, if both Leon and Paola were mistaken when they entered into the contract as to the flood-plain zoning of the property, and that zoning materially affected the value of the transaction to one or both parties, parol evidence may be admissible to establish a *mutual mistake* that would allow either party to avoid the contract. Second, if Leon should have known that the property was within the 50-year flood plain, or did not know one way or the other whether the property was outside the 50-year flood plain, parol evidence may

be admissible to establish a material *misrepresentation* that would allow Paola to avoid the contract. Third, if Leon knew that, in fact, the property was inside the 50-year flood plain, parol evidence may be admissible to establish *fraudulent inducement*. Fourth, if Paola would never have purchased the property if she had known it was zoned within the 50-year flood plain, but did so believing that she was receiving a property that was not flood-prone in exchange for her promise to pay Leon, parol evidence may be admissible to establish *lack or failure of consideration*. And, fifth, if Paola's agreement to purchase the property was conditioned on its not being situated within the 50-year flood plain, parol evidence may be admissible to establish the existence of an unsatisfied *condition precedent*.

132. **Answer (D) is the best answer**. Amendments, as with any provision of the contract they amend, are presumed to have meaning and purpose. The only meaning and purpose the December 15, 1992 amendment could have would be to require MEC to employ Lewis "for any period up to age 65." If there is a dispute over the meaning of "for any period up to age 65," the trial court should admit parol evidence to aid in interpreting the ambiguity. The facts do not indicate that the September 1, 1987 contract contained a merger/integration clause. Therefore, it should not be presumed to be fully integrated. And, even if it did and was, the parol evidence rule does not bar testimonial evidence about a *subsequent* modification. *See* R2 § 213 & ch. 9, topic 3 intro. note. Lewis alleged that (1) Washington agreed *two years after* the parties executed the September 1, 1987 contract, to amend the contract to add a promise to employ Lewis up to age 65 if he so wished, and (2) Washington reiterated that agreement *more than three years later* when she wrote it into Lewis's employment contract. Both of these events occurred after the parties executed the September 1, 1987 contract. Therefore, Lewis should be able to present extrinsic evidence of them.

Answer (C) is not the best answer because, while true, the mere possibility that new evidence will surface is not as compelling a reason for the trial court to deny MEC's motion for summary judgment as Answer (D) — which depends on a rule of law, rather than the possibility of a fact.

Answer (A) is incorrect because, as underlies the premise to Answer (D), the parties could have amended some or all of the September 1, 1987 contract, including the "at-will" clause.

Answer (B) is incorrect because, lacking an enforceable clause in the September 1, 1987 contract requiring the parties to evidence any subsequent amendments in writing (and the facts do not indicate that Lewis's contract with MEC contained such a clause), the parties may orally amend their written contract. Moreover, Answer (B) presumes that Washington did not, as Lewis alleges, amend the contract in writing. The mere fact that he has yet to put his hands on the amended version of the contract does not preclude him from testifying about its existence. One commonly recognized exception to the parol evidence rule permits a party to offer extrinsic evidence of a writing that has been lost, damaged, or destroyed. Likewise, if such a document existed, the statute of frauds will not bar its effectiveness simply because it was subsequently lost or destroyed. R2 § 137. And, in any event, even if the oral amendment was not enforceable standing alone, that does not mean evidence of it would be irrelevant to a jury construing and interpreting the contract between MEC and Lewis.

133. **Answer (D) is the best answer** because when a typewritten or printed provision in a contract conflicts with a handwritten provision, the trial court should enforce the handwritten provision, rather than the typewritten or printed one. *See* R2 § 203 cmt. f.

While resolving ambiguity often requires the services of a jury, the trial judge may be able to resolve the ambiguity as a matter of law by applying one of the primary or secondary rules of construction and interpretation. Here, the rule preferring handwritten terms to contrary typed or printed terms would allow the trial judge to resolve any ambiguity caused by the handwriting in favor of the handwriting. Therefore, **Answer (A) is not the best answer**.

Answer (B) is incorrect. Lewis gave up his claim to 20% of the proceeds of Billoway's cash-out in exchange for Washington's promise to employ him until age 65. Moreover, the promise to employ him "up to age 65" only bound MEC not to terminate Lewis before his 65th birthday; it did not bind Lewis to stay any length of time. An at-will employee gives consideration by continuing to work for his employer despite being able to leave at any time (with or without prior notice). And, in any event, even if the promise was not enforceable standing alone, that does not mean evidence of it would be irrelevant to a jury construing and interpreting the contract between MEC and Lewis.

Answer (C) is not the best answer because, while the court should try to construe the contract, as amended, to give every provision meaning and purpose, and the only way to give the handwritten amendment meaning and purpose would be to find that it binds MEC to employ Lewis for as long as he desires, up to age 65, the only way to give the pre-existing "at-will" clause in the contract meaning and purpose would be to find that MEC was not bound to employ Lewis other than at will. The two provisions conflict in such a way that the trial court *cannot* give them *both* meaning and purpose.

134.   **Answer (C) is the best answer.** A party granted an exclusive right, the exercise of which will benefit another, impliedly promises to use "reasonable efforts" on the other's behalf. *Wood v. Lucy, Lady Duff-Gordon*, 118 N.E. 214 (N.Y. 1917); *see also* R2 § 77 cmt. d & illus. 9. Here, Wallace agreed to record and perform exclusively for Vestal, and Vestal agreed to promote Wallace's music. When Chick Hanson instructed Vestal's staff to do nothing to promote Wallace — and, indeed, to try to convince radio stations to stop playing his music — Vestal ceased using "reasonable efforts."

Answer (D) is a good second choice. While not every state's law agrees, the *Restatement* imposes on each party to a contract "a duty of good faith and fair dealing in its performance and enforcement." R2 § 205. The reason why Answer (C) is a better choice than Answer (D) is that the courts seem to have a better handle on "reasonable efforts" than they do on "good faith." The *Restatement* begins defining good faith by turning to UCC § 1-201(19), which requires only "honesty in fact in the conduct or transaction concerned." *See* R2 § 205 cmt. a. (Revised Article 1 imports into the current § 1-201(19) "good faith" definition the additional requirement that all parties, not just merchants as is the case under current law, "observ[e] reasonable commercial standards of fair dealing." *Compare* Revised § 1-201(b)(20) *with* UCC §§ 1-201(19) & 2-103(1)(b). Therefore, Revised Article 2 appears to impose a higher standard of good faith than the *Restatement*.) Neither Hanson nor anyone else at Vestal lied to Wallace or anyone else about Vestal's promotional activities on Wallace's behalf after Hanson pulled the plug. The comments to R2 § 205 also mention "faithfulness to an agreed common purpose and consistency with the justified expectations of the other party." That seems more helpful to Wallace, but it is unclear that Wallace and Vestal shared much common purpose after Wallace told Hanson he wanted out, and a reasonable person in Wallace's position might have expected a negative reaction from Vestal.

Answer (A) is not the best answer because, while true, the mere fact that the contract purported to give Vestal complete discretion to promote or not promote Wallace's music is not dispositive. As the foregoing discussion of Answers (C) and (D) should make clear, unfettered factual discretion and unfettered legal discretion are two different things. Vestal still owed Wallace a duty of reasonable efforts and a duty of good faith and fair dealing.

As *Topic 9: Anticipatory Repudiation* should further illuminate, it is not clear that Wallace's statement to Hanson was a repudiation. Wallace did not say, "I'm leaving." He said, "I'm leaving as soon as the attorneys can sort it out." There was, of course, the possibility that the attorneys could not "sort it out" to everyone's satisfaction prior to the expiration of Wallace's existing contract with Vestal. There was also no real urgency in Wallace's statement. At most, Wallace's statement would have entitled Hanson to seek assurances from Wallace that he would continue to perform as promised until Vestal and Hippo could come to terms. Rather than doing so, Hanson decided to poison the well. Therefore, **Answer (B) is not the best answer**.

135. **Answer (D) is the best answer**. As does the common law (discussed in the answer to Question 134), UCC Article 2 imposes a duty on a party who promises to deal exclusively in goods to use "best efforts" to supply them or require them, as the case may be. UCC § 2-306(2). (*Revised Article 2 leaves the text of UCC § 2-306 unchanged.*) Section 2-306(1) goes further, requiring that Global produce quantities of benthahexelene not "unreasonably disproportionate to any stated estimate or . . . any normal or otherwise comparable prior output. . . ." It is not entirely clear how that language would apply in this case, because Global's contract with Byron contains no stated estimate and because this is a new plant with no prior output against which to measure what is "normal." However, the pricing structure is based on how much benthahexelene Global produced. So it would not seem unreasonable to expect that Global's output would not be "unreasonably disproportionate" to the minimum quantity specified in the pricing structure: 50,000 gallons per month.

Answers (A) and (B) are incorrect because they ignore the implied duty of best efforts. **Answer (C) is not the best answer** because, while factually correct, improving Global's bottom line is not a sufficiently compelling reason for it to avoid, in good faith, its contractual obligations to Byron.

136. **Answer (D) is the best answer** for essentially the same reasons discussed in the answer to Question 135. Just as UCC § 2-306(2) imposes a duty on an output seller to use best efforts to produce a commercially reasonable quantity of the goods it has promised to sell to its exclusive buyer, UCC § 2-306(2) imposes a duty on a requirements buyer to use best efforts to require a commercially reasonable quantity of the goods it has promised to purchase from its exclusive seller. Ascertaining a commercially reasonable quantity of hypobutatetridiene is more difficult in this Question than ascertaining a commercially reasonable quantity of benthahexelene was in Question 135 because the facts do not indicate any mention of quantity in Global's contract with Bubba Gump. Nonetheless, "a buyer which terminates its business in order to evade its obligations under a requirements contract acts in bad faith." *Schawk, Inc. v. Donruss Trading Cards, Inc.*, 746 N.E.2d 18, 25 (Ill. App. Ct. 2001). "Requirements contracts, by their nature, however, entail a sharing of risk between buyer and seller. While the buyer assumes the risk of less urgent changes in its economic circumstances, the seller assumes the risk of a change in the buyer's business that makes continuation of a requirements contract unduly costly." *Id.* Global is allowed considerable latitude to react to economic changes, but the issue here is not that honoring its contract with Bubba Gump would cause Global to lose money. Rather, Global wanted to avoid its contract with Byron, because it wanted to take advantage of higher benthahexelene prices on the spot market, which had the effect of causing Global to avoid its contract with Bubba Gump, as well.

Answers (A) and (B) are incorrect because they ignore the implied duty of best efforts. **Answer (C) is not the best answer** because, while factually correct, improving Global's bottom line is not a sufficiently compelling reason for it to avoid, in good faith, its contractual obligations to Bubba Gump.

137. **Answer (B) is the best answer.** "Satisfaction" contracts require one party to perform to the satisfaction of the other. Satisfaction contracts come in two basic varieties: those in which function dominates and those in which personal taste or aesthetics dominate. In the former, satisfaction is judged objectively, by asking whether a reasonable person in the position of the party whose satisfaction the contract required would be satisfied with the other party's performance. *See, e.g., Morin Building Products Co. v. Baystone Construction, Inc.*, 717 F.2d 413 (7th Cir. 1983). In the latter, satisfaction is judged subjectively, by asking whether the party whose satisfaction the contract required was, in fact, satisfied with the other party's performance. *See, e.g., David Tunick, Inc. v. Kornfeld*, 838 F. Supp. 848 (S.D.N.Y. 1993). Though subjective, satisfaction in the latter case is subject to the duty of good faith and fair dealing. Therefore, the party whose satisfaction is called for in the contract must be *honestly* dissatisfied with the other party's performance in order to avoid her performance obligations. *See* R2 § 205. The facts of this Question are far more like those of *Morin Building Products* (satisfactory exterior finishing of warehouse) than *Kornfeld* (forged Picasso). Absent some idiosyncrasy in the transaction that would cause a court to consider the aesthetic value of industrial paint and paneling to be more important in this transaction than its functional value, the court should apply the objective satisfaction test here, rather than the subjective test. Therefore, **Answer (A) is not the best answer.**

Neither Answer (C) nor Answer (D) is the best answer. Answer (D) could be true, yet that would not affect the outcome of this case. Answer (C) is only relevant to the extent that the "industry standard" would satisfy a reasonable person in Global's position.

138. **Answer (C) is the best answer.** Again, we have a satisfaction contract, the basic contours of which are discussed in the answer to Question 137. Here, unlike Question 137, a court is likely to apply the subjective satisfaction test, because aesthetics are likely to play a significant role in deciding whether the interior wallpapering of someone's residence is satisfactory. Therefore, **Answers (B) and (D) are incorrect** because they apply the wrong test. As between Answers (A) and (C), the facts strongly suggest that Sally was not honestly dissatisfied with the quality of Wally's performance; she was, instead, dissatisfied with *her* choice of wallpaper. She is simply trying to use her "right" to "satisfaction" as a means to remedy her own error in judgment. That is not how satisfaction contracts are meant to work. Therefore, **Answer (A) is not the best answer.**

If Sally is improperly denying satisfaction, then she is refusing to pay without cause and is in breach of her obligations under the contract. A court might couch this in terms of her duty of good faith and fair dealing in addition to, or in lieu of, finding that Wally had performed satisfactorily.

139. **Answer (C) is the correct answer**, and **Answers (A), (B), and (D) are incorrect**. The implied warranties of fitness for a particular purpose (UCC § 2-315), good title (UCC § 2-312), and merchantability (UCC § 2-314) all relate to goods sold subject to Article 2. The implied warranty of habitability relates to improvements to realty, not goods. Article 2 governs sales of goods, not realty.

The only substantive changes Revised Article 2 makes to current UCC §§ 2-312, 2-314 & 2-315 relate to a seller's ability to disclaim or a buyer's ability to waive the protection afforded by these implied warranties.

140. **Answer (A) is the best answer**. If PPP, in fact, used poor quality paint and paneling materials on the Waveland plant, the paint and paneling would not likely pass without objection in the trade, nor would it be fit for the ordinary purpose for which such paint and paneling are sold. As such, PPP would have violated the implied warranty of merchantability. UCC § 2-314.

The implied warranty of fitness for a particular purpose would not apply in this case because Falcon Crest specified the materials to be used, not PPP, and Global purchased them on Falcon Crest's advice, not PPP's. *See* UCC § 2-315. Therefore, **Answer (B) is incorrect**.

As for Answer (C), the Question asked about UCC Article 2 warranties, and the warranty of workmanlike performance is not a UCC warranty. Moreover, the facts indicate that Global's complaint is with the quality of the materials themselves, not with PPP's application or installation of them. Therefore, **Answer (C) is incorrect**.

Because Answer (A) is correct, **Answer (D) is incorrect**.

141. **Answer (A) is the best answer**. Unless explicitly waived, disclaimed, or otherwise limited, every contract for the sale of goods by a merchant includes an implied warranty that the goods, *inter alia*, are fit for the ordinary purpose for which such goods are used. UCC § 2-314(2)(b). The facts tell us that the parties have stipulated that the glitch was a problem with the GR8 computer. A computer that displays a glitch when running glitch-free graphics software is not fit for the ordinary purpose for which the computer is used, nor should it pass without objection in the trade. Therefore, Pennybakers should have a good claim under UCC § 2-314. Pennybakers should also have a viable claim for breach of express warranty under UCC § 2-313. The warranty card expressly warranted the computer against defects, other than those caused by third-party software. The seller of the computer, S&C, designed the custom software; therefore, it is not "third party" software. In addition, S&C represented before Pennybakers purchased the GR8 that it was "specially designed for graphics software." That statement may have formed "part of the basis of the bargain," which is UCC § 2-313's relaxed substitute for reliance.

Answers (B), (C), and (D) are all incorrect because they conclude that Pennybakers does not have viable claims on one or both warranty theories on which Pennybakers, in fact, does have a viable claim.

142.   **Answer (C) is the best answer, reading UCC § 2-315 literally; however, in some jurisdictions, Answer (D) is the best answer.** Unless explicitly waived, disclaimed, or otherwise limited, where the seller, at the time of contracting, has reason to know (1) the particular purpose for which the goods are sought and (2) that the buyer is relying on the seller's skill or judgment to select or furnish suitable goods, the seller warrants that the goods shall be fit for the buyer's particular purpose. UCC § 2-315. S&C knew the particular purpose to which Pennybakers would put both the custom software and the GR8 computer when S&C agreed to sell Pennybakers the GR8. Moreover, S&C knew that Pennybakers was relying on S&C's particular expertise to select or furnish the appropriate hardware on which to run the custom software, and Pennybakers did so rely. Therefore, the statutory requirements of UCC § 2-315 appear to have been satisfied. *See, e.g., Lewis v. Mobil Oil Corp.*, 438 F.2d 500 (8th Cir. 1971) (seller recommended lubricating oil for use on buyer's saw mill equipment); *Valley Iron & Steel Co. v. Thorin*, 562 P.2d 1212 (Or. 1977) (seller selected the grade of metal to use in making hoedad collars for buyer). However, some jurisdictions take to heart the notion that "'particular purpose' . . . envisages a specific use by the buyer which is peculiar to the nature of [the buyer's] business whereas the ordinary purposes for which goods are used are those envisaged in the concept of merchantability and go to uses which are customarily made of the goods in question." UCC § 2-315 cmt. 2. For example, "[s]hoes are generally used for the purpose of walking upon ordinary ground, but a seller may know that a particular pair was selected to be used for climbing mountains." *Id.* While Adam stated that the GR8 was "specially designed for graphics software," he did not state that it was specially designed to run the customized software he had created for Pennybakers. Many computers have special characteristics that enable them to run graphics software. The GR8 may have been able to run any number of graphics software applications well. It does not seem that the purpose for which Pennybakers bought the GR8, at Adam's suggestion, was sufficiently "particular" to give rise to a warranty of fitness under UCC § 2-315. *See, e.g., Mastrangelo v. Howmedica, Division of Pfizer Hospital Product Group, Inc.*, 903 F. Supp. 439 (E.D.N.Y. 1995) (artificial knee joint being used as a replacement knee joint was not being used for "other than its ordinary purpose").

       Answer (A) is incorrect because, unlike the implied warranty of merchantability (discussed in the answers to Questions 140 and 141), a seller does not have to be a merchant in goods of the kind in order to create the implied warranty of fitness for a particular purpose. **Answer (B) is incorrect** because it is incomplete. It states only one of the three statutory requirements set forth in UCC § 2-315, neglecting the foreseeable reliance and actual reliance elements.

143.   The facts make no mention of any representations about, or attempted disclaimers of, either implied warranty with respect to the software. Therefore, if the custom software is a good, then S&C will be held to any implied warranty that applies. S&C made no express warranties about the software. The problem here is that, even if Article 2 governs the transaction (presumably because the goods component predominates the services component, although it is not clear that it actually does), the custom software

is not a "good." Software design, although often yielding one or more diskettes or CDs containing the code, is primarily a service. This is particularly true in this case, because the software did not exist — and, therefore, was not identifiable, much less tangible nor movable — when the parties entered into the contract. *See* UCC § 2-105. Therefore, by their terms, neither UCC § 2-314 nor UCC § 2-315 applies. Moreover, the parties have stipulated that the defect, if any, is in the hardware, not the software. While the glitch appeared when running the custom software on the GR8, it did not appear when running the custom software on any other computer. And, when using the GR8, the glitch appeared while running software other than the custom graphics software. It would seem, then, that there is a lack of proof to support a claim that the software is unfit for either its ordinary purpose or any particular purpose known to S&C.

144. Sufficiently serious or numerous foundation cracks affect the habitability of the house or suggest unworkmanlike construction — both of which are the subject of common law implied warranties, which run in favor of the purchaser of a house, unless expressly disclaimed or waived by contract. There was no express waiver or disclaimer here. The trick is whether the Burgers can rescind their contract with the Samples based on Thomas' malfeasance. Courts are split over whether remote buyers (that is, buyers who did not purchase from the builder) are entitled to the protection of any implied warranty that runs against the builder. *Compare, e.g., Tusch Enterprises v. Coffin*, 740 P.2d 1022 (Idaho 1987); *Elden v. Simmons*, 631 P.2d 739 (Okla. 1981); *Nichols v. R.R. Beaufort & Associates, Inc.*, 727 A.2d 174 (R.I. 1999); *Gupta v. Ritter Homes, Inc.*, 646 S.W.2d 168 (Tex. 1983); *Sewell v. Gregory*, 371 S.E.2d 82 (W. Va. 1988) (all extending the builder's implied warranty to subsequent purchasers) *with, e.g., Cosmopolitan Homes, Inc. v. Weller*, 663 P.2d 1041 (Colo. 1983) (en banc); *Real Estate Marketing, Inc. v. Franz*, 885 S.W.2d 921 (Ky. 1994); *McCann v. Brody-Built Construction Co.*, 496 N.W.2d 349 (Mich. Ct. App. 1992) (all refusing to do so). So, the Burgers may be able to sue Thomas for the damage caused by the defects — but they probably cannot rescind their contract with the Samples due to Thomas' breach. What the Burgers need is for the Paradise courts to imply a warranty of habitability against *any* seller to their buyer. Courts in non-fictional jurisdictions are also split on the viability of this type of action, though the majority of jurisdictions to have weighed-in on this issue have generally refused to impose warranty liability on a used home seller. *Compare, eg., Andreychak v. Lent*, 607 A.2d 1346 (N.J. Super. Ct. App. Div. 1992) (allowing a buyer to sue a non-builder seller) *with, e.g., Haygood v. Burl Pounders Realty, Inc.*, 571 So. 2d 1086 (Ala. 1990); *Choung v. Iemma*, 708 N.E.2d 7 (Ind. Ct. App. 1999); *Miles v. Love*, 573 P.2d 622 (Kan. Ct. App. 1977); *Stevens v. Bouchard*, 532 A.2d 1028 (Me. 1987); *Logan v. Anderson*, 764 S.W.2d 116 (Mo. Ct. App. 1989); *Bernstein v. Ainsworth*, 371 N.W.2d 682 (Neb. 1985); *Everts v. Parkinson*, 555 S.E.2d 667 (N.C. Ct. App. 2001); *Arvai v. Shaw*, 345 S.E.2d 715 (S.C. 1986) (all refusing to do so).

145. **Answer (D) is the best answer.** A thief takes void title. Someone with void title can never pass anything other than void title to a subsequent purchaser, no matter how innocent.

Whether the seller knows it is selling stolen goods is irrelevant for these purposes. Therefore, **Answer (A) is incorrect**.

Because a seller of goods impliedly warrants that (1) the title conveyed is good, (2) the transfer of title is rightful, and (3) the goods are free of any encumbrance, UCC § 2-312(1), a seller who sells goods for which one or more of the foregoing statements is untrue breaches the implied warranty of good title. Neither Fennyman's establishment could have voidable title if the ring came — no matter how indirectly — from a thief. Therefore, **Answers (B) and (C) are incorrect** because Fennyman's had void title, not voidable title, and was incapable of passing good title to Romeo.

146.   No. Juliet entrusted the ring to Old Will, a merchant dealing in goods of the kind. UCC § 2-403(3). While Juliet would be entitled to recover her ring from Old Will, who had only voidable title, Juliet cannot recover it from Kent, who is a buyer in the ordinary course of business. UCC § 2-403(2).

Revised Article 2 rewords current UCC § 2-403(2) slightly, but does not change its effect on the facts of this Question.

147. **Answer (C) is correct.** In order to repudiate his promise, Shaggy must have definitely and unconditionally manifested to Fred his inability to, or his intent not to, perform as and when promised. R2 § 250 cmt. b. *See generally* Keith A. Rowley, *A Brief History of Anticipatory Repudiation in American Contract Law*, 69 U. CIN. L. REV. 565 (2001). Only in Answer (C) did Shaggy definitely and unconditionally manifest to Fred that he could not, or would not, perform as and when promised. R2 § 250 cmt. b & illus. 1.

    Answer (A) is incorrect because Shaggy's statement to Fred ("I am not sure . . .") was equivocal. *See* R2 § 250 cmt. b & illus. 3. **Answer (B) is incorrect** because, while Shaggy's statement was clear, unequivocal, and unconditional, he did not make it to Fred or to anyone acting as Fred's agent so as to give Fred constructive notice of Shaggy's repudiation. *See* R2 § 250 illus. 4. **Answer (D) is incorrect** because merely requesting more favorable terms or suggesting a modification to the terms of a contract does not repudiate the contract. *See Truman L. Flatt & Sons Co. v. Schupf*, 649 N.E.2d 990 (Ill. App. Ct. 1995). On the other hand, refusing to perform unless the other party agrees to the requested terms is a repudiation. R2 § 250 cmt. b.

148. **Answer (D) is the best answer.** After a promisor has repudiated, a promisee may (1) do nothing, subject to the promisee's obligation to mitigate damages, and await the promisor's performance at the appointed time, (2) cancel the contract, (3) act in reliance on the repudiation, or (4) immediately bring suit against the promisor. Likewise, a promisee whose promisor has repudiated his obligation may, without prejudicing the promisee's right to any other remedy for the promisor's repudiation, urge the promisor to retract his repudiation or perform in spite of it. *See* R2 § 257; *see, e.g., Mobil Oil Exploration & Producing S.E., Inc. v. United States*, 530 U.S. 604 (2000). If Fred chose to sell Morbid Manor to Mr. Greeley in reliance on Shaggy's repudiation, Fred could sue Shaggy for the difference between the contract price ($50,000) and the price at which Fred was able to sell to Mr. Greeley ($45,000), plus any incidental and consequential damages (more on those in *Topic 12: Remedies*) that Fred could prove. Therefore, **Answers (A), (B), and (C) are correct, but incomplete**.

149. **Answer (D) is the best answer.** A repudiating promisor may retract his repudiation, as long as the retraction comes to the nonrepudiating promisee's attention before the latter materially changes his position in reliance on the repudiation or indicates to the promisor that he considers the repudiation to be final. R2 § 256(1). If Fred did not act on Shaggy's repudiation before Shaggy retracted his repudiation, Fred would have lost the right to cancel, bring suit, sell Morbid Manor to Mr. Greeley, or otherwise act in reliance on Shaggy's repudiation. *See* R2 § 256 illus. 2.

Fred was entitled, but not required, to urge Shaggy to retract his repudiation. R2 § 257. Whether Shaggy retracted in response to Fred's urging or of his own volition, the effect of the retraction is the same: if Fred acted in reliance on Shaggy's repudiation prior to Shaggy's retraction, Shaggy's retraction would be ineffective, R2 § 256(1) & cmt. c; if Shaggy retracted prior to any act by Fred in reliance on Shaggy's repudiation, Shaggy's retraction would restore the contract, R2 § 256 cmt. a. Therefore, **Answer (A) is incorrect**.

Had Shaggy not retracted, Answer (B) would be correct, because Shaggy's anticipatory repudiation entitled Fred, *inter alia*, to sell Morbid Manor to Mr. Greeley. (See the answer to Question 148.) However, an effective retraction nullifies a prior repudiation. R2 § 256(1). Shaggy's repudiation prior to Fred's sale to Mr. Greeley was a necessary, but not necessarily sufficient, condition to Fred being entitled to sell to Mr. Greeley. Therefore, **Answer (B) is not the best answer**.

Even though the deadline for Shaggy's performance (July 1st) has not yet come, following Shaggy's repudiation prior to the date his performance was due, that date served only as a date beyond which Fred would have a claim for actual — as opposed to anticipatory — breach. Fred acting in reliance on Shaggy's repudiation prior to the deadline would make the deadline meaningless. R2 § 256(1) & cmt. c. Shaggy retracting prior to the deadline (and before Fred materially relied on Shaggy's repudiation), would reinstate the deadline as the date Shaggy's performance was due (provided that Shaggy's repudiation did not cause Fred to suspend his performance in a way that Fred would not be ready on July 1st). Shaggy's retraction before July 1st was a necessary, but not necessarily sufficient, condition to restoring Fred's duties under, and absolving Shaggy of liability for repudiating, the contract. Therefore, **Answer (C) is not the best answer**.

150. **Answer (D) is the best answer**. As discussed in the answer to Question 148, Shaggy's repudiation entitled Fred, *inter alia*, to sell Morbid Manor to Mr. Greeley.

Fred having done so, Shaggy's attempt to retract his repudiation came too late to be effective. *See* R2 § 256(1) & illus. 3. Therefore, **Answer (A) is incorrect**. Unlike a non-repudiating party to a contract governed by the CISG (see the answer to Question 161), Fred was not obligated to seek assurances from Shaggy before changing his position in reliance on Shaggy's repudiation. Under both American common law and Article 2, the decision to seek assurances is entirely up to the non-repudiating party. Therefore, **Answer (C) is incorrect**. And, as explained in the answer to Question 149, once Shaggy repudiated prior to the date performance is due, Fred was under no obligation to wait until that date before acting on Shaggy's repudiation. Indeed, Fred's ability to act prior to the date Shaggy's performance was due is at the very heart of the doctrine of anticipatory repudiation. Therefore, **Answer (B) is incorrect**.

151. No. Shaggy's repudiation allowed Fred to suspend his own performance, including any preparatory actions Fred had to take in order to perform his end of the contract to sell Morbid Manor to Shaggy. R2 § 253(2).

152. **Answer (C) is the best answer, except in a jurisdiction that shifts the risk of loss to the buyer of real property once the parties agree to the purchase.** Shaggy's anticipatory repudiation would have entitled Fred to sue immediately for damages. However, if something happened before Fred brought suit or otherwise acted in reliance on Shaggy's repudiation that would have substantially frustrated Shaggy's principal purpose for entering into the contract with Fred or that would have made Shaggy's promised performance impracticable, then Shaggy would no longer be liable to Fred for damages. *See* R2 § 254(2). Here, assuming that Shaggy's principal purpose was to buy Morbid Manor, rather than the land on which Morbid Manor sat, the destruction of Morbid Manor would have substantially frustrated Shaggy's principal purpose for agreeing to buy Morbid Manor. *See* R2 § 265. Likewise, the destruction of Morbid Manor would have made Shaggy's performance impracticable, through no fault of his own, because the destruction of Morbid Manor was "an event the non-occurrence of which was a basic assumption on which the contract was made," discharging Shaggy absent contrary language in the contract. *See* R2 § 261.

While some jurisdictions shift the risk of loss to real property to the buyer once the buyer agrees to purchase the property, *see, e.g., Ross v. Bumstead*, 173 P.2d 765 (Ariz. 1946); *see also Continental Insurance Co. v. Brown*, 630 F. Supp. 302 (W.D. Va. 1986) (collecting cases), the Uniform Vendor and Purchaser Risk Act provides otherwise: "When neither the legal title nor the possession of the subject matter of the contract has been transferred to the purchaser[,] if all or a material part thereof is destroyed without fault of the purchaser . . . the vendor cannot enforce the contract, and the purchaser is entitled to recover any portion of the price that he has paid." Uniform Vendor and Purchaser Risk Act § 1(a), 14 U.L.A. 471 (1990); *see also, e.g., Dixon v. Salvation Army,* 191 Cal. Rptr. 111 (Cal. Ct. App. 1983) (holding that, "where a material part of the subject property is destroyed without the fault of either party and neither title nor possession has passed to the purchaser, the vendor's performance is excused and the purchaser is entitled to the return of any consideration paid"). Because Shaggy had neither legal title to, nor possession of, Morbid Manor when it was destroyed by fire, **Answer (A) in not the best answer, except in a jurisdiction that shifts the risk of loss to the buyer of real property once the parties agree to the purchase**.

While a party's breach or repudiation of a contract for the sale of goods may shift the risk of loss to the breaching/repudiating party, *see* UCC § 2-510, there is no comparable provision in the *Restatement (Second)* for contracts, like this one, that are not for the sale of goods. Therefore, **Answer (B) is not the best answer**.

While Shaggy would have borne the risk of loss to Morbid Manor once he had legal title or possession, he was not unjustly enriched by the property being destroyed before he assumed the risk of loss. To hold otherwise would be akin to holding a buyer of goods, whose seller has yet to ship the goods, liable for damage or loss to the goods while in the seller's warehouse because the buyer did not have to pay to replace the damaged or lost goods as it would have done had the goods already been in its possession. Therefore, **Answer (D) is incorrect**.

153.   **Answer (D) is the best answer**. Unlike a buyer or seller of goods under the CISG (see the answer to Question 161), the common law does not require Fred to demand assurances before otherwise acting on Shaggy's repudiation. *Compare* R2 § 251(1) *with* CISG art. 72(2). Therefore, **Answers (A) and (C) are incorrect**. Unlike a buyer or seller of goods demanding assurances under UCC § 2-609 (see the answer to Question 158), Fred did not need to make his demand in writing — an oral demand would suffice. *Compare* R2 § 251 cmt. d *with* UCC § 2-609(1). Therefore, **Answers (A) and (B) are incorrect**. If Fred did demand assurances, he must have done so in a manner consistent with his duty of good faith and fair dealing. *See* R2 §§ 205 & 251 cmt. d. He may not have used his insecurity as an excuse to demand a material change in the contract's terms (*e.g.*, requiring Shaggy to deliver the purchase price in cash prior to July 1st).

154.   **Answer (B) is the best answer**. The bank's guarantee that it would pay Fred the $50,000 if Shaggy failed to do so was surely adequate assurance that Fred would receive the $50,000 Shaggy promised him.

       Answer (A) is incorrect because promising to "do everything I can to make sure that I have the money by July 1st" is no more (and probably less) assuring than promising to have the money by July 1st — which Shaggy had already promised. *See* R2 § 251 illus. 6.

       Answer (C) is incorrect because Fred asked for assurances by June 10th, and Shaggy did not provide them until June 14th. *See* R2 § 251 illus. 8. The fact that Shaggy's delay was due to his financial adviser being out of town should not excuse his delay. If Shaggy had a sufficient portfolio to enable him to satisfy Fred by selling off part of the portfolio, Shaggy could easily have formulated another strategy for providing assurances that did not require letting Fred's deadline pass.

       Answer (D) is incorrect because, while $50,000 cash might have assured Fred under other circumstances, because Shaggy waited until the day before performance was due to "show Fred the money," Shaggy failed to "provide within a reasonable time such assurance of due performance as is adequate in the circumstances." R2 § 251(2). The fact that Shaggy's payment of $50,000 cash on June 30th would have constituted full performance of his contractual obligation to Fred in the absence of Fred's reasonable grounds for insecurity ignores the fact that Fred properly requested assurances and that Shaggy did not give them in a timely fashion. *See* R2 § 251 illus. 5. Even if a court were to find that Fred's demand for assurances in seven days was unreasonable, the court should not find that Shaggy's decision to wait until the 59th minute of the proverbial 11th hour did not adequately assure Fred.

155.   No. Having provided Fred with adequate assurances of due performance, Shaggy did not repudiate (or, if he did, he effectively retracted his repudiation). Therefore, if Fred sold Morbid Manor to a third party or otherwise disposed of it before July 1st, *Fred* would be the repudiating party, entitling Shaggy to the same remedies Fred would have if Shaggy repudiated.

156.   **Answer (D) is the best answer**. A promisor's failure to timely provide adequate assurances of due performance, following a proper request for assurances, is, in and of itself, an anticipatory repudiation. *See* R2 § 251(2). As discussed in the answer to Question 148, a promisee whose promisor has repudiated may (1) do nothing, subject to the promisee's obligation to mitigate damages, and await the promisor's performance at the appointed time, (2) cancel the contract, (3) act in reliance on the repudiation, or (4) immediately bring suit against the promisor. Likewise, a promisee whose promisor has repudiated his obligation may, without prejudicing his right to any other remedy for the promisor's repudiation, urge the promisor to retract his repudiation or perform in spite of it. Therefore, because Fred could have done any or all of the foregoing, **Answers (A), (B), and (C) are true, but incomplete**.

157.   **Answer (B) is the best answer**, although **Answer (A) is correct**, as well. Under the contract, Romeo was obliged to make a $2,500 down payment, so one could argue that Romeo anticipatorily breached the contract by writing a check on an account with insufficient funds to cover the check. That argument should fail, however, because (1) Old Will promised to hold the check until the next day, (2) the funds would have been in the account and the bank would have honored the check if Old Will had waited as promised, and (3) Romeo neither (a) clearly and unequivocally communicated to Old Will his *intention* not to perform when performance was due nor (b) performed some act that (i) made it impossible for him to perform when performance was due or (ii) demonstrated his clear determination not to perform when performance was due. UCC § 2-610 cmt. 1. Answers (A) and (B) are both correct, but Answer (B) is more compelling and factually true.

While Old Will's investigation of Romeo's checking balance may have given him reasonable grounds for insecurity, Romeo neither clearly and unequivocally communicated to Old Will his intention not to perform when performance was due nor performed some act that made it impossible for him to perform when performance was due or demonstrated his clear determination not to perform when performance was due. As such, Romeo did not repudiate. Therefore, **Answer (C) is incorrect**, though it provides a nice lead-in to the next Question.

Assuming, without getting into a discussion of UCC Article 4 (for guidance on that subject, see, *e.g.*, William H. Lawrence, Understanding Negotiable Instruments and Payment Systems (2002), and Gregory A. Maggs & Timothy R. Zinnecker, Questions & Answers: Payment Systems (2003)) and federal and state banking and criminal laws, that Romeo's writing a check on an account that he knew did not have sufficient funds to cover the check (even though he may have arranged for sufficient funds to be in the account by the time the check was presented for payment to his bank) was illegal, it was neither a clear and unequivocal communication of intention not to perform when performance was due nor was it an act that made it impossible for him to perform when performance was due or demonstrated a clear determination not to perform when performance was due. Being arrested and imprisoned for writing a bad check may be a repudiation, but just writing the check was not. Therefore, **Answer (D) is incorrect**.

Revised Article 2 moves the definition of repudiation paraphrased above from current UCC § 2-610 Official Comment 1 into the text as Revised § 2-610(2). Otherwise, current UCC §§ 2-609, 2-610 & 2-611 are not materially changed.

158.   **Answer (C) is the best answer.** The fact that Romeo's account did not contain sufficient funds may have given Old Will "reasonable grounds for insecurity" under UCC § 2-609(1), entitling him to take action to protect his "expectation of receiving due performance." However, Old Will's actions did not comply with UCC § 2-609. Old Will failed to demand adequate assurance in writing, as required by UCC § 2-609(1) — although that requirement, admittedly, is not strictly enforced by all courts, *see* Rowley, *supra*, at 621 (collecting cases); *see, e.g., AMF, Inc. v. McDonald's Corp.*, 536 F.2d 1167 (7th Cir. 1976). More importantly, Old Will sought no assurances from Romeo; rather, he demanded a material change in the contract terms (from payment-in-installments to payment-in-full). Demanding a material change in the terms of the contract in a way that makes it obvious that the party demanding the change will not otherwise perform is, itself, an anticipatory breach. R2 § 250 cmt. b. Old Will could have demanded that Romeo make the down payment in cash (which Romeo, by the way, offered to do), but Old Will's refusal to turn over the ring without *full* cash payment repudiated the contract.

While Old Will likely had reasonable grounds for insecurity, he failed to act on them properly, repudiating the contract himself rather than giving Romeo the chance to assure him. Therefore, **Answer (A) is incorrect**.

Because Old Will did not make a proper demand — procedurally or substantively — Romeo was not obligated to give Old Will the assurances Old Will sought. Therefore, **Answer (B) is not the best answer**.

Romeo essentially told Old Will that he would not have the money for the down payment until the next day (thus, the request to hold the check). As such, we cannot say that Romeo began to perform in such a way as to foreclose a claim of anticipatory repudiation in favor of a claim of actual breach. And, in any event, accepting a check is simply accepting a promise of payment, even without being asked to hold the check for a day. Therefore, Romeo did nothing more than reaffirm his promise to perform. If, after doing so, but before actually performing, Romeo were to clearly and unequivocally communicate to Old Will his intention not to perform when performance was due or perform some act that made it impossible for him to perform when performance was due or demonstrated his clear determination not to perform when performance was due, Old Will would still be entitled to seek assurances or treat Romeo's repudiation as final and act in reliance upon it. Therefore, **Answer (D) is incorrect**.

159.   **Answer (D) is the best answer.** The news report could have given a reasonable person in Romeo's shoes grounds to feel insecure about Old Will performing as promised.

While Answer (A) may be factually true, the mere fact that "you cannot always believe what you see and hear on the news" does not mean that a news story that has hallmarks of truth is legally insufficient to give rise to reasonable grounds for insecurity. Therefore, **Answer (A) is incorrect**. (Those who have seen *So, I Married an Axe Murderer* will appreciate that some people's idea of what constitutes "the news" can be fairly bizarre; those of you who have not seen it should do so.)

The fact that the story reported only one incident involving Old Will and that the district attorney's office had declined to prosecute does not make Romeo's insecurity unreasonable. Assuming the story is based in fact, even if some of the details may be uncorroborated, the pervasiveness of the practice might suggest to a reasonable person in Romeo's shoes that the fact that Old Will had only been "caught" once did not necessarily mean that Old Will had only done wrong once. Therefore, **Answer (B) is incorrect**.

And, while UCC § 2-609(4) may give Old Will *up to* 30 days to respond to Romeo's demand for adequate assurances, it will only do so if 30 days is a "reasonable time." If a reasonable time is less than 30 days, as it might be here given the timing issues involved, Romeo did not have to wait 30 days before acting on Old Will's failure to give the assurances sought. Therefore, **Answer (C) is incorrect**.

160. Old Will should have offered and allowed Romeo, or Romeo's designated expert, to reinspect the ring using a microscope or jeweler's loupe immediately before accepting the ring. Old Will should also have warranted to Romeo that he would refund the complete purchase price if Romeo was in any way dissatisfied with the ring.

161. **Answer (C) is the best answer.** This was a contract for the sale of goods, not to be used for personal, family, or household purposes, between parties whose places of business are in different countries, both of which are signatories to the CISG, and who have not expressly opted out of the CISG. Therefore, in the absence of a contrary agreement, the CISG governs Old Will's rights with respect to his insecurity regarding Romeo's ability to perform. *See* CISG arts. 1(1)(a), 2(a) & 6. Article 71 would have permitted Old Will to suspend his performance when "it bec[ame] apparent" that Romeo would "not perform a substantial part of his obligations as a result of a serious deficiency . . . in his creditworthiness." CISG art. 71(1)(a). If Old Will had elected to suspend his performance, he would have had to immediately give Romeo "reasonable notice . . . in order to permit him to provide adequate assurance of his performance," unless (1) there was insufficient time to seek assurances, or (2) Romeo "declared that he w[ould] not perform his obligations." CISG art. 72(2)-(3). Once Romeo provided him with adequate assurances, Old Will would have had to resume his own performance. CISG art. 71(3). Here, the only urgency was on Romeo's part — and Old Will may not even have been aware of it. So there was sufficient time for Old Will to demand assurances. Nor did Romeo declare his intention not to perform. Quite the opposite, in fact. Romeo orally assured Old Will that he could pay and offered to bring the down payment in cash. Thus, Old Will had to demand assurances before otherwise acting on his insecurity. Therefore, **Answers (B) and (D) are incorrect**. Unlike UCC § 2-609, the CISG does not specify the form that Old Will's notice to Romeo must have taken. Therefore, **Answer (A) is not the best answer**. *See generally* Rowley, *supra*,

at 629-38 (discussing the CISG's anticipatory repudiation provisions and comparing and contrasting them to American common law and UCC Article 2).

162.   **Answer (D) is the best answer.** A "material breach" deprives the non-breaching party of its reasonable contractual expectations. It "is so dominant or pervasive as . . . to frustrate the purpose of the contract." *Jacobs & Young, Inc. v. Kent*, 129 N.E. 889 (N.Y. 1921). Factors to consider in determining whether a breach is material include (1) the extent to which the non-breaching party can be adequately compensated for the part of the benefit of which she is deprived; (2) the extent to which the breaching party will suffer forfeiture if the non-breaching party is excused from her contractual obligations due to the breach; (3) the likelihood that the breaching party will cure, taking into account all of the circumstances, including any reasonable assurances by the breaching party; and (4) the extent to which the breaching party's behavior comports with standards of good faith and fair dealing. R2 § 241. Russell's breach deprived Gwyneth of her expectation — two tickets to the movie premiere — at a point in time by which there was little or no possibility for Russell to cure or for Gwyneth to mitigate. No amount of money from Russell plus two tickets to the wrong show would adequately compensate Gwyneth for what she expected but did not receive. Russell would suffer no more forfeiture by excusing Gwyneth's performance than he already has suffered. And, given that Russell knew which tickets Gwyneth wanted, and he bought tickets to a different show anyway, it is difficult to cast his actions as comporting with good faith and fair dealing. Therefore, Russell's breach was material. A total breach is a material breach that the breaching party fails to cure (1) within a reasonable time or (2) within the time during which performance is possible. R2 § 242. A total breach discharges the non-breaching party's remaining duties under the contract, R2 § 237, unless (1) the non-breaching party has already performed, or (2) the non-breaching party elects to perform and then sue for damages.

Substantial performance is performance that, while not completely in compliance with the terms of the contract, is sufficient to not deprive the non-breaching party of her reasonable expectations. If Russell had told Gwyneth on March 14th that he had arranged to have two tickets to the movie premiere awaiting her at the Musik Hall's "will call" window, Russell would have substantially performed. Gwyneth would have received substantially what she bargained for: two tickets to the movie premiere, available to her before the premiere, for the price she agreed to pay. Russell's provision of two tickets to a completely different show, on the other hand, was not substantial performance. Therefore, **Answer (C) is incorrect**.

As discussed in more detail in ***Topic 12: Remedies***, receiving something she did not want, and that was of no value to her, could not unjustly enrich Gwyneth. Therefore, **Answer (B) is incorrect**. And, while Answer (A) might merit serious consideration had Russell not known, as the facts of this Question tell us he did, which *The Orange Pumpernickel* Gwyneth meant, under these facts **Answer (A) is incorrect**.

239

163.   **Answer (C) is the best answer**. While the extent of Russell's malfeasance is the same as it was in Question 162, what keeps Russell's material breach in this Question from becoming a total breach, excusing Gwyneth from her duty to perform, is that Russell still had ample time to cure his breach. Recall that a total breach is a material breach that the breaching party fails to cure (1) within a reasonable time or (2) within the time during which performance is possible. Any material breach that is not a total breach is a partial breach. A partial breach *would not* discharge Gwyneth's remaining duties under the contract, though it would *suspend* Gwyneth's duty to perform until Russell cured his material breach or failed to do so, at which point his partial breach would become total and the parties would be in the same situation as they were in the answer to Question 162. However, if a timely cure was possible, **Answer (D) is not the best answer**.

Answers **(A) and (B) are incorrect** for the reasons discussed in the answer to Question 162.

164.   **Answer (D) is the best answer**. "[A] breach by nonperformance accompanied or followed by a repudiation gives rise to a . . . total breach." R2 § 243(2). From the discussion in *Topic 9: Anticipatory Repudiation*, it should be clear that Russell's "take it or leave it" language, particularly given that the "it" was a nonconforming performance, was a repudiation.

Answer (A) is incorrect for the same reason given in the answer to Question 162. **Answer (B) is not the best answer** because, while all *other* facts are the same as those in Question 163, where we concluded that this *was* the best answer, the addition of Russell's repudiation relieved Gwyneth of any obligation to await cure before treating Russell's breach as a total breach, discharging her obligation to pay. **Answer (C) is not the best answer** because, but for Russell's repudiation, there is still ample time, as discussed in the answer to Question 163, for Russell to cure his material-but-not-yet-total breach.

165.   **Answer (B) is the best answer**. Gwyneth's breach is material and total for the same reasons Russell's was in the answer to Question 162. As such, Gwyneth's breach would have discharged Russell's duty to perform, *but for the fact that he already had fully performed at the time of her breach*. Thus, Russell was not discharged, making **Answer (D) incorrect**, and was out of pocket $150 for two tickets that Gwyneth refused to use and for which he could find no other takers. Fortunately for Russell, discharging his own duties is not the only remedy that contract law affords him. Gwyneth's total breach entitles Russell to recover his actual damages caused by the breach (more on those in *Topic 12: Remedies*), as well as any incidental and consequential damages flowing from the breach. *See* R2 §§ 236(1) & 243(1).

"Incidental" damages are costs incurred in a reasonable effort to avoid or mitigate damages caused by the other party's breach (*e.g.*, a fee paid to a realtor or agent to locate another property or performer, costs of storing goods that were to be delivered to the breaching party until a substitute buyer may be found). R2 § 347 cmt. c.

"Consequential" damages include reasonably foreseeable injuries to a person, business, or property caused by the breaching party's failure to perform, to fully perform, or to properly perform (*e.g.*, lost profits during a factory shutdown caused by the breaching party's failure to timely deliver a key piece of equipment, diminished market value of home due to defective installation of a new roof). *Id.* Assuming she can prove both with reasonable certainty, a party who has suffered a total breach may recover both incidental and consequential damages. On the other hand, a party who has suffered only a partial breach may not recover consequential damages, and may only recover incidental damages relating to that part of the performance due that was not satisfied by the breaching party. Where consequential damages are available, the non-breaching party has a duty to take reasonable steps to mitigate those damages. R2 § 350(1).

Answer (A) is not the best answer and Answer (C) is incorrect because both classify Gwyneth's breach as partial, rather than total, which mischaracterizes the facts, and because Answer (C) states that Gwyneth's partial breach would discharge Russell, which mischaracterizes the law.

166. **Answer (D) is correct**. Brown's contract with Swoop obliges him to wear Swoop shoes "for every practice that is open to the public," and more generally "in public — on and off the basketball court — . . . 'unless the occasion requires wearing a style of shoe that Swoop does not make, such as hiking boots, swim fins, and dress shoes or loafers.'" Muncie's contract with Springbok requires Muncie's players to wear Springbok shoes "during all exhibition, regular season, and post-season games." However, that contract is silent about practices, including pre-game warm-ups. Thus, Brown is complying with his Swoop contract and not putting Muncie in breach of its Springbok contract by wearing Swoop shoes prior to the opening tip-off.

Answers (A) and (B) are incorrect because they deem Brown to be in breach of his Swoop contract despite wearing Swoop shoes. "When performance of a duty under a contract is due, any nonperformance is a breach." R2 § 235(2). His wearing Swoop shoes cannot be a breach of his Swoop contract because he is obligated to wear Swoop shoes in public at all times possible, which is what he is doing. **Answer (C) is incorrect** because, while getting Brown's part of the answer correct, it misstates the effect of Brown wearing non-Springbok shoes prior to the beginning of a game.

167. **Answer (C) is correct**. Brown's contract with Swoop obliges him to wear Swoop shoes "in public — on and off the basketball court," which includes wearing them during all exhibition, regular season, and playoff games — because all such games are "in public." Muncie's contract with Springbok requires Muncie's players to wear Springbok shoes "during all exhibition, regular season, and post-season games." Therefore, if Brown wears Swoop shoes during a game, Muncie will be in breach of its contract with Springbok (and Brown will be in breach of his contract with Muncie) because "[w]hen performance of a duty under a contract is due, any nonperformance is a breach." R2 § 235(2).

Answers (A) and (B) are incorrect for the same reason given in the answer to Question 166 — although, in this case, Answer (A) is correct about Muncie's half of the equation. **Answer (D) is incorrect** because, while getting Brown's part of the answer correct, it misstates the effect of Brown wearing non-Springbok shoes during a Muncie game.

168.   Brown should honor his contract with Swoop and pay Muncie some or all of the money it will be obligated to forfeit to Springbok because of Brown wearing Swoop shoes in violation of Muncie's contract with Springbok. If the hypothetical National Basketball League plays the same 82-game schedule as the real-life National Basketball Association, plus six or eight exhibition games and (generously, considering that Muncie likely did quite poorly last year to have had such a prime draft pick this year) 10 or so post-season games, that is approximately 100 games. Even if every Muncie game were nationally televised, which is highly unlikely, Muncie would have to give $500,000 back to Springbok in order to let Brown wear his Swoops. If Muncie insisted that Brown wear Springboks during all games, Brown would have to pay Swoop $1,000,000 — assuming they did not drop him altogether, which they probably would. So the "efficient breach" result would be for Muncie to allow Brown to breach Muncie's contract with Springbok, provided that Brown reimburse Muncie for the lost income from Springbok, leaving Muncie no worse off than it would have been had Brown worn Springboks all season long, and Brown better off than he would have been had he worn Springboks all season long.

169.   **Answer (C) is the best answer**. While performing only part of a contract is generally a breach of the entire contract, if the language of the contract and the actions of the parties suggest that the parties considered the contract to be *divisible*, then performance of one part by the breaching party should entitle him to payment for the part fully performed. In order for a non-installment contract to be divisible, it must (1) be possible to apportion the performances of the parties into corresponding pairs of part perfor-mances, and (2) be proper to treat these pairs of part performances as "agreed equivalents." R2 § 240. Wallace's agreement with Bruce is, in many respects, a series of three contracts (or segments) masquerading as a single contract. Wallace fully performed the first of the three segments, and Bruce paid him $40,000 plus 5% of net ticket sales per show for his July 1-7 run. If Wallace could not perform the August 26-September 1 segment, Bruce was entitled to treat that as a divisible contract and take whatever actions were appropriate to mitigate the losses he would otherwise have suffered due to Wallace's cancellation.

Wallace, in essence, anticipatorily repudiated the August 26-September 1 segment, and Bruce was not foreclosed from exercising the rights we discussed in *Topic 9: Anticipatory Repudiation* simply because Wallace's health might have improved faster than expected. Therefore, **Answer (A) is incorrect**.

In this context, substantial performance is a bit of a red herring, unless the issue is substantial performance of a divisible segment of the whole contract. Here, Wallace fully performed the first segment and was expected to be able to fully perform the third segment; but he was unable, due to his health, to perform the second segment at all. Therefore, **Answers (B) and (D) are not the best answers**.

170. **Answer (D) is the best answer.** Now we see the flip side of divisibility: While Bruce could carve out a pair of equivalent performances — to wit, Wallace's August 26-September 1 shows and Bruce's promise to pay Wallace $40,000 plus 5% of net ticket sales for those eight shows — and treat Wallace's inability to perform his half of that pair of equivalent performances as a rationale for seeking damages or, in the case of Question 169, making other arrangements, Bruce could not use Wallace's inability to perform his half of one pair of equivalent performances as an excuse for canceling the entire contract when Wallace had already performed at least one segment and had at least one more segment to perform after Bruce carved out the August 26-September 1 segment. Divisibility aside, remember the basic rule discussed in the answer to Question 163: Only a total breach discharges the non-breaching party's remaining obligations under the whole contract. A partial breach, such as this one (because Wallace had already performed part of the contract), only entitled Bruce to a remedy based on Wallace's less-than-full performance; it did not entitle Bruce to cancel the remainder of the contract. Therefore, **Answer (D) is the best answer** and **Answer (B) is incorrect**.

Divisibility does not entitle Bruce to cancel the remainder of the contract unless Wallace repudiated or breached all remaining divisible segments — which he did not. Therefore, **Answer (C) is not the best answer. Answer (A) is incorrect**, and basically window dressing, except to the extent that it reminds you that there was more than one segment remaining to this contract when Angus called Bruce; and, therefore, you should not assume that Bruce's ability to, in essence, cancel one segment (as he did in Question 169) entitled him to cancel all remaining segments.

171. No. Substantial performance is the antithesis of material breach: If a party materially breached, they cannot have substantially performed; if a party substantially performed, they cannot have materially breached. As discussed in the answer to Question 162, a material breach so deprives the non-breaching party of its reasonable contractual expectations that it frustrates the non-breaching party's purpose for entering into the contract in the first place. The facts of this Question do not give rise to a material breach. Wallace performed every day he promised to perform. Bruce could be adequately compensated (by damages for Wallace's partial breach) for the part of the bargained-for benefit of which he was deprived (the profits from the Saturday matinee). Wallace would have suffered forfeiture if Bruce were allowed to cancel the contract due to Wallace's inability to perform one of eight scheduled shows. Wallace was not trying to get out of the second Saturday show so he could play golf or sleep late — he was genuinely unable, at least in the opinion of his doctors, to perform the extra show on Saturday — therefore, his breach was in good faith. Wallace substantially performed when he performed seven shows the week of October 14-20. Therefore, he did not materially breach his contract with Bruce.

172. Whether Boulder would be entitled to walk away from the contract due to Nester's delay would depend entirely upon whether Nester's delay constituted a material breach that could not be cured, as discussed in the answers to Questions 162 and 163. If so,

then Boulder was entitled to cancel the contract and have its obligations thereunder discharged. If not, then Boulder must have performed its part of the contract and then sought damages, if needed, to compensate it for the consequences of Nester's delay.

173.   **Answer (D) is the best answer**. This is *Jacobs & Young, Inc. v. Kent*, 129 N.E. 889 (N.Y. 1921). Boulder's use of Brown No. F-17 bricks was not a material breach, in light of the unavailability of Acme No. 63 bricks; therefore, Boulder substantially performed.

If Boulder did its best to match the color and texture of Acme No. 63 bricks when it chose Brown No. F-17 bricks, Boulder's use of Brown No. F-17 bricks to supplement the inadequate supply of Acme No. 63 bricks did not substantially deprive Wallace of the benefit of his bargain. Therefore, **Answer (A) is incorrect**.

As in *Jacobs & Young*, to the extent that there was some diminution in the value of the house because Boulder was forced to use Brown No. F-17 bricks to supplement the inadequate supply of Acme No. 63 bricks, Boulder could compensate Wallace for that diminution by paying (quite likely nominal) monetary damages. Therefore, **Answer (B) is incorrect**.

Answer (C) is incorrect because, quite the contrary, Boulder's use of Brown No. F-17 bricks to supplement the inadequate supply of Acme No. 63 bricks, rather than halting work until an adequate supply of the specified brick could be secured, was entirely consistent with its duty of good faith and fair dealing — particularly given that Wallace had made it clear that time was of the essence.

174.   **Answer (D) is the best answer**. This Question pursues the "What's the big deal about 'Reading pipe'?" query that nearly every Contracts professor asks some poor student each year while discussing *Jacobs & Young, Inc. v. Kent*, 129 N.E. 889 (N.Y. 1921). Unless Boulder knew Nester's particular purpose, *and* Wallace shared Nester's particular purpose, *and* Boulder or its masonry subcontractor purposefully laid the brick to thwart Nester's and Wallace's particular purpose, then Boulder substantially performed and Wallace would be entitled only to the diminution in value (if any) caused by Boulder's use of both Acme No. 63 bricks and Brown No. F-17 bricks, rather than Acme No. 63 bricks throughout.

Answers (A) and (C) are incorrect because Boulder substantially performed.

Answer (B) is precisely the relief that Judge Cardozo refused to award the party in Wallace's position in *Jacobs & Young*, and there is arguably less reason to award it under the facts of this Question than in *Jacobs & Young*. In either case, it would be an astounding waste. And here, unlike at least one version of the facts in *Jacobs & Young*, Boulder did not install the Brown No. F-17 bricks (or allow them to be installed by a masonry subcontractor) because of poor supervision; Boulder had to use the Brown No. F-17 bricks or some other brick because there simply were not enough Acme No. 63 bricks available given Wallace's schedule. Therefore, **Answer (B) is not the best answer**.

175. A buyer who "wrongfully rejects . . . goods or fails to make a payment due on or before delivery" commits a breach per UCC § 2-703, entitling the seller to any remedy authorized by UCC § 2-703. UCC § 2-602(3). A buyer may only rightfully reject goods if the goods themselves, or the manner of their tender, fail(s) to conform to the contract. UCC § 2-601(a). Here, neither the goods nor the tender was nonconforming, making Mercury's refusal to accept Tubular's conforming tender a breach of its contract with Tubular.

Revised Article 2 leaves current UCC § 2-602(3) unchanged, but expands current UCC § 2-703 to consolidate currently-scattered provisions detailing a seller's rights in the event of a buyer's insolvency.

176. **Answer (B) is the best answer.** Mercury could, if it discovered the nonconformity prior to accepting the tubing, have (1) rejected the entire shipment, (2) accepted the entire shipment, or (3) rejected the nonconforming part of the shipment and accepted the rest, and, in any event, sued Tubular for breach. In order to sue Tubular for breach, however, Mercury would have had to first give Tubular notice of the nonconformity — and, conditions permitting, an opportunity to cure the nonconformity — within a reasonable time following delivery. UCC §§ 2-508, 2-601, 2-602 & 2-607. Here, neither Answer (A) nor Answer (C) mentions anything about Mercury giving Tubular notice or an opportunity to cure. Therefore, **Answers (A) and (C) are not the best answers**. Because the contract required Mercury to pay in full on receipt, the mere fact that Mercury paid does not mean it accepted the nonconforming tubing. UCC § 2-512(2). UCC § 2-606(1) gave Mercury a reasonable opportunity to inspect the goods before accepting. Therefore, **Answer (D) is incorrect**.

Revised Article 2 leaves current UCC §§ 2-512, 2-601, 2-602 & 2-606 essentially unchanged. Revised Article 2 completely rewrites current UCC § 2-508, in part to clarify that a revoking buyer must afford a seller which has been acting in good faith an opportunity to cure, and in part to expressly shift any expenses the buyer incurred due to the nonconformity or the seller's attempt to cure onto the seller. Revised Article 2 amends current UCC § 2-607(3) to make a buyer's failure to timely notify the seller of a nonconformity material only to the extent that the seller was prejudiced by the buyer's failure to give timely notice.

177. **Answer (C) or Answer (D) is the best answer, depending on whether the courts of the governing jurisdiction follow the majority or minority rule on a seller's post-revocation right to cure.**

Once a buyer accepts goods, the buyer loses the ability to reject the goods. UCC § 2-607(2). Therefore, **Answer (A) is incorrect**. If Mercury did not discover the nonconformity prior to accepting the tubing, or if it failed to give Tubular the notice required by UCC § 2-602(1), and thereby failed to properly reject, it could revoke its acceptance, provided that (1) the nonconformity substantially impaired the value of the goods to Mercury; (2) Mercury failed to discover the nonconformity prior to accepting the goods because the nonconformity was not readily apparent; (3) Mercury revoked within a reasonable time after it discovered, or should have discovered, the nonconformity; and (4) Mercury timely notified Tubular of its revocation. UCC § 2-608(1)(b) & (2).

Mercury could only revoke its acceptance if, *inter alia*, it failed to timely and properly reject the nonconforming goods because (1) Mercury reasonably assumed that Tubular would cure any nonconformity that might have existed, UCC § 2-608(1)(a); (2) Tubular assured Mercury that Tubular would cure the nonconformity, UCC § 2-608(1)(b); or (3) Mercury could not discover the nonconformity until after it accepted the goods because the nonconformity was difficult to discover, UCC § 2-608(1)(b). The facts indicate that Mercury did not know of the nonconformity when it accepted the goods; therefore, the first and second options are foreclosed, and Mercury could only revoke if it could not discover the nonconformity until after it accepted the goods because the nonconformity was difficult to discover. The facts of the Question are silent. And, unlike Answers (C) and (D), Answer (B) does not mention Mercury satisfying this requirement. Therefore, **Answer (B) is not the best answer**.

UCC § 2-508 requires a *rejecting* buyer to afford the seller an opportunity to cure the nonconformity before the buyer can sue the seller. Article 2 does not explicitly require a *revoking* buyer to afford the seller an opportunity to cure the nonconformity before the buyer can sue the seller. However, UCC § 2-608(3) states that a revoking buyer "has the same rights and duties with regard to the goods involved as if he rejected them," which may impose on the revoking buyer the duty to give the seller the same opportunity to cure that the seller would be entitled to if the buyer had rejected. Courts are split on whether a revoking buyer must afford its seller the opportunity to cure. *Compare, e.g., American Honda Motor Co. v. Boyd*, 475 So. 2d 835 (Ala. 1985); *U.S. Roofing, Inc. v. Credit Alliance Corp.*, 279 Cal. Rptr. 533 (Cal. Ct. App. 1991); *Jensen v. Seigel Mobile Homes Group*, 668 P.2d 65 (Idaho 1983); *Fleet Maintenance, Inc. v. Burke Energy Midwest Corp.*, 728 P.2d 408 (Kan. Ct. App. 1986); *Head v. Phillips Camper Sales & Rental, Inc.*, 593 N.W.2d 595 (Mich. Ct. App. 1999); *Gappelberg v. Landrum*, 666 S.W.2d 88 (Tex. 1984); *City National Bank of Charleston v. Wells*, 384 S.E.2d 374 (W. Va. 1989) (all denying a seller the right to cure following the buyer's rightful revocation) *with, e.g., Fitzner Pontiac-Buick-Cadillac, Inc. v. Smith*, 523 So. 2d 324 (Miss. 1988); *Ayanru v. General Motors Acceptance Corp.*, 495 N.Y.S.2d 1018 (N.Y. Civ. Ct. 1985); *Oberg v. Phillips*, 615 P.2d 1022 (Okla. Ct. App. 1980) (all granting the seller the right to cure following the buyer's rightful revocation). Therefore, **Answer (C) is the best answer if the courts of the governing jurisdiction follow the majority rule** on a seller's post-revocation right to cure; whereas, **Answer (D) is the best answer if the courts of the governing jurisdiction follow the minority rule** on a seller's post-revocation right to cure. And, in any event, following revocation, Mercury could sue Tubular for any damages allowed by UCC § 2-714 due to the (uncured) nonconformity.

Revised Article 2 adopts the "minority" view, except when the buyer purchased the goods primarily for personal, family, or household purposes. See Revised § 2-508.

178. CISG art. 35(1) requires a seller to deliver goods "of the . . . quality . . . required by the contract." Unless the parties have otherwise agreed, goods do not conform to the contract unless, *inter alia*, they are fit for their ordinary purpose, CISG art. 35(2)(a), or any particular purpose made known to the seller, unless the buyer did not reasonably rely on the seller's skill and judgment in selecting or manufacturing the goods for that particular purpose, CISG art. 35(2)(b). The seller is liable to the buyer for any nonconformity existing when risk of loss passed to the buyer, CISG art. 36(1) — here, when PG handed the goods over to the carrier, CISG art. 67(1). A buyer must notify the seller of any nonconformity within a reasonable time after the buyer discovered or should have discovered the nonconformity, CISG art. 39(1); and, in any event, within two years after the buyer took possession of the goods, CISG art. 39(2). PG's delivery of 4,000 ft. of nonconforming glass tubing would certainly seem to be a fundamental breach under CISG art. 25. Therefore, PG's failure to delivery conforming goods entitled Mercury to "avoid" the contract, CISG art. 49(1)(a), as long as Mercury declared the contract avoided within a reasonable time after it knew or should have known of the nonconformity, CISG art. 49(2)(b)(i). Mercury could then sue to recover either cover damages, CISG art. 75, or contract-market price differential damages, CISG art. 76(1), plus incidental and consequential damages, CISG art. 74. Alternatively, Mercury could have (1) required PG to deliver substitute goods, CISG art. 46(2), but only to the extent that forum law would permit specific performance, CISG art. 28, or (2) sued to recover its "expectation" damages, plus incidental and consequential damages, CISG art. 74. (Technically, Mercury could also demand repair, CISG art. 46(3), but it is unclear whether such a demand would be reasonable.) If Mercury elected to pursue "expectation" damages, it must have taken reasonable steps to mitigate its damages, CISG art. 77.

179.   **Answer (D) is the best answer.** A "promise" is "a manifestation of intention to act
        or refrain from acting in a specified way, so made as to justify a promisee in
        understanding that a commitment has been made." R2 § 2(1). A "condition" is "an
        event, not certain to occur, which must occur, unless its nonoccurrence is excused,
        before performance under a contract becomes due." R2 § 224. The parties to a contract
        can agree to specifically condition one or both parties' performance on the occurrence
        of some event. *See* R2 § 226.

        Conditions may be either express or constructive. An express condition is set forth
        explicitly in the parties' agreement. A constructive condition is implied into the
        agreement as a matter of fact, law, or equity. Tiffani and Colt having expressed the
        condition in their agreement, the condition must have occurred before Colt could
        enforce Tiffani's obligation to pay rent. R2 § 225(1). The non-occurrence of the
        condition, unless Tiffani is responsible for it failing to occur, deprives Colt of the
        expected performance, but does not give him a remedy against Tiffani. R2 § 225(3).
        Colt, having been willing to make his contract with Tiffani conditional on her
        (hopefully early) release from the LexCentre lease, could not treat the contract as
        unconditional and begin charging rent. Therefore, **Answer (A) is incorrect.**

        The facts do not indicate that Tiffani promised to induce LexCentre to let her out of
        their lease agreement. She may have promised to try. But, having tried and (apparently,
        at least) failed, she is not liable for the non-occurrence of the condition. Therefore,
        Answer (B) is incorrect.

        While the law generally abhors a forfeiture, *see UNUM Life Insurance Co. v. Ward*,
        526 U.S. 358 (1999), any forfeiture Colt suffered between September 1st and December
        31st, 2002 was pursuant to the terms of the agreement into which he freely entered.
        Therefore, **Answer (C) is incorrect.**

180.   **Answer (C) is the best answer.** Colt promised to make space available for Tiffani
        as early as September 1st. Admittedly, his promise was conditional (as was hers) on
        Tiffani securing an early release from her LexCentre lease. But, as soon as she did
        (or as soon thereafter as Colt received notice that she did), Colt would have been bound
        to his promise to Tiffani. Therefore, **Answer (A) is incorrect.**

        While David & Galati's occupancy of the space Colt agreed to lease to Tiffani
        complicated Colt's performance, and may even have made it temporarily impracticable
        (depending on whether Colt had other space available that suited Tiffani's needs), *see*
        R2 § 269, that impracticability did not discharge Colt's obligation to perform as soon
        as he could and to answer to Tiffani for any damages caused by his delay in performing.
        Therefore, **Answer (B) is not the best answer.**

The 30-day notice provision in Colt's lease agreement with David & Galati only binds Colt and David & Galati. It does not bind Tiffani. Therefore, **Answer (D) is incorrect**.

181. Yes. In the first place, as discussed in the answer to Question 179, Tiffani's obligation to begin paying Colt rent on September 1, 2002, was conditional on LexCentre releasing her early from her existing lease. Until that condition occurred (or the lease expires), Tiffani was not obligated to perform her lease contract with Colt, *see* R2 § 225(1), nor was she liable to him for breaching their lease agreement, *see* R2 § 225(3). Moreover, a party who prevents the occurrence of a condition precedent to the other party's liability under a contract cannot bring suit despite (or because of) the failure of that condition to materialize. Doing so is, *inter alia*, inconsistent with the latter party's duty of good faith and fair dealing. R2 §§ 205 & 225 cmt. b. The prevention doctrine does not require proof that the condition would have occurred "but for" the wrongful conduct of the promisor. Instead, it only requires the conduct to "contribute materially" to the non-occurrence of the condition.

182. **Answer (D) is the best answer**. The condition that LexCentre release Tiffani from her lease, or that her lease with LexCentre expire, before she must begin paying rent to Colt was clearly for Tiffani's benefit, not Colt's. In the spirit, if not the letter, of R2 § 227, Colt promised to make space available to Tiffani at any time on or after September 1, 2002, provided that Tiffani took the space, or at least began paying rent on it, as of January 1, 2003. While Colt assumed a duty to stand ready to have space for Tiffani, Tiffani assumed no duty to try to escape her lease with LexCentre. Colt and Tiffani certainly could have drafted their agreement to impose such a duty. But, they did not. As such, Tiffani was under no obligation to perform her agreement with Colt until January 1, 2003, unless she chose to, and was able to, obtain a release from LexCentre. Therefore, **Answer (A) is correct, but not the best answer**. Moreover, **Answer (C) is correct, but not the best answer** because LexCentre refused Tiffani's request to terminate her lease early.

Good exam-taking skills should tell you that, when two of four possible answers are clearly correct, and the fourth option is "all of the above," that must be the correct answer. But, rather than marveling at our magnificence, let's run it out. Moving consumes time and energy, and is particularly difficult to do in the middle of a large, document-intensive project. (If you have not yet had the pleasure, take my word for it, as well as my wishes that you never have to do so.) So much so that, for a small-firm practitioner like Tiffani, moving might be impracticable, but only temporarily so. This impracticability, as discussed in the answer to Question 180, did not discharge Tiffani's obligation to perform her lease with Colt, it merely suspended that obligation until the impracticability ceased. R2 §§ 261 & 269. **Answer (B) is correct, but not the best answer**.

183. **Answer (C) is the best answer**. A novation is a new agreement that replaces one or more parties to the existing agreement with one or more new parties acceptable to all parties to the existing agreement who continue to have rights or obligations under the new agreement. R2 § 280.

Modifications and substituted agreements, by contrast, involve the same parties as the contract they modify or replace. *See* R2 §§ 89 & 279. Therefore, **Answer (B) is incorrect and Answer (D) is imprecise.** Because Slate promised to cease collection efforts against Bamm Bamm in exchange for Betty's promise to assume Bamm Bamm's debt, the novation was supported by consideration and Slate's promise was not illusory. Therefore, **Answer (A) is incorrect.**

184.   No. A novation discharges the original agreement and any breach of the novation would not give Slate the right to revive and enforce the original contract against Bamm Bamm. *See* R2 § 280 & cmt. b.

185.   **Answer (C) is the best answer.** This is a contract for the sale of goods for at least $500 (or $5,000, applying Revised Article 2). As such, Betty must have signed some writing evidencing the contract in order for Slate to enforce the contract against her. UCC § 2-201. The facts indicate that there was no such writing.

There is nothing to suggest that Betty entered into her contract with Slate under duress or undue influence. Therefore, **Answer (A) is incorrect.** Unlike common law, which often requires separate consideration to make a modification, substituted agreement, or novation binding, there is no such requirement for modifications in Article 2. *See* UCC § 2-209(1). Article 2 does not specifically address whether substituted agreements and novations require separate consideration, but the logic of UCC § 2-209(1) says "no." And, in any event, as discussed in the answer to Question 183, this novation *was* supported by consideration. Therefore, **Answer (B) is not the best answer.** For much the same reason that Answer (A) was incorrect, **Answer (D) is incorrect.** There is nothing in the facts to indicate that Betty had no meaningful choice but to agree to the novation. And, in any event, $10,000 or thereabouts is not an unfair price to pay for a $10,000 pool table and accessories. So, even if there was procedural unconscionability, there was no substantive unconscionability. Lacking the latter, a court almost certainly would not find this novation runs afoul of UCC § 2-302.

Revised Article 2 leaves current UCC §§ 2-209 and 2-302 essentially unchanged.

186.   **Answer (D) is the best answer.** ATG's acceptance of prior late deliveries without protest may have waived ATG's right to complain about the tardiness of those deliveries. UCC § 2-209(4) provides that an attempt to modify contract terms can, if not objected to, operate as a waiver, even though it may not satisfy the writing requirements of the contract, UCC § 2-209(2), or UCC § 2-209(3). Here, Basin attempted to modify the performance schedule of the contract. ATG's failure to object and its acceptance of the tardy goods appear to be a waiver under UCC § 2-209(4).

While correct in the absence of waiver, **Answer (C) is not the best answer** because it overlooks UCC § 2-209(4). Likewise, **Answers (A) and (B) are neither the best answer** because, while correct statements of UCC § 2-209(2) and UCC § 2-209(3), respectively, they fail to take into account UCC § 2-209(4).

187.   Article 29 of the CISG provides that, in the absence of a clause like the one in this contract, the parties can agree to modify or terminate their contract after formation. CISG art. 29(1). However, where the contract at issue requires written modifications agreed to by both parties, any other form of attempted modification is ineffective *except that* "a party may be precluded by its conduct from asserting [a no modification without both parties' signature] provision to the extent that the other party has relied on that conduct." CISG art. 29(2). Thus, as is the case with UCC § 2-209(4), ATG may be estopped from insisting that Basin strictly adhere to the delivery schedule, given that ATG previously accepted numerous late deliveries without objection.

188.   **Answer (D) is the best answer**. The inability of Gromit's to perform due to commercial impracticability — that is, the occurrence of a contingency the non-occurrence of which was a basic assumption on which ATG and Gromit's made the contract — will excuse Gromit's from performing for the duration of the occurrence, UCC § 2-615(a), or until ATG cancels the contract, *see* UCC § 2-616(1)(a), provided that Gromit's seasonably notifies ATG of the delay, UCC § 2-615(c). Elsewhere the UCC defines commercial impracticability as "supervening circumstances not within the contemplation of the parties at the time of contracting," UCC § 2-615 cmt. 1, and "some unforeseen contingency which alters the essential nature of the performance," such as "a severe shortage of raw materials or of supplies due to a contingency such as war, embargo . . .," UCC § 2-615 cmt. 4.

If Gromit's fails to seasonably give ATG notice, it cannot avoid liability due to the impracticability. UCC § 2-615(c). Therefore, **Answer (C) is incomplete**. If Gromit's seasonably notifies ATG, and the impracticability will "substantially impair the value of the whole contract" to ATG, then ATG may terminate the contract, thereby discharging Gromit's. UCC § 2-616. Until ATG does so, however, the impracticability will only suspend Gromit's performance, not excuse it. Therefore, **Answer (B) is not the best answer**.

Answer (A) is incorrect. Unless the parties expressly excluded the UCC when they choose the law of a jurisdiction that has adopted the UCC to govern their transaction, then Iowa's version of the UCC is part of "Iowa law."

Revised Article 2 makes no material changes to current UCC §§ 2-615 or 2-616.

189.   As to any delivery affected by an event of impracticability under UCC § 2-615, or as to the entire contract if the impracticability substantially impairs the value of the whole contract, ATG could (1) terminate any unperformed portion of the contract, or (2) modify the contract to reflect ATG's quota of Gromit's available supply or capacity. UCC § 2-616(1)(a)-(b). If ATG fails to modify the contract within a reasonable time after receiving notice from Gromit's, but in any event within 30 days after notice, then the contract will lapse with respect to any deliveries affected by the event of impracticability. UCC § 2-616(2).

190.   **Answer (C) is the best answer**. Due to circumstances beyond his control or contemplation, Russell was unable to purchase any tickets to the movie premiere. As

such, absent contrary language in the contract, Russell's duty to perform would be discharged as a matter of law. R2 § 261.

The availability of tickets could be viewed as a condition precedent to Russell's performance, just as waking up alive could be viewed as a condition precedent to every employment contract that does not have an "until death" clause in it. However, because neither Russell nor Gwyneth expressly conditioned their own or the other's performance on the availability of tickets, **Answer (A) is not the best answer**. A court might imply such a condition, if doing so was necessary to insulate Russell from liability; but, as long as Russell pleads impracticability, the court need not do so.

Frustration of purpose does not apply to Russell's part of the contract. Therefore, **Answer (B) is not the best answer**.

Given that Russell has an impracticability defense and, perhaps, a failure of condition defense, **Answer (D) is incorrect**.

191.   No. A mere increase in ticket price would not excuse Russell from performing. A party's performance is not excused by the occurrence of a foreseeable event that makes a contract unprofitable for that party. *See, e.g., Karl Wendt Farm Equipment Co. v. International Harvester Co.*, 931 F.2d 1112 (6th Cir. 1991). When he agreed to provide Gwyneth with tickets he did not already possess for $100 each, Russell assumed the risk that they would cost him more than $100 each to buy.

192.   Russell's death or incapacitation prior to performing a personal services contract would excuse his performance as objectively impossible or impracticable. R2 § 262. A change in circumstances that makes his performance temporarily impossible or impracticable would, as discussed in the answers to Questions 180 and 182, suspend, *but not excuse*, Russell's performance. R2 § 269. So, if Russell was hospitalized only for a few days, he might still have been obligated to perform after his release. Likewise, if Russell was sufficiently coherent while hospitalized, he may have had a duty to attempt to delegate his performance to someone who was capable of performing.

193.   **Answer (D) is the best answer**. While Cameron's presence at the movie premiere may have been a condition precedent to Gwyneth's *desire* to perform, because she did not express that to Russell, she cannot use the failure of that condition to avoid her *duty* to perform her end of the bargain. Therefore, **Answer (A) is not the best answer**. As discussed in the answers to Questions 187-190, impracticability requires the occurrence of an event the non-occurrence of which was a basic assumption on which Russell and Gwyneth made their contract. R2 § 261. Nothing in the facts suggest that Cameron's presence at the premiere was such a basic assumption to *both* Russell and Gwyneth that Cameron's failure to appear would discharge Gwyneth's duty to perform once Russell had fully performed. Therefore, **Answer (C) is not the best answer**.

Gwyneth's best argument is frustration of purpose, along the lines of *Krell v. Henry*, [1903] 2 K.B. 740 (C.A. 1903), and R2 § 265. If Gwyneth can convince the court that her primary purpose for agreeing to purchase the tickets was to schmooze Cameron at the premiere, then, like the defendant in *Krell* who no longer wanted to rent the room overlooking the parade route when he learned that the parade had been cancelled, Gwyneth may be excused from performing her part of the contract. *Krell*, however, is an old case, and the court will more likely apply R2 § 265, which provides that a party's duty to perform may be discharged if (1) an event occurs the non-occurrence of which was a basic assumption on which the contract was made, and (2) as a result, the party's principal purpose was substantially frustrated. Gwyneth may argue that Cameron not attending the premiere was, to paraphrase R2 § 265, the non-occurrence of an event the occurrence of which was a basic assumption on which she made her contract with Russell and, as a result, her principal purpose was substantially frustrated. This argument will likely fail, however, because, for Gwyneth to take refuge in a frustration of purpose defense, Russell must have known that Gwyneth's purpose in making the contract was specifically to schmooze Cameron, not just to attend the premiere and "hob nob" generally. Therefore, while frustration of purpose is the most viable of the defenses listed, **Answer (B) is not the best answer**.

194. **Answer (B) is the best answer, if the court will enforce Gwyneth's promise.**
Reliance damages reimburse the non-breaching party for any expenses actually
incurred, *inter alia*, in reliance on the breaching party's promise to perform. Reliance
damages seek to put the non-breaching party in as good a position as he would have
been in had he never entered into the contract. *See* R2 § 344(b) & cmt. a. While the
parties' failure to mean the same *The Orange Pumpernickel* may have kept a contract
from forming, as discussed in the answer to Question 13, it did not negate the effect
of Gwyneth's *promise* to pay Russell for tickets to *The Orange Pumpernickel*. Russell
should be able to recover the $150 he paid for the play tickets as reliance damages
under R2 § 349, unless the court finds that enforcing Gwyneth's promise is not
necessary to prevent injustice, **in which case Answer (D) would be the best answer**,
and Russell would be without a remedy.

Answer (A) is incorrect. Expectation damages seek to put the non-breaching party
in as good a position as he would have been in had the breaching party fully performed
by awarding the non-breaching party the difference between the value of the performance promised by the breaching party and the performance, if any, actually received.
See R2 § 344(a) & cmt. a. Russell cannot recover his expectation damages — the
$200 he expected Gwyneth to pay him under the contract — under R2 § 347, because
there was no contract to breach. As discussed in the answer to Question 13, the parties
failed to mutually assent; therefore, there is no contract based on their exchange of
promises that unwittingly related to different subjects.

Restitutionary damages seek to ensure that Gwyneth is not unjustly enriched by her
refusal to pay Russell for the tickets. *See* R2 § 344(c) & cmt. a. Restitutionary damages
would restore to Russell the "reasonable value" to Gwyneth of the play tickets "in
terms of what it would have cost [her] to obtain [play tickets] from a person in
[Russell's] position." R2 § 371(a). However, Gwyneth has not been enriched —
unjustly or otherwise — by Russell's performance. He delivered tickets she did not
want, did not use, and did not dispose of for value. Moreover, R2 § 373(2) forecloses
restitutionary damages for breach of contract where the non-breaching party has fully
performed (even if his performance is unsatisfactory) and all that remains is for the
breaching party to pay a "sum certain of money." Russell fully performed by delivering
the tickets to Gwyneth. All that remained was for Gwyneth to pay Russell the $200
she promised him. Therefore, **Answer (C) is incorrect**.

195. R2 § 378 gives Russell the right to elect, from among the remedies to which he is
entitled, the remedy that affords him the most complete relief. Therefore, if more than
one of options (A)-(C) is available to Russell, and if Russell is a rational actor (excuse
the pun), he will choose the most lucrative remedy.

Unlike Question 194, Russell should be able to recover his expectation damages here, because a court should find that Gwyneth formed a contract on Russell's terms when she used the play tickets. If so, then Russell would be entitled to recover $200 as his expectation damages (unless the tickets indicated a different face value, in which case a court may find that his counteroffer was not only for play tickets, rather than movie tickets, but also for the price stated on the play tickets, rather than the $200 Gwyneth previously offered for the movie tickets). Therefore, **Answer (A) may be correct, but it will be the best answer only if Answer (C) is incorrect.**

For the same reasons discussed in the answer to Question 194, Russell should be able to recover the $150 he paid for the play tickets as reliance damages under R2 § 349. Therefore, **Answer (B) is correct, but will be the best answer only if Answers (A) and (C) are incorrect.**

Unlike Question 194, using the play tickets, for which she had not yet paid, has unjustly enriched Gwyneth. Russell's restitutionary damages would be $250, what it would have cost Gwyneth to obtain tickets to the play on the day of the play. R2 § 373(2) seems to still be a stumbling block. Russell fully performed by delivering the tickets to Gwyneth. All that remained was for Gwyneth to pay Russell for the tickets. If Gwyneth accepted Russell's counteroffer to sell her play tickets, rather than movie tickets, Russell may be able to argue that, while all Gwyneth had left to do was pay him for the tickets, the amount she had to pay him was not a "sum certain of money." If Russell prevails on this theory, he would be entitled to recover restitutionary damages in the amount of $250; and, as a rational actor, Russell should elect this remedy over either expectation damages or reliance damages because restitutionary damages are the most lucrative. Therefore, **if Answer (C) is correct, then it is the best answer.**

In any event, **Answer (D) is incorrect.**

196. **If Gwyneth can prove any actual or incidental damages and Russell cannot prove that she failed to mitigate her damages, then Answer (D) is the correct answer; otherwise, Answer (C) is the correct answer.**

Russell and Gwyneth formed a contract for tickets to the movie premiere because Russell knew, and was therefore bound by, Gwyneth's meaning. R2 §§ 20(2) & 201(2). Therefore, Gwyneth can recover her expectation damages from Russell, including any incidental damages and any foreseeable, unavoidable, and sufficiently certain consequential damages caused by Russell's breach, less any costs she avoided by reason of Russell's failure to perform as promised and any loss she avoided or should have avoided by mitigating, or

Loss in Value + Other Loss – Cost Avoided – Loss Avoided,

where Other Loss is the sum of Gwyneth's incidental and consequential damages. *See* E. ALLAN FARNSWORTH, CONTRACTS 795 (3d ed. 1999).

Incidental damages are costs incurred in a reasonable effort to avoid or mitigate damages caused by the other party's breach (*e.g.*, a fee paid to a ticket broker to purchase desired tickets that the broker or the broker's client have already purchased or to sell undesired tickets to the broker or the broker's client). R2 § 347 cmt. c. Consequential damages include reasonably foreseeable injuries to a person, business, or property caused by the breaching party's failure to fully and properly perform (*e.g.*, lost income due to the loss of a job as a result of the other party's breach). *Id.* Where consequential damages are available, the non-breaching party has a duty to take reasonable steps to mitigate those damages. R2 § 350(1).

Under R2 § 347, Gwyneth should recover the difference between the value of the performance she expected and the value of the performance she received, plus any incidental damages and any foreseeable, unavoidable, and sufficiently certain consequential damages, minus the $200 she promised to pay Russell. What did Gwyneth expect? She expected two tickets to the movie premiere and the chance to meet, dazzle, and be cast by Cameron in his upcoming movie. What did she receive? She received two tickets to a play she did not want to see and no tickets to the movie premiere — and, therefore, no chance to meet, dazzle, and be cast by Cameron in his upcoming movie. So, Gwyneth lost the enjoyment value of attending the movie premiere. She also "lost" the movie role she coveted to Belle Harry. What did Gwyneth expect to pay? $200. What did she pay? Nothing.

Her odds of recovering the estimated value of the movie role (extrapolated in some way from the $15 million reportedly to be paid to Belle), are slim, because such damages do not appear to have been reasonably foreseeable to Russell (there are no facts indicating that he knew why Gwyneth wanted to attend the movie premiere), sufficiently certain (even if she went to the movie premiere, there was no guarantee that she would meet, much less dazzle, much less be cast by Cameron), nor caused by Russell's breach (Cameron did not announce in advance that he would cast the coveted role at the premiere, he obviously could have filled the role after the premiere, he may have chosen Belle even if she had not been at the premiere, and he may have not chosen Gwyneth even if she were). Therefore, **Answer (A) is incorrect**.

The money Gwyneth spent on the dress, shoes, jewelry, personal care, and transportation, even if reasonably foreseeable to Russell, is neither incidental nor consequential damages because she did not incur those expenses trying to mitigate her damages nor as a consequence of Russell's breach. Those are reliance damages, not expectation damages. Therefore, **Answer (B) is incorrect**.

The choice between Answer (C) and Answer (D) turns on whether Gwyneth can prove any actual or incidental damages and whether Russell can prove that she failed to take reasonable steps to mitigate her damages. Gwyneth will have a difficult time establishing the enjoyment value of attending the movie premiere — the only actual damage Gwyneth can claim — particularly given that she had the chance to attend the play premiere and elected not to do so. The facts do not suggest that Gwyneth had any incidental damages. However, if she incurred any expenses trying to procure tickets to the movie premiere or trying to sell the tickets to the play premiere, those expenses would be incidental damages. Mitigation is not much of an issue, because the facts tell us that there were no other tickets to the movie premiere commercially available when Gwyneth realized that Russell had delivered the wrong tickets. Gwyneth may have had a duty to attempt to sell the play tickets to someone who would use them.

197.   **Answer (A) is correct**. Rescission relieves Gwyneth of any obligation to pay Russell for the tickets he delivered, if he knew they were the wrong tickets. Sad as it may seem, this is likely to be the most favorable among Gwyneth's electable remedies.

Gwyneth has not yet paid Russell for the tickets; therefore, she is not "out of pocket" anything for them. However, she has incurred significant expenses in reliance on attending the premiere. She spent $8,350 on the dress, shoes, jewelry, personal care, and transportation. Those are reliance expenses, less whatever she was able to recover, or could have recovered, by returning items or canceling reservations. The problem is that, if Russell can prove that Gwyneth would have incurred those reliance expenses, and that they would have gone uncompensated, even if he had performed as promised, R2 § 349 will preclude Gwyneth from recovering them as reliance damages. Given the unlikelihood that Gwyneth would have realized any monetary gain by attending the premiere, she would have been net out of pocket the $8,350 (plus the $200 for the tickets) even if Russell had performed as and when promised. Therefore, **Answer (B) is correct, but is not likely the best answer**. Had Russell initially agreed to drive her to the premiere, and then backed out of that promise because of another engagement, the expense Gwyneth incurred for a limousine and driver would be recoverable reliance damages. However, the facts do not indicate any promise by Russell other than to deliver the tickets in exchange for $200.

Gwyneth has not unjustly enriched Russell in any way (other than, perhaps, giving him a good laugh), so she should not be able to recover any restitutionary damages. Therefore, **Answer (C) is incorrect**.

Specific performance orders the breaching party to perform (or refrain from performing, in "negative enforcement" cases) as is called for in the contract. For example, if the contract calls for the sale of a certain parcel of land, an order of specific performance would require the breaching party to sell the land. Generally, specific performance is disfavored. Courts should not award specific performance (1) if there is any other adequate remedy available, *see* R2 §§ 359-60; (2) if the contract terms are not sufficiently specific to support an order directing the breaching party to do or not do a particular act, R2 § 362; or (3) if enforcing or supervising the (non-)performance would impose burdens on the court disproportionate to the benefit to be gained by the non-breaching party, R2 § 366. Specific performance is a discretionary remedy that courts will typically award only in cases involving the sale of — but generally not creation of (see below) — unique goods or the sale of real property (and fixtures thereon). Courts should never award specific performance where the contract requires personal services, including the creation of a unique good, because to do so smacks of involuntary servitude, R2 § 367; however, courts may enforce a covenant not to compete or a covenant not to disclose or to use trade secrets if the restriction imposed by the covenant is not unconscionable or contrary to public policy. Specific performance is unavailable here, because the movie premiere has long since come and gone (and the facts tell us that there were no tickets to the movie premiere to be had even before it came and went). Therefore, **Answer (D) is incorrect**.

198.   Unlike Question 194, Russell may be able to recover his expectation damages here, because a court may find that Gwyneth formed a contract on Russell's terms when she used the play tickets. If so, as discussed in the answer to Question 195, then Russell would be entitled to recover $200 as his expectation damages (unless the tickets indicated a different face value, in which case a court may find that his counteroffer was for play tickets for the price stated on the play tickets rather than for movie tickets for $200). Can Russell sue Gwyneth for a portion of her salary from *Fritz*, on the theory that she would never have gotten the role but for him giving her the play tickets? No. What was Russell's expectation? At most, it was that Gwyneth would pay him $200 for the play tickets. Period. Therefore, **if Answer (A) is correct, then it is the best answer**.

For the same reasons discussed in the answer to Question 194, Russell should be able to recover the $150 he paid for the play tickets as reliance damages under R2 § 349. Therefore, **Answer (B) is correct, but it will be the best answer only if Answer (A) is incorrect**.

Unlike Question 194, using the play tickets, for which she had not yet paid, has unjustly enriched Gwyneth. Russell's restitutionary damages should be at least $250, what it would have cost Gwyneth to obtain tickets to the play on the day of the play. R2 § 371(a). Unlike Question 195, there is a second possible element of unjust enrichment damages: the $500,000 that Sam Quentin promised to pay Gwyneth to star in his new production. R2 § 371(b) provides that the sum of money awarded to protect Russell's restitution interest may be measured by "the extent to which the other party's property has been increased in value or h[er] other interests advanced." Gwyneth walked in to the play with nothing but the hope that going to the play would prove more entertaining than sitting at home and watching *Gladiator* for the 53d time. She walked out with a job and the promise of at least $500,000 pay for that job. Surely, that constitutes advancing her other interests. However, she did not win the $500,000 as a door prize. Surely the amount Quentin offered to pay Gwyneth to perform in his production was due to her talent, rather than the mere fact that she showed up at the same David Marmoset play on the same night as he did. Therefore, while Russell delivering play tickets instead of movie tickets has enriched Gwyneth, that enrichment is not *unjust*, because Gwyneth will have to earn that $500,000. Moreover, a close reading of R2 § 371 makes clear that Russell could recover either the value to Gwyneth of the tickets or the extent to which Gwyneth's interests were advanced, not both. Therefore, **Answer (C) is incorrect**. However, do not dismiss the significance of the $500,000 contract too quickly. To the extent that Gwyneth would otherwise be entitled to recover some damages resulting from Russell's breach, Russell should be able to reduce those damages by at least $500,000 (unless Gwyneth can prove that she could have performed both for Cameron and Quentin on terms all three parties would find satisfactory) by claiming that she is now getting more benefit than she could have reasonably expected had Russell performed as Gwyneth intended. Gwyneth's ability to get the role in the *Titanic* sequel was by no means certain; now she has a sure deal.

Because reliance (and possibly expectation) damages are available to Russell on these facts, **Answer (D) is incorrect**.

199. **Answer (D) is the correct answer.** The measure of Gwyneth's expectation damages is the difference between the price Gwyneth had to pay for the tickets and the price she expected to pay, plus any incidental and consequential damages ($0, because the broker's fee was rolled into the ticket price), minus any cost avoided as a result of Russell's breach, minus any loss avoided by mitigation (the $150 she received from Kate for the play tickets). So, Gwyneth's expectation damages are

$$(\$1,000 - \$200) + (\$0 + \$0) - \$0 - \$150 = \$650.$$

Gwyneth cannot recover the entire cost of the replacement tickets from Russell, because she expected to pay him $200 in the first place. Letting her attend the movie premiere for free (by making Russell pay the entire price of the replacement tickets) would put her in a better position than she would have been in had Russell performed. That is contrary to R2 § 344(a)'s intent to put Gwyneth "in as good a position as [s]he would have been in had the contract been performed." R2 § 347 cmt. a. Therefore, **Answer (A) is incorrect**.

For purposes of calculating Gwyneth's expectation damages, the benchmark is the price for which Russell promised to sell her the tickets, not the price he paid for them. Therefore, **Answer (C) is incorrect**. And, while Answer (B) uses the correct benchmark, it fails to reduce Gwyneth's recovery by the $150 windfall she received by selling the play tickets to Kate — something she could not have done had Russell performed as promised. Therefore, **Answer (B) is incorrect**.

200. This is trickier than Question 199 because the facts do not indicate that Kate gave Gwyneth any value for the play tickets. Therefore, Gwyneth's expectation damages are $800 — the difference between the price she expected to pay for the tickets and the price she ended up paying for them. Or are they? If Kate or a third party was willing to pay $150 or more for the tickets, Gwyneth may have had an obligation to mitigate by selling the tickets rather than giving them to Kate. *See* R2 § 350(1). If so, then her expectation damages would be reduced to the extent of the ignored opportunity to mitigate. Is Russell entitled to an offset for Kate's use of the tickets? The answer to Question 195 discusses Russell's right to restitutionary damages to the extent that using the play tickets without paying for them unjustly enriched Gwyneth. Here, though, Gwyneth does not appear to be unjustly enriched. R2 § 71(4) is clear that consideration can still be consideration even if a party other than the promisor receives it. The *Restatement* provisions addressing restitutionary damages do not offer similarly clear guidance with respect to whether the unjust enrichment of a third party entitles a party to recover restitutionary damages. Taking R2 § 370 at face value — "[a] party is entitled to restitution . . . only to the extent that he has conferred a benefit on *the other party* by way of part performance or reliance" (emphasis added) — Russell

does not appear to have conferred any benefit on Gwyneth. R2 § 370 cmt. a states, in relevant part, that "[t]he other party is considered to have had a benefit conferred on him if a performance was rendered at his request to a third person." *See also* R2 § 370 illus. 5. However, Kate was not in the picture when Russell and Gwyneth reached their agreement; therefore, Russell's actions do not appear to fall within the ambit of R2 § 370 cmt. a & illus. 5.

201. Because Gwyneth had a reasonable opportunity to mitigate and failed to do so, she may not recover any consequential damages to which she might otherwise have been entitled due to Russell's breach. She can only recover, if at all, her actual loss, less a $200 offset in Russell's favor.

202. **Answer (D) is the best answer**, although **Answer (C) is also correct** because UCC § 2A-219 places the risk of loss to leased goods, absent a contrary agreement between the parties, on the lessor: Winny Hairston. The reason Answer (D) is the better of the two is that it would be equally true if Gwyneth had purchased the jewelry from Winny Hairston and was mugged on her way home from the store; or, for that matter, if Gwyneth had purchased the jewelry from Winny Hairston, was unable to wear it to the premiere, and could not return it to the store.

Much like the oft-maligned counter clerk in *Hadley v. Baxendale*, 156 Eng. Rep. 145 (Ex. 1854), to whom, in the opinion of Baron Alderson (as opposed to the opinion of counsel), Hadley's agent did not explain the urgency of having the mill shaft repaired, unless Gwyneth told Russell before they concluded their contract that she would need to acquire a whole new ensemble for the premiere, her actions (other than arranging transportation, and perhaps hiring a sitter to stay with her pet Pomeranian) would not have been reasonably foreseeable to Russell. Therefore, **Answer (A) is incorrect**.

While Answer (B) may be factually correct, if Gwyneth's lease or purchase of the jewelry was reasonably foreseeable to Russell when they made the contract (suppose, for instance, that Russell promised to accompany her to the premiere — remember, she asked for two tickets — and said "I want you to look fabulous. Get yourself a new dress and some jewelry to go with it."), then the fact that he is not the guardian of all of Gwyneth's possessions would not relieve him of liability for the cost of the necklace and earrings, damaged or otherwise, unless Gwyneth intentionally damaged them in order to thwart any attempt to mitigate. Therefore, **Answer (B) is not the best answer**.

203. **Answer (A) is the best answer**. Russell should have a viable breach of contract claim against Gwyneth. He offered to sell her two tickets to the movie premiere for $100 each, to be delivered on March 14th, she accepted, there was an exchange of consideration — their mutual promises, and there is no statute of frauds issue. So, Russell ought to be able to recover the greater of his expectation damages (R2 § 347) or reliance damages (R2 § 349). His expectation damages would be the contract price, $200, plus any costs incurred in trying to mitigate, less any cost avoided by Gwyneth's

breach and any loss avoided by mitigation. Russell attempted to mitigate after Gwyneth breached by refusing to pay for the tickets; but, due to circumstances beyond his control, he was unable to use, sell, or return the tickets. The facts do not indicate that he incurred any expense trying to mitigate. And, because he had already purchased the tickets when Gwyneth breached, there was no cost to avoid. Thus, his expectation damages are $200.

Russell's reliance damages would be his out-of-pocket expense incurred in reliance on Gwyneth's promise to buy the tickets from him: the $150 he paid for the tickets. Because R2 § 378 permits Russell to elect the remedy that is most beneficial, **Answer (B) is not the best answer**.

While it appears that Russell might have restitutionary damages as high as $300 to $350, based on the "fair market value" of the tickets on the day of the premiere or the day he delivered them, respectively, R2 § 373(2) forecloses restitutionary damages for breach of contract where the non-breaching party has fully performed and all that remains is for the breaching party to pay a "sum certain of money." Russell fully performed by delivering the tickets to Gwyneth; all that remained was for Gwyneth to pay Russell the $200. Therefore, **Answers (C) and (D) are both incorrect**.

204.   **Answer (D) is the best answer**. Hilda is obligated to mitigate her damages. R2 § 350. However, she is not required to choose the mitigation option that most reduces her economic losses, if another reasonable choice is available that is more comparable to the performance of which Missy's breach of contract is depriving her or that is better suited to Hilda's reasonable needs. In this case, she may reasonably mitigate her damages by accepting the teaching job at SLS, although it pays less than the job at Valet Rain and involves moving costs and higher housing costs than staying in Magnolia and working for Valet Rain, because the job at SLS is the closest substitute to another year of teaching at Missy's. Likewise, if Hilda decides to return to practice, she may choose to take the lower-paying job at Valet Rain, in order to avoid the expense and hassle of moving again, or the higher-paying job at S&P, despite the expense and hassle of moving again, because she is fully licensed in South Mesquite, but not in Magnolia, and may have better professional opportunities in a jurisdiction where she is licensed than one in which she is not. **Answers (A), (B), and (C) are all viable options, each for a different reason, but none is so compelling as to foreclose the other two**; therefore, Answer (D), which allows Hilda her choice among the options presented in Answers (A), (B), and (C), is the best answer.

205.   **Answer (C) is the best answer**. If Hilda can overcome the statute of frauds and state a claim for breach of contract, she may be able to recover the difference between the value to her of the performance that she expected from Missy's — $100,000 for two years' worth of teaching — and the value of the performance actually tendered by Missy's — $50,000 for one years' worth of teaching — or $50,000, plus any costs she incurs in attempting to mitigate her damages ($8,000 in unreimbursed moving expenses + the $10,000 lost on the sale of her house in Magnolia), less any cost avoided ($0, because her monthly rent in Orange will be the same as her monthly housing

cost in Magnolia). Because Missy's only partially breached the contract, Hilda would not be entitled to recover consequential damages. Hilda is obligated to mitigate her damages, R2 § 350, and so her $68,000 loss will be reduced by the $55,000 SLS will pay her to teach for one year (loss avoided). Therefore,

$$($100,000 - $50,000) + ($18,000 + $0) - $0 - $55,000 = $13,000.$$

Answer (A) is not the best answer because it includes Hilda's unreimbursed expenses moving to Orange and the increased salary she will earn at SLS, but it fails to account for the loss she will take upon selling the house in Magnolia. **Answer (B) is not the best answer** because it includes Hilda's unreimbursed expenses for moving to Orange, but fails to account for either the increased salary she will earn at SLS or the loss she will take upon selling the house in Magnolia. **Answer (D) is not the best answer** because it includes the higher price Hilda would have to pay to purchase a house in Orange comparable to the one she purchased in Magnolia. It might have been reasonable for Hilda to purchase a house in Magnolia when she went there for two years, with a remote possibility of staying longer, particularly given her (mistaken) belief that federal tax law required her to roll the gain from the sale of her house in South Mesquite into the purchase of a house in Magnolia in order to avoid paying taxes on the gain. It seems unreasonable for Hilda to purchase a house in Orange when she is going there for only one year with no possibility of her position being extended and has no gain on the sale of the house in Magnolia to worry about shielding from federal tax.

206. **Answer (A) is the best answer**. A non-breaching party has the right to recover expenditures incurred preparing to perform or in performing, less any loss the breaching party can prove with reasonable certainty the non-breaching party would have suffered had the breaching party fully performed. R2 § 349. Hilda incurred both actual (out-of-pocket) and (foregone) opportunity costs in preparing to perform, and in performing, her agreement to teach at Missy's. She quit her lucrative job at LSBB, giving up $50,000 per year of income; she sold her house in South Mesquite for $25,000 less than its appraised value (but $25,000 more than she paid for it); she incurred $5,000 in unreimbursed moving expenses; and she spent $135,000 on a house in Magnolia. Of those, what can she recover? The purpose of reliance damages is to reimburse the plaintiff by putting her in "as good a position as [s]he would have been in had the contract not been made." R2 § 344. But for Missy's promise of a two-year appointment, Hilda would not have quit her job at LSBB ($100,000/yr.) to take the job at Missy's ($50,000/yr.), nor would she have sold her house in South Mesquite, bought a new house in Magnolia, or incurred the unreimbursed moving expenses. The salary part is tricky, because she obviously chose to take a pay cut in order to teach. That seems to fall within the ambit of R2 § 349, which offsets against reliance damages losses that would have been incurred with full performance. The problem is that all of the other expenses, likewise, seem to fall within the ambit of R2 § 349, because she would have sold the South Mesquite house for less than its appraised value, incurred the unreimbursed moving expenses, and spent $135,000 on a house in Magnolia if Missy's had fully performed. The key to understanding why they *do not* fall within

R2 § 349 is to pay careful attention to the language of the *Restatement (Second)*: while Hilda's lower salary is a "loss," her expenses relocating to Magnolia are "costs." So, Hilda can recover her unreimbursed moving expenses ($5,000), the costs incurred selling her house in South Mesquite ($15,000), and at least the difference between what she owed on the house in South Mesquite when she sold it ($125,000) and the price she paid for the house in Magnolia ($135,000).

Answer (C) is not the best answer because it adds the difference between the salary Hilda would have made during the year she spent at Missy's if she had, instead, stayed at LSBB and the salary she was, in fact, paid by Missy's. Despite the fact that Hilda would not have taken the teaching job — and, hence, the salary cut — had she known that Missy's would only employ her for one year, she would have "lost" the $50,000 (indeed, she would have "lost" $100,000 or more) had Missy's fully performed. Therefore, R2 § 349 prevents the income she voluntarily foreswore from her reliance damages.

Answer (D) is not the best answer because, in addition to erroneously adding the $50,000 difference between Hilda's salary the year she taught at Missy's and what she would have earned if she had stayed at LSBB, Answer (D) compounds the error by including the other $50,000 difference between what Hilda's salary would have been had she taught a second year at Missy's and what she would have earned that year if she had never left LSBB.

Answer (B) is not the best answer because you must have committed a mathematical error, erroneously considered only Hilda's "lost" income, or just guessed to choose $50,000.

207. **Answer (B) is the best answer**. Regardless of the jurisdiction, a plaintiff who successfully claims promissory estoppel is entitled to recover the greater of (1) reliance damages, representing the expenses and opportunity costs incurred by the plaintiff in performing or preparing to perform in reliance on the defendant's promise, less the value of any loss the breaching party can prove with reasonable certainty that the plaintiff would have suffered even without the breach, R2 § 349, or (2) restitutionary damages, representing the value of any benefit the plaintiff conferred on the defendant, R2 § 371.

Specific performance should be unavailable because the combination of a substitute job and damages are adequate to make Hilda whole. (Hilda might, were the facts otherwise, convince the court that she could only be made whole by teaching, and, in the absence of another teaching job, that ordering Missy's to employ her as promised might be the only viable remedy. However, she has been offered another teaching job, so specific performance should be unavailable.) Therefore, **Answer (D) is incorrect**.

The *Restatement* specifically provides for restitution in cases where an otherwise enforceable contract is unenforceable because of the statute of frauds. R2 § 375. R2 § 371(a) provides that restitutionary damages equal "the reasonable value to the other party of what he received in terms of what it would have cost him to obtain it from a person in the [plaintiff]'s position." R2 § 370 further provides that "[a] party is entitled to restitution . . . only to the extent that he has conferred a benefit on the other party by way of part performance or reliance" for which the party has not already been compensated. The problem here is as follows: Hilda has been paid for her services under the written contract; the only services for which she has not been compensated are those she has not yet performed; and, at least under the facts known to us, she has not conferred and would not confer any benefit on Missy's by agreeing to teach for the second year until she actually did teach the classes. (This might be different if her presence induced some students to go to Missy's or some donors to give money to Missy's who would not have otherwise done so, but we have no facts to support such a claim.) As a consequence, while legally Hilda may be entitled to seek restitution, factually there does not seem to be any grounds to award restitution. Therefore, **Answer (C) is incorrect**.

Courts are split regarding a promisee's ability to recover expectation damages under R2 § 90 (or § 139), *compare, e.g., Tour Costa Rica v. Country Walkers, Inc.*, 758 A.2d 795 (Vt. 2000) (awarding expectation damages where doing so was the only means by which the court could avoid injustice, given the inadequacy of any other available remedy) *with, e.g., Jarboe v. Landmark Community Newspapers of Indiana, Inc.*, 644 N.E.2d 118 (Ind. 1994) (holding that the plaintiff's remedy for promissory estoppel "is limited to damages actually resulting from [his] detrimental reliance"), though the weight of modern authority seems to be in favor of awarding expectation damages where they are reasonably ascertainable and afford the plaintiff a better remedy than the alternative(s). *See* Richard Craswell, *Against Fuller and Perdue*, 67 U. Chi. L. Rev. 99 (2000). The *Restatement (Second)* does not clearly take a particular side in this debate, which has been ongoing since before the ALI published the <u>first</u> *Restatement of Contracts* in 1932, other than to provide in both R2 § 90 and R2 § 139 that any remedy granted should be "limited as justice requires." Opponents of awarding expectation damages seize upon this language, upon the requirement of actual reliance under R2 §§ 90 and 139, upon the explicit language in R2 § 375 making restitutionary damages available to a party who is relegated to R2 § 139, and upon the fundamentally equitable nature of promissory estoppel (as opposed to the fundamentally legal nature of breach of contract), to support their view that expectation damages are unavailable to a plaintiff who cannot establish the defendant's breach of an enforceable contract. Proponents of awarding expectation damages echo Professor Williston's oft-repeated argument that, if promissory estoppel makes a promise legally binding, despite the absence of consideration or a required writing, then the legally binding promise ought to be enforced as a contract. *See* Mary E. Becker, *Promissory Estoppel Damages*, 16 Hofstra L. Rev. 131 (1987). If the Magnolia courts have held that expectation damages are unavailable to a plaintiff who can establish promissory estoppel, but cannot establish the breach of an enforceable contract, **Answer (A) is incorrect**. On the other hand, if the Magnolia courts have held that expectation damages are available to a plaintiff who can establish promissory estoppel, but cannot establish the breach of an enforceable contract, **Answer (A) is correct, but not the best answer** because Hilda's expectation damages ($13,000) are substantially less than her reliance damages, which are at least $30,000 (and could be much more), as discussed in the answer to Question 206.

208.   Joaquin's expectation damages are $70,000 ($100,000 value lost – $30,000 cost saved). Joaquin's reliance damages are $60,000 (the amount Joaquin spent without reimbursement). Joaquin's restitutionary damages are $40,000 (the value of the benefit Joaquin has conferred on Estrella without compensation).

209.   **Answer (C) is the best answer**. Because the second paragraph of the contract quoted above appears to be a valid liquidated damages clause, *see* R2 § 356(1), the contract clearly provides Wally the choice between (1) repairing any defective wallpaper, which would cost Wally $250; (2) removing the wallpaper and repainting, which would cost Wally $800; and (3) refunding the contract price, less the cost of any nondefective wallpaper and materials, which would cost Wally $350. Alternatively, Sally can demand payment of $500. While Wally's best choice might appear to be repairing the defective wallpaper, it is easy to imagine that saving that $100 (as compared to refunding the contract price, less the cost of any nondefective wallpaper and materials) might lead to an endless cycle of dissatisfaction claims from Sally that would require additional responses from Wally. Therefore, **Answer (A) is not the best answer**. If Wally wants to be able to walk away from Sally, his best choice will be to refund the contract price ($1,000), less the cost of any nondefective wallpaper and materials ($650). However, if Sally is rational, she will not accept Wally's tender of $350 when she can demand $500 as liquidated damages. Therefore, **Answer (B) is not the best answer**. Wally would only be on the hook for $1,250 if he has to pay Sally to hire WallCo to remove the "nymph and satyrs" wallpaper and install replacement wallpaper. Because that is not one of the four remedies (three at Wally's option and one at Sally's) set forth in the contract, **Answer (D) is incorrect**.

210.   **Answer (C) is the best answer**. Marlowe offered to sell Romeo the same ring at a price ($7,500) significantly below both the market price ($11,000) and the contract price ($10,000). Romeo's explanation for rejecting this offer is unpersuasive. There is relatively little post-sale service on a $10,000 diamond ring; and, in any event, Romeo would have been able to find some alternate source for whatever minor service might have become necessary (*e.g.*, cleaning, re-sizing).

Any attempt by Romeo to recover the difference between the $12,000 he paid for the replacement ring and the $10,000 for which Old Will agreed to sell him the original ring will prove problematic. The "cover" remedy requires that the replacement purchase be "reasonable." UCC § 2-712(1). Paying $12,000 for a ring with a market value of $11,000 may or may not be reasonable, depending on what information Romeo had at his disposal, the cost involved in searching elsewhere for a better price, etc. In any event, Romeo will be foreclosed from recovering the difference between the contract price and the cover price because, as explained below, he failed to mitigate. Therefore, **Answer (A) is incorrect**.

Alternatively, Romeo may be limited to the difference between the market price at the time and place of tender ($11,000) and the contract price ($10,000). *See* UCC

§ 2-713(1). That $1,000 difference is the financial benefit of Romeo's bargain. Even this claim will fail, however, because Romeo had and spurned a reasonable opportunity to mitigate his financial loss. Therefore, **Answer (B) is incorrect**.

Answer (D) is incorrect. Romeo is not bringing a tort claim against Old Will's Jewelers for overcharging him for Juliet's ring. Even if he were, Marlowe's subsequent offer to reduce the price of the ring could as easily have been an attempt to fend off a lawsuit by Romeo as an admission that Old Will had overpriced the ring to begin with.

Revised Article 2 does not materially change current UCC §§ 2-712 or 2-713, although it does subdivide § 2-713 to address damages for non-delivery, rejection, or revocation separately from damages due to the seller's repudiation and to afford the buyer a commercially reasonable time after the buyer learns of the seller's repudiation to determine the buyer's damages.

211. **Answer (D) is the best answer**. A buyer, unlike a seller, can recover consequential damages under Article 2. UCC § 2-715(2). Therefore, **Answers (A) and (B) are incorrect**. Section 2-715(2)(a) requires that Old Will had reason to know that Romeo had "particular requirements and needs . . . which could not reasonably be prevented by cover or otherwise." Old Will may have had reason to know about Romeo's planned Maui trip, and the facts tell us that Romeo (1) did not have sufficient time after Old Will's breach to secure a replacement ring before leaving on the trip, and (2) could not cancel the airline tickets to save their expense. The problem for Romeo is that he took the trip; he just did not enjoy it as much. Essentially, Romeo seeks to recover for the decreased pleasure of the trip made versus the trip planned. This kind of recovery is outside the scope of Article 2. Therefore, **Answer (C) may be correct, but it is not the best answer**.

Revised Article 2 leaves current UCC § 2-715 unchanged. However, it extends to sellers the right to recover consequential damages, except in consumer goods transactions. See Revised § 2-710(2)-(3).

212. Mercury's wrongful rejection entitled Tubular to cancel the contract. In addition, Tubular could (1) sell the goods to another buyer and sue Mercury for contract-resale damages, under UCC § 2-706; (2) sue Mercury for contract-market damages, under UCC § 2-708(1); (3) sue Mercury for lost profits, under UCC § 2-708(2); or (4) sue Mercury for price, under UCC § 2-709.

Revised Article 2 does not materially change current UCC §§ 2-706, 2-708 or 2-709, although it does subdivide § 2-708 to address damages for non-acceptance separately from damages due to the buyer's repudiation and to afford the seller a commercially reasonable time after the seller learns of the buyer's repudiation to determine the seller's damages.

213. **Answer (A) is the best answer**. UCC § 2-706 entitled Tubular to resell the goods in good faith and in a commercially reasonable manner, and having done so, to recover

from Mercury the difference between the contract price (KP) and the resale price (RP), plus any incidental damages (ID) permitted by UCC § 2-710, minus expenses saved (ES) by Tubular as a result of Mercury's nonperformance. So,

$$(KP - RP) + ID - ES = § 2-706 \text{ damages.}$$

Here, KP = $25,000; RP = (4,000 x $6.00) = $24,000; ID = $500 (the cost of transporting the glass from Mercury's plant back to Tubular's plant) + $250 (the cost of storing all 5,000 ft. of tubing for the month of May); and ES = $0 (Tubular had already manufactured and shipped the tubing before Mercury breached). So, Tubular's § 2-706 damages are:

$$(\$25,000 - \$24,000) + \$750 - \$0 = \$1,750.$$

However, in order to recover resale damages, Tubular must have notified Mercury of Tubular's intent to resell the goods prior to its resale to Video Matrix. UCC § 2-706(3). Because Tubular failed to satisfy the requirements of UCC § 2-706(3), it would not be able to recover under UCC § 2-706, but might recover under UCC § 2-708(1). Therefore, while Answer (C) reflects a proper calculation of Tubular's resale damages as of June 1st, because Tubular did not provide Mercury with proper notice of resale, **Answer (C) is incorrect**.

Answer (B) is incorrect because, even if Tubular were entitled to recover under UCC § 2-706, Answer (B) fails to include in Tubular's incidental damages the cost of storing the glass tubing until Video Matrix, or its designated carrier, picks up 4,000 of the 5,000 feet of tubing on or after June 2, 2003. **Answer (D) is incorrect** because, even if Tubular were entitled to recover under UCC § 2-706, Answer (D) includes in Tubular's incidental damages the cost of transporting the 4,000 feet of glass tubing Video Matrix bought. However, the facts indicate that Video Matrix, not Tubular, bore that cost.

214.   **Answer (A) is the best answer**. Under UCC § 2-708(1), Tubular may recover the difference between the contract price (KP) and the market price *at the time and place for tender* (MP), plus any incidental damages permitted by UCC § 2-710 (ID), minus expenses saved by Tubular as a result of Mercury's nonperformance (ES). That is,

$$(KP - MP) + ID - ES = § 2-708(1) \text{ damages.}$$

If this remedy is insufficient, UCC § 2-708 also permits the wronged seller to sue for lost profits. UCC § 2-708(2).

Here, KP = $25,000; MP = (5,000 x $5.50) = $27,500; ID = $750 (the cost of transporting the glass from Mercury back to Tubular, plus the cost of storing all 5,000 ft. of tubing for the month of May); and ES = 0. So,

$$(\$25,000 - \$27,500) + \$750 - \$0 = -\$1,750.$$

Because the market price was greater at the time and place of tender (May 1st) than the contract price, Tubular will not have any recoverable damages unless the cost of storing the tubing exceeds $1,750 — which will not happen until December 1, 2003, if Tubular continues to store all 5,000 feet at $0.05 per foot per month, or December 1, 2005, if Tubular stores 5,000 feet at $0.05 per foot for one month (until Video Matrix or its authorized carrier picks up the 4,000 feet it agreed to purchase) and the remaining 1,000 feet originally destined for Mercury for another 30 months. All that said, it is not entirely clear that Tubular can even include storage costs in its calculations because UCC § 2-708(1) presumes a hypothetical sale at the market price at the time of tender (May 1, 2003). If such a sale took place, Tubular would not have incurred any storage costs, and may not have had to pay to ship the goods back to its factory as it did following Mercury's breach. And, if Tubular is not entitled to recover storage costs, its market-differential damages would be

$$(\$25,000 - \$27,500) + \$0 \text{ (or } \$500) - \$0 = -\$2,500 \text{ (or } -\$2,000).$$

In any event, Tubular will not have to pay negative damages resulting from Mercury's breach to Mercury. So, no matter which negative number is correct, the net result is $0 damages.

Answer (D) is incorrect because it makes the all-too-common mistake of assuming that the difference between KP and MP is an absolute number — that is, it is a positive number, generated by subtracting the smaller number from the larger number whichever happens to be which. KP -MP is *not* an absolute number, it is a positive number if the market price is lower than the contract price and a negative number if the market price is higher than the contract price. **Answer (C) is incorrect** because it measures MP as of the date Mercury breached — April 15th, when MP = $5.00 per foot — instead of the date of tender — May 1st, when MP = $5.50 per foot. **Answer (B) is incorrect** because it conflates the two errors of Answers (C) and (D), measuring MP on the wrong date — here, the date Tubular and Mercury formed their contract, April 2nd, when MP = $5.25 per foot — and treating KP -MP as an absolute number.

215. Yes, because the recovery permitted Tubular under UCC § 2-708(1) appears to be inadequate to put Tubular in as good a position as it would have been absent Mercury's breach. Tubular would also be entitled to recover under UCC § 2-708(2) if Tubular is a "lost profit" seller, who could have satisfied both Mercury's and Video Matrix's orders.

216. **Answer (D) is the best answer if Tubular is a "lost profits" seller, while Answer (A) is the best answer if Tubular is not a "lost profits" seller.** UCC § 2-708(2) allows Tubular to recover any profits (B) that Tubular would have realized had Mercury performed, plus any incidental damages (ID) permitted by UCC § 2-710, minus expenses saved by Tubular as a result of Mercury's nonperformance (ES), minus any credit due Mercury for partial payment (PP), and minus any profit Tubular made on the resale to Video Matrix (RP) *if* Tubular could not have otherwise sold to both Mercury and Video Matrix. So,

$$B + ID - ES - PP - RP = \text{§ 2-708(2) damages.}$$

Here, B = KP – DC (direct cost of producing the tubing) = \$25,000 – (5,000 x \$4.50) = \$2,500; ID = \$750 (the cost of transporting the glass from Mercury back to Tubular, plus the cost of storing all 5,000 ft. of tubing for the month of May); ES = \$0; and PP = \$0. The trick is, what is the value of RP? If Tubular could have sold to both Mercury and Video Matrix, then RP = \$0 and

$$\$2,500 + \$750 - \$0 - \$0 - \$0 = \$3,250.$$

Thus, if Tubular is a "lost profits" seller, Answer (D) is the best answer.

If Tubular could not have sold to Video Matrix but for Mercury's breach, then RP = \$6,000 (4,000 x \$1.50) and

$$\$2,500 + \$750 - \$0 - \$0 - \$6,000 = -\$2,750.$$

If RP = \$6,000, Tubular will not be able to recover any damages under UCC § 2-708(2) unless the cost of storing the tubing is greater than \$3,000, which will not happen unless Tubular stores all 5,000 feet until May 1, 2004, or until December 1, 2007, if Tubular stores 5,000 feet at \$0.05 per foot for one month (until Video Matrix or its authorized carrier picks up the 4,000 feet it agreed to purchase) and the remaining 1,000 feet originally destined for Mercury for another 55 months. Article 2 does not contemplate a seller whose buyer has breached having to pay damages to the buyer if the buyer's breach ultimately results in a profit to the seller. Therefore, if Tubular is not a "lost profits" seller, Answer (A) is the best answer.

Answer (B) is incorrect because it only calculates (KP – DC) using the 1,000 feet of tubing not resold to Video Matrix. **Answer (C) is incorrect** because it fails to account for Tubular's incidental damages.

217. **Answer (C) is the best answer.** If its buyer fails to pay when due, a seller suing under UCC § 2-709 may recover any incidental damages permitted by UCC § 2-710 (ID), plus the price of (1) accepted goods; (2) conforming goods lost or damaged within a commercially reasonable time after risk of their loss passed to the buyer; and (3) goods identified to the contract (a) if the seller is unable after reasonable effort to resell them at a reasonable price, or (b) circumstances reasonably indicate that such effort will be unavailing.

As to goods identified to the contract that Tubular is unable to resell after reasonable effort at a reasonable price, Tubular may recover the price (P) of those identified, un-resold goods, plus any incidental damages permitted by UCC § 2-710 (ID). So,

$$P + ID = \S \text{ 2-709 damages.}$$

Here, because Tubular was able to resell to Video Matrix 4,000 feet of the tubing originally identified to its contract with Mercury, Tubular can only recover the price of the unsold 1,000 feet. So, P = (\$5.00 x 1,000) = \$5,000; and ID = \$800 (the cost of transporting the glass from Mercury back to Tubular, plus the cost of storing all 5,000 ft. of tubing for the month of May, plus the cost of storing the un-resold 1,000 ft. of tubing for the month of June). So,

$$P + ID = 5,000 + 800 = \$5,800.$$

It is easy to focus on the price of the unaccepted, unsold, conforming goods and ignore Tubular's incidental damages, but doing so would not accord with the measure of damages that UCC § 2-709 affords. Therefore, **Answer (B) is incorrect**.

It is tempting to say P = $25,000, because that is the entire contract price. But Tubular could only recover $25,000 if Mercury accepted the shipment and did not pay for it or if the entire shipment of identified and conforming goods was destroyed within a commercially reasonable time after risk of loss shifted to Mercury. UCC § 2-709(1)(a). Otherwise, Tubular is limited, as here, to suing for the price of unaccepted, unsold, conforming goods — here, the 1,000 ft. of glass tubing originally slated for Mercury which Tubular was not able to resell to Video Matrix. Therefore, **Answer (D) is incorrect**.

If Tubular eventually resells any or all of the remaining 1,000 feet, it must credit the proceeds (less $0.05 per foot per month storage cost) against its judgment against Mercury. It is tempting to treat the $24,000 sale to Video Matrix as proceeds to be credited against Tubular's damages under UCC § 2-709(2). But, again, the only goods for which Tubular can seek price are the ones that it did not resell to Video Matrix. So, there is no offset against the unsold 1,000 feet unless Tubular eventually sells that 1,000 feet to someone else. Therefore, **Answer (A) is incorrect**. Mercury will likely bear the burden of proving that any tubing subsequently sold by Tubular is part of the 1,000 not accepted by Mercury and not sold to Video Matrix.

218. **Answer (A) is the correct answer**. Chandler's cover damages would be

$$(CP - KP) + ID + CD - ES,$$

where CP = the price of the replacement mangoes, KP = the contract price between Monica and Chandler, ID = incidental damages under UCC § 2-715(1), CD = consequential damages permitted by UCC § 2-715(2), and ES = expenses saves as a result of Monica's repudiation. Here, Chandler had no consequential damages because Ross could provide Chandler with the mangoes he needed by the date he needed them. Likewise, Chandler does not appear to have incurred any expenses mitigating the effects of, or to have saved any expenses due to, Monica's repudiation. So, Chandler's cover damages = $700 -$600 + $0 + $0 -$0 = $100.

Chandler's contract-market differential damages would be

$$(MP - KP) + ID + CD - ES,$$

where MP = the market price of mangoes when Chandler learned of Monica's repudiation, and the other variables are the same as in UCC § 2-712. So, Chandler's contract-market differential damages = $650 – $600 + $0 + $0 – $0 = $50. Therefore, **Answer (B) is not the best answer**.

Because Monica failed to deliver the goods under the contract, UCC § 2-711 governs. Chandler may: (1) cancel the contract; (2) recover any money already paid to Monica;

(3) purchase replacement mangoes from another supplier, per UCC § 2-712, and recover the difference between the cover price and the contract price, plus any incidental and consequential damages; (4) recover the difference between the market price when Chandler learned of the breach and the contract price, per UCC § 2-713, plus any incidental and consequential damages, less any expenses saved by Monica's breach; (5) seek specific performance, per UCC § 2-716; or (6) agree to modify the contract and allow Monica to deliver the contract quantity at the contract price on or before September 8th. The one buyer's remedy unavailable to Chandler is UCC § 2-714, which only applies to accepted, nonconforming goods. Therefore, **Answer (C) is incorrect**.

Chandler is unlikely to convince a court to award him specific performance under UCC § 2-716, because there is no evidence that Monica's mangoes are unique and other suppliers, no doubt, exist. *See* UCC § 2-716(1) & cmt. 2. Therefore, **Answer (D) is not the best answer**.

Revised Article 2 expands the availability of specific performance as an agreed remedy, unless the breaching party's sole remaining duty is to pay money or the contract is for consumer goods. See Revised § 2-716(1).

219. Because Pennybakers did not discover S&C's breach(-es) of warranty until after accepting both the software and the GR8 computer, the only remedy Article 2 affords Pennybakers is to sue S&C for breach under UCC § 2-714, which permits Pennybakers to recover its expectation damages — that is, the difference at the time and place of acceptance between the value of the (nonconforming) good accepted and the value the good would have had if it had performed as warranted — plus any incidental and consequential damages recoverable under UCC § 2-715 that can be attributed to the nonconformity, provided Pennybakers gave S&C proper notice of the non-conformity, as required by UCC § 2-607(3)(a). Here, Pennybakers should be able to recover the difference between the $2,500 paid for the GR8 and its fair value in light of the nonconformity. What about the $25,000 of lost profits on the Garfield Fan Club account as consequential damages? According to UCC § 2-715(2), that will depend on whether Pennybakers could have prevented the lost profits "by cover or otherwise." Because the custom software ran without a glitch on other computers — a fact that Pennybakers should have known, given that Petunia's assistant, Cleo, "loaded the software onto another computer and ran it for several weeks without ever encountering the glitch" — Pennybakers may be barred from recovering the lost profits. It probably boils down to a timing question. When they lost the account, did Pennybakers know that they could run the software on another computer; and, if so, when did they know it?

Revised Article 2 does not materially change current UCC § 2-714.

220. Under the CISG, a buyer may "avoid" its contract if the seller has committed a fundamental breach, CISG art. 49(1)(a), but only if the buyer declares the contract avoided within a reasonable time, CISG art. 49(2)(b). A "fundamental breach" by a seller is one that substantially deprives the buyer of what it is entitled to expect under

the contract, unless the seller did not foresee and a reasonable person in the seller's circumstances could not have foreseen such a result. CISG art. 25. A buyer who successfully avoids the contract may sue to recover either "cover" damages, CISG art. 75, or contract-market price differential damages, CISG art. 76(1), plus incidental and consequential damages, CISG art. 74. A malfunctioning computer certainly deprives Pennybakers of what it is entitled to expect under its contract with S&C, and neither S&C nor a reasonable person in S&C's position should expect otherwise. The problem is that Pennybakers most likely did not declare the contract avoided within a reasonable time. Therefore, Pennybakers does not appear eligible to avoid its contract with S&C. That being the case, Pennybakers may choose between (1) specific performance, CISG art. 46(2), but only to the extent that forum law would permit specific performance, CISG art. 28, and (2) expectation damages, plus incidental and consequential damages, CISG art. 74. For much the same reasons that Pennybakers could not obtain specific performance under UCC § 2-716 in the answer to Question 219, unless Pennybakers brought this suit in Mexico (not likely) and Mexican law was more inclined toward specific performance than U.S. law (quite likely), Pennybakers would not be entitled to specific performance under the CISG. If Pennybakers elects to recover expectation damages, it must have taken reasonable steps to mitigate its damages. CISG art. 77.

221.   **Answer (D) is the correct answer**. Noah is an *intended* beneficiary because Methuse-
        lah formed his contract with Keynes *for Noah's benefit*. *See* R2 § 302(1) & cmt. a.
        On the other hand, if Methuselah had formed his contract with Keynes *for someone
        else's benefit*, but Noah benefited as well, Noah would be an *incidental* beneficiary.
        See R2 § 302(2) & cmt. e. Therefore, **Answers (A) and (C) are incorrect**. When
        it is unclear whether a third party is an intended or incidental beneficiary, courts
        typically ask whether a *reasonable person* in the promisor's (Methuselah's) position
        would have intended to confer on the third party (Noah) the right to bring suit to enforce
        the contract. *See* R2 § 304. In so doing, courts consider whether: (1) performance was
        rendered directly to the third party, (2) the third party has the right to control details
        of the performance, and (3) the third party is expressly designated in the contract. Here,
        the first and third prongs are clearly met at the outset, and the second prong will be
        met when Noah assumes control of the ranch, if not sooner.

        Noah is a *donee* beneficiary, rather than a *creditor* beneficiary, because Methuselah
        made his contract with Keynes as a gift to Noah (and the rest of the family, present
        and future, who are "incidental beneficiaries" under these facts), R2 § 302(1)(b) &
        cmt. c, rather than to satisfy some obligation Keynes owed to Noah, R2 § 302(1)(a)
        & cmt. b. Therefore **Answer (B) is incorrect**.

222.   **Answer (D) is the best answer**. While Methuselah would have the right to enforce
        the contract against Keynes as soon as Keynes signed it, Noah's rights in the contract
        do not vest — and, therefore, Noah could not bring an action to enforce the contract
        and Methuselah and Keynes were free to change the terms of or to rescind the contract
        — until (1) Noah manifests his own assent to the contract (*e.g.*, writes a letter
        acknowledging his awareness of and consent to the contract for his benefit), (2) Noah
        materially alters his position in detrimental reliance on the contract (*e.g.*, sells his
        automobile in anticipation of receiving a new automobile pursuant to the contract),
        or (3) some contractual condition for vesting occurs (*e.g.*, an insured dies vesting the
        policy beneficiary's rights). *See* R2 § 311(2)-(3); *see, e.g., Olson v. Etheridge*, 686
        N.E.2d 563 (Ill. 1997). Here, the facts do not indicate that Noah acknowledged his
        awareness of, and consent to, the contract at any time, nor did the contract set forth
        any vesting condition — Methuselah's transferring control of the ranch to Noah at
        or before death changed the hourly rate at which Keynes was entitled to be compensated
        and the number of hours per week he was expected to make himself available to Noah,
        but neither of those are vesting conditions within the contemplation of R2 § 303 &
        cmt. a. Noah's rights in the contract did not vest until he gave up his free time the
        first afternoon Keynes came to tutor him, and thus materially changed position in
        detrimental reliance on the contract. His detrimental reliance was not as dramatic as

selling his car, admittedly, but a court should find it to have been sufficient to give Noah the right to enforce the contract.

In the absence of some manifestation of assent by Noah or the occurrence of a vesting condition, neither of which is evident in the facts of this Question, neither Methuselah's and Keynes's exchange of promises, nor their actions, vested Noah with the right to enforce the contract until Noah detrimentally relied. Therefore, **Answers (A), (B), and (C) are incorrect** because they are premature.

223. **Answer (C) is the correct answer.** Keynes owed both Noah and Methuselah a duty to perform, *see* R2 §§ 304 & 305(1), empowering either or both to sue Keynes (though, of course, they can receive only one satisfaction, *see* R2 § 305 cmt. b). Once Noah's rights in the contract vested, he was entitled to enforce it. *See* R2 § 304. Therefore, **Answer (A) is incorrect.** Despite the fact that Noah was the recipient of Keynes's performance, Keynes's promise was to Methuselah, and Methuselah was the one paying the freight. Therefore, Methuselah could sue to enforce the contract, *see* R2 § 305(1) & cmt. a, making **Answer (B) incorrect.** The irresistibility of the teaching position at TISU may have made it worth Keynes's while to breach his contract with Methuselah and Noah, but it would not excuse that breach, unless Methuselah renounced, *see* R2 § 277, and Noah disclaimed, *see* R2 § 306, the remainder of the contract. The facts of this Question do not suggest either renunciation or disclaimer; therefore, **Answer (D) is incorrect.**

224. Yes. Once Noah's rights in the contract vested (see the answer to Question 222), any non-performance by Methuselah that excused Keynes from performing the contract for Noah's benefit would have given Noah a cause of action against Methuselah. *See* R2 § 309 illus. 5; *see also* R2 § 310(1).

225. **Answer (C) is the best answer.** GHI's promise to pay $500,000 to Susanna and her children on Methuselah's death was conditioned on Methuselah making all premium payments due prior to his death (barring policy language to the contrary). Methuselah's non-performance relieved GHI of its duty to perform for the benefit of Susanna and her children to the extent of the breach. *See* R2 § 309(2) & cmt. b. (If this were a whole life policy, it would have accumulated some cash value prior to the time Methuselah stopped paying the premiums, and GHI would be liable for that cash value. However, the facts of this Question were that the policies were term life policies. Term life policies, unless they explicitly provide a "cash surrender value," pay no benefit unless the insured dies during the term and premiums were current at the time of the insured's death.)

Answer (A) is not the best answer. R2 § 308 allows beneficiaries who are not identified when a contract is made to benefit from it, nonetheless, if they can be identified when the time comes for GHI to pay the death benefit.

Answer (B) is not the best answer because the facts do not indicate an agreement between Methuselah and GHI to cancel the policy in favor of Susanna and her children.

This was not an agreed modification, subject to R2 § 311(2); this was a breach by non-performance, subject to R2 § 309(2).

Answer (D) is incorrect. While a policy on Susanna's life might reduce or eliminate benefits if she committed suicide, absent some bizarre language in Methuselah's policy, how Adam and Eve came to be the primary beneficiaries of 100% of the policy on Methuselah's life, rather than 50%, is irrelevant (unless, perhaps, they were responsible for Susanna's death).

226. **Answer (D) is the best answer**. Barring language in the contract restricting Noah's right to assign, or prohibiting Noah from assigning, his rights under the contract to another, Noah could assign them to Samuel, because substituting Samuel for himself would not (1) materially change Keynes's duties, (2) materially increase the burden imposed on Keynes by the contract, (3) materially impair Keynes's chance of being paid as promised, nor (4) materially reduce the value of the contract to Keynes. R2 § 317. Noah was not required to give Keynes prior notice, much less get his consent. *See* R2 §§ 323 cmt. a & 336(2). Therefore, **Answers (B) and (C) are incorrect**. And, while the personal nature of the services Keynes was rendering might preclude him from delegating his responsibilities to anyone else, there is nothing in the facts to suggest that there is anything particularly personal about Noah's receipt of these services that would have precluded him from assigning them to Samuel. (Keynes did not, for example, agree to handle Wallace Williams's business and financial affairs, on a commission basis, only to have Wallace assign his rights under the contract to a member of his road crew or to a security guard at one of the concert venues.) Therefore, Noah's rights fall under the general rule of R2 § 317(1) permitting assignment, and **Answer (A) is incorrect**.

227. Generally speaking, an assignment extinguishes the assignor's rights under the contract and transfers them to the assignee. *See* R2 § 317(1). However, until Keynes received notice of Noah's assignment to Samuel, Noah would have had the power to discharge or modify Keynes's remaining obligations under the contract, provided Keynes gave Noah some value in return. *See* R2 § 338(1). Until Keynes received notice of Noah's assignment to Samuel, Noah would also have had the right to accept performance by Keynes in satisfaction of Keynes's contractual obligation to perform for Noah's benefit.

228. As a general rule, all contract duties may be delegated, *except* where: (1) the delegator owes the obligee fiduciary duties or other duties arising from a special trust in the delegator; (2) performance depends on the unique personal skills or talents of the delegator (*e.g.*, Greg Maddux cannot delegate his pitching duties to Tiger Woods); (3) performance by the delegatee would vary materially the performance expected by the obligee (*e.g.*, Sue Smith contracts with Tiger Woods to give her golf lessons; Tiger cannot delegate those duties to Butch Harmon, Tiger's own golf instructor, because Sue wanted Tiger's personal performance); or (4) the contract specifically forbids delegation. *See* R2 § 318(1)-(2). Here, the facts do not indicate that the contract forbade delegation or that Keynes's owed Noah any type of fiduciary duty. And, while Keynes's personal skills and talents were, doubtless, part of why Methuselah chose him to be

Noah's tutor and consultant, unless there is a "substantial reason" for Noah and Methuselah to object to Malthus's assumption of Keynes's duties, *see* R2 § 318 cmt. c, Keynes should have been free to delegate them without Noah's and Methuselah's consent. *But see* R2 § 318 illus. 5-7.

229.   **Answer (C) is the best answer**. If the delegation was enforceable, Noah and Methuselah must have accepted Malthus's performance. But, if Malthus failed to perform adequately, Keynes remained liable for Malthus's breach, *see* R2 § 318(3) & cmt. d, and Malthus was also liable for his own breach, *see* R2 § 318 cmt. d & illus. 10. Therefore, **Answers (A) and (B) are incorrect**. And, as was the case with Question 223, while the irresistibility of the teaching position at TISU may have made it worth Keynes's while to breach his contract with Methuselah and Noah, it did not excuse that breach, unless Methuselah renounced, *see* R2 § 277, and Noah disclaimed, *see* R2 § 306, the remainder of the contract. Again, the facts of this Question do not suggest either renunciation or disclaimer; therefore, and because it incorrectly relieves Malthus of liability for his own malfeasance, **Answer (D) is incorrect**.

230.   **Answer (B) is the best answer, unless Jared benefits from Yubotah's warranty disclaimer, in which case Answer (D) is the best answer.**

Because Methuselah purchased the Yubotah mower from Jared (as opposed to buying it used), to whom Yubotah sold or consigned it for resale, vertical privity should not bar Keynes's claim against Yubotah, and vertical privity is a non-issue against Jared because he was the direct seller. Horizontal privity is also easy for Keynes to establish, because UCC § 2-318 (Alternative C) extends all Article 2 quality warranties to "any person who may reasonably be expected to use, consume or be affected by the goods and who is injured by breach of the warranty." Keynes was a "person who may reasonably be expected to . . . be affected by" Methuselah's riding mower, because riding mowers are often used in relative proximity to people other than the mower operator and to things other than the mower itself, and Keynes was "injured by the breach of the warranty" when the defective mower sent a rock hurtling through his windshield, his rear view mirror, and the upholstery of his driver's seat. The trick for Keynes would be overcoming the last sentence of UCC § 2-318 (Alternative C), which reads: "A seller may not exclude or limit the operation of this section with respect to *injury to the person* of an individual to whom the warranty extends." Yubotah's warranty disclaims liability to anyone other than the purchaser (Methuselah) for anything other than personal injury. In other words, it disclaims everything the last sentence of UCC § 2-318 (Alternative C) allows it to disclaim, and nothing more. As such, Keynes does not have a colorable claim against Yubotah. Therefore, **Answers (A) and (C) are incorrect**.

Merchant sellers, like Jared, make the implied warranty of merchantability to their purchasers whether or not they manufacture the goods they are selling. Therefore, Answer (B) appears to be the correct answer. However, we need to know whether Jared receives the benefit of Yubotah's warranty disclaimer. The facts do not indicate whether Jared sold the mower to Methuselah making "no warranty other than the manufacturer's express warranty" or "as is." If he did, then he should be shielded from liability for anything other than personal injury to anyone other than Methuselah, as is Yubotah. **In that case, Answer (D) would be the best answer**. But, because the facts do not indicate one way or another whether Jared disclaimed his implied warranty of merchantability, the more prudent course would be to not assume facts not in evidence and conclude that Jared is liable, under UCC § 2-318 (Alternative C), for the property damage Keynes suffered due to the defective riding mower Jared sold to Methuselah, **making Answer (B) the best answer**.

Revised Article 2 substantially restructures current UCC § 2-318, though not in a way that would appear to change the answer to this Question.

PRACTICE FINAL EXAM: ANSWERS

231. **Answer (C) is the best answer**. This contract should be governed by the CISG. The U.S. and Mexico are both signatories to the CISG; Tempus knew or should have known from the faxed acknowledgment and the shipping documents that FC's place of business is in Mexico; Tempus' place of business is in the U.S.; Tempus did not purchase the precision gear works primarily for personal, family, or household use; and the fact that the gear works may be custom-made, rather than ready-made, does not take the contract outside the scope of the CISG. *See* CISG arts. 1(1)(a), 1(2), 2(a) & 3(1). The twist in this Question is that Tempus (the U.S. purchaser) did not contact FC (the Mexican manufacturer). Instead, Tempus contacted GEARZ, which is located in New Mexico. Can GEARZ's Albuquerque office be considered a "place of business" for FC? If so, we would have to consult Article 10 to determine FC's "official" place of business for this transaction. Article 10 provides that, when a party has more than one place of business, that party's place of business for purposes of Article 1(1) is that "which has the closest relationship to the contract and its performance, having regard to the circumstances known to or contemplated by the parties at any time before or at the conclusion of the contract." Here, unless Tempus had no reason to know that it was ultimately contracting with FC (and that should have been obvious when it received the confirming fax from FC's Nuevo Laredo factory), the place of business with the closest relationship to this contract is FC's Nuevo Laredo factory.

Because this contract falls within the scope of the CISG, the UCC, UETA, and Arizona common law all yield to the CISG, to the extent that the CISG addresses a particular issue, because the UCC, UETA, and Arizona common law are all state law, and the CISG is a treaty of the United States. As such, under the Supremacy Clause, it "trumps" contrary state law. *See, e.g., Filanto, S.p.A. v. Chilewich International Corp.*, 789 F. Supp. 1229 (S.D.N.Y. 1992) (holding that the CISG "trumps" Article 2 in cases where the CISG applies), *appeal dismissed*, 984 F.2d 58 (2d Cir. 1993). Therefore, **Answers (A) and (B) are incorrect** — Answer (A) doubly so because, even if the CISG did not govern, UCC Article 2 would "trump" Arizona common law because this is a sale of goods. The CISG is not among the bodies of substantive law specifically excluded from the scope of UETA; so, to the extent that Tempus and FC both evidence a willingness to transact electronically, UETA may *supplement* the substantive rules of the CISG, to the extent UETA is not inconsistent with the CISG. But, UETA's scope is so narrow that it cannot be properly described as governing any *transaction*; and, even if it could in theory, it could not govern this transaction because, again, it is state law that yields to the CISG. Therefore, **Answer (D) is not the best answer**.

232. **Answer (B) is the best answer**. The "majority rule" with respect to mixed contracts is the "predominant purpose" test. Here, it appears that Pennybakers' predominant purpose was to pay S&C to design customized graphics software. Pennybakers only purchased the GR8 computer because S&C recommended it to run the software that Pennybakers engaged S&C to write. This reading of the facts is supported by the relative expenditures on the software and hardware: Pennybakers paid S&C $25,000 to design the software and only $2,500 for the computer. Software design, although it often yields one or more diskettes or CDs containing the code, is primarily a service, rather than a good. This is particularly true in this case, because the software did not exist — and, therefore, was not identifiable, much less tangible or movable — when the parties entered into the contract. *See* UCC § 2-105. Therefore, if Pennybakers' predominant purpose was to purchase services — to wit, the custom software — then Article 2 would not apply to the transaction if the court applied the predominant purpose test, making **Answer (B) a correct answer** and **Answer (A) incorrect**.

If the gravamen of the action test applied, Article 2 would govern Pennybakers' action against S&C. The parties have stipulated that the Dogbert glitch is a "hardware" problem, rather than a "software" problem — that is to say, the defect originated with the GR8 computer, rather than with the customized software. The computer is clearly a "good" under UCC § 2-105. However, because the Question instructed you to assume that the law of a jurisdiction whose courts follow the majority rule with respect to mixed contracts governs this dispute, **Answer (C) is not the best answer**. And, in any case, **Answer (D) is incorrect**.

233. **Answer (D) is the correct answer**. Because Beauford told Sanjay he could only accept by means of a writing, which Beauford *received* on or before April 1st, only Sanjay's April 1st fax, which Beauford received on April 1st, is sufficient to constitute an acceptance of Beauford's offer to purchase Sanjay's house for $200,000.

A contract requires, among other things, offer and acceptance. "Acceptance" is "the offeree's assent to the terms of the offer, demonstrated 'in a manner invited or required by the offer.'" R2 § 50(1). The *Restatement* further provides that, if an offer prescribes the time, place, or manner of acceptance, the offeree must *strictly comply* with those requirements to create a contract. R2 § 60. Here, Beauford, as offeror, specifically required that Sanjay's acceptance be communicated *in writing*. Therefore, neither Sanjay's March 5th phone call, nor his March 31st phone call, could operate as an acceptance of Beauford's offer. Therefore, **Answers (A) and (C) are incorrect**.

What about Sanjay's March 10th letter? Beauford specifically required that he *receive* Sanjay's written acceptance no later than April 1st. Because acceptance was conditioned on Beauford's receipt of the written acceptance, and Beauford never received the March 10th letter, Sanjay's March 10th letter would not operate as an acceptance. Therefore, **Answer (B) is incorrect**. Note, however, if Beauford's offer had *not* been conditioned on Beauford's receipt of the written acceptance (*e.g.*, "This offer will expire unless you accept in writing no later than April 1st."), then Sanjay could have relied on the "mailbox rule" to make acceptance effective on the date Sanjay posted the letter if (1) Sanjay correctly addressed the letter and properly placed it in the mail, and (2) it was reasonable, under the terms of the offer, for Sanjay to accept by mail. Here, Beauford asked for a written acceptance, so using the mail seems quite reasonable. So, if Sanjay properly addressed the written acceptance to Beauford and placed it in the correct type of mailbox before April 1st, there would have been a contract, *but for the receipt requirement in Beauford's offer.*

234.	**Answer (D) is the best answer.** An offeror is free to revoke his offer at any time prior to the offeree's acceptance, if the offeror has no actual or constructive knowledge of that acceptance. Because Sanjay had not effectively accepted Beauford's offer as of March 31st, as explained in the answer to Question 233, Beauford was free to revoke the offer during the March 31st phone call. The only situation in which this would not be true is if the offer could be deemed to have given Sanjay an exclusive option to accept or reject until April 1st. Such an option must have been supported by separate consideration. There is no evidence here of separate consideration; therefore, there was no option. In the absence of a valid option, supported by separate consideration, Beauford was free to revoke his offer at any time prior to Sanjay's acceptance. Because Beauford revoked prior to receiving Sanjay's written acceptance on April 1st, Beauford's revoked offer was no longer subject to acceptance on Beauford's receipt of Sanjay's written acceptance.

Answers (A) and (B) are incorrect for the reasons given in the answer to Question 233. **Answer (C) is incorrect** because nothing Sanjay said during the March 31st phone call could satisfy Beauford's requirement that he receive Sanjay's written acceptance of his offer by April 1st.

235.	**Answer (D) is the best answer.** It is very easy to get caught up in the "mailbox rule," the variation on the "mailbox rule" that occurs when an offeree dispatches a rejection or counteroffer before dispatching an acceptance, and whether Ross's offer was a firm offer that estopped him from revoking his offer before the deadline or before Joey terminated his own power to accept. While you should consider all of those things, resist the urge to let them obscure the simple truth that Ross offered to sell Joey *goods*; and, therefore, Joey's July 5th letter was an acceptance, despite the fact that it changed the price term and added a delivery deadline, *because Joey did not expressly condition his acceptance of Ross's offer on Ross's assent to Joey's different and additional term.* Therefore, under UCC § 2-207(1), supplemented by the common law "mailbox rule," Joey accepted Ross's offer when he properly dispatched his July 5th letter.

Answer (A) is incorrect because a revocation is not effective until the offeree *receives* it, *see* R2 § 42, and Joey did not receive Ross's revocation until after he had accepted

Ross's offer by means of *either* his July 5th letter or his July 8th fax. **Answer (C) is not the best answer** because it implies that Joey's July 5th letter was not an acceptance — when, in fact, it was, because it was a "definite and seasonable expression of acceptance . . . sent within a reasonable time" after receipt of the offer, and it was not "expressly made conditional on [Ross's] assent to the additional or different terms" contained in Joey's acceptance. UCC § 2-207(1).

Answer (B) is not the best answer. It correctly states that Ross's offer was a firm offer, subject to UCC § 2-205, because (1) he made it in writing, (2) he is a merchant in goods of the kind, and (3) the offer contained language of non-revocability. It also correctly states that Joey accepted Ross's firm offer before Ross was legally entitled to revoke it and before Joey did anything to terminate his own power to accept. But, it mischaracterizes (as discussed above) Joey's first response as a counteroffer.

236. **Answer (D) is the best answer.** Ecuadorian pygmy shrimp are goods. *See* UCC § 2-105. Ross and Joey contracted, respectively, to sell and buy goods. The contract price was $5,000. Therefore, the contract is within the scope of UCC § 2-201 (as well as Revised § 2-201).

Answer (C) is not the best answer because, while Ecuadorian pygmy shrimp are personal property (at least once caught) as well as being goods, the Article 1 statute of frauds only applies to personal property that is not subject to a statute of frauds in another Article of the UCC. Because this contract is subject to UCC § 2-201, UCC § 1-206 is inapplicable. (*Recall that Revised Article 1 does not include a counterpart to § 1-206, making this answer clearly incorrect in a Revised Article 1 jurisdiction.*)

Answer (B) is not the best answer because, while the pygmy shrimp are Ecuadorian, Ross is not; and Joey's contract is with Ross, not with some Ecuadorian shrimper. Therefore, the CISG would not apply, because the key to its application is the location of the parties, not the location of the goods. *See* CISG art. 1(1)(a).

Answer (A) is not the best answer because, while a true statement, it overlooks the fact that UCC Article 2 governs this contract, not common law.

237. The agreement between Joey and Ross, as represented by Ross's July 1st firm offer and Joey's July 5th (or July 8th) acceptance, satisfies the statute of frauds. The statute of frauds is "in play" because this is a contract for the sale of goods valued at $500 or more. UCC § 2-201. The statute requires a writing signed by the party against whom enforcement is sought, which evidences that a contract has been made, and which states the quantity of goods being bought and sold. UCC § 2-201(1). Here, Joey is trying to enforce the contract against Ross, so he needs a writing Ross signed that evidences the contract Joey is seeking to enforce. Ross's July 1st firm offer is written and identifies the quantity of goods to be sold. Even if it is not signed in the formal sense of the word (*i.e.*, a signature), it most likely was made on Ross's letterhead, an invoice with Ross's name printed on it, or some other document attributing it to Ross. The

comments to UCC § 2-201 indicate that any of these would satisfy the "signature" requirement. Moreover, if necessary, Joey can satisfy the statute, under the composite document rule, by using more than one document. Here Ross's firm offer plus Joey's written acceptance should leave no doubt as to the terms of the deal or the parties' intent to enter into an agreement on those terms.

238.   **Answer (C) is the best answer**. There was no "bargained for" consideration. Mary did not bargain for the Museum's promise, as required by R2 § 71. The Museum did not offer to name the new wing after Mary or her designee in exchange for Mary's pledge of $4,750,000. Had another, larger pledge been made during the fundraising campaign, Mary would not have been given the naming rights. The Museum's offer to name the new wing after the first $5,000,000 bidder or the highest bidder thereafter smacks of both a "reward" offer, like that in *Carlill v. Carbolic Smoke Ball Co.*, [1893] 1 Q.B. 256 (C.A. 1892), and a first-come, first-served offer like that in *Lefkowitz v. Great Minneapolis Surplus Store, Inc.*, 86 N.W.2d 689 (Minn. 1957). Both "reward" offers and "first-come, first-served" offers are routinely enforced. Therefore, **Answer (A) is not clearly untrue**.

To the extent that the Museum made a valid offer, Mary accepted in one of the two manners invited by the offer. While she did not pledge $5,000,000 earmarked for the new wing, she did make the largest earmarked pledge. Therefore, **Answer (B) is not untrue**.

The statute of frauds should not be implicated because Mary could fully perform the contract within one year. And, even if she could not, she signed a pledge card evidencing the amount of her pledge. That should be sufficient to enable the Museum to satisfy the statute of frauds, particularly when coupled with the pledge solicitation letter and brochure under the composite document rule. Therefore, **Answer (D) is not untrue**.

239.   **Answer (D) is the best answer**. Dionne's promise to pay could not have induced Callie to paint, because Callie painted before Dionne promised; therefore, Callie has no promissory estoppel claim, making **Answer (A) incorrect**. Callie's actions were not necessary to preserve Dionne's property without asking Dionne's permission; therefore, *Restatement of Restitution* § 117 does not apply, making **Answer (B) incorrect**. Callie might have a claim under R2 § 86 for promissory restitution, but only if enforcing the after-the-fact promise is necessary to prevent injustice, which it probably is not, making **Answer (C) not the best answer**.

240.   Probably so. This would seem to fall within *Restatement of Restitution* § 117, provided that (1) Callie acted lawfully and without any pre-existing duty owed to Dionne as a result of their relationship or Callie's own acts or omissions; (2) Callie acted without Dionne's permission out of necessity; (3) Callie had no reason to believe that Dionne would not consent if asked; (4) Callie intended to be compensated for her services; and (5) Dionne accepted the benefit of Callie's services. Callie might also be entitled

to recover under R2 § 86, which provides that a promise, made in recognition of a benefit already received, is binding to the extent necessary to prevent injustice, as long as (1) Callie did not render the benefit gratuitously, (2) not enforcing the promise would unjustly enrich Dionne, and (3) Dionne's promise is not disproportionate to the benefit she received.

241.   **Answer (A) is the best answer**. If the Burgers can prove they were only obligated to complete their purchase of the Samples' house if Ham's mother sold her house in Tennessee, they will be excused from performing the contract to purchase the Samples' house due to failure of a condition precedent. R2 § 225(1). The parol evidence rule will not exclude extrinsic evidence of the condition precedent — despite it not being mentioned in the written contract — even if the writing is fully integrated (and here the explicit reference to facts outside the agreement, *i.e.*, "the furniture in the upstairs game room," belies the meaningfulness of the integration clause in paragraph 20), because the parol evidence rule does not exclude extrinsic evidence of a condition precedent even to an otherwise fully integrated, unambiguous agreement.

Answer (B) is not the best answer. As discussed in the answer to Question 144, sufficiently serious or numerous foundation cracks affect the habitability of the house or suggest unworkmanlike construction — both of which are the subject of common law implied warranties, which run in favor of the purchaser of a house unless expressly disclaimed or waived by contract. There was no express waiver or disclaimer here. The trick is whether the Burgers can rescind their contract with the Samples based on Thomas' malfeasance. Courts are split over whether remote buyers (that is, buyers who did not purchase from the builder) are entitled to the protection of any implied warranty that runs against the builder. So, the Burgers may be able to sue Thomas for the damage caused by the defects — but they probably cannot rescind their contract with the Samples due to Thomas' breach. What the Burgers need is for the Paradise courts to imply a warranty of habitability against *any* seller to their buyer. Courts in non-fictional jurisdictions are also split on the viability of this type of action.

Answer (C) is incorrect. Even if the solar screens and/or the washer and dryer were part of the sale, the Samples' failure to deliver them to the Burgers would not be a material breach entitling the Burgers to rescind the contract. At most, the Samples' breach with respect to those items would entitle the Burgers to damages — most likely either return of the specified items or money damages in the amount of their reasonable replacement cost, plus any incidental damages, such as the cost of going to the laundromat.

Answer (D) is not the best answer. The Samples knew or should have known about the light display because they had been living in the house for two years (including two Christmas seasons). The question is: Did the Samples have a duty to disclose this fact to the Burgers?

Generally, neither party to a contract has a duty to volunteer information unless the other party asks — and there is nothing in the facts to suggest that the Burgers asked the Samples about seasonal light displays or the like. However, common and statutory law create a duty to speak in certain situations, including where the disclosure is required to (1) keep something that was said (or done) from being misleading (one cannot tell another only half of the story); (2) correct a basic assumption of the other party; (3) satisfy the duty of good faith and fair dealing; (4) correct a mistake about a writing; (5) satisfy a trust, confidence, or fiduciary duty; or (6) alert an innocent party to a serious defect or serious risk of injury. The Samples did not tell a half-truth. The absence of neighborhood seasonal light displays (unlike the absence of toxic waste) was not a basic assumption on which the Burgers agreed to buy the house. There was no mistake in the writing on this issue. The Samples did not owe the Burgers any fiduciary duty. The neighbor's Christmas lights were not a serious defect in the Samples' house nor did they pose any risk of serious injury. All that is left is the duty of good faith and fair dealing. That is problematic for at least two reasons. First, the duty does not extend to contract formation, only to performance and enforcement, and any duty to speak would have arisen before the Burgers agreed to buy the house. Second, all that the duty of good faith required of the Samples is honesty in fact. They do not appear to have acted dishonestly.

There is also a question of materiality. Any duty the Samples had to disclose would only obligate them to disclose a material fact — that is, a fact that the Samples reasonably assumed would likely induce a reasonable person in the Burgers' position, or would likely induce the Burgers due to some idiosyncrasy known to the Samples, to assent or to withhold their assent. People put up Christmas lights. Some displays are tasteful; some are garish. Some people are offended only by garish displays, some are offended by any display, and some do not care. Even among those who might be offended, what is the likelihood that they would choose not to purchase an otherwise ideal house because of an obnoxious seasonal display? Factor in that there may be any number of neighborhoods whose homeowners' association imposes restrictions on such displays, and that the Burgers have decided to purchase a house that is apparently not in one of those neighborhoods, and we begin to see that this claim is going to stand, if at all, on some idiosyncrasy of the Burgers actually or constructively known by the Samples.

If the Burgers can prevail on a claim against the Samples for fraudulent or negligent misrepresentation based on the Samples' failure to disclose the Christmas-season rhubarb, the Burgers should be able to avoid the contract under R2 § 164(1). However, given the uncertainty whether the Samples had a duty to disclose and whether the Christmas light display was a material fact, **Answer (A) is a superior choice to Answer (D)**.

242. No, Wallace would not be justified in refusing to perform, absent some defense to the otherwise binding February 15th agreement. There is no evidence that Wallace agreed to the February 15th contract on account of some mental defect or illness or other incapacity, or under duress or undue influence. There is no evidence that Bruce defrauded or negligently misled Wallace with regard to any fact material to their

agreement. There is no evidence that Wallace was "dominated" by Bruce or lacked any meaningful choice or that the terms of the contract were grossly unfair to Wallace *when the contract was formed*. Nor is there any evidence to support a claim by Wallace that the contract should be set aside on the ground of mistake, frustration of purpose, impossibility, or impracticability. Basically, he's stuck.

243. **Answer (B) is the correct answer**. Wallace's statement constituted a definite and unequivocal manifestation of his intent not to perform the contract. As such, Bruce was entitled to treat Wallace's statement as an anticipatory breach and was, as discussed in the answer to Question 148, entitled, and perhaps obligated, to make other arrangements.

      Answer (A) is incorrect because, while Wallace did not repudiate by asking Bruce for more money (as discussed in the answer to Question 147), Bruce did not repudiate by refusing to discuss Wallace's proposed modification. **Answer (C) is incorrect** because, while Bruce was entitled to urge Wallace to retract his repudiation, R2 § 257, Bruce was not required to do so. **Answer (D) is incorrect** because, having exercised his right following Wallace's repudiation to book a replacement act in reliance on Wallace's repudiation (*i.e.*, materially changing his position), Bruce was entitled to refuse Wallace the right to perform when he showed up despite his prior repudiation.

244. The first question, here, is whether this case more closely resembles *Alaska Packers' Association v. Domenico*, 117 F. 99 (9th Cir. 1902), or *Schwartzreich v. Bauman-Basch, Inc.*, 131 N.E. 887 (N.Y. 1921) — that is to say, does this appear to be a (forced) modification or a (voluntary) substituted agreement? If it is a modification, then it requires additional consideration, because this contract does not fall within the ambit of UCC § 2-209(1). If it is a substituted agreement, then any consideration not yet performed that would have been sufficient to support the original contract will support the substituted agreement. Also, *Schwartzreich* suggests that the mutual rescission of the old agreement is sufficient consideration to support the new one. The facts here suggest that the June 8th agreement replaces the February 15th agreement. There is no indication that the terms of the June 8th agreement were "subject to" the earlier agreement (even though the June 8th agreement does contain the identical terms, except for compensation, as the February 15th agreement). Furthermore, Bruce and Wallace destroyed the old agreement when they executed the new one. Therefore, as long as Wallace still owed Bruce unperformed consideration under the original agreement, that unperformed consideration would support the substituted agreement. Finally, if for some reason the court were to find that the June 8th contract was merely a modification that was not supported by separate consideration, Wallace may have a claim in promissory estoppel for the unpaid balance. Bruce's promise to pay Wallace $50,000 — even if he was not required to do so as a matter of contract law — induced Wallace to rely to his detriment on the promise by performing. Wallace's response to Bruce's promise to pay him $50,000 was reasonably foreseeable to Bruce when he made the promise. The question for the court will be whether Wallace would have performed

anyway for the original $25,000 if he had not secured Bruce's promise to pay him $50,000.

245. **Answer (B) is the best answer**. While Mitsubishi is one of the world's largest manufacturing concerns, and it makes hundreds, if not thousands, of different products, Jason later clarified the ambiguity by confining the promise to a new Mitsubishi car, truck, or SUV and by stating that the contest winner would be responsible for any vehicle registration fees. There is no parol evidence rule problem here for two reasons: first, the contract was never in writing, so the parol evidence rule does not apply; second, even if it did, Jason's subsequent statements would not be excluded by the parol evidence rule because he made the statements after the written agreement had been formed. Therefore, a court should permit Jenny (and one or more of her co-workers) to testify about Jason's subsequent statements that would have led a reasonable person to conclude that the "new Mitsubishi" was, in fact, a new Mitsubishi car, truck, or SUV.

Answer (A) is not the best answer because it fails to account for Jason's subsequent statements and Jenny's ability to present testimony regarding them.

Answer (C) is incorrect because the contest-prize agreement between Owl's Nest and Jenny was not written; therefore, the parol evidence rule would not apply. Moreover, even if the parol evidence rule did apply, it would not, as discussed in the answer to Question 132, bar evidence regarding statements Jason made after the contract was formed.

Answer (D) is not the best answer because, while it correctly states the effect of the parol evidence rule on the admissibility of evidence regarding statements made after the contract was formed, it mistakenly assumes that the parol evidence rule applies to this oral contract.

246. **Answer (A) is the best answer**. If she can establish a breach of contract, Jenny can recover her expectation interest: namely, the price of a new Mitsubishi car, truck, or SUV. Because Jason's promise did not specify what model Mitsubishi the winner would receive, we cannot put a specific number on this measure of damages, but we can establish the baseline: the purchase price of the least expensive Mitsubishi on the market on or about May 1, 2002. Ultimately, it will be up to the trier of fact to decide whether to award that price or some greater amount up to, but not exceeding, the purchase price of the most expensive Mitsubishi on the market on or about May 1, 2002 (plus attorneys' fees and costs, if recoverable by statute).

In the alternative, or in lieu of expectation damages in the event that Jenny (1) does not prevail on her breach of contract claim or (2) prevails on her breach of contract claim, but the court decides that her expectation damages are too uncertain, Jenny can recover her unreimbursed out-of-pocket expenses and the unreimbursed reasonable value of her efforts incurred in reliance on Jason's promise or the contract formed, in part, by Jason's promise. The facts tell us that Jenny worked 10 more hours per week during the contest period than usual. However, Owl's Nest paid her $5.00 per hour for each additional hour she worked, and she collected an additional $300 in tips compared to her average month. Therefore, it is hard to characterize her effort as unreimbursed. She did incur $70 per week of babysitting expenses, which she might claim as unreimbursed. But, since paying that $70 per week allowed her to earn an extra $125 per week, she may have a hard time recovering that, too. Therefore, **Answer (B) is not the best answer**.

As an alternative to expectation or reliance damages for breach of contract, Jenny may attempt to recover either (1) the reasonable value of the services she performed for Owl's Nest, in terms of what it would have cost Owl's Nest to pay someone else for those services, or (2) the extent to which Owl's Nest's interests were advanced by Jenny's extra efforts. R2 § 371. Jenny will likely not be able to recover the first measure, because Owl's Nest and its customers have paid her for the extra hours she worked. So, as long as she is earning market wages and tips, Owl's Nest has not been unjustly enriched. As for the second measure, that will depend on whether she was providing extra or replacement services. Owl's Nest's interests were advanced by its share of the extra tips Jenny earned. But if Jenny was merely replacing another waitress who could have earned those same tips, then it is not clear that Owl's Nest has been unjustly enriched. If, instead, she was working in addition to the normal wait staff, and her presence allowed Owl's Nest to collect more "tip tax" than it would have had she not been there, then she should be able to recover Owl's Nest's share of the additional tips she generated. Jenny does not run afoul of R2 § 373(2) because, while she has fully performed, Owl's Nest's only remaining obligation is not to pay "a definite sum of money." Nonetheless, **Answer (C) is not the best answer**.

Whether Jenny can get specific performance depends on whether damages are adequate to protect Jenny's expectation interest, if any. If they are, she cannot recover specific performance. R2 § 359(1). If they are not, she can. She would also have to prove a reasonably certain basis for awarding specific relief. R2 § 362. This might be a problem, because Jason did not say what kind of Mitsubishi, so what does the court specifically award? If Jenny can prove breach of contract and recover her expectation damages, then she should be foreclosed from recovering specific performance. Therefore, **Answer (D) is not the best answer unless Jenny cannot recover her expectation damages**. If she cannot, then specific performance may be appropriate — and would certainly be her preferred remedy.

247. **Answer (D) is the best answer.** KOOK's offer was to perform over a five-year period. As such, the contract could not, on its own terms, be fully performed within one year from the date of making — which in this case would be the date on which Harry and Lloyd accepted the offer by getting the tattoos and then notifying KOOK that they had done so. Therefore, the contract, if there is one, is unenforceable against KOOK. R2 § 110(1)(e).

Boulder, KOOK's agent, offered Lloyd and Harry the chance to be paid $30,000 a year for five years in exchange for getting KOOK's logo tattooed to their foreheads. Lloyd and Harry accepted by getting the logo tattooed on their foreheads. KOOK sought the publicity it would gain by having people walk around with its logo tattooed to their foreheads. Lloyd and Harry sought the $30,000 per year for five years KOOK offered to anyone who would so publicize the station. Therefore, each party's consideration was "bargained for" by the other. Therefore, **Answer (C) is not the best answer**. There is a legitimate question whether Boulder's statement qualified as an offer under R2 § 24, as it did not limit the number of people who could accept it or the time within which they could accept it. (By comparison, the backstage pass offer was limited in number and had to be accepted by showing up at KOOK's booth at the concert on the date of the show.) As such, it lacked the "first come, first served" aspect of *Lefkowitz*. However, it should qualify as a "reward" offer, like that in *Carbolic Smoke Ball*, which was similarly neither limited as to the number of people who could claim the reward nor the time within which they had to claim it. Therefore, **Answer (A) is not the best answer**. Assuming that KOOK made an offer capable of acceptance, Harry and Lloyd did exactly what the offer required them to do: present themselves at the station with the station's logo permanently tattooed to their foreheads. Therefore, **Answer (B) is not the best answer**.

248. R2 § 90 would govern Lloyd's and Harry's claims if the court found that KOOK's promise was not an offer, Lloyd and Harry improperly accepted, or Lloyd and Harry did not give adequate consideration to bind KOOK to its contract. R2 § 139 would govern Lloyd's and Harry's claims if the court found that the parties had a contract but the contract was unenforceable under the statute of frauds. R2 §§ 90 & 139 both require proof of (1) a promise, (2) that the promisor could reasonably foresee would induce action or forbearance by the promisee, (3) which does induce such action or forbearance, (4) as a result of which injustice can be avoided only by enforcing the promise. As discussed in the answer to Question 87, many courts add that the promisee's actual reliance must be reasonable. Three of the elements are easy: Boulder promised the chance to win a prize, Lloyd and Harry did what was required to claim the prize, and injustice would result if the promise was not enforced because Lloyd and Harry's actions in reliance on Boulder's promise were definite and substantial and Lloyd and Harry lack any other remedy because they cannot prove the existence of an enforceable contract, nor can they prove that KOOK was unjustly enriched by their actions. The harder issue will be whether their decision to get KOOK's logo permanently tattooed to their foreheads was reasonably foreseeable to Boulder, and thus to KOOK. While it is true that Boulder invited the actions that Lloyd and Harry undertook, he may well have thought that no one would be foolish enough (1) to have the logo tattooed on their foreheads and (2) to do so with the honest belief that the station would pay them for doing so. The fact that no one else attempted to claim the reward suggests Lloyd and Harry may not have acted in a reasonably foreseeable manner. On the other hand, the facts that Lloyd and Harry repeatedly asked for confirmation that the offer was genuine, and that KOOK repeatedly confirmed its genuineness, should make Lloyd's and Harry's actions reasonably foreseeable.

249.   **Answer (D) is the best answer.** As discussed in the answer to Question 207, specific performance should be unavailable because money damages should be adequate to make Harry and Lloyd whole. *See* R2 §§ 359-360. After all, KOOK never promised them anything other than money in the first place.

As discussed in the answer to Question 207, a plaintiff who successfully claims promissory estoppel is entitled to recover the greatest of (1) reliance damages, (2) restitutionary damages, and, if the law of the governing jurisdiction so allows, (3) expectation damages. Harry and Lloyd incurred expenses in reliance on KOOK's promise; the publicity attendant to their performance would unjustly enrich KOOK if KOOK were not required to compensate them; and a reasonable person in their position likely would have expected KOOK to pay as promised. Therefore, **neither Answer (A), Answer (B), nor Answer (C) is the best answer**.

250.   **Answer (B) is the correct answer.** Under certain circumstances, a seller can gain a windfall profit by suing to recover the market price-contract price differential under UCC § 2-708(1) even though the seller is entitled to sue for price under UCC § 2-709 or for contract-resale differential damages under UCC § 2-706. Here, Monica is eligible to seek any of the Article 2 measures of seller's damages. However, one yields a better result for Monica than the others.

Recall (from the answer to Question 214) that UCC § 2-708(1) damages = (KP – MP) + ID – ES, where KP = contract price, MP = the market price at the time and place for tender, ID = incidental damages permitted by UCC § 2-710, and ES = expenses saved by Monica as a result of Chandler's nonperformance. Here ($1,000 – $400) + $0 – $0 = $600.

Recall (from the answer to Question 213) that UCC § 2-706 damages = (KP – RP) + ID – ES, where RP = the price at which Monica resold to the third party, and the other terms are unchanged from the UCC § 2-708(1) formula. Here ($1,000 – $500) + $0 – $0 = $500. Therefore, **Answer (A) is incorrect**. Recall (from the answer to Question 217) that UCC § 2-709 damages = P + ID, where P = the contract price of, in this case, accepted goods. Here, $1,000 + $0 = $1,000. But, that is not the end of the story. While it did not figure into Question 217, UCC § 2-709 requires Monica to deduct the $500 paid by the new purchaser from its $1,000 claim against Chandler, reducing Monica's UCC § 2-709 recovery to $500. Therefore, **Answer (D) is incorrect**.

It is not entirely clear that Monica is eligible to recover under UCC § 2-708(2). There are no facts to suggest she is a "lost profit" seller of Moroccan kumquats. However, because UCC § 2-708(2) is also available when UCC § 2-708(1) fails to adequately compensate Monica, one should determine the result under UCC § 2-708(2) to determine whether UCC § 2-708(1) fails to adequately compensate Monica. Recall (from the answer to Question 216) that UCC § 2-708(2) damages = B + ID – ES – PP – RP, where B = KP – direct cost, PP = any portion of the purchase price the Chandler prepaid, and RP = profit on resale. Here ($1,000 − $750) + $0 − $0 − $0 − (−$250) = $500. Therefore, **Answer (C) is incorrect**.

So, in this case, Monica would be entitled to a more generous remedy under UCC § 2-708(1) than under UCC §§ 2-706, 2-708(2), or 2-709.

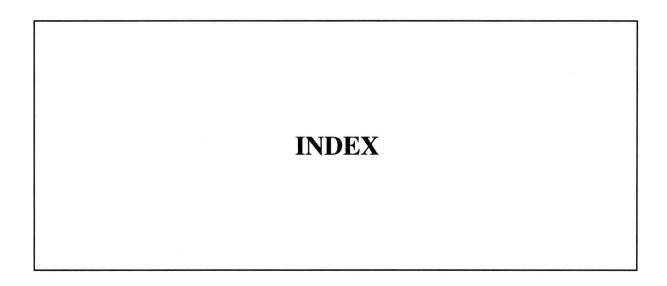

INDEX

INDEX

TOPIC   **QUESTION**

299

TOPIC	**QUESTION**
Habitability	139, 144, 241
Merchantability	122, 123, 139, 140, 141, 142, 143, 230
Workmanlike Performance	140, 144, 241